APE-MAN

THE UNOFFICIAL AND UNAUTHORISED GUIDE TO
100 YEARS OF TARZAN

APE-MAN

THE UNOFFICIAL AND UNAUTHORISED GUIDE TO
100 YEARS OF TARZAN

SEAN EGAN

First published in the UK in 2012 by
Telos Publishing Ltd
17 Pendre Avenue, Prestatyn, Denbighshire LL19 9SH
www.telos.co.uk

Telos Publishing Ltd values feedback. Please e-mail us with any comments you
may have about this book to: feedback@telos.co.uk

ISBN: 978-1-84583-067-0

Ape-Man: The Unofficial and Unauthorised Guide to 100 Years of Tarzan ©
2012 Sean Egan

Internal design, typesetting and layout by Arnold T Blumberg
www.atbpublishing.com

Printed in the UK by Berforts Group Ltd

British Library Cataloguing in Publication Data.
A catalogue record for this book is available from the British Library.

ACKNOWLEDGMENTS

My grateful thanks to the following for granting interviews or providing quotes for this book: Robert R Barrett, Al Bohl, Andy Briggs, Danton Burroughs, Gerry Conway, Gary Goddard, Thomas Grindberg, Bill Hillman, Hugh Hudson, Len Janson, Micheline Keller, Robert Kline, Joe Kubert, Joe Lansdale, Robin Maxwell, Denny Miller, Michael Moorcock, RA Salvatore and Roy Thomas.

Thanks also to the following people for helping me with queries: Robert W Lamb, Jim Sullos and Cathy Wilbanks.

Robert R Barrett kindly granted his expertise in matters ape-man by reading through my manuscript and correcting errors.

Last and emphatically not least, I extend my vast gratitude to lifelong Edgar Rice Burroughs fan Bill Hillman, who provided assistance over and above the endless queries he patiently answered simply via maintaining his multitude of ERB sites, the main one of which – erbzine.com – constitutes a staggering Burroughs resource.

CONTENTS

INTRODUCTION

Edgar Rice Burroughs' Tarzan is one of the great fantasy figures of modern times.

He made his first appearance in the issue of *The All-Story* magazine cover-dated October 1912. The public immediately took to the tale of an English lord raised by a previously undiscovered type of great ape in the African jungle after his parents are shipwrecked and who grows up both to claim his inheritance in civilisation and to adhere to the principles and skills he has learnt in the wild. The ape-man was such a cultural phenomenon that he was responsible for many firsts: after conquering the printed word, he proceeded to triumph in other media and markets almost as soon as they were invented, from movies to comic strips to radio to merchandising. Burroughs' tally of two-dozen Tarzan novels was impressive but was dwarfed by the multiplicity of film adaptations of his character. Though they weren't exactly faithful to the source, these were so pleasing to the public that, Sherlock Holmes excepted, they constitute the longest-running movie franchise of all time. The character's popularity crossed national boundaries, with boys from America to India to Russia miming swinging on a vine while emitting a deafening yodel. Not only was it global, the popularity was enduring: the boys in the early part of the 20th Century who imitated their idol grew up and spawned a generation to whom the character was even more revered. Though inevitably the Tarzan craze lessened in intensity, it continues in some form to this day, with an archive of Tarzan films and TV series in rotation on television screens across the planet, a comic strip still circulating and new Tarzan stage plays and films continuing to be scheduled.

Yet ironically, almost from the moment he created him, Burroughs was bored by his character, seeing him as having little story potential. He continued to crank out his adventures only through financial necessity. Even more ironically, many of those resentfully-written stories were high-quality.

Over the course of the hundred years of his existence, there have been many societal changes that have had a potential impact on the ape-man, from the de-colonisation of the African continent to the rise of ecological concerns and animal preservation movements to the abolition of the heredity principle in the House of Lords: all of these things change the landscape for the Lord of the Jungle and may possibly undermine his very premise.

Ape-Man: 100 Years of Tarzan explores the Tarzan phenomenon across all cultural media. With the aid of writers, actors, directors and other creative talents who have been involved in purveying the ape-man to the world, it examines the history, appeal, impact and uncertain future of a truly remarkable icon.

PART ONE: THE CREATOR

Edgar Rice Burroughs was a restless soul.

Born to a well-to-do Chicago family in 1875, by 1911 he had been among other professions, a cavalry officer, a cowboy, a goldminer, a store proprietor and the manager of a large Sears catalogue office. 'He tried just a huge number of jobs,' says Bill Hillman, lifelong Burroughs fan and supervisor of the official ERB website. 'He did all this stuff and then a lot of failed things as well. I guess he was a daydreamer.'

'He wasn't a failure,' Burroughs' grandson Danton insisted to this author in his last ever interview, conducted four months before his death in his sleep from heart failure in May 2008. (All Danton Burroughs quotes presented in this book are from that interview unless stated.) 'He just wasn't interested in those lines of work. When he took over the stenographic department at Sears and Roebuck, he shaped that place up. They'd never experienced anybody like my granddad. And then when he worked at Michigan Military Academy, he was manager of the football team; the horsemanship, he took care of that; he taught geology. He had so many varied jobs. He didn't fail at them, he just was moving on to what he really wanted to do.'

Burroughs himself seemed to be of the inclination to beg to differ, noting 'I am a flop' of the years 1905-11 in an outline for an unwritten autobiography.

Hillman points out that Burroughs was always artistic as an adult: 'In the Michigan Military Academy back in the early 1890s, he was editor of the school paper. He wrote quite a bit of stuff. He was an excellent cartoonist and artist. He wrote a lot of little-known stuff before he was published, mainly for family or for newspaper submissions with poetry and things like that. He turned to professional writing at a very late age.'

Danton: 'He was starting to write around the turn of the century, when he wrote *Minidoka*.'

Minidoka was a fairytale-come-fantasy not submitted for publication anywhere. In 1911, however, Burroughs decided to do more than just write for fun. He was currently attempting to make a living as a pencil sharpener agent. The business wasn't going well and he found he had empty hours to fill. He decided to try his hand at devising something for the 'pulp' fiction magazines that in an era before movies and TV were massively popular. Hillman continues: 'He had dreams, nightmares and stuff and it all came together – all his past experiences. He thought, "I can write this drivel as well as the pulp authors." In his spare time he looked over some pulp magazines and checked out the advertising in them. *Under the Moons of Mars* or *A Princess of Mars* was the result.'

Under the Moons of Mars was written on the backs of pages carrying the mastheads of a previous failed Burroughs business. Its protagonist John Carter is on Earth merely a mustered-out Civil War soldier turned gold prospector. On Mars – Barsoom in native parlance – he becomes a fearsome warrior through the lighter gravity, which enables him to make 20-yard leaps over the heads of the brutal six-limbed green men he soon finds himself in battle against on the side of the planet's more cultured red race. Carter finds his way to the titular planet by the pat manoeuvre of wishing himself there, and learns the language of Mars preposterously swiftly. Nonetheless, Burroughs' first foray into his new profession – serialised across six issues of *All-Story* magazine cover-dated from February to July 1912 – saw him exploiting superbly the then still widely-held belief that Mars was either inhabited or had been. He created an evocative and intricately imagined picture of a planet whose culture was of a decaying majesty.

Burroughs had finally alighted on a career that didn't make him restless. It was one that would ultimately see him hailed as a pioneer of science fiction and fantasy, become one of the most popular authors of all time and, if that wasn't enough, create an imperishable cultural icon. Said Danton, 'He was unique … My grandfather could describe action so vividly that the reader literally couldn't put the book down.' Danton was biased of course, but his comments reflect those of many with no blood link to ERB.

There would be ten Mars tales printed in Burroughs' lifetime. The initial trilogy – the first story was printed in book form as *A Princess of Mars* in 1917 and was followed by *The Gods of Mars* and *Warlords of Mars* – are the strongest. However, unlike others of his series that were demeaned by incrementally less interesting sequels, Burroughs maintained a consistent quality and invention in the Barsoom franchise, with only *Synthetic Men of Mars* (1939) considered to be truly bad.

When Burroughs' most enduring creation made his debut in *All-Story* in October 1912, he initially earned him $700. It was a goodly sum in those days, but the character would before long become a multi-million dollar industry. The magazine version of *Tarzan of the Apes* saw Burroughs incorrectly place tigers in Africa, but otherwise it was an amazingly convincing tale of a child brought up in the jungle by a species – which the author would later name Mangani – halfway between apes and man, after his blue-blooded parents are stranded and subsequently die there. Noted Danton, 'He created the name Tarzan from nonsense syllables. You could see him in his original handwritten draft where he scratches out different names and things.' That manuscript shows Burroughs toying with 'Zantar' and 'Tublat-Zan'. Danton: 'And he finally hits on "Tarzan". It's just amazing how that man's mind worked.' In time, Burroughs would evidently realise that such a non-guttural word was not the sort of sound that naturally emanates from the mouth of even a man-like simian and would do a little backtracking when he came up with a Mangani name for the ape-man's son, explaining that the word Korak was 'as near as it may be interpreted into human speech.'

The tiger references were corrected when *Tarzan of the Apes* became Burroughs' first published book in 1914. 'A book was just really beyond reach at that time, certainly with his imaginative stuff,' says Hillman. 'It took quite a number of years before actually they published some of his stuff in hardcover. The pulp magazines were the available market for him. Before that [book publication], he serialised things in American newspapers.'

Though Burroughs had little trouble placing work with book publishers from hereon, he – ever a canny businessman – still ensured his works appeared in the pulps first for the extra remuneration. Hillman: 'He serialised things first, and he learned after his first effort to keep the publishing rights, which a lot of [other pulp writers] didn't do. And then he expanded and collated some of these serialised chapters into the finished product. He did that all his life.'

Burroughs unashamedly wrote for money, playing hardball over fees and measuring out a story's worth in the time it took him to complete it more than any aesthetic consideration. Nonetheless, not all Burroughs stories made the transition from pulp to book in his lifetime, which is why all first appearance dates given in this section are for magazine publication, unless otherwise stated.

Burroughs' third franchise was Pellucidar, a physically inverted world he imagined (far) beneath our very feet, whose rising horizons are ruled over by repulsive winged reptiles called Mahars. *At The Earth's Core,* the first of seven Pellucidar books (filmed pulpily in 1976, with Doug McClure in the role of protagonist David Innes), appeared in 1914.

Burroughs' fourth series was Caspak, which debuted with *The Land That Time Forgot* (1918). Though clearly inspired by Arthur Conan Doyle's *The Lost World,* Burroughs' own undiscovered land in which dinosaurs still place their thunderous steps also features real originality in the form of an ingenious truncated internal evolutionary system spanning not millennia but an individual's lifetime. A film appeared in 1975, with a sequel in '77, made by Amicus, the same company responsible for the *At The Earth's Core* film. A new movie adaptation of *The Land That Time Forgot* materialised in 2009.

These series and others have garnered Burroughs the title the Grandfather of Science Fiction. Bill Hillman offers, 'I've always qualified that by saying "American science fiction". Of course, H G Wells and Jules Verne and earlier people come before.' But Burroughs was not just the first major US SF novelist, Hillman notes: 'And science fantasy or science fantasy adventure, somewhere in a niche there, you could put him as a pioneer, as a first.'

Burroughs could also claim to have brought significant female characters into SF and fantasy for the first time. Danton observed: 'He combined the science fiction with romance, and you really took the part of his heroes and heroines.' Hillman adds: 'He's a much easier read. He's more captivating. He moves the plot along much faster than H G Wells or Jules Verne … He was the launch pad for so many authors to come. Pulp authors and authors right into the Golden Age of science fiction. They drew so heavily on his ideas. And he's always been criticised for not being scientific, but I've done a number of features where I've listed some of the inventions that he has come up with, and so many of these have eventually come true, like body transplants and x-rays and navigation devices, and it goes on and on.'

Burroughs was never fêted by the critics. 'He was panned a lot,' admitted his grandson. 'I think the bottom line was, if he wasn't a great author he wouldn't have been so damn popular.' Danton also said, 'He would always downplay it. He was pretty humble about it.'

'I don't think you can take that at face value,' says Hillman of Burroughs' 'I'm-a-simple-storyteller' line. 'He put a lot of work into his writing and he was very successful and I think he was very proud of what he had accomplished … He never really admitted that, but I think it bothered him when critics didn't realise the type of writer he was.' John Taliaferro's Burroughs biography *Tarzan Forever* certainly portrays a man frustrated by his inability to make the step up from the low-rent pulps to the respectable 'slicks'. Hillman: 'He was writing for a certain market and he was top of his field. In his own way, he was a great writer.'

Burroughs' other major series was Amtor, which debuted with *Pirates of Venus* (1932). Opinion on these stories – four of which were published in Burroughs' lifetime – is sharply divided. Many find them dull and their blundering protagonist Carson Napier irritating. As Danton pointed out, 'He was on his way to Mars. He ended up on Venus.' Others feel Napier's pointedly unheroic nature was an indication of Burroughs' development as both writer and human being, the glorification of battle – and at times homoerotic celebration of muscle-bound heroes – of his earlier books giving way to a more mature outlook, just as his writing style had become leaner and less inclined to floridity down the years. 'Sure,' said Danton when asked if Burroughs was satirising hero novels. 'Probably to show the vulnerability of the character being normal. And you're talking about a period of time where Ed was going through some changes in his life also. He was divorcing my grandma, Emma, marrying a younger woman, Florence Gilbert. It was just a time of turmoil. He lost the [El Caballero] country club. They launched the huge radio programme and [Tarzan movie actor Johnny] Weissmuller had come on the scene. It was a bizarre early 1930s adventure for Ed and for Carson Napier of Venus.'

'It came later,' says Hillman. 'Burroughs' peak writing seemed to be in the ['10s] and early '20s and then he had a lot of personal problems after that and financial problems and things like that. A lot of people misinterpret the Amtor series, because in a few of them he really satirised Nazi Germany and people took it at face value.'

Certainly a mature outlook was evinced by *Beyond the Farthest Star* (1942), which depicted a planet, Poloda, in the midst of a hundred-year war that is a matter for depression rather than derring-do. Ironically, Burroughs became World War II's oldest war correspondent after being an eyewitness at the bombing of Pearl Harbor.

Other Burroughs SF and fantasy novels are: *The Moon Maid* trilogy, an anti-communist alien invasion story collected in one volume in 1926; *Beyond Thirty* aka *The Lost Continent* (1915), a rare Burroughs future-set story; *The Eternal Lover* aka *The Eternal Savage*, a high-quality pair of stories from 1914 and 1915 concerning a primeval man who awakens in modern Africa; *The Monster Men* (1913), a cross between *Frankenstein* and *The Island of Doctor Moreau* with a romance thrown in; and *The Resurrection of Jimber-Jaw* (1936), a battle-of-the-sexes story featuring a reawakened preserved caveman.

Danton said of his grandfather, 'He would inject quite a bit of himself in all of his work,' but he also admitted, 'He stayed away from the realistic.' Even several books in the quasi-naturalistic Tarzan series feature science fiction elements. However, Burroughs' *oeuvre* is not exclusively fantasy and SF. The prolific author tried his hand at virtually every writing genre imaginable. The least interesting of his non-fantasy fare are jungle-set Tarzan variants like *The Cave Girl, Jungle Girl* and *The Lad and The Lion* and naturalistic works such as *The Oakdale Affair* (filmed in 1919), *The Efficiency Expert, The Girl From Hollywood, The Girl from Farris's* and *Marcia of the Doorstep*. The latter was a novel with an ingénue protagonist written in 1924 that was by far his longest piece of work. Nobody could bring themselves to publish it, including Burroughs himself when he acquired his own imprint. It saw the light of day only in 1999. Danton offered, 'I like *The Girl from Hollywood* because you could see the family background there.' In the so-so category of non-SF Burroughs are *The Prisoner of Zenda*-homage *The Mad King*, the realistic play *You Lucky Girl!* (published in 1999) and 13th Century England-set *The Outlaw of Torn*.

I am a Barbarian was also historical but its narrative of a slave of Caligula is high-grade and it's surprising that this 1941 novel didn't see print anywhere in Burroughs' lifetime. Also impressive is the uncategorisable (and possibly intentionally parodic) *The Mucker*, the story of a no-good bum who discovers an inner moral fortitude when he is swept up in high sea adventure.

The Wild West was no mythological place to ex-cavalryman Burroughs so it's unsurprising that his Westerns are the most interesting of his non-fantasy works. *The War Chief* (1927) and *Apache Devil* (1928) are not only fine reads but predate *Dances With Wolves* by a good half-century in their sympathetic portrayal of Native Americans. 'He did a lot of research on those,' said Danton.

Burroughs was one of the most widely-read English language authors of the first half of the 20th Century. Reliable sales figures for the era are difficult to find but it is generally accepted that of his contemporaries only Zane Grey outsold Burroughs in America. Moreover, almost nobody can name a Zane Grey character today, whereas there are still few people on the planet who don't have at least a vague idea who Tarzan is. Burroughs naturally made a fortune from his vast readership. However, his revenue streams came from many sources other than his writing. His works, Tarzan especially, spawned industries left, right and centre. Tarzan movies were phenomenally lucrative for him. Additionally, points out Hillman, 'He was one of the first big merchandising people.'

Unfortunately, Burroughs also lost large chunks of his fortune via over-spending, the '29 Wall Street crash and divorce. He continually had to sell off parts of the 540-acre San Fernando Valley estate that he bought in March 1919 and turned into a ranch named Tarzana. Nonetheless, in the shape of the town of Tarzana – founded in 1928 on parts of the property he had sold off – he left an enduring monument in this world in addition to his 80-odd books. 'He had a dream and he told his brother Harry that he wanted to start a community and name it Tarzana,' recalled Danton. 'And by God he did it. He wrote diligently to the postal department and got a post office brought here and got telephone service. He got a bus service, stage line. He really put this whole community on the map. He got the chamber of commerce going. We're thriving today with about 60,000 residents.'

Towards the end of Burroughs' life, a certain fatigue began to set in to both his writing and his private life. (His estrangement from his wife seemed to coincide with the disappearance from the Tarzan series of the character's own wife Jane.) His Tarzan books particularly became increasingly formulaic, featuring an endless procession of lost cities (all, with one exception, white settlements), safaris in trouble and implausible Tarzan look-alikes. When he returned to civilian life after World War II, Burroughs' publishing company – which he had set up in 1931 because by his own admission his hardball playing had cut his previous publishers' profit margins to counterproductive levels – issued three more books, one each in the Tarzan, Mars and Venus series, before he passed away. The cause of his death on 19 March 1950 was a Parkinson's disease-related heart attack. Said Danton, 'My granddad was diagnosed with Parkinson's in 1949 – I've got the letter from the doctor – and then my dad acquired it in 1959 and I got Parkinson's in 1999.' This sad genetic fact does rather blow asunder Edgar Rice Burroughs' pride in his family's pure gene pool. (He was horrified during the Second World War to discover a Japanese man named Burroughs was living in his adopted home of Hawaii.) It also complicated his belief in eugenics, distasteful manifestations of which litter his work, and nature-over-nurture, which forms the bedrock of the Tarzan character: the belief that an English lord brought up amongst wild beasts will retain an innate nobility. Yet Burroughs was no idiot. He admitted in correspondence that if a child really had been raised like Tarzan, far from exhibiting nobility, he 'would develop into a cunning, cowardly beast' and, in contrast to the preternatural beauty he gave the ape-man, would be 'under-developed' through lack of nourishment and rest.

By the time of his death, a new generation of SF writers who had idolised Burroughs as kids were already making a mark. His swashbuckling blend of fantasy and SF is clearly evident in the works of Robert E Howard, Ray Bradbury and Michael Moorcock. H P Lovecraft and Isaac Asimov were also evidently devotees. Superman – one of the few fictional characters as iconic and enduring as Tarzan – would not have been possible without John Carter and by extension neither would any other costumed superhero. Observes comics writer Roy Thomas of Superman's creator, 'Jerry Siegel was a Burroughs fan. The main Martian city is Helium and Siegel made his Krypton, which is another inert gas, and of course the idea of leaping that distance and being stronger in a weak gravity – there's an awful lot of John Carter in there.' Another fictional hero was also clearly indebted to John Carter. Burroughs had been trying to place a John Carter strip with both United Feature Syndicate and King Features Syndicate, and three days after negotiations fell through with the latter agency, newspapers began running their Flash Gordon strip. Gordon – in his original newspaper strip incarnation – was a fearsome swordsman who found himself able to make giant leaps on a planet with lighter gravity. Meanwhile, Philip José Farmer, though a considerable SF talent himself, wrote what was almost Burroughs fan fiction throughout his career, with several of his novels featuring Tarzan-esque characters. Burroughs even influenced hack Western writer J T Edson, who wrote a series of novels about one Bunduki, Tarzan's adopted grandson. 'So many were inspired in their early years,' says Hillman. 'Even Carl Sagan for example. They attribute so much of the wonder they have to Burroughs. Some people started as fan writers. Like Mike Resnick. Lin Carter. Even Leigh Brackett – she wrote the screenplay for *The Empire Strikes Back* – was a major Burroughs fan and wrote almost Burroughs pastiches.' Hillman also mentions the rumour that George Lucas wanted to make a John Carter film and wrote *Star Wars* when stymied in this endeavour. 'And a multitude of pulp authors, most of them forgotten now,' Hillman adds of the devotees.

In 2012, fully one hundred years after the publication of Burroughs' first novel-length story, an adaptation of it finally hit the cinema screens in the form of Disney/Pixar's *John Carter*. Though ERB's work has fallen in and out of print, deluxe editions of his Tarzan books appeared for his hundredth anniversary year, as well as fresh ape-man books by other authors and a new comic. A Warner Brothers Tarzan movie was on the horizon. A Disney Tarzan musical continued to wend its way successfully around the world. Even Carson Napier was rumoured to be the subject of a forthcoming film adaptation.

Burroughs' brand of SF and fantasy may today seem old-fashioned to some, with its Victorian morality, an over-reliance on coincidence and a flamboyancy of dialogue. However, his captivating, pacy narrative, futuristic visions leavened with romance, and universes imagined to the tiniest detail could still teach a thing or two to contemporary writers of speculative and fantasy fiction who may feel a sense of superiority about their more edgy styles. Moreover, a patina of age has not precluded much of Burroughs' work possessing an immortal status: who of his disciples have created the likes of Tarzan and John Carter, characters so iconic that they are still the subject of adaptations when the world in which they first made an appearance is barely recognisable as our own?

PART TWO: BIRTH OF THE APE-MAN

In the early years of the 20th Century, the market for the printed word was vast.

While then, as now, the educated classes had their books and periodicals, they were, unlike now, in a minority in their love of reading. In an era when there was no TV or radio and where cinema was in its silent, histrionic infancy, the working classes kept themselves entertained via vaudeville/music hall and – on the domestic front – consuming prose, especially fiction. The modest of pocket gravitated to dime novels and to magazines. In the American market, magazines were divided into the 'slicks' and the 'pulps'. The former were more highbrow, printed on good-quality paper and priced accordingly. The pulps cost (originally) just a dime because they were printed on low-grade paper (pulp). Their content – stories, often book-length, of adventure, crime, science fiction, cowboys, romance or a combination thereof – were also geared toward the reader with a less sophisticated palate. Modern sensibilities might scoff at its moral, structural and stylistic simplicity, but while much pulp writing can now really be taken seriously only by children and teens, it remains a quite sobering fact that a century ago, poorly educated people devoured words in volume unimaginable to their modern, nominally more sophisticated counterparts.

The All-Story Magazine was a monthly title that began life in 1905. (It dropped the '*Magazine*' part of its title in 1910 and became a weekly in 1914.) It was published by Frank Munsey, who pioneered the pulp format with *Golden Argosy* aka *Argosy*. Burroughs was well-acquainted with the Munsey magazines from when he had daily handled them in his time as a newsagent. Though, like much of Burroughs' science fiction, *Under the Moons of Mars* was ingenious, one wonders whether this secondary *All-Story* feature would have ever made it to book form had it not been for the slipstream of success created by the second novel-length narrative the magazine accepted from him. Three other, much shorter, stories appeared in that edition of *All-Story* cover-dated October 1912, which went on sale on 27 August; but whereas 'The Spaniard' by Frank Comstock, 'The Goat of Dolores Valdez' by John D Swain and 'On the Zodiac Turnpike' by Ella B Argo have now disappeared into history, *Tarzan of the Apes* emphatically has not. Even Clinton Pettee's cover illustration – a headbanded Tarzan astride a rearing lion, preparing to plunge a knife into its flank as a cowed visitor from civilisation looks on – has persevered, remaining one of the definitive images of the ape-man (something assisted in recent years by it becoming public domain).

Burroughs himself stated in a letter to a scholar who inquired about his inspirations for the work, 'It may have originated in my interest in Mythology and the story of Romulus and Remus. I also recall having read many years ago the story of a sailor who was shipwrecked on the Coast of Africa and who was adopted by and consorted with great apes to such an extent that when he was rescued, a she-ape followed him into the surf and threw a baby after him. Then, of course, I read Kipling; so that it probably was a combination of all these that suggested the Tarzan idea to me.' The Kipling story to which Burroughs refers is *The Jungle Book,* which like *Tarzan of the Apes* featured an animal-reared young man alternately romping with and endangered by wild animals with generic names different from those conferred by man. Burroughs scholars like Richard A Lupoff spent chunks of their lives searching in vain for the shipwrecked sailor story, and indeed some have concluded that Burroughs heard a piece of folklore rather than saw it in print. Some have also cited the possible influence of *Captured by Apes* (1888) by Harry Prentice, although this tale of a sailor shipwrecked on an island who becomes king of the resident simians by wearing the hide of the former ape king only seems persuasive as an influence in combination with the similarity of the same author's later *Captured by Zulus* to the plot of the Burroughs Tarzan book for children *The Tarzan Twins.* A 1910 *All-Story* inclusion titled 'The Monkey Man' and the 1906 Jack London novel *Before Adam* also contain elements that are reminiscent of components of *Tarzan of the Apes.*

The centuries-old story of Romulus and Remus being raised by a she-wolf before founding Rome was of course known to be a myth but it's difficult to believe that Burroughs was not also influenced, if only subliminally, by real-life stories of feral children, i.e. human young who by virtue of a combination of rural location and abandonment/tragedy lived for a period cut off from humanity, in some cases reputedly in the company of wild animals, before re-entering human society. Stories about the likes of Wild Peter of Hanover, the Bear Girl of Hungary and the Wild Boy of Aveyron had been appearing in print for hundreds of years and in more credulous times tended to be accepted at face value. Subsequently (mostly after Burroughs' time), many of the stories were exposed as false, with motives for the falsity ranging from a determination to prove the non-existence of God to altruism (raising funds for an orphanage in which feral children were supposedly housed) to mischief to ignorance to simple financial profit. However, even a hundred years ago it was widely known that even in the confirmed cases, if a child was feral during its baby-to-toddler years, it was never able to re-assimilate fully into society: speech faculties are irreparably impaired, as is a perception of being human.

In order to tell the story he had in mind of the triumph of nature over nurture, Burroughs had to ignore all of this latter evidence.

Tarzan of the Apes reads surprisingly like Jane Austen in places, what with its often courtly narrator's voice, belief in idealised love and talk of marriage based on financial imperatives. Sometimes it reads like a parody of Austen, what with its flowery prose ('But what of Alice and that other little life so soon to be launched amidst the hardships and grave dangers of a primeval world?') and laughably stilted dialogue ('Hundreds of thousands of years ago our ancestors of the dim and distant past faced the same problems which we must face, possibly in these same primeval forests. That we are here today evidences their victory'). In other places, though, the story reads like Conrad, with much exciting shipboard intrigue and ferocious jungle conflict. If Burroughs did take his cue from Kipling, his vision is a somewhat more blood-drenched variant of his cosy-ish tableau, for the world traversed by Tarzan is a far more savage one than that negotiated by *The Jungle Book*'s Mowgli. In one passage, Tarzan's scalp is left hanging over his eyes during a fight with an ape. In another, a squabble amongst pirates sees the point of a pick-axe brought fatally down upon a head. Jane is narrowly saved from being raped by a bull ape.

The tale begins with Burroughs informing the reader, 'I had this story from one who had no business to tell it to me, or to any other.' Though the framing device is illogical – Burroughs cannot possibly have had the manifold and minutely detailed events that follow related to him in mere conversation – it is also clever, drawing in the reader with its tone of a shared secret and its intriguing implication of being a true story. The basic plot runs as follows. In the year 1888, John Clayton, Lord Greystoke, accompanied by his pregnant wife Alice, is sailing to 'a British west coast African colony' to investigate on behalf of the British Colonial Office the maltreatment of natives. The brutality of the captain of their vessel the HMS *Fuwalda* provokes a mutiny, and it is only the concern Greystoke previously displayed about the conditions on board that sees his and Lady Greystoke's lives spared. They are put ashore with their (considerable) belongings in a place identified only as 'West coast of Africa, about 10° degrees south latitude.' Greystoke doesn't believe the mutineers' promise that they will alert the authorities as to their whereabouts and throws himself into creating a safe haven for Alice and their imminent child. Alice shortly gives birth to a healthy baby boy in the sturdy log cabin Greystoke has constructed. They call him John. However, a frightening encounter with one of the apes they have frequently espied lurking in the vicinity sends Alice into a bed-ridden delirium from which she never quite recovers until her death a year after giving birth. The cause of death is never specified; the perception of the time of women's general fragility is apparently sufficient explanation. Greystoke follows Alice into the afterlife shortly thereafter when the cabin is invaded by the human-like apes. His baby, however, is spared due to the coincidence of a female amongst the apes named Kala having lost her own baby only hours before when Kerchak, the king of her tribe, embarked on a bad-tempered rampage that culminated in it falling to the jungle floor. Kala snatches up the crying babe and, to the derision of her hairy friends, nurses and raises the child as her own. The tribe give the new, strange, hairless baby the name Tarzan, which in their language means 'White-Skin'.

Burroughs depicts the primates who raise young Clayton not as a known species such as chimpanzees (which barely appear in any Burroughs Tarzan book) or gorillas. Instead, he renders them 'a species closely allied to the gorilla, yet more intelligent; which, with the strength of their cousin' makes them 'the most fearsome of those awe-inspiring progenitors of man.' In later books he would flesh out his vague classification, explaining that they were a hitherto undiscovered type of ape. He also belatedly gave this species a name, which was – confusingly – Great Apes, ordinarily an umbrella title for the larger primates: chimps, gorillas, orangutans and, indeed, humans. The Manganis' name for themselves distinguishes them in their language from 'Tarmangani' – 'white people' – and 'Gomangani' – 'black people'. Though they can grow to a height of seven feet, Burroughs' apes swing through the upper branches of the trees like chimps and (though the world did not understand this at the time) unlike gorillas. However, they engage in rituals similar to those of primitive man, such as the fevered, drum-beating Dum-Dum, designed to mark milestones like tribal killings or the ascension of a new king. They are also omnivores, and quite bloodthirsty ones: they ceremoniously place one foot upon the necks of vanquished enemies and emit a blood-curdling victory cry before sinking their teeth into their flesh.

We follow Tarzan's progress amongst his primate peers from helpless infant to nervous child to mischievous teen and finally to an adult who becomes king of his tribe after a battle to the death with Kerchak. Outside of his tribe, Tarzan's best friend is Tantor, Burroughs' generic Mangani name for elephant. Over time, Burroughs would establish that Tarzan held no respect for Gimla the crocodile, was naturally wary of Numa the lion, felt the closest thing he knew to fear when contemplating Histah the snake and despised Dango the hyena for his cowardly scavenging.

Burroughs' jungle opera is, on one level, ludicrous. However, we in the main part buy into it because the narrative is engagingly written by an author who displays no embarrassment about the unlikely picture he is weaving. By investing the apes with human-like personalities and motivations, Burroughs keeps the narrative compelling without indulging in the more sentimental aspects of anthropomorphism, even if their vocabularies are absurdly wide ('Let us leave him quietly sleeping among the tall grasses, that you may bear other and stronger apes to guard us in our old age'). He even has us half-believing that Tarzan really could unlock the mysteries of the written word by spending hours poring over the children's primers and books owned by his parents, which have been preserved in the rudimentary house his father built. In fact, these sections of head-scratching absorption leading to enlightenment are rather sweet. The spell is broken only when the grown Tarzan leaves a note for foreigners who have taken over his treasured cabin signed in his ape name, and we recall that Burroughs has already explicitly stated that his silent, solitary studies mean that Tarzan doesn't understand the connection between the written word and speech, so would not know how to write 'Tarzan'.

Less sweet are Tarzan's murderous games with a black tribe who set up camp in his part of the jungle. He has learned from his father's books that he is not an *ape* but a *man*, hence his impulse to shave his face with his father's hunting knife. But when the first human he can ever recall having laid eyes on kills his adoptive mother Kala, he wreaks terrible revenge. Fair enough in regards to the actual killer, perhaps, but Tarzan then torments the man's tribe, who are characterised – according to Burroughs – by 'yellow teeth … filed to sharp points…', 'great protruding lips' and an overall appearance of 'low and bestial brutishness.' It would probably be unwise to be over-sensitive about depictions of cannibalism – such phenomena did exist – but the way that Tarzan kills these 'savage natives of the interior' whenever he desires arrows or jewellery or a loincloth (another self-conscious adoption of the trappings of men) is somewhat disturbing. Burroughs does at least posit the savagery of the natives partly as a legacy of their bitterness at their treatment by 'that arch hypocrite, Leopold II of Belgium, because of whose atrocities they had fled the Congo Free State …'

Sabor the lioness took the place in the book version of the tiger Burroughs erroneously placed in Africa in the *All-Story* version. However, it would have been just as apt to object to the presence of Numa and Tantor in the African bush, which creatures overwhelmingly tend to inhabit the continent's plains. Because of Tarzan's popularity, this mash-up became the real state of African fauna to millions in the West. As Hillman notes, 'His Africa is not a real place: to swing from the upper terraces of the rainforest and [have] lions and elephants running through the rainforest. But his Africa was picked up by so many films and authors later on.'

The adoption of the family knife puts Tarzan on equal footing with the ferocious animals by which he is surrounded, and he is able to defend himself from gorillas and lionesses. Not that Tarzan can use only physical power to overcome his opponents. Burroughs emphasises that he buys into the idea of the beneficial effects of a noble lineage with comments on 'the hallmark of aristocratic birth, the natural outcropping of many generations of fine breeding and hereditary instinct of graciousness.' It is just as much Tarzan's intelligence as his brawn that leads him to work out that he can kill a lion or ape with a full-nelson. Though investing such stock in noble blood seems preposterous from a modern perspective wherein lords are more likely to be perceived as upper class twits than a superior breed, it should be noted that the word 'lord' in 1912 and for a long time thereafter was as synonymous with glamour to the majority of people as the word 'princess'. It might be the case that even as Burroughs was writing *Tarzan of the Apes*, peers were losing a certain allure: the 1911 Parliament Act took away the House of Lords' ability to reject the legislation of the democratically elected Commons. However, only after the Second World War and the arrival into the mainstream of leftist politics did 'lord' begin to tip over into a pejorative. The word and concept never really regained its previous allure even as the political fashions lurched back to the right.

Burroughs' description of Tarzan is idealised to the point of homoerotic. He is a giant of six foot (even today, after a century of increasing average height, western men tend to be around 5' 10') with a 'straight and perfect figure, muscled as the best of the Roman gladiators must have been muscled, and yet with the soft and sinuous curves of a Greek god.' By the time two paragraphs later Burroughs is enthusing over 'the noble poise of his handsome head upon those broad shoulders, and the fire of life and intelligence in those fine, clear eyes' we imagine he is all but slavering. (For the record, Burroughs had three children and there seems no obvious indication of a gay leaning.)

Act II of the book starts at around the 100-page mark when a party of civilised outsiders is put ashore almost exactly where Tarzan's parents were marooned 21 years previously and in almost identical circumstances (the spared survivors of a ship mutiny). This event is just about plausible but by a quite astonishing/ridiculous coincidence one of the party is Tarzan's cousin, William Cecil Clayton, who has inherited his title and estates on the assumption that the Greystokes who disappeared on the high seas are dead. Another of the party is Miss Jane Porter of Baltimore, a young woman by whose beauty the observing Tarzan is immediately enraptured. When Tarzan recues Jane from mortal danger and takes her on an exhilarating swing through the tree-tops, she begins feeling the same way about him. The presentation of such attraction as pure love is a sign of times in which lust was a reality that dared not speak its name. Another indication of olde worlde mentality is the fact that the only profanities throughout – uttered by the sailors – are rendered as black lines. Additionally, some of the expressions used in the text have long passed out of the language. (Burroughs tells us that 'Tarzan sat in a brown study' to indicate that he is absorbed in thought.)

The book's comedy elements are its weakest parts. The 'Lawdy'/'No sah!' speech patterns of Jane's black maid Esmeralda might in isolation be simple colloquialism but combined with her attempting to jam her bulk into cupboard shelves and fainting away at every sign of danger become part of a bad taste cartoon. In fairness, Burroughs also portrays Jane's intellectual father Professor Archimedes Q Porter and his secretary and assistant Samuel T Philander as effete and absurd, even if the burlesque chapter in which they engage in intellectual babble about a lion that is trailing them is risible.

Burroughs employs a stately pace as he tells a varied and sometimes complex tale. He is often ornate, but such is the quality of his penmanship that the reader can sink into this stylistic plushness quite happily: 'For a moment he scrutinised the ground below and the trees above, until the ape that was in him by virtue of training and environment, combined with the intelligence that was his by right of birth, told his wondrous woodcraft the whole story as plainly as though he had seen the thing happen with his own eyes.' The omniscient narrative voice that was so prevalent in literature of the time and that can be insufferable to the modern reader is here the only apt method to relay a story that must explain the motivations of not just civilised humans but also savage beasts and a feral boy.

The story begins to unravel when Tarzan starts his transformation into a gentleman, which process is not only absurdly accelerated (maritime man Paul D'Arnot – the rescuer of the Porter/Clayton party – has him eloquent in French within weeks) but also makes him intrinsically less interesting and likeable: when Tarzan kills a lion to win a bet, he suddenly seems less a noble savage than a glorified big game hunter. Burroughs also misses a trick in not showing Tarzan's reaction to his first metropolis (Paris). Tarzan expertly driving a car not long after reaching America, meanwhile, is just too much for even the most credulous to swallow.

Burroughs does at least introduce an impressive twist at the end when a miserable Jane is contemplating marriage to a man she hates but to whom her father is financially indebted. Tarzan rescues Jane from a forest fire and then from her marriage, both by brute physical force. However, Tarzan doesn't get the girl, nor the title and estates that he knows his fingerprints prove are rightfully his. When Jane subsequently tells him she has promised to marry William Cecil Clayton, Tarzan keeps his counsel rather than take away status and riches from his beloved's intended. Asked by William Cecil about his background, he says, 'My mother was an ape … I never knew who my father was.' It is a pleasingly unusual and poignant conclusion in an era in which a manufactured happy ending would have been expected by much of the readership. This is in keeping with the book as a whole, for despite its expedient gaps in logic and the idealised nature of the hero – and he is a hero, not a protagonist – it sidesteps simplistic patterns. One example is Tarzan being given the handicap of initially not being able to speak the words he has learnt to read. Even Jane's improbable instant love for Tarzan is undercut by her subsequent apprehension that he will eat like an animal at table and her realisation back in civilisation that context was the main reason for her feelings for her 'forest god.'

Burroughs' story was not only engaging and exciting, it was also highly unusual – something that quite quickly became forgotten through the over-familiarity of the Tarzan character in the culture. Unsurprisingly, *Tarzan of the Apes* was an immediate sensation with *The All-Story*'s readers. Burroughs very cannily sold Munsey only the first magazine publication rights. It was a move so unusual that it could be said to have jeopardised publication – there was considerable correspondence between the magazine and the author about it before Munsey acquiesced – but by sticking to his guns Burroughs laid the foundation stone of his fortune.

Thomas Metcalf, managing editor of *The All-Story*, virtually begged Burroughs for a sequel to *Tarzan of the Apes*. However, when the author did acquiesce to the resumption of the adventures of the hero who had enraptured the magazine's readership like no other, Metcalf dismissed it as unprintable.

Burroughs was so distraught at the rejection of the tale he first titled *Monsieur Tarzan* that he told Metcalf he was going to give up writing. 'I put a lot of work on it,' he wrote. 'Mapped it out carefully so that I was quite sure that it would be smooth and consistent. You approved of the plans, and I did not deviate from them except in such minor details as seemed necessary … I certainly cannot afford to put months of work into a story thinking it the best work that I had ever done only to find that it doesn't connect. I can make money easier some other way … I think I'll chuck it.' Metcalf wrote back to implore him, 'For the love of Mike! Don't get discouraged!' Burroughs was actually a bit of a drama queen when it came both to rejection and to what he felt to be unjustly low remuneration, and it's doubtful that he contemplated abandoning his new writing career longer than a few minutes. After all, he had already suffered knock-backs: his historical novel *The Outlaw of Torn* had been rejected by *All-Story* following the acceptance of *Under the Moons of Mars*. Perhaps Burroughs was a little fed up with Metcalf: he had rejected *The Outlaw of Torn* after being the one to suggest an historical novel to him, and likewise it was at his suggestion that Burroughs transplanted Tarzan to an urban setting for his second adventure.

Burroughs sent what he now retitled *The Ape-Man* to *New Story Magazine*, published by Munsey rival Street & Smith. Though it was accepted, it's highly probable that it was simply the acclaim and profit the first Tarzan adventure had yielded for Munsey that engendered this happier result for the author. Nonetheless, Burroughs – who, however creatively inventive, would always demonstrate an apparently genuine prioritisation of profit over art – was probably less concerned by this than the fact that his payment was three hundred dollars more than he had secured for his first Tarzan story.

Approaching what was eventually serialised in *New Story* from June to December 1913 as *The Return of Tarzan* in terms other than those of naked commerce, it becomes understandable why Metcalf was not impressed. It's laughable. Technically, the juxtaposition of a wild man's savagery with the mores and customs of civilisation is a valid idea for fiction. However, as had already been demonstrated by the last sections of *Tarzan of the Apes*, Burroughs did not know how to bring off this literary conceit. Here, the faults of the way he depicted his urbanised Tarzan in the first book are magnified several-fold. A year or so after his first glimpse of white people, Tarzan is cruising through society enjoying cigarettes and absinthe ('… it was because he took civilisation as he found it'), attending libraries and picture galleries, devouring books and doling out personalised cards declaring 'M JEAN C. TARZAN.' Barely a year after first speaking, he is preternaturally eloquent ('I am convinced that their enmity is a sufficient guarantee of the integrity of its object,' he pronounces at one point) and steeped in American culture ('She is from an old southern family in America, and southerners pride themselves on their loyalty,' he observes of Jane's promise of marriage to his cousin). Meanwhile, the book is riven with unlikely coincidences, from Jane's best friend Hazel Strong being on the same liner as the ape-man at a critical juncture, to Tarzan after being thrown overboard said liner finding himself washed ashore – of all the places in the world – at the log cabin where he was born. Elsewhere, there are lapses more grave than offences against probability: '… the black men … to my mind are in most ways lower in the scale than the beasts,' offers Tarzan easily.

The plot begins with Tarzan loafing around Paris under the aegis of D'Arnot. His honourable behaviour in a duel – engineered by his new nemesis, high society criminal Nikolas Rokoff – lands him a job as a secret agent for the French government in Algeria. It is Rokoff who arranges for Tarzan to be thrown over a ship's rail when he is headed for Cape Town on business. Back in the Africa in which he feels far more comfortable than the metropolis, even despite a lukewarm welcome from the Mangani and the lack of cigs and absinthe, he becomes head of the Waziri tribe, who will feature in many Tarzan adventures to come. It is the Waziri who take Tarzan to a lost city from which they obtain their ornaments: Opar. This is the first and for many the best of the numerous isolated and antediluvian civilisations that will occur in Tarzan stories, not least because of its high priestess, the beautiful La. Cut adrift from its (imputed) motherland Atlantis after the latter's well-known watery fate, Opar is populated by repulsive savage men, who are the result of carnal relations with apes, and physically perfect women, who are the result of careful breeding. Little wonder that La – a recurring character in the series – would forever hold a torch for the buff Tarzan. It is rumoured that Burroughs always regretted not pairing the two. Though Jane did develop into a resourceful woman and character in her own right rather than the prim cypher she was in danger of appearing in the debut, La – with her haughty demeanour, steely determination, scantily clad sensuality and facility in the Mangani language – is arguably a far better match for Tarzan.

Tarzan finds Jane on his patch again when she, her intended and Rokoff are, in another ludicrous coincidence, washed ashore on the stretch of the African coast where he grew up. Jane's Southern loyalty of which Tarzan has spoken evaporates when her fiancée fails to try to protect her from a lion (leaving a hidden Tarzan to save them with a spear). Tarzan subsequently rescues Jane from Opar's blood-drenched sacrificial altar. William Cecil Clayton ensures the happiness of Tarzan and Jane by telling them on his fevered African deathbed that he knows Tarzan to be the real Lord Greystoke; although the treasures Tarzan has looted from Opar mean they won't be skint anyway. At book's end, Tarzan and Jane are married by Jane's father. They sail to civilisation, Tarzan comfortable in the knowledge that his love for his new 'mate' will quell his misgivings about never seeing the jungle again.

There are occasional flashes of good writing in *The Return of Tarzan*, such as the depicted terror of the inhabitants of an upmarket house through which rings the victory cry of the bull ape after Tarzan has pitilessly dealt with an antagonist. Generally, though, the prose is utilitarian and stiff. It also suffers from the comic book-like tenor of action scenes in which we never feel any anxiety over Tarzan's fate. In fact, sometimes we wish for harm to befall the ape-man, such is the pompousness of his assumption of the mantle of do-gooder. Additionally, the omniscient narration that was so appropriate in *Tarzan of the Apes* is here somewhat suffocating: four points of view are represented in the first three pages alone.

Despite its hectic plot, throughout *The Return of Tarzan* Burroughs just doesn't seem to know what to do with the character he had dreamed up in a fit of sublime creativity. That and the poor writing and utter lack of believability will confirm to some that *Tarzan of the Apes* – with its now ruined perfect, tragic ending – never needed a sequel.

The phenomenal success of Tarzan in the pulps created a commensurate demand for more. Yet that demand was in a way illogical. Tarzan was intrinsically a one-off. Once the concept of a noble raised in the jungle and then being reclaimed by civilisation had been depicted, there was, apparently, nowhere else to go with it. For this reason, it's probable that Burroughs had not even considered *Tarzan of the Apes* to be anything other than self-contained when he was writing it. The Tarzan universe was far more limited than those of the two other franchises he had begun. In neither of the two sequels to *Under the Moons of Mars* that had seen magazine publication by 1914 had Burroughs been visibly straining for a way to perpetuate his original idea. Similarly, the ideas on which he had begun expounding in *At the Earth's Core* would be ingeniously, rather than forcedly, elaborated on in half a dozen further volumes set in Pellucidar. We should also note that Tarzan at this juncture was probably not a huge priority for Burroughs. Between the first and the third Tarzan stories, Burroughs had published in the pulps the novel- or novella-length stories *The Cave Girl*, *A Man Without A Soul* (later re-titled *The Monster Men*), *The Mucker*, *The Mad King* and *The Eternal Lover*. These tales – which don't even include some unpublished short stories dating from this period – range from science fiction to a form of dirty realism. Burroughs was clearly enjoying his newly assumed status of author, and Tarzan was just one of the characters whose stories he was veritably cranking out. He may well have been thinking that there was no reason to believe he could not create something just as popular as Tarzan.

Yet as a cold-eyed realist and someone with a family to support, Burroughs was naturally happy to accede to public demand for more Tarzan. Moreover, sandwiching the third *bona fide* entry in the Tarzan series were two stories that shamelessly exploited the ape-man's success. Burroughs first shoehorned Tarzan into the otherwise unrelated *The Eternal Lover* by making the protagonist a big-game hunter visiting the estate of Lord and Lady Greystoke at the start of a fantastic adventure wherein he is transported back to primitive times – in so doing creating severe continuity problems, as Burroughs' depiction of the Claytons' son Jack as a babe in arms doesn't chime with the way he subsequently placed him in the thick of the action in the First World War. The other sandwiching story, *The Lad and the Lion*, in fairness ties in just as much to *The Mad King*, but with it Burroughs effectively gave himself another bite of the Tarzan cherry by proffering what is essentially a re-tooled *Tarzan of the Apes*: the young heir to a European crown is washed up on an African shore and has to fend for himself in the company of only a lion he has befriended onboard; ultimately he returns to his noble birthright.

Despite its warmed-over nature, in 1917 *The Lad and the Lion* became the first-ever Burroughs story to be adapted to the young medium of the moving picture. The première of the five-reel movie of the same name occurred simultaneously with the story's magazine publication, an indication both of the short turnaround times for films back then and of Burroughs' business canniness in proactively pitching his wares at movie studios. Sadly, no print of *The Lad and the Lion* is known to survive and there is almost certainly nobody alive on this planet who would have seen the picture, which was very loosely remade in 1936 as *The Lion Man*. Curiously in retrospect, at first no movie studio seemed interested in *Tarzan of the Apes* itself.

The inherent limitations of Tarzan were made almost embarrassingly manifest by *The Beasts of Tarzan*, published in May-June 1914 by the magazine that was, following a merger, now called *All-Story Cavalier Weekly*. Even expanded for book publication in 1916, it would be one of the slimmest of Burroughs' Tarzan volumes. It is just as insubstantial aesthetically.

At the beginning of the story, a shadow is cast over the nuclear family bliss in which Tarzan, Jane and Jack are living by news that Nikolas Rokoff has escaped from prison. Naturally, the villain from *The Return of Tarzan* is out for revenge. He abducts both Jane and Jack and strands Tarzan on a remote island, giving him something on which to dwell in his new home by telling him he is going to allow Jack to be raised by cannibals in Africa while Jane's fate 'I shall leave to your imagination.'

The beasts of the title are the creatures on the island that Tarzan enlists to help him get back his family. One is a form of Mangani with whom Tarzan is able to converse. Somewhat less comprehensible is how he is able to communicate with Sheeta the panther, who becomes his obedient (if admittedly edgy) ally after he rescues him from beneath a fallen tree. The final ally he picks up is the warrior Mugambi, and if his implicit bracketing with 'beasts' will set the antennae twitching of those who have already perceived racism in Burroughs, it has to be said that the character is at all times depicted as noble and brave, with it actually being stated that he is the ape-man's 'black counterpart.' Tarzan battles a crocodile for the first time in the series prior to reaching Africa, killing Rokoff and saving Jane and Jack from their respective fates-worse-than-death.

If Tarzan has become far too civilised for plausibility over the previous two stories, Burroughs at least tries to keep him true to his savage upbringing: at one point Tarzan smears his face almost orgasmically with his quarry's hot blood, at another he dismisses Jane's pleading for an enemy's life as he methodically breaks his neck. Such realism is rather spoilt by a feeble ending in which Burroughs takes his penchant for sometimes annoying omniscience to the farthest degree by speaking directly to the reader like some vaudeville turn. Referring to Tarzan's African estates, on which the ape-man is proposing to allow Mugambi and his woman to live, he writes, 'Possibly we shall see them all there amid the savage romance of the grim jungle and the great plains where Tarzan of the Apes loves best to be. Who knows?'

This hardly enthusiastic closing remark is in keeping with the tentative and aimless air surrounding *The Beasts of Tarzan*, a book that sums up a problem that Burroughs would really face for the rest of his days. Within its pages, he gropes for something to do with a character who stubbornly persists in being his most successful invention.

The tight constraints in which Burroughs found himself *vis a vis* Tarzan presumably explain why the ape-man did not return to the newsstands for another 18 months. Though the author's solution to his creative impasse was not quick in coming, it was clever. *The Son of Tarzan* – serialised in *All-Story Weekly* (the *Cavalier* component having now been dropped from the title) in six parts in December 1915 and January 1916 and the longest Tarzan story so far – was streets ahead of its predecessor and is one of the most enduringly popular of all Tarzan adventures.

One wonders how much of the renewed inspiration evident in Burroughs' Tarzan writing was due to the fact that a month after *The Beasts of Tarzan* began its serialisation, he had received confirmation that *Tarzan of the Apes* was to become his first published novel. This was no small achievement. Burroughs might have bristled throughout his life at the fact that his magazine writing almost never made it out of the pulps, but a proper bound book was on a higher plateau than occupied even by the slicks. It was A C McClurg who finally consented to publish *Tarzan of the Apes* after several other publishers –

as well as, previously, McClurg – had rebuffed Burroughs' entreaties to rescue it from its literary ghetto.

Once again, Burroughs was displaying his grounding as a businessman. Most other writers would simply have been bowled over to see their name in print, yet though Burroughs was no doubt pleased to get published in *All-Story*, he was also cognisant of the fact that despite the estimated 200,000 pairs of eyes that had seen the edition in which Tarzan made his debut, it was a transient success: the shelf-life of the magazine was precisely one month (and it was presumably not the kind of periodical favoured by libraries). A serialisation of *Tarzan of the Apes* started in January 1913 in the *New York Evening World* newspaper in a deal brokered by Munsey's had brought welcome extra exposure and income. (The vast number of city and state newspapers in America prepared to pay to run a story already published elsewhere would afford a nice little bonus for Burroughs in coming years.) Though the shelf-life of an edition of a newspaper was even shorter than that of a magazine, the serialisation was an elongated one: it ran for 46 daily episodes (except Sundays). More to the point, it was newspapers that gave Burroughs his foot in the door of book publishing: friend Albert Terhune, fiction editor at the *Evening World*, did Burroughs a favour by testifying to publishers how popular were Burroughs' stories were with its readers.

McClurg, based in Burroughs' home town of Chicago, published *Tarzan of the Apes* on 6 June 1914. The approximately 10,000 copies printed of the novel's first edition may not sound too impressive considering that the readership of the *All-Story* stood at around 20 times that figure, nor might Burroughs' $250 dollar advance on a royalty of ten percent (with escalator) of the $1.30 cover price immediately scream 'big time.' However, a book, if it remained in print, would generate money for many years. There was an additional benefit incalculable in monetary terms. The *Tarzan of the Apes* McClurg hardback had a red binding on which the title and author's name were embossed in gold lettering. Over this was positioned a quietly dignified dust jacket whose wraparound illustration by Fred J Arting went in the other direction to Clinton Pettee's dramatic, full-colour cover art for the same tale when featured in *All-Story*, showing simply a human silhouette sitting in a tree, with a lion wandering around in the distance. Inside the covers, the crisp, thick pages were a world removed from the second-rate paper from which the pulps had taken their name. This whole artefact was the type of thing that would sit very nicely alongside the handsome volumes on the shelves in the learned Burroughs' ever-expanding library. Burroughs was now a *bona fide* author. Book versions of *The Return of Tarzan*, *The Beasts of Tarzan* and *The*

Son of Tarzan followed at annual intervals thereafter.

This did not mean, though, that Burroughs began to spurn the likes of *All-Story*, especially when by no means all of his stories made the jump from magazines: *The Lad and the Lion*, for instance, couldn't be placed with a book publisher even despite having become a movie. However, Burroughs' main series – Tarzan, Mars, Venus, Pellucidar and Caspak – now all found book publishers pretty effortlessly, as did several other mini-series and one-offs. The previously small McClurg became rich as Burroughs' – and especially Tarzan's – fame spread exponentially.

That Burroughs decided to re-invigorate the Tarzan franchise by giving the ape-man's son an adventure of his own in *The Son of Tarzan* was on one level a dangerous move. A Tarzan with a teenage progeny is by definition getting on a bit, which can't help but diminish the hero's aura of physical perfection. On the other hand, the coming-of-age story – with its built-in vulnerability, youthful vigour and journey of discovery – is the very thing to inject life into an arid literary landscape. Additionally, the 'family' tableaux it creates can't help but be touching. Burroughs himself had two sons and, though there doesn't seem any evidence that he loved Hulbert (born 1909) and John Coleman (1913) any more than his daughter Joan (1908), his patent fondness for his boys shines through the text.

Jack Clayton's age is not specified, but at the start of this book we infer he is in his early teens. He disturbs Jane with his obsession with Africa, his superhuman strength and his penchant for climbing trees despite having been told nothing of his father's jungle upbringing. The romantic notion that Jack would have somehow inherited the simian-like agility that was his father's only via conditioning has, of course, no basis in science, but such conceits are common even in today's more rationality-suffused culture.

A performing ape at a music hall transpires to be a captured Akut, Tarzan's simian friend from the last adventure. In this book, Burroughs begins properly fleshing out the concept of the Mangani, describing them as an 'almost extinct species of ape.' (In one of the stories in the later book *Jungle Tales of Tarzan*, he will explicitly differentiate them from chimpanzees and gorillas by stating that unlike them they 'walk without the aid of their hands quite as readily as with.' In *Tarzan and the Leopard Men*, two decades after Tarzan's first appearance, a character will observe of the species, 'It was evident that they were not gorillas, and that they were more man-like than any apes he had seen.') After making secret visits to see Akut, during which he learns his language, Jack ends up with the ape's owner's hands around his throat. In a classic Burroughs example of unlikely coincidence, said owner is Alexis Paulvitch, former accomplice of Rokoff, who ended up in Sheeta's belly in the previous story. Akut kills Paulvitch to protect Jack. Jack then smuggles Akut onto a ship bound for Africa. Once there, Akut again resorts to killing to defend Jack after a man tries to fleece him at a sleazy hotel. Jack flees with Akut into the jungle to escape a murder rap.

A relationship reminiscent of that of Mowgli and Baloo in *The Jungle Book* is then enacted as Jack learns the ways of the wild in sections equivalent to those sweet parts of *Tarzan of the Apes* in which we saw the wonder and simple pleasures of his father's forest-based formative years. Jack loses in stages the pyjamas in which he has fled. He also loses his name, as Akut can't pronounce it. Instead, the ape dubs him 'Korak', an approximation of the Mangani for 'killer'. Korak's first kill is a native who has committed no crime worse than being a member of a village that had made him and Akut unwelcome. This is a hallmark of a bloodthirsty and sometimes distinctly nasty book. Later on, Korak massacres an entire village in the mistaken belief that they have eaten somebody he cares about. Though Burroughs shows Korak learning to recognise the smell of jungle animals and acquiring other survival instincts, he doesn't totally overdo it, depicting him chastened after cockily attempting to take on Numa before he is ready. Ultimately though, Jack becomes 'a creature of marvellous physical powers and mental cunning.' He is having such a ball with Akut that he only idly resolves to make his way back to civilisation at some hazy point in the future.

Korak's life becomes even more blissful when he happens upon a beautiful, nut-brown girl his own age named Meriem, who is being held prisoner in an Arab stockade. Korak rescues the grateful, abused girl and the two turn the jungle into a veritable Garden of Eden as they embark upon a love affair, communicating via the Mangani that Korak teaches Meriem. The love affair becomes sexual (or as close to sexual as the prim Burroughs ever depicted anything) only after a passage of time we assume to be years.

In the second half of the book, Korak and Meriem are separated, with Meriem being cared for by a kindly couple who at book's end are revealed to be Tarzan and Jane, looking for their lost son. Before that revelation, memorable scenes include Korak mustering an army of 3,000 baboons in a quest to find Meriem, and Korak being rescued by a summoned Tantor from a burning at the stake. At the conclusion, Korak and Meriem are married on board the ship that is taking the Greystoke clan back to England, by which point arch-snob Burroughs has emphasised that Meriem is no mere Arab waif but a princess.

Perhaps because of the above-mentioned diminution of physical perfection in the father that a grown son implies, Burroughs did no more with Korak after this book than feature him in a secondary role in a trio of novels in the middle of the series. Having said that, beyond this 'origin story', there wasn't much potential for him, as demonstrated by Gold Key and DC Comics, who both later gave the character his own regular title but failed to convey much more than an ersatz Tarzan. Burroughs himself only really differentiates Jack from his father by having him spurn the victory cry of the bull ape for a silent exultation. It must also be admitted that *The Son of Tarzan* relies for much of its appeal on being a rehash of the first Tarzan book. Nonetheless, it covers old ground adroitly and often charmingly.

The fifth Tarzan adventure was *Tarzan and the Jewels of Opar*, serialised in *All-Story Weekly* in November and December 1916 and published in book form in 1918.

This story both showed Burroughs finally apprehending how he could prolong the ostensibly limited Tarzan concept and set the template for the series. With a few exceptions, ape-man novels would from now on involve lost cities, imported ne'er-do-wells, separate safaris with similar objectives but morally contrasting motives and a Tarzan who is the man with the key to the relevant issue or – as a man in his element – the key to the survival of the good guys. Burroughs would in future years dot Africa with a most unlikely number of missing metropolises. Though those lost cities were sometimes marked by authorial ingenuity and though Burroughs juggled and dovetailed the stories of the separate parties seeking or stumbling upon them quite impressively, in time this whole approach ossified into a rigid, groan-inducing formula, often incorporating the device of a man and a woman in the 'good' safari falling in love. *Jewels of Opar*, though, is one of the better examples, even if it does feature another of the tut-provoking elements of that formula in the shape of Tarzan temporarily losing his memory after a blow on the head.

The beautiful but deadly La is central to the proceedings in a tale that sees Tarzan looting Opar because – in an example of the way Burroughs depicted the ape-man as someone with a foot in both the jungle and high society – his African estate has become a bit strapped for cash. Also seeking Opar's treasures is a Belgian army deserter named Albert Werper, who is in cahoots with Arab villain Achmet Zek. (Burroughs had a penchant for cosmopolitan villainy.) Zek decides to sell Jane to a harem (a common threat to Lady Greystoke in the Tarzan stories) but when she is abducted, the feisty Mrs Clayton turns out to be equal to the challenges she faces. That Tarzan manages to remain immune to La's lustful charms (surprisingly candidly drawn by the often moralistic author) despite an amnesiac state that means he has no knowledge of having sworn marriage vows may provoke a response of, 'Mister, you're a better man than I.'

A dying witchdoctor croakingly predicting doom and a rhinoceros with attitude (he takes on seven lions) are amongst the thrills in a roller-coaster ride that has a whimsical twist in the tail.

In the autumn of 1916, a Virginia teenager named Herman Newman set up the Tribe of Tarzan, the first association relating to the ape-man. Newman explained in a letter to Burroughs that Tarzan had made a man out of him. The organisation had a Tribe room for their meetings and played with grass ropes, hunting knives and bows and arrows. A delighted Burroughs obtained them publicity in *All-Story* and had bronze medallions struck for them to give out for achievement of tasks. (The medals were designed in imitation of the locket Tarzan wore around his neck with photographs of his parents inside that he had found in the log cabin back in the first story.) Truthfulness, honesty, manliness, courageousness, health and cleanliness were among the values listed on the back of Tribe membership cards. In other words, a Tarzan-inflected variant of the Boy Scouts, then a very young organisation (formed by Baden-Powell in 1907). Such a code of honour might seem pretty square, but this was several generations before questioning of society's mores was perceived as more admirable than steadfast adherence to them. Branches of the Tribe of Tarzan soon sprang up across the country, and 13 years later – long after Herbert Newman had grown up, joined the army, been demobilised and dropped out of the picture – it was going strong enough to be talking of striking out internationally.

All of this was significant because having inspired such formalised devotion only five magazine stories/three books in indicated that the ape-man already had the makings of a phenomenon.

From its issue cover-dated September 1916, *Blue Book* magazine began publishing new Tarzan short stories by Burroughs at a rate of one per month up to the issue dated August 1917. They were subsequently collated and published in book form as *Jungle Tales of Tarzan* (in the UK, *Tarzan's Jungle Tales*).

The word 'midquel' was not in currency in 1916/17 (and some lovers of the English language might suggest it shouldn't be today) but that is what the stories – and book – constitute, with Burroughs going back to the point in *Tarzan of the Apes* when Tarzan was an adolescent roaming the jungle aware of the world beyond it only in the sense of what he had seen in the books in his parents' cabin. The author's opting for such fragmented and nostalgic Tarzan writing at this juncture may have been down to a combination of a form of repetitive strain disorder diagnosed as neuritis and a desire to work on other projects, especially motion picture adaptations of his work. Another possibility is that the stories were a way for him to work around his uncertainty about how to continue the Tarzan franchise. However, even if this book represents a holding action, it is a delightful entry in the Tarzan canon.

All these stories occur after the death of Kala but before Tarzan becomes king of his tribe by killing Kerchak. The 12 chronologically-presented stories are each self-contained but the fact that they are interlinked – some subtly, some overtly – creates an episodic novel in all but name. They see Tarzan develop his first crush (on a comely Mangani), engineer his own rescue from hostile natives by calling on Tantor (a device from *The Son of Tarzan* that would become a tedious cliché of Tarzan movies), win round a hostile mother in his tribe by rescuing her baby from danger, tussle with the notion of God, kidnap a young boy from the local village as a surrogate son before returning him when overcome with compassion for the homesick child, defeat the nefarious plans of an abhorrent witch-doctor consulted by the distraught mother of the boy Tarzan had abducted, turn the witch-doctor's plans for his grisly death back on him, try to teach his Mangani tribe the virtues of vigilance with regard to potential predators only to have his machinations blow up in his face, confuse dreams with reality after becoming feverish though food poisoning, get rescued from peril by bullets taken from his parents' log cabin, murderously torment the local villagers with both a lion skin and a real lion and obtain a hero aura among the frightened Mangani for seeming to retrieve a disappearing moon that is actually in eclipse.

This lesson-learning against a wilderness backdrop as well as the title of the book serves to strengthen the impression of the influence on Burroughs of *The Jungle Book*. Only the mean-spirited anti-black strain running through the stories diminishes the overriding air of sweetness and innocence.

When Burroughs had insisted on selling them only magazine publication rights to *Tarzan of the Apes*, a bewildered Frank Munsey Company had asked him what other possible rights there might be. According to writer Gabe Essoe, the author had seemed vague himself: 'I don't know. Maybe moving picture rights or something else.' Burroughs' inchoate hunch proved right, for successful though his novels already were, in 1918 it was the new medium of the 'movies' that was the true making of both him and his ape-man creation.

Lost in the mists of time is how influential in several respects the first

Tarzan movie was on the young medium of the moving picture. When *Tarzan of the Apes* (1918) was released, it was, apart from *Birth of a Nation* (1915) and *Intolerance* (1916), the longest theatrical cinema film up to that point. In an age when most movies were of two reels (each reel lasting between 13 and 15 minutes), this one ran to ten reels. However, it wasn't just length that rendered *Tarzan of the Apes* remarkable. Though like so many pictures from the silent era it looks comical to modern eyes, it was an amazing spectacle at the time, innovative in camerawork and production values. Its promotional campaign was a precursor of modern hype. It also spawned one of the first movie sequels. There is even an argument for saying that it was the greatest cinematic cultural sensation up to that point, for grand and successful though *Birth of a Nation* was, its exposure was restricted by the bans that its controversial content acquired it in many places, while *Intolerance* was a commercial flop.

The National Film Corporation of America bought the film rights to *Tarzan of the Apes* four years after that aforementioned exchange between author and magazine publisher, for a then-massive $5,000 advance, $50,000 in company stock and five percent of gross receipts. Grand though their title was, the National Film Corporation of America was actually a start-up venture by a man with no cinema experience. Previously, William Parsons had been a life insurance salesman. He had inked a deal with Burroughs after the latter had been unsuccessful in persuading anyone to make a Tarzan picture when the idea was put into the author's head by a New York play broker in 1913. Parsons' plan was to found a film company and shoot the picture with the money he made by selling its stock.

Parsons is listed as producer of *Tarzan of the Apes,* which was directed by Scott Sidney. Edgar Rice Burroughs is, along with Fred Miller and Lois Weber, credited as a writer. Al Bohl, the producer of *Tarzan: Lord of the Louisiana Jungle,* a 2012 documentary about the movie, explains that this billing reflected an actual contribution to the script by Burroughs rather than just being a courtesy credit: 'He was really part of the production at the start, but when they began to change the story a little bit he backed out. They didn't want him to leave. They felt like he had a good name … Even though people act as if [Parsons] was a snake-oil salesman, from all the things I've read from the Burroughs family it looked like he was a pretty nice fella [who] really, sincerely wanted Burroughs to be part of it. But, see, Burroughs just didn't understand that a book and a movie [are] two different things.' In correspondence with Parsons, Burroughs asserted that to change Tarzan would be to 'ruin' it for the million or so people who he estimated had read the story by then, even if 'the change made a better story of it.' Prior to the movie's release, a disgruntled

Burroughs made enquiries about the feasibility of removing his name and even Tarzan's from the picture.

Bohl is fairly sure that *Tarzan of the Apes* was the first major American motion picture formally shot on location. 'By that time, film had pretty much settled into two coasts, either New York or California,' he says. 'At first they were just shooting *Tarzan* in California but they just felt like it didn't have that natural feeling. They couldn't go to Africa, because you couldn't get around like you can now.' (For the same reason, Bohl dismisses publicity of the day that suggested that an excursion had been made to Brazil.) 'So they sent out scouts to find a place that had three deals.' Morgan City, Louisiana, fit the bill in having jungle-like greenery, a large black population and reliable transportation.

The 'scenario' (as screenplays were then called) for the most part follows the plot of the first Burroughs Tarzan novel. Ten-year-old Gordon Griffith plays the jungle lord as a young boy in the first sections of the movie. Elmo Lincoln was the adult Tarzan, although not without a hiccup when his brinkmanship over a demand for a fee of $100 per week rather than $75 led to the studio re-casting Stellan Windrow in the role. The latter athletic vaudeville actor spent several weeks shooting jungle scenes in Louisiana, but when America entered what we now call the First World War, Windrow decided to enlist in the Navy, necessitating his replacement. A recalled Lincoln got his extra $25. Windrow can still be seen in the occasional tree-top in the finished film, but agreed to waive a place in the credits for $1,000. Bohl: 'Anytime they're high up in the trees, he's there. He did all the arboreal stuff. He left the shoot four weeks into it. Down on the ground or lower limbs, you see Elmo Lincoln. Now they say it's because Elmo Lincoln was afraid of heights, but I've interviewed his daughter and she said he had never indicated to her that he was scared of heights at all … It was probably that they'd fought so much of the elements – they had malaria – they probably thought, why shoot it all over again?'

The film comes in different running lengths. Explains Bohl, 'Originally the film was two hours and ten minutes. They had to cut it down.' Much of the footage excised from the longer version was non-jungle material. *Variety* complained in February 1918, 'The early sections are almost wholly devoted to planting the underlying theme of the story … Much time is devoted to the reason for the parents of Tarzan going to South [sic] Africa, also a tremendous footage is held by the succeeding holder of the title of Lord Greystoke, his escapades, marriage to a barmaid (Bessie Toner) and subsequent heir (Colin Kenny) …' Bohl: 'The only thing that the English part really did was to show that the Clayton character that was trying to get Jane to marry him was pretty much of a womaniser and that he was a scoundrel, which he really isn't in the books, which may have made Burroughs mad. Burroughs was pretty much an idealist. Most of his characters, they could be bad but not jerks like that.' He adds, 'Most people enjoyed the jungle parts but not the rest of it, so they took out the English part and kept most of the jungle scenes and made it about 71 minutes long. They called it a digest version. Even though it was cut down to 71 minutes, the story still holds together.'

Sadly – and rather amazingly, considering hundreds, even thousands, must have been in circulation throughout the world – there is no surviving print of the first, 130-minute, version of *Tarzan of the Apes*. Bohl: 'They would melt them down to get the silver nitrates out and remake film with. They just didn't really think about saving movies. It was so new a medium, they didn't really think much that it would survive.' Bohl adds that if any copy remains extant, it is highly likely that it will be severely corroded, but he does think that one may turn up: 'It's very possible when they tear down some old movie houses or something throughout the world, they'll find it.'

The movie gets underway with a montage of shots of African wildlife that is indiscriminate about jungle dwellers or denizens of the plains but at least sticks to the fauna of the right continent. Bohl says, 'It wasn't that unusual at that time to have travelogue-type footage made; stock footage. They went and bought that and edited it in. They did a pretty good job of splicing all that footage together. It does look a little different, but not so much that someone in 1918 would have looked at it and said, "You know, that doesn't look as good as I've seen before." Even with the Weissmuller films later on, it's very evident that they were doing rear-screen projection on some of that, but audiences accepted it.'

The film's story for some reason starts two years before that in the book. After some England-set scenes featuring members of the Greystoke clan, we see the shipboard mutiny. Cut to the Greystokes hugging each other in fear against the backdrop of a departing ship. Binns, the sailor who saves the Greystokes from the same fate as the crew, is unable to join them ashore as he wishes, because he is captured by Arab slave traders. A decade before talking motion pictures, these plot developments are, of course, helped along with title cards, some of which are quite literary ('Only the leopard outside the door hears the cries of the new-born heir of Greystoke'), others colloquial ('I wonders if they died a thinking old Binnsey broke 'is promise to 'em.')

In this narrative, Kala's baby isn't killed by Kerchak but dies of natural if unexplained causes. This death sends the ape king into a 'frenzy of rage', causing him to lead an invasion of the cabin wherein the Claytons' baby is stolen. The apes – described as exactly and merely that – are acrobats dressed in furry costumes, although the murky film quality and sepia tones of the era prevent them from looking too risible. The men in suits alternate with baby chimps, used in close-up. Bohl: 'The way it reads to me, they saw if they wanted to have any interaction with apes, it would be best to use the men in costumes as far as acting, because back then they didn't have animal wranglers like they do now.'

The name Tarzan is used in the title cards but its origin is not explained, at least not in the surviving condensed version. The boy Tarzan is shown swinging on handily situated and conveniently numerous vines, inaugurating that Tarzan tradition that movies just cannot seem to shake off and that contrasts with the ape-man's more plausible and exciting swinging from bough to bough in the books. Griffith is expressive and impressive, perfect in his mixture of innocence and animalistic guile. In an era before the censorship imposed by the Hays Code, the producers were relatively free of moral restrictions in capturing Burroughs' tale. As Bohl notes of Griffith, 'He probably has the longest – in a major feature film, not a blue film – nude scene of anyone in film history.' He adds, 'The females, the natives, they were nude to their waist.'

Young Tarzan steals a loincloth after apprehending from the sight of his reflection in a pool that he is not an ape. Meanwhile, realising he is near the Claytons' cabin following a decade of imprisonment, Binns escapes his captors and heads for it. He swears to the skeleton of Lady Alice he discovers therein that he will find her child and take it back to England. The boy Tarzan comes upon Binns asleep on the cabin floor. It is Binns who teaches Tarzan to read while Tarzan nurses him back to health. The returning Arabs thwart Binns' plan to take Tarzan home: he tells the boy to run for it and says he will look up his folks if he makes it back to England.

Following another African animal-and-landscape montage, we are then introduced to 'TARZAN - -, THE MAN. ELMO LINCOLN.' A similar caption had coincided with the first screen shot of Griffith. Lincoln is a screen presence less conducive to the viewer's comfort than the latter, however. His build would be impressive in an urban setting, but a barrel torso does not seem the type of physique a lifetime spent in the trees would produce, and that's not even mentioning the strong suspicion the viewer has that the actor is carrying a bit of ballast: one of the first shots of Lincoln finds him moving hand-over-hand across a horizontal jungle creeper that is wobbling rather alarmingly. Having said that, in long-shot he is occasionally handsome, and the *Variety* reviewer – who was perceptive enough to snort at 'cut-ins of animal stuff' and who said of the apes, 'very foolishly a number of close-ups are shown which kill the illusion' – saw no shortcomings in Lincoln, whom she described as 'all that could be asked for.'

'The only [contemporaneous] criticism I've heard of Lincoln is that Burroughs didn't really care for him,' says Bohl. 'Even though they became friends eventually. The Stellan Windrow version of Tarzan was closer to what Burroughs envisaged Tarzan as being, but if you really go back and read the book, he does talk about him having the long sinewy muscles and this sort of thing, but also he describes him as a forest giant, and so as many times as I've read the book *Tarzan of the Apes*, I think Lincoln fits that bill.'

Long hair on men in early cinema almost always looked ridiculous because – as society then frowned on growing out for real – it was represented by wigs. Lincoln's bushy-thatch-and-headband affair is no exception. 'It's so horrendous,' says Bohl. 'I think it added to what we would consider more a comical look. At that time, over-dramatisation was the way you did it. … They were still so close to stage plays that it wasn't unusual for him to act as he was acting; but that wig was so terrible.' It has been suggested that Lincoln was going bald, but Bohl says, 'Actually he had a really good head of hair.' Bohl counted Lincoln playing at least six characters in *Birth of a Nation* and says, 'He plays two characters in *Tarzan of the Apes*. He's one of the mutineers on the ship. I don't think they really thought that films had that big an impact. It was almost like just having fun somewhat.'

Binns does indeed make it back to England, and a group of scientists and relatives of Tarzan's parents – Jane in tow – decide to set sail to check out his story of the jungle waif. It's rather ironic that such tampering as this with the original story is possibly what caused ERB to walk. The Tarzan movies would eventually build up a massive history of misrepresenting Burroughs' key character, but not only is this movie very faithful to the source, but what tweaks there are improve the tale profoundly. Bohl says of Binns, a character not seen in the original novel, 'He was the glue that tied the story together, in that he [was a composite of] several characters in the book and also gave some plausibility to different things in the film. He escapes and comes back and finds Tarzan and teaches him how to read … Then Binns leaves and goes to England and tells them that he's found the heir to the Greystoke fortune, and that prompts the safari to go find him, whereas in the book they're not looking for him at all, they're looking for gold … It streamlined the story, and I think it made it better.'

The safari discover Tarzan's cabin and are presented with the same don't-touch-my-stuff note that the ape-man leaves in the book. Tarzan saves Jane from the aggressive amorous intentions of her fiancé, and Jane and Esmeralda from a big cat trying to enter the cabin (a lion here, as opposed to the book's lioness). Legend has it that Lincoln killed the lion for real, but others have dismissed this as hype. Bohl: 'I do believe after hearing pros and cons that the lion was killed for the production of the film. [Lincoln] says that he did [kill it] and his daughter believes he did...' This is not as impressive as it might sound, for as Bohl points out, the producers used 'animals that were real old.' Though they would probably have been in a minority amongst the public a century ago, some found the feat repugnant rather than impressive. Bohl: 'Lions breed really well in captivity so they had a lot of them. The Humane Society, while it was a fledgling organisation, was against this, because Parsons announced that he was looking for six lions to kill for this film and some other things. When they found out about it they got all upset about it, and so he backed it down to just that one lion.'

Jane is kidnapped by natives, one of whose number has been shot dead by a fearful member of her party. Tarzan rescues her and carries her off before burning down the natives' village. The movie ends rather limply with the very-much-in-love Tarzan and Jane sitting on a log, Tarzan pointing out the delights of his jungle home. As *Variety* noted, 'The audience is left in the dark as to whether or not he has come into his birthright, whether he has won the girl or not, or, if he has, did he keep her in the jungle wilds...'

It's easy for modern audiences to laugh at that uncertain ending (written at a time when screenwriters were still feeling their way with narrative film). Ditto Lincoln's gurning expressions and peculiar hops off screen. On top of all that, the introduction of sound in the '20s made films like this and their exaggerated, eye-rolling 'vocabulary' instant period pieces. Yet, for the era, this is often sophisticated stuff. The production values obtained by an extremely high budget of $250,000 are exceptional and the sets for stately homes, ships and Tarzan's cabin impressively believable. Meanwhile, we can just imagine the gasps of the audiences in the picture houses as lions, leopards, elephants and giraffes paraded across the screen. Though it can be naïve, the camerawork is sometimes imaginative (for instance, a cutaway to startled birds taking flight as Tarzan kills the killer of Kala is of a technique that could have come direct from any modern picture). Bohl: 'The editing really showed a lot of understanding, even for that time period ... There are a lot of high-angle shots. They had to build platforms up in trees and get all that equipment up there.'

One is struck by just how similar is this movie to *Greystoke* (1984). Though this is inevitable on one level, for the latter is the only other Tarzan motion picture to closely follow the plot of Burroughs' first Tarzan book, it still seems remarkable that two movies separated by 66 years and vast changes in film technology and societal mores feature the same juxtapositions of Victorian society and naked jungle frolicking.

With such a high investment having been made in this extravaganza, naturally the stops were pulled out promotion-wise, if mainly in New York, where the première took place on 27 January 1918. A symphony orchestra provided the accompaniment in the form of a specially-written jungle-themed score. Says Bohl, 'It was the first time – [and only] time – they've ever stretched [a banner] all the way across Broadway promoting a film. They say that they put the original stuffed lion in the lobby that they killed in the movie. They put a lot of fake foliage and stuff in the lobby and they released monkeys up in there. There's even one thing saying that they had a gorilla that was taking tickets – I don't know if it's true or not.'

Even at this early stage in cinema's development, the host form had developed the parasite of critics, many of whom had moved over from reviewing stage plays to the new-fangled 'photo plays'. Bohl reports that *Tarzan of the Apes* generally got good notices: 'They were just really excited by it.' More importantly, if probably related, it was also a hit with the public, becoming one of the first half-dozen movies to gross over a million dollars. Bohl: 'I believe they made more than that. I think that's a domestic [figure] but that film played all over the world. Most movie tickets of that time cost a nickel – that's why they're called nickelodeons – but *Tarzan*, they charged anywhere from a dollar to two dollars 50 cents per ticket, which was astronomical at that time. But the people paid it. There's even one advertisement I saw that said people stayed up all night just to see it. It was a little bit like *Star Wars* when it came out: people would just go see it, get back in line and see it again.'

Gordon Griffith succumbed to a heart attack in 1958. He was only 51, but it's a measure of how long ago the film was produced that if he were still alive he would be over a hundred now. Bohl: 'He was in two of the movies with Charlie Chaplin, so as a child actor he was really gaining ground, but like many child actors he fell out of favour. He stayed in the movie business and eventually became a producer. He directed some too.

'Enid Markey, who played Jane, was a stage actress, and after *Tarzan* it's my understanding from talking to her daughter that she didn't want to be stuck as being seen as Jane. Whereas Elmo never really broke away from Tarzan. She went on to New York and starred in a number of really well-known plays, and eventually she went into television and she made more films.' Bohl also says, 'As far as I know, no-one from the production side did much of anything else.' This surprises him: 'It was just away ahead of its time. It's hard to believe that a guy like Parsons could pull something together so magnificently as he did.'

The link in the public's mind between a Tarzan picture and an enthralling spectacle had been set. *Tarzan of the Apes* kicked off a film franchise that would be amongst the most successful of the first half of the 20th Century and that continues, if in less all-conquering form, to this day. The transition to movies completed Tarzan's progress from merely successful product – one estimate has about 600,000 combined sales of the five Tarzan books in print at this point – to cultural phenomenon.

'The original film came out in January 1918 and by April they were making a sequel,' says Al Bohl.

News of the shooting of the sequel – which would be released in October 1918 as *The Romance of Tarzan* – incurred the ire of Edgar Rice Burroughs, ever mindful of the value of his intellectual property. Bohl: 'When Burroughs found out they were making a sequel to *Tarzan of the Apes*, he said, "Why didn't you come to me and get a clearance to do that?" Well, they had the right to make the entire book but they only shot half of it and so they said, "Well, we have the rights to the book so we're going to make a second film out of it." Burroughs' attorney said, "You really don't have any leg to stand on …" They rushed into production on this. They wanted to stay true to the original story where there's a big forest fire. They were going to shoot that in California and they couldn't because of a burn ban. They used a lot of the original footage for Louisiana … that they'd already shot [for the first film].'

Lincoln, Markey and Griffith all reprised their roles in a movie that lasted 96 minutes and – according to the publicity – took four months to shoot. It was loosely based on the latter stages of the *Tarzan of the Apes* novel but seems to have had more in common with the wild-man-in-civilisation concept of the book *The Return of Tarzan*. Flashbacks to the first movie explained who the ape-man was and how he came to be in California. Some critics mocked the sight of Tarzan in dress-suit, and Lincoln himself later said, 'They made a mistake when they put Tarzan in clothes. Tarzan is a wild man and he does not belong in a drawing room.'

Exhibitor's Trade Review described *The Romance of Tarzan* as 'a lively, romantic drama with thrilling situations accumulating at a breathtaking rate.' *Variety* was less charitable, dismissing it as 'a meller of the veriest sort' – sheer melodrama in modern parlance. We are unable to adjudge who was right for, as Bohl explains of the film, 'There is no print left of it.' However he does add, 'There's some belief that somewhere in Europe someone has an actual copy of the film.' Such are the vagaries of early cinema, though, that one part of *The*

Romance of Tarzan is still extant. Says Bohl, 'The only portion which remains of that is actually now part of the *Tarzan of the Apes* film.' The producers belatedly rectified the feeble and inconclusive ending of the first movie by tagging on a scene from *The Romance of Tarzan* wherein Jane, having been delivered to the cabin by her forest god, calls him back when she sees him forlornly about to step into the jungle. Says Bohl, 'It was a better, more romantic ending, and people liked that.'

Though *The Romance of Tarzan* was both far less well-received and commercially successful than its predecessor, as with the first Tarzan movie, it broke new – or new-ish – ground. Bohl: '[It's] one of the very first sequels made.'

Edgar Rice Burroughs was quite a war enthusiast. Politically conservative and intensely patriotic (though, almost conversely, anti-organised religion), he had no misgivings about America's entry in April 1917 into what was then known as the Great War. However hard-right some of his beliefs, though, one would hesitate to suggest that he saw the war as a godsend for the Tarzan series that he had been trying to manoeuvre out of creative cul-de-sacs since almost the moment the first instalment was published. Nonetheless, it can't be denied that said conflict gave a handy new sense of purpose to the ape-man.

Tarzan the Untamed was published in six parts in *The Red Book* from March to August 1919, and *Tarzan and the Valley of Luna* in five parts in *All-Story Weekly* in March and April 1920. When McClurg collected the two tales in book form in 1920 under the title *Tarzan the Untamed* (the first time any Tarzan novel was published in the same year that any part of its story had been printed in a magazine; from hereon this would be the norm), it was a great fat tome – in fact, the longest Tarzan book there would ever be – full of barbarity and borderline fascism, most of it, surprisingly, coming from Lord Greystoke. The war impinges upon Tarzan's world when the German army visits his estate in British East Africa in 1914 during his absence. When Tarzan returns from a trip to Nairobi, he finds the dead body of his murdered wife. Tarzan incrementally goes insane, embarking on a quest for vengeance against not just the killers of his wife but all German soldiers, before turning to complete misanthropy.

While one can understand Tarzan's grief-stricken fury, and while allowances must be made for an era when dissent about the war was taboo, Burroughs' demonisation and degradation of Germans is shocking. One scene in the book sees Tarzan forcing the Hun who he thinks is responsible for Jane's death to march for miles at spear-point, grimly unyielding as the German literally sobs and pleads his innocence, before leaving him to the mercies of a lion. We are invited to draw no adverse inference from the fact that it turns out that this man is indeed innocent and merely the brother of the real killer. Not only is this heavy, vicious stuff with a built-in sell-by date (albeit later temporarily given an unexpected extension by the Second World War), but Tarzan's aligning himself with the Entente powers is impossible to reconcile with what we know of the ape-man. Though it wouldn't be true to say he had never before killed for sport or vengeance as opposed to food or self-defence, no part of Tarzan's jungle upbringing would make him inclined to take sides in a conflagration that historians now consider a territorial squabble bereft of ideological differences. The only things that can be said for this bizarre out-of-character behaviour are that it at least creates a counterbalance to the similar treatment Tarzan doled out to blacks in most of the previous books and that the grim tone is an antidote to the later 'soft' Tarzan presented in the likes of the Weissmuller movies. Such arguments, though, cut no ice with Germans.

The first foreign translation of Tarzan was a Danish version of *Tarzan of the Apes* in 1918. It unleashed a highly lucrative revenue stream. In 1967, Burroughs biographer Robert W Fenton counted 26 languages into which Tarzan books had been translated plus four Indian dialects. Though German was one of the languages, *Tarzan the Untamed* was deliberately not translated into Deutsch at the time. However, when outraged German journalist Stefan Sorel 'exposed' the book's contents, it caused a huge Teutonic backlash against Burroughs, destroying the market for his work there for an extensive period – somewhat ironically considering that the war was long over by the time either *Untamed* or the similarly Hun-baiting *The Land That Time Forgot* came out in book form.

In light of all this, how ironic that *Tarzan the Untamed* marks the start of the peak of the Tarzan novels. It is possibly the finest of all Tarzan books, even if it slightly betrays its origin as two separate stories and even despite the presence of a bewildering unresolved episode in which Tarzan discovers on an ancient skeleton a cylinder containing a Spanish manuscript and a map. Though the first part of the book is taken up by Tarzan devising ingenious and cruel ways to help the British army kill Germans, the second follows his adventures in the lost city of Xuja, whose denizens arguably have an even greater rapport with animals than he but who are also completely loopy as a consequence of in-breeding.

The book version ends with the revelation that Jane may still be alive, the discovery of the body depicted in *The Red Book* altered so that it was one charred beyond recognition and identifiable as Jane's only via rings on fingers.

Her magazine death was almost certainly related to the problems in Burroughs' crumbling marriage to his wife Emma. Ironically, it was 'commuted' at the urging – according to their daughter Joan – of Emma herself, though some sources also cite the concern of Burroughs' editors. Either way, it makes even more unforgivable Tarzan's slaying of the alleged murderer's brother.

The large supporting roles for an English spy disguised as a Fraulein, Bertha Kircher, and a marooned RAF pilot, Harold Percy Smith-Oldwick, and the fact that they fall for each other, set the pattern for future Tarzan books in which the ape-man would play a diminished role that sometimes amounted to little more than a combination of *deus ex machina* and unwitting matchmaker. Also setting a pattern, *Tarzan the Untamed* is the first Tarzan novel whose title bolts a superlative to his name. These superlatives would come to seem arbitrary, then lazy, as the series sagged, but this one was perfectly descriptive.

Silent movie actors did not need to know how to act as we would define the term. In a field in which thespians were still to learn that the type of histrionics that even the untrained could deliver were not necessary, it seemed perfectly natural that Joseph C Pohler, a New York fireman with no cinematic experience beyond bit parts, should be cast in the lead for the film adaptation of *The Return of Tarzan* when Elmo Lincoln had to decline to reprise his role for contractual reasons. The assumptions of the era ensured that the fact that Pohler was over six foot two and built like a tree trunk were the major requisites – although it's surprising that even nearly a hundred years ago his cowlick and gormless expression don't seem to have raised eyebrows. Some things, however, become comical only retroactively. For instance, an impetus for 'decency' saw the skimpy outfits of Lincoln dispensed with in favour of an over-the-shoulder pelt – smirk-inducing ever since 1960 when the Flintstones were first depicted wearing similar apparel.

The movie was made by the Weiss Brothers, whose tender Burroughs liked the best. Some sources state the picture started circulating from 30 May 1920, others 20 July, symptomatic of the problem of pinning down reliable release dates for early movies. In any event, by then Pohler had been re-styled as Gene Pollar and the movie renamed *The Revenge of Tarzan*, the latter partly because it was feared that people would assume it was merely a re-release of the first Lincoln movie – understandable in light of the different versions of *Tarzan of the Apes* by now floating around. Not that scenario-writer Robert Saxmar's 'picturisation' was that chronologically faithful to Burroughs' second Tarzan tale, although most of its elements were ultimately deployed across its seven reels. (The nine-reel version shown at previews was cut down for wider release.) Harry Revier directed.

Once again, no print is known to survive. Though the claims in the film's publicity that the three-month shoot involved location work in New York, Florida and California may even be true, the trio of Weiss brothers, who set up a company called Numa to make this picture, were renowned for knocking off low-budget quickies. The contemporaneous testimony suggests that this showed on the screen, despite the usual panoply of wildlife, including lions, elephants and – puzzlingly – an example of the non-African ape the orangutan. For what it's worth, though the film accrued mixed notices, Pollar was well-received, and it did sufficiently good box office for Universal to offer him a then-princely weekly wage of $350 to make further Tarzan pictures for them. However, extortionate demands by Numa to release Pollar from his contract saw the deal collapse. Pollar – by all accounts a sweet-natured gentle giant – returned to his fireman's job. His Jane – Karla Schramm – turned up in the next Tarzan cinematic venture but eventually drifted back into her profession of musician and musical tutor. Burroughs later revised his politic contemporaneous praise for Pollar and *The Revenge of Tarzan* ('I have no criticism, and am very proud to be identified with the offering') to, 'As an actor, Gene was a great fireman.'

The franchise returned to the National Film Corporation for the next Tarzan movie project, a move facilitated by the death of William Parsons – whom Burroughs hated for reasons over and above disagreements over script – from kidney failure in September 1919. As if to underline its insubstantiality, *The Beasts of Tarzan* was skipped over for adaptation in favour of the fourth book in the series.

It was decided that *The Son of Tarzan* should be not a single motion picture but a serial, or chapter play – a form common then, now obsolete. The mathematics give an idea of the extra potential profit involved: 15 episodes of two reels each (around five hours of material) meant audiences having to return week after week. Perhaps it was anticipation of such profits that caused National to agree to pay Burroughs a whopping $20,000 advance, approaching a quarter of a million dollars in today's coinage.

Manilla Martan, a popular singer of the day, was cast as the adult Meriem. P Dempsey Tabler was Tarzan. Gordon Griffith – the boy Tarzan in the first two Tarzan flicks – was cast as the young Jack Clayton. Ex-stuntman Kamuela Searle bagged the prize role of the adult Korak, and this piece of casting at least was good. The toned Hawaiian was a fine figure of a man, a matter made easier to ascertain by his skimpy loincloth. Searle's long hair is perfect, presumably because – unusually – it seems real.

The serial took a reported cumulative seven months to shoot. Locations included San Bernardino, Pico Rivera, the San Francisco and Los Angeles coasts – and the Tarzana ranch. Without said ranch, it's possible that Burroughs would not have continued writing the stories of the character after whom it was named, for the financial burdens it imposed on him made a high workrate necessary, and of course the ape-man was by far the most lucrative of his characters.

The photodramatist – another early term for scriptwriter – was Roy Somerville. Burroughs, smarting at some of the liberties taken with his stories by the movies, made sure that he was guaranteed a close involvement, visiting the sets regularly and consulting with Harry Revier, who shared directing duties with Arthur J Flaven. Despite the consequent faithfulness to the source, inter-title cards referred to 'Lord Greystone'. Meanwhile, Burroughs could do nothing about the pitiless gaze of the camera: though possible to sidestep in a book, the potential faults with a project involving Tarzan's progeny are painfully manifest here. Gordon Griffith is quite patently a child, making his character's overpowering of an adult Arab while rescuing Meriem preposterous. Meanwhile, Tabler's wig is idiotic beyond parody, as is his distended belly. The uncredited performer playing Akut looks absurd and almost offensive in his blackface, although that problem with convincingly depicting Mangani is admittedly not unique to this Tarzan film in this era. Nevertheless, there is some impressive stuff here, especially the scene where Tantor the elephant rescues Korak and trots off with him attached to the stake at which he was intended to burn.

The one unequivocal virtue of the enterprise is Searle, and it's difficult not to come to the conclusion that he would have assumed the lead role in the next Tarzan movie had he not been put out of action for a while via an injury incurred during the filming of the Tantor rescue scene and then been debilitated by the cancer to which he succumbed in 1924. Quite simply, he was the first adult actor to play Tarzan – which Korak was in all but name – who didn't look ridiculous.

The serial started appearing in cinemas in December 1920 and did good business, recouping its costs within three months. Burroughs, though, was disappointed at its poor showing in the United Kingdom and said privately that he thought the film market had been flooded with Tarzan. Perhaps this is why he personally edited a two-hour movie version of the serial footage titled *Jungle Trail of The Son of Tarzan*, released in 1923. This still exists but in partial and degraded form. Ten parts of the original serial, however, are extant and have been commercially released on DVD. There was an overdubbed European 'sound' release of the serial in the 1930s, though this now appears to have been lost.

There were some interesting innovations attached to *The Son of Tarzan*. Via tinting effects, the serial was given a form of prototypical cinema colour. It was also provided with what we now call multi-media promotion via the commissioning of a special song, 'Tarzan, My Jungle King', written by Norman Stackey and Osborne Tedman and sold as sheet music (though never recorded). Its most important innovation was something that had a profound influence on the serial form: by showing slivers of preceding episodes before each new one, it accidently invented the soon *de rigueur* 'Previously ...' serial précis.

4 October 1920 saw the ape-man make his inaugural appearance in a further medium when the *Tarzan of the Apes* stage play opened in England.

Many will instantly find ridiculous the notion of a theatrical presentation of a tale largely set outdoors and involving inbuilt obstacles to credibility such as the potentially risible sight of real people impersonating animals. However, prior to television, radio and talkies, theatre was still a huge part of people's lives, and little if anything would have been assumed to be beyond its parameters.

Methuen of London had been the first publisher outside the USA to publish a Tarzan novel, so it was natural that the British should wish to mount a play about the character, not least because he was an English lord. Brixton was the location for Tarzan's entrée to the boards in a production that featured a prologue and four acts written by Major Herbert Woodgate and Arthur Gibbons. Elements of *The Return of Tarzan* were incorporated into the script. One doesn't know how seriously to take the report sent to Burroughs by his UK agents Curtis Brown about the opening night. As they had brokered the deal for the production, they could be said to have had a vested interest in not being critical. However, for what it's worth, they claimed, 'The jungle scenes were effective and proved distinctly to the taste of the audience. The parts of Tarzan and Kala were both played extremely well, Kala being particularly good.' A bit of gender switching was going on in the casting, with a man – Edward Sillward – playing Kala and a young girl named Gwen Evans depicting the ten-year-old Tarzan.

It was initially stated that the show had ten weeks' worth of provincial bookings following a fortnight's showing in Brixton. Reports are confusing as to how the tour progressed. Though Burroughs was notified at one point that it was to be curtailed in the week of 14 December, there are claims of sporadic stagings through to the following June. Adding to the confusion is American unfamiliarity with English geography. Irwin Porges stated in *Edgar Rice Burroughs: The Man Who Created Tarzan* that one performance of the play was scheduled for London on Boxing Day 1920 but that these arrangements fell through and '*Tarzan* was never staged in London', apparently unaware that Brixton is in south-west London and not, as he stated, 'in the provinces'. (This mistake was repeated by Taliaferro.) It would seem to be true, though, that the show never played the all-important West End. However, the fact that Gibbons agreed terms with Burroughs for a follow-up stage production in the form of *The Son of Tarzan* as late as February 1921 suggests he was happy enough with the takings, even if that production seems not to have been mounted. Gibbons and his business partner Arthur Carlton also thought their property valuable enough to go to court to prevent one Dick Mortimer continuing to perform a sketch titled *Warzan and his Apes* consisting of Tarzan scenes done in 'dumb show.' Though the legal action failed – the judge's ruling mainly based on the fact that the sketch had been seen in music halls for six years – and though it might be viewed from today's perspective as unfairly attempting to suppress what was parody rather than 'passing-off', it is notable as possibly the very first civil case brought to prevent something that would be viewed by Burroughs and/or his licensees as an increasing menace in coming years: people jumping on a very lucrative, loin-clothed bandwagon.

Also suggestive that *Tarzan of the Apes* was a British stage success is the fact that the following year it transferred to Broadway, where it opened on 1 September. As he had in the English production, Ronald Adair – an actor with a boxing background – took the title role. Photographs of the time suggest he was pretty well cast, possessing matinée-idol (if blond-ish) looks and a trim physique. Only his costume – looking more like leopardskin hotpants than an animal pelt loincloth – conforms to the comical patina overlaying so many Tarzan actors of the era. As Woodgate and Gibbons' original script was adapted for the American market by the Broadway show's producer George Broadhurst, it's reasonable to assume that this version of the play was significantly different from what UK audiences had seen. Certainly there was a new element in the form of live lions padding the stage. *The New York Times* felt Burroughs' source material posed 'almost insurmountable stumbling-blocks to the playwright' and that the story was told 'episodically and not always convincingly.' However both Adair's athleticism and his depiction of 'the gradations of the savage's education in the English language' came in for praise, as did the enterprise of Broadhurst and Mrs Trimble

Bradley, the latter credited with having 'staged' the production: '[They] have lavished upon it a wealth of care, patience and attention to detail. They have created several jungle scenes that are striking in the extreme and have in general done their best to make this bizarre tale a convincing piece of theatre.' *Life* was far less generous, describing it as 'almost too bad to be true.' It ridiculed Tarzan being taught by Kala to wear a loincloth by the age of five so that the show could conform to civilisation's definition of decency, described Howard Kyle – head of an expedition from 'Greystoke Castle' to find the Claytons – as 'America's premier ham' and mocked the convenient coincidence that saw the Greystoke party arrive just as young Tarzan was in the vicinity. Having said that, it does seem as though the *Life* reviewer was almost looking for a target for his sarcasm: 'To those of our little band of condors who earn their living by making comical cracks about other people's plays it came like a visit from St Nicholas.' Reviews, incidentally, answer in the affirmative the question of whether or not Adair spent some time on stage in trees, or at least approximations thereof.

The New York production closed after 14 performances, a paltry figure that justified Broadhurst's comment in a telegram to Burroughs that it was 'a complete failure.' Curtis Brown reported to Burroughs that Broadhurst was not going to pursue another course of action open to him – taking the show on the road to less merciless audiences than those to be found on the Great White Way – because he felt the Broadway run had demonstrated it had little appeal to Americans. Burroughs seemed sanguine. He had taken receipt of a $1,000 advance and 10% royalties for the British production, and presumably an advance for the American version, and all in all felt – according to his private correspondence – 'it will do the books no harm.'

Burroughs added, 'Most of the critics seem to think that the impossible has been attempted and I rather imagine they are right.' He opined that a stage Tarzan should be a 'real, honest-to-God Burlesque.' He would be proved wrong in his belief that it was impossible to mount a successful Tarzan stage presentation that was non-comedic – but not for eight decades.

By 1920, with several million copies of Tarzan books in print in the United States alone and the character the subject of an ongoing series of movies/serials, it would have seemed axiomatic to the public – especially those left on tenterhooks at the end of *Tarzan the Untamed* by the revelation that Jane was almost certainly alive – that a new Tarzan book was high on the list of Edgar Rice Burroughs' priorities. In fact, Burroughs found the idea a deadening imposition and the execution a bore.

His recent correspondence had seen him confessing, '… for the last few years it has been a case of rearranging and camouflaging threadbare situations.' He admitted that he would never write another Tarzan story 'if it wasn't for the lure of filthy lucre' – also indicating that his weariness extended to the Mars tales, of which he had so far turned out four. When writing the follow-up to *Tarzan and the Valley of Luna* in Autumn 1920, Burroughs confessed to his McClurg editor Joe Bray that it was 'awful hard work' and that it was 'very possible that I shall never be able to finish this.' Hardly the most promising preamble to what became *Tarzan the Terrible*. Even the book's title seems a subliminal expression of the author's resentment of being chained to his most famous creation. Yet it turned out to be one of the best and most ingenious Tarzan tales of all.

Tarzan the Terrible – published in seven parts in *Argosy All-Story Weekly* in February and March 1921 – takes the Tarzan franchise fully into the realm of fantasy. Though this works to negate the effect of *Tarzan of the Apes* – whose events could just about be posited as rooted in reality – it's difficult to argue with the fine result. In this thrilling, unique novel, Burroughs brings to Tarzan the incredible detail and visualisation that had always marked his Mars and Pellucidar universes, describing as though witnessed personally, invented customs, dwelling conditions and language (of which a glossary is printed at the back 'from conversations with Lord Greystoke and from his notes').

Tarzan follows the trail of Jane, who has escaped her German abductors and made her way to Pal-ul-don, a land in a valley isolated by a huge bog. Pal-ul-don is 'Land of Men' in the native lingo. The natives are the hairless, white skinned Ho-don and the hairy, black-skinned Waz-don. Despite their physical differences, the two races have in common the fact that they possess tails. The way Burroughs uses the philosophical and bodily differences of the 'dons' to mock racism would almost seem calculated to throw off the scent people who had begun to suspect the author himself of that offence, were it not for the fact that he was operating at a time when there was no incentive to care about such things – which, confusingly, must mean he was sincere. The local wildlife is even more remarkable, including the jato, a lion/sabre-tooth tiger hybrid (one of whom the ape-man inevitably battles to the death), and the gryf, a carnivorous form of triceratops (which Tarzan learns to ride in a way he finds exhilaratingly reminiscent of straddling Tantor). A seized Tarzan so impresses his captors with his fighting prowess that he is given the title 'Tarzan-jad-guru' – Tarzan the Terrible. Jane has her own chapters, which show her being resourceful and brave in the midst of religion-based skulduggery and intrigue.

Tarzan leaves a trail of dead bodies as he works his way toward her, but he and his wife seem doomed until the dramatic arrival of a mysterious Enfield-wielding man glimpsed in previous chapters and now revealed to be Korak, who like a good son has been on their trail. The nuclear family depart Pal-ul-don on the back of a gryf.

Even leaving aside our contemporary knowledge of the way Burroughs snatched this artistic triumph from the depths of ennui, *Tarzan the Terrible* is an amazing achievement. Though elements have antecedents in his Caspak series (which itself owed a debt to Arthur Conan Doyle's *The Lost World*), one is left almost open-mouthed at ERB's inventiveness. Men with tails who live in cliffs honeycombed with caves reached by nailed pegs? Triceratops brought under control by a smart rap on the snout with a pole? A language thought through to an almost insane degree ('the names of all male hairless pithecanthropi begin with a consonant, have an even number of syllables, and end with a consonant')? Where does this stuff come from?

It all seems to show that sometimes it is not necessity but 'the lure of filthy lucre' that is the mother of invention.

'Picturised from the concluding chapters of "The Return of Tarzan"' read a poster for *Adventures of Tarzan*, the ape-man's cinematic appearance of 1921/22.

The Weiss brothers/Numa Films had decided to exercise their option to make a second film from the book upon which they had based *The Revenge of Tarzan*. When they learned that the Great Western Picture Company were keen to produce a new Tarzan project directly and had, via their associations with Universal to whom he was contracted, access to Elmo Lincoln, Numa agreed merely to distribute a product made by Great Western. Eyeing the success of the *Son of Tarzan* serial, Great Western decided to make the project a chapter play. The result was, according to some reports, the fourth highest-grossing cinema release of 1921 – quite extraordinary if true, for the first episode of *Adventures of Tarzan* apparently didn't play until 1 December that year. (The claim is more plausible if the alternative date – 1 October – given by Robert W Fenton, author of *The Big Swingers*, is the correct one.) Amazingly for those who thought he looked ridiculous – which number included Edgar Rice Burroughs himself – the fact that Elmo Lincoln was restored to the Tarzan role seems to have been the major reason for the big box office. No less comical than his not-very-trim physique and noticeable double-chin is his costume, which is a return to the just-one-nipple-please primness of the over-the-shoulder Pollar pelt. Moreover, the pelt is an elaborate two-part, trailing affair that is somewhat more feminine than Jane's leopard-skin dress. At this point in history, though, Lincoln was still the definitive Tarzan to much of the public, which appears to have welcomed him back with open arms. Sixteen year-old Louise Lorraine is a charming Jane. Lillian Worth plays La. Robert F Hill and Scott Sidney directed.

The serial again consisted of 15 episodes. All were two-reelers except the first, which had an extra reel. There was also a ten-chapter 1928 version and a ten-chapter 1935 release, the latter with dubbed sound effects. The 1935 version is the only version known to be still in existence. For *Adventures of Tarzan,* the ante was upped with regard to on-set wildlife, particularly lions, and, as was by now standard, stories abound of on-set lion-related fights-to-the-finish and escapes from maulings, which from this distance are impossible to separate into truth and publicity hype. The drawbacks of the serial format are sorely in evidence if the project is viewed in one or two sittings: manufactured cliff-hangers and a necessity for a quotient of thrills-per-episode make for a disjointed, if frenetic, experience.

Promotion-wise, the Weiss brothers recommended to theatre owners men dressed in ape costumes and jungle flora in the lobbies to drum up interest, while Lincoln went on a lion-wrestling supporting tour. Another interesting facet of the promotion is the fact that the script by Robert F Hill and Lillian Valentine was adapted for a newspaper serial. It has been said that segments of this print version, written by Maude Robinson Toombs, were published to coincide with each episode of the serial hitting the screen, but this doesn't seem consistent with the fact that it appeared in some places as early as March 1921. In 2006, with the Toombs serialisation long out of copyright, its chapters were collated by ERBville Press in book form (something said publisher also did with the Arthur B Reeve-written serialisation of the 1928 chapter play *Tarzan the Mighty*).

For various reasons, there would now be a six-year gap before Tarzan returned to the screen. This would seem to have played a part in the eclipse of the career as a featured actor of Elmo Lincoln, who became too old to plausibly don the pelt again once the franchise resumed and whose body-orientated talent was dealt a further blow by the arrival of talkies.

Edgar Rice Burroughs had an answer ready whenever a journalist or correspondent (he replied to his fan letters) asked him about his literary abilities. It was a formula of words amounting to 'I'm a storyteller, me, and the public seem to love my stories.'

Behind that ostensible easy-going attitude toward the many reviewers and reporters who poured scorn on his purple prose, un-colloquial dialogue, creakingly obvious *deux ex machina* and convenient plot coincidences was a simmering resentment at not being taken as seriously as he thought he should. However entertaining it (and much of the rest of his oeuvre) is, *Tarzan and the Golden Lion* – serialised in seven parts in *Argosy All-Story Weekly* from December 1922 to January 1923 – does rather demonstrate that Burroughs would always be a pulp writer.

The story literally begins where *Tarzan the Terrible* left off, with Tarzan, Jane and Korak making their way back from Pal-ul-don. The fact that they are strolling through the jungle as though Africa – Burroughs doesn't bother with country delineations – is a little principality in which home is a gentle amble away from any specific point is the first sign herein of Burroughs' irredeemable, if quite endearing, pulp sensibility. Also charming is the little scene where the ape-man suggests to Jane – after winking at Jack – that he may have had simian parents. 'John Clayton, I shall never speak to you again if you don't stop saying such hideous things,' protests Lady Greystoke. This exchange occurs after the trio discover an orphaned lion cub and Tarzan, by virtue of a rapport with wildlife that even the jungle-trained Korak admits he lacks, wins its trust prior to adopting it. The lion is christened Jad-bal-ja, Pal-ul-don for 'the Golden Lion', and will become Tarzan's equivalent of a Rottweiler: loyal to its master and enough to drive terror into the hearts of its master's enemies.

When Tarzan returns to his estate, he finds the Waziri – depicted as showing him pretty much the same unconditional affection as Jad-bal-ja – rebuilding it. Because the war and the rebuilding have reduced his resources drastically, Tarzan decides to embark on another of his guiltless looting trips to Opar, whose denizens have neither appreciation of nor use for the treasures that surround them. Unbeknownst to him, also headed for Opar is a party at whose core lies Flora Hawkes, a one-time maid of the Greystokes infected by money lust, and her partner-in-crime Esteban Miranda, a Spanish actor whom she has retained because his remarkable resemblance to her former employer will make easier her plans to plunder the lost city. That Miranda is the spitting image of Tarzan is unlikely enough: Burroughs has told us enough times of an amplified level of physical beauty about the ape-man (from *Tarzan of the Apes*: 'His face was very handsome – the handsomest, thought D'Arnot, that he had ever seen') that would make it impossible for him to have a *doppelganger*. Burroughs piles on the absurdity yet further by making Miranda such a convincing look-alike that he fools Tarzan's wife, the Waziri and even the animals of the jungle – with which, remember, even Korak has admitted he doesn't have Tarzan's affinity. Then there is the unaddressed issue of the Spanish accent in which Miranda presumably speaks. Burroughs never disclosed to us the Mangani word for 'bollocks', but this is surely its definition. The literary writers with whom Burroughs secretly desired to be bracketed would never use such a comic-book look-alike device even once but, astoundingly, this was far from the last time Burroughs would.

That La still carries a torch for Tarzan is demonstrated by her rescuing him (not for the first time) from the sacrificial altar when things go wrong at Opar. Meanwhile, it turns out that Opar has an adjacent site, the city of the Bolgani in the valley of the Palace of Diamonds. These Bolgani are not the common-or-garden gorillas we have previously understood this Mangani word to describe but a mutant offshoot with the bodies of apes but the sensibilities of the more pretentious type of human. The narrative sees Tarzan take up arms on the side of the less developed Gomangani whom the Bolgani oppress, and also restore La to her place as ruler of Opar, assisted by Jad-bal-ja and his formidable jaws. Esteban – whose portrayal by Burroughs as an actor ultimately not up to the job of depicting the ape-man may be his way of having fun at the expense of Elmo Lincoln – ends up a prisoner of cannibals who are enemies of Tarzan.

Tarzan and the Golden Lion was the first Tarzan tale Burroughs did not physically write. A dictating machine became, after a few teething problems and a switch from his initial Ediphone to a Dictaphone, his 'writing' tool of choice.

Tarzan and the Ant Men appeared in seven parts in *Argosy All-Story Weekly* in February and March 1924. Burroughs wrote it in fits and starts. Once again he confessed that he hated the process, and once again he snatched inspiration from the jaws of lethargy.

Tarzan and the Ant Men gets off to an unpromising start with the reappearance of Esteban Miranda, who recurs – along with his ludicrous *doppelganger* premise – throughout, albeit almost never on the same page as Tarzan. Already so mad in the last adventure that he believes he really is Tarzan, he now wheedles his way out of captivity and stumbles through a series of adventures before winding up at the Greystoke estate, where Jane welcomes him as her husband and has to be disabused by someone less intimate with the real Lord Greystoke, Flora Hawkes.

Tarzan's own adventure begins when he disappears after going out in an aeroplane. A scene on the veranda of his African bungalow involving him,

Korak, Meriem and the latter pair's young son Jackie communicates to us that son has taught dad to fly and that the trip on which Tarzan is about to embark is the ape-man's first solo voyage. Tarzan dips too low when inspecting the legendary Great Thorn Forest and his plane crashes into a mysterious land that has always been kept isolated by that impenetrable thicket. We are soon knee-deep in another of the lost worlds that apparently pepper the African continent.

Tarzan discovers the Alali, a primitive race whose women brutally dominate their men. Burroughs' own marriage problems seem to be manifested in this subplot. Although it – and indeed the ant men premise – was the idea of his *All-Story* editor Bob Davis, Burroughs does seem to hammer out with some enthusiasm a scene wherein a woman who has been struck with both spear and foot by a newly assertive Alali male hugs his legs as though in gratitude for putting her in her rightful place. Tarzan then encounters the ant men. Their title is misleading, as the Minunians are up to 18 inches in height. Nonetheless, they and their society are as ingeniously thought through as Pal-ul-don and its residents, once again right down to the language, whose word constructions are completely different from those of Pal-ul-don's and involve some real tongue-twisters. (Two warring ant men tribes are called Veltopismakusians and Trohanakalmakians.) If anything, Burroughs goes into too much detail, with page after page devoted to ant man housing, history and dress. Certainly it's difficult to imagine readers in their twenties and under – or those of any age merely seeking jungle-based thrills – finding much of interest in such dense pseudo-sociology. One would imagine that titches like the Minunians would not be particularly aggressive, but their giant ant-hills are in a constant state of war with each other literally as a point of virtue. They ride nobly into battle on the backs of small antelopes.

Tarzan is temporarily shrunk to Minunian size in an experiment whose science is not defined sufficiently even to warrant the description questionable. Tarzan retains his normal strength even as an ant man. His ability to leap over heads is reminiscent of John Carter's superman abilities in the Mars series. Those who consider this tale a Lilliputian yarn are given some ammunition by another plot strand in which Burroughs depicts the Minunians as oppressed by taxation – although the knowledge that Burroughs was having money problems through over-reaching himself via the Tarzana ranch makes the passage seems less Swiftian satire than a profligate man's whinge.

For many fans, this event- and idea-packed work was the final aesthetically credible Tarzan. From hereon, with few exceptions, Burroughs' weariness with the character, his wife and possibly even writing were often painfully apparent.

If one subscribes to this supposition, it was at least a good way to go out, with even such a learned Burroughs scholar as Richard A Lupoff remarking in his book *Edgar Rice Burroughs: Master of Adventure*, 'If anything keeps *Tarzan and the Ant Men* from being the perfect Tarzan novel, it is perhaps the embarrassment of riches of the book ...'

PART THREE: CONQUERING THE FUNNIES

The increasingly Tarzan-weary Burroughs did not publish a new ape-man tale until 1927. As if to underline how intertwined his life now was with his creation, that was the year that Tarzan came back with a bang, with the first Tarzan cinema release for six years and two new Tarzan tales from Burroughs, one of which took the character into the uncharted territory of juvenile literature.

The hiatus in Tarzan pictures was partly due to the National Film Corporation, producers of *The Son of Tarzan*, going under following tax problems. Burroughs decided to take up the slack – as was his self-promotional wont – by agitating for a new picture himself. R-C Pictures – whose parent company was a precursor of RKO – took the bait and decided to film *Tarzan and the Golden Lion*, presumably adjudging the war content of *Untamed* dated and the otherworldly elements of *Terrible* and *Ant Men* unfilmable. Burroughs was even responsible for the casting of the title role. His daughter Joan introduced him to her friend (and future husband) American football coach and ex-player Jim Pierce at a party at Tarzana. Pierce was six foot four and very well-built, as the fact that he was in a swimming costume afforded Burroughs the opportunity to appreciate. Shooting took three months, although it's not clear if that includes a month in which Pierce was said to be recuperating after an on-set accident. Direction was by J P McGowan. Jane was played by Dorothy Dunbar. A then little-known Boris Karloff took several villainous roles.

It has been suggested that William E Wing's adaptation was faithful to the novel, but Opar is excised – replaced by a diamond city – along with Flora Hawkes. That Esteban Miranda is played by Frederick Peters and not by Pierce demonstrates that the ape-man impersonation plot strand has been amended. Even Jad-bal-ja's Pal-ul-don name is changed to the all-American sounding 'Jab'. Tarzan is also given a sister, Betty. On the plus side, Pierce is the most impressive Tarzan yet, even if his distinctly '20s short blond haircut with an emphatic parting is more reminiscent of F Scott Fitzgerald than a jungle man. (His over-the-shoulder leopard-skin pelt is an improvement on Lincoln's prior feminine outfit, though still looks demure compared with the logical breechcloth.) The interior sets for the diamond city are lavish and exotic, as are the denizens' costumes. Jab is a magnetic presence: a pet lion sitting as calmly as a hearthside dog in the Greystokes' drawing room is quite a sight.

The six-reel *Tarzan and the Golden Lion* – variously stated as having been released in January, February and May 1927 – was a box office success but widely panned by the critics. In his '70s-published autobiography *The Battle of Hollywood*, Pierce said, 'Tarzan and the Golden Lion hit a terrible market because "talkies" were coming in ... The studio considered dubbing in the sound-voice over the film and adding sound effects, but gave it up as too expensive ... The major chain houses had to turn it down as they were equipped for sound. However, many small towns and independent theatres had not yet wired up for sound, due to the great expense, and continued to screen silent films for two or three years after talkies. The picture proved to be a big hit on the B circuit.' Pierce also gave *Tarzan of the Movies* author Gabe Essoe some comments (which appear from their construction to have been written answers) in which he blamed the film for the end of his career as a featured player: 'Because of poor direction, terrible story treatment and putrid acting, the opus was a stinkeroo. I emerged with nothing to show for my strenuous effort except being typecast as Tarzan. I was out of a job.' That he was never again cast as the ape-man (at least on film) must have been particularly sickening for Pierce, as he had passed up the starring role in the epic aviation movie *Wings* to play him. Burroughs certainly seemed to think it was an injustice, and this can be put down neither to his usual public expression of support for a current cinema Tarzan nor to loyalty to his son-in-law: in private correspondence long before Joan married Pierce, he wrote, 'We have found a man who really is Tarzan, and whom I believe will be raised to the heights of stardom.'

The fact that for several decades *Tarzan and the Golden Lion* was considered a lost film – though Pierce was informally told a print existed in 1976, one was confirmed as extant only in the '90s – gives reason to hold out hope that earlier astray Tarzan pictures may one day turn up.

Though Edgar Rice Burroughs was fairly used to book publishers declining to print stories he had successfully placed with pulps, up until October 1927 he never experienced the reverse. When the children's book *The Tarzan Twins* was published by P F Volland Co that month, it marked the unfortunate milestone of being the first Tarzan story that no magazine had deemed fit to publish, as well as being the first Burroughs book *per se* to not appear in a magazine beforehand. Admittedly, with a far smaller market existing for juvenile prose, Burroughs had few other places to go when *Youth's Companion* rejected the story.

The book was not the author's idea but that of J C Flowers, an employee of the company that owned Volland. Burroughs seems to have been enthused by the idea because it constituted new territory: though he had written whimsical stuff for his family that could be posited as juvenile fare, this would be his first book for children of any professional description. He admitted as much to the Volland president Theodore Gerlach, to whom he described it as 'in the nature of an experiment.' However, despite embracing the idea of a new discipline, Burroughs proceeded to ignore just about all the suggestions and requests of his publisher, aiming his story at 14-year-olds instead of the eight-to-12 age range originally proposed, declining to make one of his child protagonists a girl on the grounds that it would be indecent to have a female child running around a jungle half-clothed, and tetchily declining to increase the word count or make good the deficiencies Volland felt existed in his submitted manuscript.

Fourteen-year-old Dick and Doc, the twins of the title, are not really twins but cousins who were born on the same day and who, different hair colour aside, look very much alike. The Tarzan part of their joint nickname came about when the kids at their 'excellent English school … learned that Dick's father was distantly related to Lord Greystoke, who is famous all over the world as Tarzan of the Apes …' Lord Greystoke being famous all over the world as Tarzan of the Apes only via the sole place he exists – the media – Burroughs was here breaking the fourth wall. It would not be his last piece of post-modernism in a Tarzan story.

The plot of this slim read involves Dick and Doc being invited to stay at Tarzan's African estate, wandering off into the jungle after their train crashes, learning to take refuge in trees from hostile wildlife, being captured by cannibals who plan to cook them even despite Doc's awe-inspiring magic tricks and escaping before they end up in a pot. Tarzan and the Waziri arrive to rescue Dick and Doc when they are on the brink of recapture. The book's informal, paternalistic tone is quite sweet and actually appropriate for that eight-to-12 age range originally envisaged. Quite how a father of three thought sentences like 'One could almost start a guessing contest with a conundrum like this, but the trouble is that no-one would guess the correct solution, though the answer is quite simple' would be greeted with anything but derision by a 14-year-old is a mystery. It's not quite clear that Volland did target the book at an age range as high as 14 – its heavily illustrated format and grinning cover illustration of the ape-man and the two protagonists suggest not – but the fact that it sold so poorly that it didn't even allow the publishers to recoup the author's small advance of $500 was probably more down to its surprising lack of local colour. The vivid jungle description at which Burroughs was usually so adept – and which would have been particularly appreciated by children, the world's most ardent zoo lovers – is mysteriously absent.

Burroughs' ambiguity on race issues is once again in evidence: 'Many other things they came to understand during the days of their captivity, not the least of which was a new conception of the Negro. To Doc, whose experience with colored people had been limited to a few worthless specimens of the Northern States, it came as a revelation. Even among the warriors of the cannibal Bagalla, he encountered individuals who possessed great natural dignity, poise and evident strength of character.'

Perhaps the most interesting thing about this book is the cultural warp and weft that it reveals to have been engendered by history. So much has Tarzan become the preserve of children in recent decades that many will be surprised to learn that there is any such thing as a designated Tarzan children's book. Tarzan novels are from today's perspective wholesome. At the point *The Tarzan Twins* appeared, though, their ornate prose and blood-splattered and occasionally sexually suggestive nature (including the discussion of bestiality in the books featuring Opar) unquestionably made them adult fare.

December 1927 saw the ape-man's third media appearance of the year when *Blue Book* began their six-part serialisation of the new Tarzan story for adults, *Tarzan, Lord of the Jungle*.

Some might posit an unintended metaphor residing in the fact that the book starts with the ape-man lounging lethargically on the back of an elephant before being dragged into other people's problems against his will. (The lounging-on-Tantor opening and the unwilling adventuring would crop up again in the series.) However, though a reluctant Burroughs was after a gap of three years being forced once again to devise a Tarzan story through financial necessity, and though we are again presented with a lost city peopled with intriguing and fantastic inhabitants as though his tested methods are now a veritable grid, the reader yet again can't help but admire his inventiveness. Moreover, that facility for storytelling – by now so well-honed – remains impressive. Even Burroughs' preposterous dialogue can sing, so slickly stylised is it. Additionally, the po-face that Burroughs often wore for his Tarzan writing refreshingly gives way here to a bit of twinkle-eyed merriment.

The comedy element comes from the scenes involving James Hunter Blake, a safari member who wanders into a lost valley in which are located two castles containing rival factions of the Knights Templar who – like stranded Japanese soldiers still fighting World War II – are under the impression that the Crusades are still going on. The juxtaposition of Blake's wiseguy personality and low-born manners with the verily-verily syntax and behavioural courtliness of the knights is amusing. However, as Blake is assimilated into the antediluvian society, wins friends – including an Arthurian princess – and engages in such local customs as a duel, one can't help but think that it is Tarzan who should be having these adventures. Intensifying the idea that he is merely a supporting character in the book whose title bears his name and does so in such an ornamental manner – something that will afflict Tarzan stories more and more – are the chapters involving the Arabs who are plotting to kill him. Impatience begins to mount at these characters for keeping Tarzan off the stage. There is also an emotional hole at the heart of the story; one that would be apparent in all Tarzan tales to a greater or lesser degree from hereon. Jane was at least fleetingly referred to in the previous book but she is not even mentioned here; a symptom, it has been surmised, of Burroughs' desire for his wife to be similarly absent from his own life. Korak, Meriem and anyone else who might provide a tender or human side to the ape-man are, and would henceforth be, absent, and the occasional presence of Jad-bal-ja – who appears at the end of this story – and Nkima – a mean little bugger of a monkey friend who would be first seen in *Tarzan and the Lost Empire* (1928) – hardly make up for this deficiency. In what seems a related matter, Tarzan himself becomes less likeable, compassion for his fellow man being replaced by impatience.

Incidentally, Burroughs 'real' medieval book *The Outlaw of Torn* (magazine 1914, book 1927) featured a walk-on role for a character called Lord Greystoke, who is postulated by some at the more intense end of the fan spectrum as an ancestor of Tarzan.

When the first episode of the film serial *Tarzan the Mighty* appeared in the summer of 1928, a new actor was in the title role, but one whose potential the creator of Tarzan had long before recognised.

Though Frank Merrill had appeared in Tarzan cinema ventures before, his roles in *The Son of Tarzan* and *Adventures of Tarzan* were as stuntman and extra. It may have been *Adventures of Tarzan* from which director Jack Nelson remembered him when he had to re-cast *Tarzan the Mighty* when first choice Joe Bonomo had to pull out of the lead role after breaking a leg on the third day of filming. Burroughs himself had reputedly already noted Merrill's suitability about seven years before, remarking, 'That is the man to play Tarzan' when on a set during a Hollywood visit. A weightlifter and national gymnastics champion prior to his movie career, the six-foot, hard-bodied Merrill was in some respects the most convincing Tarzan yet, with no hint of the flab, gormlessness, inappropriate hairstyle or effeteness that had detracted – singularly or in combination – from the look of all previous cinematic Tarzans. (For the purposes of this Korak-less argument, Kamuela Searle can be said not to count.) He was let down only by his wardrobe, a knee-length over-the-shoulder leopard pelt that was unmistakably dress-like. Also incongruously feminine were his leopard-skin headband and boots, the archetypal matching-accessory-and-shoes.

The franchise returned to Universal for *Tarzan the Mighty*. Jack Nelson and Ray Taylor directed Ian McClosky Heath's script, to which they are also said to have contributed. Advance publicity stated that the serial was based on *Jungle Tales of Tarzan*, and some of the incidents and issues from that collection do crop up. However, the chapter summaries (no print of the serial is known to exist) suggest that if *Tarzan the Mighty* was a loose adaptation of anything it was *Tarzan of the Apes*. The details of the first book are recounted – and taken liberty with: it is Tarzan's uncle who comes looking for the lost Greystoke and Jane is excised from the scene, the love interest for the ape-man now castaway Mary Trevor (Natalie Kingston). Al Ferguson plays Black John, a pirate with a plan to pass himself off as the heir to the Greystoke fortune. Though the author himself had airbrushed Jane out of the picture in his last published Tarzan book, after a visit to the set he was furious at Universal's tampering with his creation and even contemplated legal action to stop the serial's release. The public, though, couldn't get enough. Like many serials, its first episode was distributed before filming of the series had wrapped, and box office was so good that its planned 12 episodes were extended to 15. It was an example of the process to which Burroughs would become wearily used: Joe and Jo Public loved Tarzan movies no matter how much they watered down or maligned his stories.

Though Tarzan had been shown swinging on tree vines in movies before, it was Merrill who installed it as a signature of the franchise. As someone who had done his fair share of high bar work and rope climbing, he had his own ideas about how Tarzan could be depicted making his way from arboreal a to b. A hidden loop he devised enabled him to swing with one-arm, with Kingston chivalrously tucked under the other. Future cinematic ape-man Johnny Weissmuller was shown film of Merrill's swinging as an example of what we now call 'best practice'.

It is this serial that inaugurated what would become a tradition in Tarzan films and TV shows. Mary Trevor's little brother Bobby (played by Bobby Nelson) provides Tarzan – as would later Boy, Tartu, Jai and others – with a junior but unrelated version of himself to protect and mentor. A part of this was presumably a studio desire to appeal to a female demographic unmoved by derring-do and to provide a kiddie audience someone with whom to identify.

Though by 1928 writing Tarzan stories had long ago become a chore for

Burroughs, the exercise must have struck him as even more unfulfilling than usual that year, for recently he had been alternating the jobs-of-work with projects that were of sentimental value and even, relatively speaking, high art.

In the latter category were his two Apache novels, *The War Chief* (written in the second half of 1926) and *Apache Devil* (written in the second half of 1927), almost certainly the most heavyweight stories for which he was ever responsible. In the former category was *You Lucky Girl!*, Burroughs' one and only full-length play. Written to try to advance his daughter's acting career, it's not the greatest play in the world, but Burroughs must have enjoyed the fact that its creation taught him a new dimension to the craft of storytelling. Moreover, for the duration of its three acts, Burroughs impressively goes against the grain of the chauvinism-cum-misogyny he betrayed elsewhere in his work as he places himself on the side of two women with showbusiness hankerings whose traditionalist fiancés object to their careerist leanings. (The play was unproduced until 1997 and unpublished until 1999.) By January '28, he was hunched miserably (it seems safe to assume) over his desk knocking out a sequel to *The Tarzan Twins* that wasn't even wanted (and would not find a publisher for eight years). His next formulaic adult Tarzan novel followed that in March. The title under which it sagged said it all. *Tarzan and the Lost Empire* must surely have inspired many a sarcastic response of, 'Wot? Another one?'

Yes indeed, and there is a strong feeling of familiarity about the events and situations: two cities at war, a time-warp, a charismatic Western interloper who has to be rescued by Tarzan, a romance between two supporting characters and a new language and set of exotic word constructions, in this case Latin. There are additional absurdities to overcome for the reader who doesn't easily suspend disbelief, over and above the fact that even an unexplored Africa in the late 1920s could not hold so many isolated cities as Burroughs had already posited. For instance, Tarzan becomes conversant in a new language (as characters routinely do in Burroughs fiction) in mere weeks. Moreover, though he is progressively kinder to black people in the books, Burroughs' growing belief in eugenics rears its ugly head in a passage where a character advocates a bud-nipping approach to crime involving executing people simply for being related to wrongdoers.

Yet when that fluid if florid storytelling gets going, and one becomes absorbed in the intrigues of rival outposts of the Roman Empire left behind by history, misgivings melt away. What schoolboy (or overgrown schoolboy) doesn't adore tales of centurions and gladiatorial arenas (where Tarzan startles the crowd by emitting the victory cry of the bull ape after taking out a lion)? Burroughs' impish humour can be easily missed amongst his general solemnity and occasional nastiness, but how can one not love names like Dion Splendidus and Fulvus Fupus or the fact that they are instantly recognisable as the handles of respectively a good guy and a baddie?

Tarzan and the Lost Empire was serialised in five instalments in *The Blue Book Magazine* from October 1928 to February 1929. When it made the usual graduation to book form, the publisher's name on the spine was not McClurg. The only time this had previously happened with a Burroughs novel was when Macaulay had published his Tinsel Town exposé *The Girl from Hollywood* in 1923 after its magazine appearance the previous year. The setting up of Metropolitan Books was Burroughs' response to his growing financial problems. In 1923, he became one of the first writers to follow in the footsteps of Mark Twain by incorporating himself, but the implied financial canniness of this needs to be set against the fact that though Edgar Rice Burroughs, Inc grossed $60,000 in 1928 – equivalent to over three quarter of a million dollars in today's money – most of this sum was swallowed up by taxes and such things as the expense of a large household staff at Tarzana. He had embarked on a convoluted method to retain a property he couldn't really afford that involved selling 125 acres to a country club – named El Caballero – of which he became a director. In 1928, Burroughs had to foreclose on the club, but that increased his problems, because Tarzana's other 350 acres were tied up in a bond the club had issued. It was a head-spinning mess and Burroughs had responded to it via increasingly desperate financial demands on those who published his work. Burroughs and McClurg had been good for each other, but financially desperate men have little time for sentiment, and Burroughs was pleased by the fruits of a recently formed relationship with Metropolitan Newspaper Services, who had succeeded in selling a Tarzan newspaper strip. He was the only author Metropolitan Books would ever have on its lists.

By 1929, Tarzan had placed his right foot upon the necks of the media of pulp magazine, book and film and let forth the victory cry of the bull ape over their conquered forms. His encounter with the stage had left him in the unfamiliar position of having to retreat to lick his wounds, but he was still in vigorous cultural health and ready to take on new challenges.

He had racked up more than one first in his 17 years, and when advertising man Joe H Neebe had suggested to Burroughs in June 1927 a daily Tarzan newspaper strip it seemed that the ape-man was now destined to constitute both the first example of a work from literature to be licensed for such exploitation and the first drama-based American strip. In the end, he had to share both honours with *Buck Rogers in the 25th Century*, which strip by a remarkable coincidence debuted on the same date, 7 January 1929.

The well-known statistic (at least among newspaper strip and Tarzan buffs) that the Tarzan strip has been in continuous publication for over 80 years gives an inaccurate impression that it was a sensation from day one. Burroughs agreed with Neebe – an acquaintance of his brother Harry – a 50-50 split on any sales Neebe might manage to secure. The Hearst newspaper empire turned a Tarzan strip down because film rights weren't available as an adjunct, and an out-of-pocket Neebe had to bring in people with more experience in the field in the form of the Metropolitan Syndicate. Metropolitan artist Rex Maxon told Gabe Essoe that once his company's president and general manager Max Elser had set the 7 January publication start date for *Tarzan*, 'He … had to come through, but it wasn't easy to sell.' With no precedent for an adventure-based newspaper strip – all previous examples had been jokey ones colloquially referred to as 'funnies' – the reticence of papers was perhaps understandable. Maxon added, 'Finally Max made a deal with the North American Newspaper Alliance. If their papers would use the strip for ten weeks and then ask their readers if they wanted the strip continued, then Max would give them the entire ten weeks for what amounted to practically nothing.'

By that 7 January deadline, Metropolitan had sold the idea to the UK *Tit-Bits* magazine, 13 American newspapers and two Canadian papers. Despite those successes, there were no dividends that January of '29 to pay shareholders in Famous Books and Players, the incorporated company Neebe had set up to sell the strip. Possibly one of the reasons for the initial low take-up was that the strip started out with an adaptation of *Tarzan of the Apes* that was almost dogmatic in its faithfulness to the source. With the intrigues on board the HMS *Fuwalda* dominating the early days, and nothing resembling the Tarzan with which people were familiar from the nickleodeons appearing until into the third week, this would have been hard-going for fans of the thrill-packed films and serials.

Though the Tarzan newspaper strip didn't immediately reap Burroughs the dividends of the movies, it at least performed the role of pushing Tarzan's name and presence into a new quadrant of the mass media. Furthermore, Burroughs' close involvement meant that the results did not make him wince or consider reaching for his lawyers as the cinema Tarzan on more than one occasion had. Artist Hal Foster, an employee of the Palenske-Young Advertising Agency who had come to Neebe's attention, rendered Tarzan as the author had envisaged him, apart from the fact that his ape-man wore that ridiculous semi-singlet again. Though Foster's art was scratchier at this point than it would later become, it was stylish and evocative. At Neebe's request,

Foster spurned speech balloons for explanatory text and dialogue beneath the five panels of each instalment, something that added to a feeling of class. This format lasted for a decade before the more conventional comic strip traditions took over.

The *Tarzan of the Apes* adaptation was concluded in 60 daily episodes (Monday to Saturday) and was anthologised in August 1929 in *The Illustrated Tarzan Book No. 1*. (There was no *No. 2*.) Following that conclusion, there was a three-month gap before the adaptation of *The Return of Tarzan* was ready. Foster withdrew from the strip to concentrate on his advertising work, replaced on 10 June 1929 by Rex Maxon. The 'continuity' – effectively abridgement – of *The Return of Tarzan* was handled, like the first adaptation's had been, by R W Palmer. Maxon would draw the dailies almost continuously for the next 18 years, initially working his way through adaptations of the original Burroughs novels, although not always chronologically. The *Tarzan the Ape Man* strip that started in March 1933 was an adaptation of the previous year's Johnny Weissmuller movie of the same title, while *Tarzan and the Fire Gods*, beginning February 1935, was the first daily strip unrelated to either a Burroughs book or a Tarzan film. By 1938, the strip was adapting Burroughs manuscripts yet to appear in the pulps. Like Foster, Maxon took a while to develop the style for which he is most famous, and his early work was not to everybody's taste: Tarzan's face often seemed like that of a waxwork in its expressionlessness, and Burroughs in particular took exception to Maxon's slapdash approach to figure drawing and research. Nonetheless, such was the power of the Tarzan name that a mass hypnosis seemed to occur, with people assuming that *ipso facto* the strip was good because it featured Tarzan. It proceeded to pick up increasing numbers of licensees around the country – 44 US newspapers were running it by April and over 70 by the second half of '29 – and around the world. The strips gained a second lease of life when reprinted in the long-running series of Tarzan Big Little Books.

On 15 March 1931, the strip made an important expansion with the advent of a Sunday edition. The Sunday 'funnies' were more prestigious than the daily strips. Not only did they have their own section, but each strip took up an entire page and furthermore was in full colour. In *Tarzan*'s case, the Sunday page consisted of 12 panels, plus a logo accompanying a unique illustration. (Unlike in the daily strip, captions appeared within frames.) Curiously, the first instalments of the Tarzan Sunday strip featured the ape-man rescuing and proceeding to look after Bob and Mary Trevor, characters seen in the *Tarzan the Mighty* serial, although Mary here was not Tarzan's love interest but a child like Bob. Tarzan explained that he was taking them under his wing because he had 'lost a son whom I seek in the jungle.' This mangling of the Burroughs Tarzan stories was not a good start after the daily strip's faithfulness to the books. Burroughs wasn't completely happy about this, although didn't get around to voicing his concern for a while because he was distracted by illness. He eventually complained, '... the only Tarzan story that I ever wrote which is a flop is a juvenile called *The Tarzan Twins*, written around two boys ... The thing that bothered me was the possible effect that the juvenile element in the colour pages might have on my book sales ... I am constantly endeavoring to impress on the public that the stories are primarily stories for adults and I am afraid that these Sunday colour pages are going to pull some of the pegs out from under my contention.'

Burroughs, though, was far more concerned by Maxon's art, and repeatedly stated his unhappiness with it. Some think that this is the reason why by 27 September 1931 Maxon was confined to the daily strip. Maxon himself implied a mutual consent scenario, stating that doing the Sunday strip as well 'was too much work.' Whatever the truth, when Hal Foster returned to Tarzan to take up the reins on the Sunday strip mid-story, it inaugurated what many consider to be the first golden age of Tarzan comic strips. Foster's craft seemed to grow with his bigger canvas and colour (even if the latter was added after he submitted his work). His lines became cleaner as his Tarzan became more credible and animalistic. He mercifully dispensed with that wretched quasi-circus strongman's leotard, even if its replacement more closely resembled leopardskin briefs than a loincloth. Foster's continuity was supplied by R W Palmer (March 1931 to November 1931), George Carlin (November 1931 to June 1934) and Don Garden (from July 1934).

Foster only stopped working on Tarzan in 1937 because he was given the opportunity by the Hearst papers to write, draw and own the copyright on his *Prince Valiant* strip. An indication of just how beloved was Foster's ape-man is a recollection from Joe Kubert, a young fan at the time who grew up to become a draughtsman and Tarzan illustrator himself: 'I was reading this stuff when I was about eight or nine years old, and on a Sunday I'd wrap myself around that paper and I'd be in another world. The kind of work that Foster did in terms of telling a story really grabbed me out of wherever I was living in Brooklyn and took me to another place. The way he drew Tarzan made him live.'

When Foster's eight-year stint on the Sunday Tarzan strip came to an end, a replacement was found who was in some eyes even better. Though 26-year-old Burne Hogarth was two decades Foster's junior, his method was arguably more sophisticated, going in the opposite direction to Foster's quasi-impressionism to embrace a style almost overwhelming in its detail. Hogarth's first strip was published in May 1937. One of his amusing signatures was the way he would render Tarzan's very long (for the era) hair standing up almost in a cone as he descended from a height on an antagonist. Hogarth also at times wrote the scripts. He left the job in 1945 in a dispute over his lack of remuneration for book anthologies but returned in August 1947 after being given a pay rise, even if conditional on supervision of the daily strip. Unable to balance his workload at his School of Visual Arts with the daily's obligations, he quit *Tarzan* again in August 1950. He would work on the ape-man's adventures again in the future, but in the less restrictive parameters of comic books.

When Russ Manning took over the daily strip in December 1967 and the Sunday in January '68, it was an attempt by United Features Syndicate – who had been administering since March 1930 after buying out Metropolitan – to get a wayward strip back on track. (Tarzan had been given an orphan child and the strip had featured an island called Tarzanland.) They had clearly been impressed by Manning's illustrations of Gaylord DuBois' faithful adaptations of Tarzan novels for Western comics and his work on DuBois' original stories on the same publisher's *Korak* title. Manning's dozen-year stint, in which he employed a style even more burnished than Hogarth's, was marked by utter respect for the character's history. That he wrote as well as drew makes his seven-day workload even more impressive.

Manning was probably the last of the artists who made their name via the Tarzan strip, as opposed to being an artist drafted in because of pre-existing fame such as successors Gil Kane and Mike Grell. Gray Morrow became what looks like being the final *Tarzan* newspaper strip artist in 1983, when he took over both daily and Sunday jobs.

At its peak in the late '30s, the *Tarzan* strip was running in about 300 newspapers. For whatever reason, its appeal seemed to diminish significantly after World War II, with domestic sales dropping by a third between 1949 and 1959. Meanwhile, foreign sales peaked post-war at 55 countries. The handful of newspapers that take the Tarzan strip today are running reprinted material. However, this is enough to keep the strip's unbroken run staggering on and the hope burning in Tarzan fans that it will one day outpace the longest-running newspaper strip in the world, *The Katzenjammer Kids*.

Their other hope for the strip – a return to new work – looked as though it might have a chance in 2012 through the aegis of Roy Thomas and Thomas Grindberg. The latter well-known comic book artist approached United Features Syndicate with the idea of revivifying the Tarzan strip. After a long wait (Grindberg: 'United Features was going through a merger takeover from one of the largest syndicates in the world, Universal Uclick') his work was seen.

Explains Grindberg, 'They actually thought it looked top-notch but they were more interested in one-line-gag strips and not action adventure. The continuity strips such as Tarzan are not big sellers like they used to be.' Not wanting the work he and Thomas had invested in their samples go to waste, he offered ERB, Inc a deal whereby the two would produce a strip to be featured on ERB, Inc's website: 'The costs would be next to nothing, no printers bills no need to license the strip to newspapers or do much other than some advertising to let the fans know. I told ERB, Inc to waive any upfront fees towards my contribution. I essentially wanted to get the strip up and going and if it were a bust then no hard feelings. However I did negotiate that they compensate Roy's writing until we see a profit. We have produced almost three months' worth of material and [are] waiting for the "go" signal from ERB, Inc. Once we get moving on this project my hopes are to reprint the entire year's worth of material into one Tarzan book. Fans only seeing the work online and not in print, I believe they would snatch this item up quickly.' Adds Thomas, 'What's amazing is that, while it still remains a great desire of mine to one day do things like John Carter and Carson of Venus and the like, I'm happier being back involved with Tarzan now probably than I was at Marvel in the '70s, when I was distracted by the attention I had to give to Conan.'

The Tarzan comic strip, incidentally, bequeathed an important part of the Tarzan universe. The distinctive Tarzan logo that is now a registered trademark of Edgar Rice Burroughs, Inc – upper case 'T', all other letters lower-case, all letters double-outlined, the tail of the two instances of 'a' melding into the next letter – first appeared (in a more primitive version) atop the opening instalment of the Sunday Tarzan strip.

When Burroughs set to the task of writing the next Tarzan novel, he may have decided to send the ape-man to Pellucidar because he thought that to have him stumbling upon yet another lost city or civilisation in Africa would be taking the mickey a little. Or perhaps it was mammon rather than art behind his reasoning and he realised that if he dovetailed his jungle stories with his parallel tales of the world at the Earth's core it would reap the financial double-whammy of appealing to fans of both series.

This sort of crossover – the only one of Burroughs' career, unless you count the likes of Tarzan's cameo in *The Eternal Lover* – was a precursor of the kind of thing that the medium of comic books practises *in extremis* today and that has seen the ape-man cross paths there with the likes of Batman, Superman and cinema's Predator. Because such team-ups are the stuff of fantasy to the aficionado, it is to many Burroughs fans' chagrin that the author never wrote a tale in which the ape-man met the only one of his other creations to approach his popularity, John Carter. Had Burroughs produced a Martian-set Tarzan story, it might have taken the ape-man's adventures too far into the realm of science fiction for the tastes of some – but perhaps Burroughs strayed over that line with *Tarzan at the Earth's Core* in any case. Whereas with few exceptions the fantastical elements of previous Tarzan tales could be reasoned to be unlikely but just about plausible, by 1929 – in September of which year *Blue Book* began its seven-part serialisation of *Tarzan at the Earth's Core* – the idea of our planet having a hollow centre in which life could be maintained was already generally known to be not scientifically credible. Straining credibility further insofar as it militates against artifice, the story's prologue contains an example of the breaking of the fourth wall: Jason Gridley – seen in the previous Pellucidar novel, which Burroughs had written immediately before this one – picks up a message on his radio set while in Burroughs' office in the real-life town established the previous year that was named after the author's most famous creation.

The message reveals that David Innes – hero of the Inner World novels – is in peril. Gridley travels all the way to Africa (again, the particular country of that vast continent is not specified, although the ape-man helpfully verbally identifies it as 'Tarzan's country') in order to persuade Lord Greystoke to help him recue Innes, currently languishing in a dark dungeon in the land of the villainous Korsars. 'I believe that you are peculiarly fitted to lead such a venture as I have in mind,' Gridley explains when the ape-man's trained nostrils pick up the spoor of his safari and he goes to ask them what they are doing on his turf. The (unanswered) question this raises is how Gridley has heard of Tarzan: as a figure in real life or as a cultural phenomenon that gave rise to the town of Tarzana (referred to three times in the narrative altogether). Though at this stage of the series Tarzan is usually reluctant to help people in trouble, he consents to go in a dirigible all the way to the north polar icecap on the offchance that a then-current theory that it contains a hole transpires to be true and will enable him to help a man he has never met.

The hole transpires to exist and provides an ingress to Pellucidar for a party comprised of Tarzan, Gridley, Waziri and Germans. Both latter groups are shown in a good light, as though Burroughs is trying to appease in one fell swoop those who had objected to his depictions of the indigenous population of Africa and the inhabitants of Deutschland (though it should be pointed out that at the time his treatment of black people didn't create anything like the furore surrounding his demonisation of Germans). When the party gets separated in Pellucidar, Tarzan isn't too perturbed, finding he loves this savage place and its outlandish fauna. The fact that he comes across Sagoths, ape-like men who speak Mangani, makes him feel even more at home, though the havoc the eternal daylight wreaks on his usually impeccable sense of direction throws somewhat the perennial self-confidence that at other points sees him utter lines like, 'I am Tarzan – mighty hunter, mighty fighter.'

Gridley falls in love with one of the natives, the beautiful but impetuous Jana. The crushing predictability and banality of their romance is offset by less familiar Tarzan novel components. The backdrop makes for a refreshing change from the now predictable parade of Bolgani, Numa and Tantor wandering across Tarzan's literary landscape. Instead we are treated to a pteranodon swooping on Tarzan and carrying him off, sabre-toothed tigers laying waste to woolly mammoths and other animals before snarlingly turning on each other and – a species from Burroughs' own brain – the Horibs, who despite their slightly comical name are rather unsettling in their storing alive and fattening up in dank dungeons their prey.

Clearly past its peak the series might now be, but *Tarzan at the Earth's Core* sees Burroughs yet again pulling off his regular trick of subverting and defying impossibly limited narrative confines to create a compelling story.

The *Blue Book* illustrations for *Tarzan at the Earth's Core* by Frank Hoban portrayed the ape-man in an over-the-shoulder leopardskin pelt. Other pulp illustrators had depicted the ape-man similarly. Though this apparel had never been part of Burroughs' stories, ERB surprisingly had no objection to it. Hoban had previously put Tarzan in a leopardskin loincloth for *Blue Book* serialisations but made the switch, in Robert Barrett's opinion, at Burroughs' suggestion. 'I have a piece of original art drawn by Burroughs [of] the various characters in *Tarzan at the Earth's Core* showing just how he thought they should look, and Tarzan is dressed in this same over-the-shoulder attire,' says Barrett. Courtesy of Hoban and fellow artist Herbert Morton Stoops, *Blue Book* would continue portraying Tarzan in this rather straitlaced way past the point when cinema had settled on the loincloth.

Tarzan the Tiger was the ape-man's introduction to 'talkies' – sort of.

The second 15-part Tarzan serial to star Frank Merrill boasted sound, but only in the sense that some audiences saw a version that was distributed with an accompanying record containing sound effects and music. Said record featured the victory cry of the bull ape. Those who had read the books must have been stuck by how feeble was Merrill's cry ('Yaa! Yaa! Yaa!') compared with the berserk ululation they had heard in their heads. The Weissmuller yodel soon to be unveiled to the world was more of an announcement of the ape-man's presence or a form of communication but would have made a far more appropriate post-battle exultation.

Tarzan the Tiger's first episode was released in October 1929. Direction was by Henry McRae. Ian McClosky Heath ('continuity') & William Lord Wright ('supervision') adapted the script from the Burroughs novel *Tarzan and the Jewels of Opar*. Both Merrill and Natalie Kingston reprised their roles from *Tarzan the Mighty* though Tarzan's lady love was named not Mary Trevor but Jane again. Also confusingly, while Al Ferguson took on the role of the villain once more, it was in the form of the book's Albert Werper rather than the previous serial's pirate Black John. Kithnou played 'Queen La of Opar'. As the plot follows that of the novel fairly closely, it's mystifying why the serial wasn't given the book's title rather than the stupid name it was. After a bump on the head in the early chapters, Tarzan loses his memory and 'reverts to his old life as Tarzan the Tiger' we are told. There were plenty of other superlatives that could have been attached to the ape-man's name without rousing an army of pedants cognisant of the continent to which the striped big cat is indigenous. Also stupid is the depiction of an ape being intelligent and dextrous enough to truss Jane.

Though many are under the impression that it wasn't until the Weissmuller era that Jane was shown swimming nude in a Tarzan picture, in fact it was *Tarzan The Tiger* that first saw this occur; and, unlike that later instance in *Tarzan and his Mate*, the scene wasn't cut to appease the censors, even if the only nudity on display (rather than merely hinted at) is a distant shot of a dive. Another treat for the dads who accompanied their children was some exotic dancing by the bikini-clad women of Opar as La prepares to sacrifice Jane. Such sultry sights make Tarzan's modest leopard-skin dress look ever more ridiculous. On a related note, a scene in which the ape-man descends from a vine and daintily and smilingly hops in his bootees over to Jane must surely have had even audiences of 1929 rolling in the aisles.

After Tarzan calls his animal friends (including tigers) to rescue him and Jane from peril and plunders Opar to save his (English) estate, the serial ends with some kissy-kissy stuff between Lord and Lady Greystoke, dressed once again in the finery of civilisation.

Merrill had been pencilled in to appear in a third Tarzan serial – *Tarzan the Terrible* – but the sound era that he helped inaugurate was his undoing. He became one of the many silent era actors who it was adjudged possessed a voice that did not have the heroic qualities of his visual image. Merrill, however, indicated that he voluntarily bowed out of motion pictures for a career as Recreational Director for Los Angeles Parks because of his anxiety about the influence actors had on the impressionable. Either way, the decks had been cleared for what would become the most famous Tarzan of them all.

Tarzan, Guard of the Jungle was a pretty ungainly title for the story that was serialised in seven parts in *Blue Book* starting in October 1930. The substituted *Tarzan the Invincible* for book publication seems little better, being a Tarzan title interchangeable with so many others. Or perhaps that's appropriate for such an identikit affair.

The furious but empty plot of *Tarzan the Invincible* doesn't bear repeating in depth, but: a once again rootless ape-man with no family in sight goes up against a group of communists in league with Arabs intent on looting Opar in order to finance their plans for global revolution. The feeling of over-familiarity is suffocating. Tarzan throws the same shapes we've seen him throw so many times before, whether it be lazing on the back of Tantor, following up his hunting and devouring of prey with a treetop snooze or fending off the advances of the throbbingly passionate La. Meanwhile, yet again a swell couple of kids fall in love against the exotic, hectic backdrop. Exacerbating that rigidly adhered-to pattern this time though is bad writing, in terms both of a staccato plot and of didacticism. Burroughs had already written an anti-communist allegory in the shape of *The Moon Maid* and this Tarzan tale is cut from the same red-baiting cloth. Despite having experienced poverty and despite a penchant for huge financial generosity to friends and family, Burroughs was virulently anti-left, opposed not just to the cruelty of communism but the very principle of organised labour. The communists here are pantomime villains, with no suggestion permitted that any of them might be motivated by genuine concern for victims of social iniquity. The extremism and the soporific plot result in the first truly bad ape-man story since *The Return of Tarzan* 17 years before.

La and Opar would never be seen again in an adult Burroughs book. The author's increasingly desperate shoehorning in of the lost Atlantean outpost might make that a good thing on a surface level, but with La went passion and colour that the series desperately needed.

When this story appeared in book form in 1931, it became the first publication of Edgar Rice Burroughs, Inc. Financial returns on Burroughs' books had been disappointing of late – although this was true of just about every business in the Depression – and Burroughs was always looking for ways to increase his profit margins. He now cut out the middle man completely. Though Grosset & Dunlap continued in their role as distributors of his 'popular editions' – hardbacks bound in cloth that were the precursors of paperbacks – all Burroughs' first editions for the rest of his life would be self-published.

In October 1931, Edgar Rice Burroughs presented to the world just what it wasn't hungering for: another Tarzan story featuring a scheming communist, a lost race in the African jungle and a young couple who take time off from fighting peril to fall in love. Called *The Triumph of Tarzan*, it ran in six instalments in *Blue Book*. Its title was changed to *Tarzan Triumphant* for book publication.

Although Burroughs almost always planted references to previous stories in his Tarzan tales (if not always chronologically consistent ones), *Tarzan Triumphant* is unusual in that its events occur as a direct consequence of its predecessor. Joseph Stalin, premier of the Soviet Union, is so enraged by Tarzan thwarting the Bolshevik plot in the story told in *Tarzan the Invincible* that he swears vengeance and sends an assassin Africa-wards. Tarzan meanwhile has taken up the case of the 'Bangalo people of Bungalo' who hail from 'toward the north' and who have sought out the ape-man because *shiftas* resident in Abyssinia have come into their country and started seizing their people and selling them into slavery. Tarzan decides to help by accompanying a safari to the trouble-spot, him disguised as 'Lord Passmore'. On the way, Tarzan inevitably stumbles across a lost city full of intrigue and historical throwbacks. Midian is nestled in a dead volcano and its denizens are descended from a follower of the apostle Paul. Their Christianity has become perverted down the eons into vicious puritanism of which human sacrifice is a component. A mixed-sex trio end up in this insalubrious environment and, as ever for Tarzan stories, the experience is the making of them and, as ever, one of them falls for a native (named – yes – Jezebel) and, as ever, Tarzan makes sure they all get home safely once their inexperience in this neck of the woods exposes them to peril. Also as ever, Burroughs throws in an unlikely coincidence: Tarzan's would-be assassin has fallen in with the *shifta* with whom he already has an appointment.

Just as *Tarzan the Invincible* began with a lot of waffle that suggested that what one was about to read was true, so the opening of *Tarzan Triumphant* is attended by similar whimsy, with Burroughs musing on the ripples spread through the generations by our ancestors.

Burroughs uses this book to score points against not just collectivism but also religion, and not for the first time in one of his novels. Ironically, many of the Soviet politburo would have applauded his depiction of irrational behaviour generated by sheep-like obedience to religious doctrine as chiming with their perception of the 'opiate of the masses'. They might also have had something to say about how Burroughs, in the supposed land of free speech, doesn't dare do anything more than make the religion he condemns generic.

PART FOUR: ENTER WEISSMULLER

With Burroughs' Tarzan books now having fully entered their long arc of decline and the Tarzan cinema franchise having lain dormant for three years in the new and uncertain age of talking pictures, the early 1930s is the point at which the ape-man could have died a cultural death. Though he wouldn't necessarily be forgotten about today, Tarzan might easily have ended up occupying the same cultural backwaters as figures with comparable origins like Doc Savage or the Shadow: well-known to pulp aficionados but of little relevance to subsequent generations. Fortunately, Johnny Weissmuller was about to come – on a vine, of course – to the rescue.

There are conflicting accounts of how Metro-Goldwyn-Mayer (MGM) came to shoot the first proper Tarzan 'talkie'. Some sources state that the idea originated with the studio, who were anxious to find a vehicle in which to employ African wildlife and location footage left over from their 1931 film *Trader Horn*, the first cinema drama shot on location in the 'Dark Continent'. Other sources state that ERB, Inc general secretary Cyril Ralph Rothmund approached MGM himself with the idea. It may even be that those two stories don't conflict. Initially, the film was actually intended to be a sequel to *Trader Horn*. A story outline depicted the eponymous Trader Horn character agreeing to lead an expedition to search for a lost tribe and *en route* encountering Tarzan, who kidnapped a female scientist in the party. Eventually the Trader Horn story element was dispensed with.

First choice to play MGM's Tarzan was weightlifter and shot-putter Herman Brix, but he was another prospective ape-man who had to pull out due to an injury, this one incurred on a prior job. (Unlike Joe Bonomo, though, he would get a second chance.) The studio's replacement casting was inspired and crucial. Memories of him in later Tarzan pictures in which he had begun to go out of shape have blurred just how physically perfect was Johnny Weissmuller in the early years of his occupancy of the loincloth. He was as low in body fat and as toned of muscle as would be expected of someone who had won five gold medals for swimming across the 1924 and 1928 Olympics. Importantly, unlike with Universal and Frank Merrill, MGM didn't hide this glorious bod. Though he was depicted as wearing an over-the-shoulder pelt in the artwork for the movie poster of his 1932 debut *Tarzan the Ape Man*, Weissmuller's costume in the film was the diametric opposite of such modesty: not only did he sport just a loincloth but, slit as it was to the hip on both sides, it showed unprecedented flesh. On top of that was not just his handsomeness but his *appropriate* handsomeness. Unlike Jim Pierce, Weissmuller did not have urban good looks that made him appear as though he had just swapped a dress suit for an animal hide but instead appeared genuinely wild. Yes, he had a side-parting, and even a hint of a blow-wave early on, but there was enough of an unruliness and greasiness about his barnet to make us believe that his domicile really was the jungle.

The casting came with an example of the type of serendipity that seems to confirm that something is just meant to be. The famous yodel that Weissmuller produced and that was never matched let alone bettered by any Tarzan actor has been claimed to be his imitation of a product of MGM's sound department that melded the bleat of a camel, the howl of a hyena, the growl of a dog and the pluck of a violin string, each played a fraction of a second after the other. That the powerful, ululating and intrinsically human noise that emerged from Weissmuller's throat resembles none of those components instantly provokes the suspicion that this was the kind of public relations guff that in a less sceptical age tended to be reproduced unquestioningly by the media and lapped up by the public. Far more plausible is the theory that the yodel is a savaged-up version of the kind of thing that Weissmuller – of Germanic origin – was used to hearing in *bierkellers*. In private conversation unmoored to the requisites of publicity announcements, he told his daughter of yodelling contests at *schlacht*s that pre-dated his film career, even if he acknowledged to her that he learnt to imitate a studio souped-up version of his own holler. It is unlikely that MGM knew that Weissmuller possessed the capacity for such a vocal signature when they selected him without supposedly even bothering with a screen test, but his yodel – instantly imitated in school playgrounds around the world – would become the single most famous thing about the cinema ape-man. So much so that it has become a trademark in more than a metaphorical sense. The name 'Tarzan' was trademarked by ERB, Inc in 1965 for books and other paper products, and the trademark was extended to other items of merchandise at intervals thereafter. However, in the 20th Century, ERB, Inc – at the urging of legal firm Fross Zelnick – trademarked the Tarzan yell preparatory to entering into a US licensing agreement for a Tarzan action figure toy. Had he been alive, Weissmuller might have been amused – or possibly had some less benign emotion – to find that the relevant soundfile on Fross Zelnick's website was his own ululating voice. The EU rejected the corporation's attempt to file the same trademark across the Atlantic on the grounds that the spectrogram submitted as evidence did not clearly explain the sound.

Yet though the talkies gave Tarzan an instantly recognisable vocal signature, they also made him an idiot. In all Tarzan pictures hitherto, the dual nature of a man who was jungle-raised but articulate heir to the seat of Greystoke had been faithfully transferred over from the books. With the Weissmuller era, the character's origin went unexplained and his speech became pidgin English. The consequent innocent man-child persona was endearing to an extent, but it traduced the nature of the literary character. Though he loved the money that began to pour in from MGM, Burroughs hated what they did to his creation: Joan Burroughs recalled her father shaking his head sadly in his seat after a cinema showing of a Tarzan picture by which the rest of the audience had been enthralled. Said Danton Burroughs, 'The producers always went in their own direction thinking they knew the character without reading the books. That frustrated him, but the money was good and he allowed the distortion. Every time he tried to get involved and steer these writers and producers in the right direction, they'd promise him something, then do something completely different.' Yet the traducing was a more complicated issue than that. As Bill Hillman says, 'Some of that is [Burroughs'] fault. He stipulated to some degree that the stories and some of the elements of the novels not be duplicated.'

Another change made to Tarzan by talking pictures was the pronunciation of his name. Burroughs' had always said 'Tar-zun,' but the makers of *Tarzan the Ape Man* had the actors enunciate the character's name as 'Tar-*zaan*.' The stress on the second syllable sounds less Western and therefore more appropriate, but it was the power of cinema rather than logic that ensured that that's what it instantly and permanently became. Stateside at least. British inclination was to stick to the short second 'a' – as was, strangely, Weissmuller's.

Trader Horn director W S Van Dyke was logically enough assigned *Tarzan the Ape Man*. The screenplay was 'adapted' by Cyril Hume (another alumnus of *Trader Horn*) with dialogue written by none other than Ivor Novello, a British thespian and composer now chiefly remembered through having given the UK's most prestigious songwriting award its name. The plot sees explorer James Parker (C Aubrey Smith) on a quest to find the fabled elephant's graveyard. Jane (Maureen O'Sullivan), his beloved flibbertigibbet daughter with an incongruous deadly aim with a rifle, insists on accompanying him. Irishwoman O'Sullivan opting to play Jane as an English girl started a tradition in Tarzan movies that has continued off and on to this day.

At 99 minutes, it is a long movie for the time, and things get off to a boring start, with early sections having to rely on, of all things, some weird, incestuous banter between Jane and her father to provide the only sign of vitality amongst family reunion soap opera and a flat travelogue. Meanwhile, even in its era it would have raised an eyebrow that when a laden native bearer falls screaming to his death from a mountain, the 'Poor devil' uttered by Parker's employee

Holt doesn't come until *after* he demands 'What was in that pack?' Elsewhere, the view is explicitly stated that natives are mindless savages.

If the leftover *Trader Horn* material was indeed the impetus for the film, it's somewhat ironic, because its use is risible: Jane and her father laughably stand remarking on local customs in front of an obvious back projection of natives, while it was clearly acres of unused hippo material that compelled the producers to commission the writing of a quite distasteful aquatic slaughter section. Fourteen years on, things don't seem to have advanced much beyond the cut-ins employed in Elmo Lincoln's first film. Apart, that is, from the technological leap of sound that enables the deployment of that yodel. It is first heard as a mysterious noise carrying to the safari from the depths of the jungle. Though wonderful, it is somewhat overused, ringing out in situations where the ape-man couldn't possibly muster sufficient lung power, such as when he is wresting a lion or executing a breaststroke.

Tarzan makes his first visual appearance round about the half-hour mark. His acrobatics in the jungle canopy are quite impressive here and throughout – but is that a trapeze swing we discern in the treetops? Tarzan snatches Jane and carries her off to his tribe (men dressed as apes, apart from baby chimps portraying the young ones). One particular chimp makes his first of many appearances in the franchise. The name of Tarzan's famous chimpanzee friend has variously been spelt 'Cheetah', 'Cheeta' and 'Cheta' in movie credits, and variously implied to be male and female. The character has also been retrospectively claimed by various often conflicting sources to have been played by animal actors in their care. No attempt will be made here to settle the issue of who the simian thesp was, but the spelling 'Cheeta' and the male pronoun will be used henceforth for the sake of convenience. There is a funny tussle between Cheeta and the ape-man over Jane's handkerchief, while Miss Parker sits unamused between them. Tarzan then stabs to death an encroaching leopard. How a knife of forged steel ever came to be in his possession is not explained. As to his backstory, the closest it comes to being addressed is when Mr Parker later remarks, 'I can't make it out – how did he get here?' Jane's response of, 'Oh, what does it matter?' blithely dispenses with any intention of supplying an origin. Tarzan is none too gentle or polite to Jane, but does tuck her safely into a tree nest before chivalrously posting guard outside.

The next day, Tarzan frees an elephant from a trap before breakfast (freshly killed gazelle). Jane explores his vocabulary, which so far has consisted of 'Umgawa!', an instruction to his animal friends and foes as all-purpose as that yodel. The famous phrase 'Me Tarzan, you Jane' originates here, even though it was never quite said but rather is a colloquial simplification of an exchange involving pointed fingers and repetitions of 'Me,' 'You,' 'Tarzan,' 'Jane' and various other words.

The safari catches up with Tarzan. In the ensuing battle, one of Tarzan's tribe is shot dead. A distraught ape-man starts taking revenge, picking people off one by one. Jane has begun to fall for Tarzan and defends him to his detractors in her party. A bullet-grazed Tarzan fights a lioness to the death, after which her mate attacks him. Elephants respond to Tarzan's yodel for assistance. He is nursed back to health by Jane, who has been snatched by one of his tribe. The two frolic together, including a scene designed to show off Weissmuller's swimming prowess as he cuts through water faster than Jane can run parallel along the river bank. Jane starts to feel blissfully relaxed in the company of her innocent forest god, but she knows how important she is to her dad. There is a genuine moment of sadness when a forlorn-looking ape-man steps back into the bushes after returning her to her party.

Jane's party is captured by bizarre diminutive natives. 'Pygmies?' the question is asked. 'Dwarves,' comes the accurate reply – though 'in blackface' is left unsaid. Jane espies Cheeta and tells him to alert Tarzan, which Cheeta does, although he has his own mini-adventure on the way. Resorting to his yodel again, Tarzan rustles up a herd of elephants to help him, though on the way to fulfil the role of saviour he encounters a barrier of crocodiles, which he ultimately evades by scrambling onto a hippo's back. In the dwarves' village, the safari is being thrown to the mercies of a giant, ferocious caged ape. The filmmakers' accomplishment of making this beast vaguely scary even though it is clearly a man in costume is undermined somewhat by the moment Tarzan throws his knife in the ape's face: the lodged weapon bounces about as only rubber can. The elephants invade the village and show savagery unheard of in real life before carrying Jane, her father and Holt to safety. One of the elephants is fatally injured and duly takes the party (via an entrance hidden by a waterfall) to the elephant's graveyard, where Jane's father expires in the realm of his dreams. Jane meanwhile decides to stay with her ape-man. She and Tarzan wave off Holt, who heads for civilisation astride an elephant.

The film is very clunky in places from today's perspective, but at the time, the miracle of synchronised sound was as awe-inspiring as 'moving pictures' had been at the turn of the century and would have provided *Tarzan the Ape Man* a real allure. Just when Western audiences had become blasé about the sight of African wildlife, now one could hear roars, grunts, growls and chatters accompanying it. While O'Sullivan's short hair means she is not yet possessed of the lustrous beauty for which she would soon become renowned in Tarzan flicks, Weissmuller looks like a million dollars.

Tarzan the Ape Man was one of the ten biggest box-office hits of the year. The best was yet to come for a revivified icon.

Simultaneous with the première of *Tarzan the Ape Man, Argosy* magazine – in its issue dated 12 March 1932 – began a six-part serialisation of the latest Burroughs Tarzan story, *Tarzan and the City of Gold*.

Burroughs might have felt disdain for Tarzan movies but MGM's revitalising of the franchise – however cockeyed – was the kind of thing clearly beyond the character's creator, who turned in possibly the dreariest, stalest Tarzan tale yet. The lost cities this time are Athne (City of Ivory, whose inhabitants worship elephants) and Cathne (City of Gold, whose denizens bow down to lions). Tarzan seems strangely blasé about stumbling upon these places – but then maybe it would have been less realistic if Burroughs had depicted surprise on the ape-man's part after having shown him in this situation so often before. The queen of Cathne is Nemone. She resembles La in that she is fiery, half-bonkers and totally in love with Tarzan, who as usual with such temptresses is immune to her charms despite there being the now predictable Jane-sized hole in the proceedings. Tarzan once again learns the native language sufficiently speedily for easy story development but far too quickly to engender any sense of realism. Meanwhile the spiritual aridity continues apace, with the increasingly aloof and superior Tarzan musing his most misanthropic thoughts yet, even if the conventions of the adventure story dictate that he shakes himself out of them long enough to help people in danger, in this case a young woman called Doria who is due to be put to death by Nemone because she is prettier than she.

It's not all by-numbers stuff: just when we are expecting the sort of tussle to the death with a lion we have already seen 101 times in Tarzan tales, Burroughs provides a new spin by having a knife-less Tarzan turning and running away because he knows that Numa tires after a hundred yards. (His plan goes wrong because this is a lion specially bred for endurance, but a dramatic entrance by Jad-bal-ja saves the day.) Aside from little flashes of lateral thinking like that, though, this is clearly the product of a bored, uninterested author and an unhappy human being.

The next Tarzan story was serialised in *Blue Book Magazine* in five parts starting from August 1932. Despite its quick appearance after *City of Gold*, *Tarzan and the Leopard Men* is enveloped by sluggishness and inertia, perhaps symptomatic of which is the fact that it didn't appear in book form until *after* the following Tarzan magazine serial, *Tarzan and the Lion Man*, had been published as a novel, and this despite the fact that Burroughs wrote on the flap of the first edition of the latter book, 'Mr Burroughs believes this to be the poorest Tarzan novel he has ever written ...'

In a sense, it's a surprise that *Leopard Men* doesn't work, for it sees Burroughs trying something a little different, at least in the sense that he appears to have decided (albeit temporarily) that any more lost cities would be just too much. Instead, he sets up an intriguing and potentially highly dramatic scenario involving the secret society of the title who draw their members from various villages and whose fairly realistic activities – conducted in ceremonial robes and claws – involve cannibalism. Somehow, though, Burroughs manages to throw away the interesting concept, starting with the ostensible Ku Klux Klan metaphor of the Leopard Men: this book contains some of Burroughs' most racist material yet.

Back in 1915, *All-Story* editor Bob Davis had complained to Burroughs of *Tarzan and the Jewels of Opar*, 'You have introduced the old wallop-on-the-bean idea for the purpose of sidetracking Tarzan's intelligence.' A device that was hoary 17 years previously is here deployed again, and to no greater dramatic purpose than to have Tarzan fall in with the supposition of native Orando – who finds him after he has been knocked out by a storm – that he is a *muzimo*, or protective spirit. When Tarzan inevitably undergoes a second, process-reversing wallop, he is as ever miraculously devoid of brain damage or physical trauma. Meanwhile, with the exception of the contents of a cooking pot yielding up a grisly secret, the Leopard Men are a somewhat less scary (and active) proposition than we are at first led to assume by Orando, who persuades Tarzan to join him in his lonely resistance to their malign influence. Burroughs also throws in the obligatory fractured group of Westerners whom Tarzan is obliged to rescue from danger. The romance that predictably develops between two of them is as uninteresting as the revelation that one of the party is the long lost younger brother of another. Philip José Farmer – the science fiction author and Burroughs fanatic who went as far as to proclaim himself 'the greatest authority on Tarzan' – described *Tarzan and the Leopard Men* as 'the dullest' of the Burroughs Tarzan novels. So leaden is the storytelling that we feel almost as though we are reading this in real time, following minute-by-minute the drudgery Burroughs experienced as he wearily ground out another entry in the series he had long ago concluded was exhausted.

It's rather ironic that the deeper Edgar Rice Burroughs went into his rut with Tarzan, the healthier was the character elsewhere: on 10 September 1932, radio could now be added to magazines, books, films and comic strips as media conquered by the ape-man.

Because film is a 'fuller' medium in that we use our main sense – sight – to experience it, the temptation is to assume that radio is a more primitive form to which cinema is the successor. In fact, radio is younger, with public broadcasts dating back only as far as 1920 (i.e. two years after the first Tarzan movie was released). Radio really took off in the Christmas of 1924 when the consumer buying trends came down on the side of 'wirelesses' rather than gramophones or phonographs. Though music was radio's bedrock, drama became very important in the medium in an era in which it could otherwise be obtained only at the nickelodeon or theatre house. Radio dramas had originated in meaningful form in the late 1920s. *Little Orphan Annie*'s transference from comic strip to radio in April 1931 was pioneering, but the entry into the medium of a figure of such vast cultural recognition as Tarzan was more significant. It brought sorely needed income in bleak economic times: sponsors and advertisers were keen to attach themselves to him on this broadcasting expedition.

Burroughs had been considering for a while the idea of reading his Tarzan stories over the air, but Joe Neebe, who had first floated the idea of the Tarzan newspaper strip, was responsible for the ape-man swinging into radio, where Neebe was now employed. Neebe acted as Burroughs' broker in a deal with LA's American Radio Features syndicate for adaptations of Tarzan stories, starting with the first book. Burroughs had approval of the scripts and was able to veto the inaccuracies about wildlife about which he had been sensitive ever since being ridiculed for including tigers in the first version of *Tarzan of the Apes* and about which Rex Maxon's carelessness infuriated him. He was also able to prevent the ape-man becoming the kind of cartoon character into which MGM were beginning to turn him. It was presumably also the author who was responsible for the fact that each episode began with the piece of quasi-advertising: '*Tarzan of the Apes* – brought to you from off the pages of Edgar Rice Burroughs' thrilling book.'

Each show was 15 minutes long (ten without the commercials) and was designed to run three days a week. As with film and comic strips, Tarzan was in the vanguard on radio, pioneering new methods. Radio dramas were usually broadcast live, but radio stations who subscribed to *Tarzan of the Apes* were circulated 16-inch transcription discs of the programme, an innovation that meant it could be – and was – bought by many English-speaking nations around the world. Though circumscribed in needing to suggest rather than depict action (especially early on when Tarzan could not speak English), the producers were conversely unhindered by the requirement to import real or replicated animals, lost cities and weaponry, and could go to town on what they included. The listeners staring at their grilles were treated to all manner of evocative roars, burbles, gunshots and screams between the intense (if a little pompous) present-tense description of Fred Shields. That the radio series began with an adaptation of the first Tarzan book, just as cinema, stage and newspaper strip versions had done, might seem like overkill on that story, but with the origin-less Weissmuller movie in circulation, perhaps now, of all times, such a reiteration was appropriate.

The publicity that claimed that a high-and-low search had been conducted for the radio Tarzan and Jane was somewhat eyebrow-raising, for after their supposed scouring of the country, the producers had decided to cast none other than Jim Pierce as Tarzan and Joan Burroughs Pierce as Jane – son-in-law and daughter of the ape-man's creator respectively. Burroughs, ever loyal to his family, had already given Jim Pierce a marriage gift enabling him to appear in a Tarzan movie, which was to cause Burroughs some legal problems later on. That the Pierces worked not for the five dollars per show the other actors were paid but royalties would ultimately make them a wealthy couple. Joan was a trained actor but the fact that Pierce had got into the profession only because he was cast for his build in an era where sound did not exist in cinema was sometimes painfully apparent on the radio show. A photograph released to publicise the programme was also unfortunate: though still only 32, Pierce was now too rotund a figure to be stripped to a loincloth, and he was clearly carrying a safari-suited Emma in his arms only to hide his pre-middle-age spread. However, this didn't matter too much with a product you couldn't see. Nor did the fact that Pierce's bull ape victory cry was serviceable rather than awe-inspiring like Weissmuller's yodel. (It may also have been dictated by Burroughs, for it seems to consist of an elongated version of the word 'Tarmangani.') For a quarter of an hour, the public – kids especially – were enraptured as drama, thrills and exotic sounds filled a living room that might otherwise be resounding only with the rustle of a newspaper or a family's bickering. Ratings were excellent.

The publicity cross-fertilisation between versions of Tarzans in different media was now at its apex. The ape-man was simultaneously to be found on screen, on radio, in comic strips and in books. In a world with a profoundly smaller media than today, the impact of this was commensurately greater. The consequences were predictable. When ERB, Inc claimed in 1936, 'Tarzan is the best known and best loved fictional character in the world today,' they were not exaggerating. Burroughs even had a feeling that he had reserved a space on a juggernaut that was going to make his novels obsolete. By 1935, he was writing, 'There is one factor that may have more effect on reducing book sales than any number of depressions, and that is radio ... Already, with two programmes, we are netting more than we do from the sale of all our books, which, taken in connection with the fact that there are hundreds of similar programmes on the air, suggests that people are taking their fiction this way instead of through books.' He was partially right: it would be the medium that effectively superseded radio – television – that decimated reading as a leisure activity.

The advent of the Tarzan radio show marked the point where ape-man merchandising truly took off. Tarzan merchandise – or at least official Tarzan merchandise – went back to 1922 when Burroughs granted permission to New York toy manufacturer Davis & Voetsch to market toy simians with the ape-man's name attached, including a large ape with flexible fingers. Perhaps the fact that Burroughs' royalty for the first year totalled just $120 is what initially made him relaxed about unauthorised merchandise such as the watermarked Tarzan bond paper that came to his attention in 1926: he wrote an unsolicited letter of forgiveness to the manufacturer, in which he revealed he was using the paper for the manuscript of his latest novel. A Berlin café, German chocolates and an amusement park freak all appropriated the Tarzan name without incurring more than bemusement from the author: he seemed to perceive them as involving the same sort of tribute communicated by dogs and race horses (including one owned by the Prince of Wales) named after his creation. He became more business-minded as he realised just how much money merchandising rights could generate.

With merchandising, the Tarzan character was once again in the vanguard of a hitherto unknown phenomenon, or at least unknown on this scale. Acting on his own initiative, Burroughs commissioned statuettes of Tarzan characters and creatures from a company that had previously made figures based on the *Our Gang* film series. ERB, Inc sold these statuettes to sponsors of the Tarzan radio series, who in turn offered them as loyalty incentives to their customers. Though he had always been business- rather than art-orientated, it was the fact that half a million of these figurines had been shipped within the first 18 months of the Tarzan radio show that made Burroughs apprehend fully the need to protect his intellectual property. From now on, he would employ somebody especially to license the Tarzan name, which was now so embedded in the language as a synonym for both strong-man and uncouth that it was in danger of being perceived as generic and public domain. (One synonym made the jump from colloquial to formal in the 1940s when Webster's dictionaries started defining the word Tarzan as 'a well-built, agile and very strong man.') He had hit yet another goldmine. The Tarzan name appeared on commercial products in unquantifiable numbers. Some were logical (Tarzan singlets, swimming trunks, chest expanders, action figures, phonograph records, posters, bubblegum cards, stickers, transfers, colouring books, board games, toy knives and archery sets) or at least semi-logical (jungle helmets, animal jungle masks). Some were simply fatuous and examples of the way a brand name could lend allure to anything (crockery, schoolbags, shoes, shirts, foodstuffs from ice cream to chewing gum to bread).

The sponsorship of the radio programme by Signal Oil played a huge part in this process. Having hosted a première event for the show (Weissmuller was invited despite having nothing to do with it), the petrol company milked their connection to the ape-man for everything it was worth – which was plenty – via promotions like the Tarzan Jig-Saw Puzzle Contest (in which people could build up free of charge a four-colour Tarzan puzzle week by week by stopping into a Signal Service Station, with prizes awarded at the end). The pester-power factor was cranked up by the formation of the Signal Tarzan Club, a membership requirement of which was to bring a new customer to Signal. The club provided access to Tarzan badges, membership cards, photos and competitions, and awarded points redeemable against various consumer desirables for persuading others to buy Signal products.

Signal's blurring of the demarcation between cinema and radio Tarzans continued when in 1933 the company used its space on the radio programme to promote the new Tarzan picture *Tarzan the Fearless* and bought screen advertising time and lobby A-boards at theatres to emphasise the link (which didn't exist) between Signal and the movie. The illogicality of all this was hardly going to bother Signal: within a year, the club's membership-card logo of a hollering Tarzan had been circulated to a reported 100,000. As well as the calculable financial benefit of causing so many people to fill up at Signal stations who otherwise would not have, there was the unquantifiable but undeniable benefit of the goodwill engendered by being associated with a brand that gave people a warm feeling. Signal furthered this goodwill by sponsoring baseball teams formed by Tarzan club members, creating another dimension to the Tarzan phenomenon that, though it might have been rooted in consumerism, actually ended up injecting a participatory and activist principle inherently absent in the consumption of art.

Yet by 1934, Signal seemed to think they had created a monster that was out of control. With membership of the club running at 415,000, the administration involved was so considerable that they took the decision to end their sponsorship of the radio show.

Or perhaps the severing of the tie was down to unexpected changes. In March of that year, the 130-episode adaptation of *Tarzan of the Apes* had finished and the show was part-way through *The Return of Tarzan*, which ran to 156 episodes. At that point, Burroughs decided not to renew his contract with American Radio Features. He had either concluded that even his power of veto over unsatisfactory elements wasn't sufficient or he wanted once again to cut out the financial middle man. There were other changes afoot. It was announced that Pierce and his wife would not be returning to their roles. Pierce later wrote, 'Toward the end of our contract, Joan became pregnant with Mike and the producer … was afraid that Joan would not have time to do justice to the job. I felt that we could get ahead a few episodes and Joan wouldn't be out long … They wanted me to continue with a new Jane, but I told them that Joan was just as important to the programme as I and resigned.' Burroughs felt compelled to write to the clients of the show emphasising that it would continue.

Tarzan and the Diamond of Asher, produced by ERB, Inc, debuted on 10 August 1934. There were 39 episodes of 15 minutes each written by Rob Thompson, who was personally chosen by Burroughs and whose chapter outlines the author would amend and approve before he went ahead and wrote a full script. Carlton KaDell played the ape-man. Jane did not appear. Unfortunately, the success Burroughs had had in publishing his own books – he reported in correspondence that his self-published novels were making a profit, and in coming years he would issue previously unsold manuscripts as well as magazine stories that had not previously transferred over to book form – did not apply to the radio medium. This seems to have been for no good reason. Though the story *Diamond of Asher* told of a missing man who is a Tarzan lookalike and a lost expedition may sound same-old, same-old, its production values and execution are generally considered superior to those of the Pierce Tarzan show in almost every way. Though it was pushed hard by Burroughs, who commissioned a glossy brochure to sell it, it found far fewer outlets than the Tarzan radio show was used to. A follow-up 39-part series, *Tarzan and the Fires of Tohr*, copyrighted in 1936, fared even worse. A Thompson-written Tarzan and D'Arnot adventure involving a lost expedition, ivory smuggling, a hidden city and a strange yellow race who engage in human sacrifice, it was bought by only a handful of domestic stations plus a Hawaiian one, an Australian one and a Canadian one. More Tarzan radio scripts were commissioned and recorded but not broadcast: two chapters of *Tarzan and the Tower Of Ho* by Rob Thompson and two chapters of *Tarzan in Pellucidar* by Jerry Cady.

Perhaps the public had simply got used to Pierce as the 'voice' of Tarzan. Whatever the reason, the '30s radio Tarzan flared sensationally for 18 months but then quickly and quite dramatically faded.

In late 1931, a rather unseemly incident occurred on the doorstep of Edgar Rice Burroughs' home.

Jules Goldstone, a lawyer working for film producer Sol Lesser, handed the author $10,000. When Burroughs asked what this money was for, Goldstone explained that it was payment for a Tarzan movie to which Burroughs had previously agreed. Burroughs literally threw the money back at the lawyer and told him the relevant contract had lapsed. While the author closed his front door, Goldstone was left chasing thousand dollar bills. That was the version of events of Lesser. Burroughs, in notes to himself, told a more sedate tale that also involved one Walter Shumway, comments about the nice weather and a polite but firm statement by Burroughs that he knew what the two men were here to discuss and that he had no intention of doing so. Somewhat unconvincingly – as though in preparation for a court case – Burroughs wrote, 'He did not show me any money nor any cheque.' Either way, a dormant contract had come back to bite the author on the backside.

It originated in a deal Burroughs had agreed in January 1929 – at a point between the two Frank Merrill Tarzan cinematic ventures – with a pair of producers, Jack Nelson and the aforementioned Shumway, who proposed a Tarzan movie or serial called *Tarzan the Fearless*. The agreement stipulated that the venture must be released within seven years. In what amounted to a wedding present to his new son-in-law, Burroughs also insisted on a clause that stated Jim Pierce be cast as Tarzan. Since then, the rights to the project had been bought by a third party, a consortium headed by film producer Sol Lesser, responsible for the likes of an early *Oliver Twist* adaptation and *The Mine with the Iron Door*. Lesser's lawyer had discerned a legal loophole: though Nelson and Shumway were in breach of the contract by not having paid Burroughs the $10,000 advance that he was due to receive, Burroughs had failed to inform them of their breach, which itself could be made good by rendering payment to him. Hence the doorstep contretemps.

Burroughs' alleged refusal to accept the money made no difference to the contractual loophole, and when Lesser took legal action against Burroughs both he and MGM – shortly to start work on Weissmuller's first Tarzan picture, which had been assigned a very large budget – were faced with a cinematic release that might queer their pitch. Though he might have acted in good faith – his cash advance was more than two years overdue, so he might have thought the project was dead – Burroughs must have felt more than a little awkward at the fact that he had assured MGM they had exclusive Tarzan movie rights. The most MGM could do – short of dropping their own film and suing Burroughs – was to grease Lesser's palm in order to persuade him to at least delay production of his own Tarzan project. Lesser agreed to the latter and, due to the box office success of *Tarzan the Ape Man*, by the time he was ready to exercise his option found himself in an even better position than he had been. Some have posited the theory that it was Burroughs' mortification at this whole scenario that was behind his not objecting – at least in public – to what an idiot MGM proceeded to portray Tarzan as.

Though Lesser made his Tarzan different from the MGM version in that the romantic interest was not Jane but one Mary Brooks (Jacqueline Wells, later called Julie Bishop), he also stipulated that his Tarzan movie should portray the ape-man as the monosyllabic man-child seen by so many millions in *Tarzan the Ape Man*. That he cast an Olympic swimmer as Tarzan might also have been perceived as – ahem – monkey-see, monkey-do, but it seems to have been as much inspired by the fact that Clarence 'Buster' Crabbe – Gold medallist in the 1932 competition – had done very well in a 1933 Tarzan rip-off movie *King of the Jungle*, portraying Kaspa the Lion Man.

The fact that Crabbe ended up in the picture was a saga in itself. When Burroughs had stipulated his son-in-law be cast in *Tarzan the Fearless*, Pierce was a fine figure of a man. As mentioned previously, a physical decline as shocking for its pace as its extent had afflicted Pierce since then. Though once the *Tarzan The Fearless* project was resurrected Pierce tried gamely to shed the approximately 50 pounds by which he was overweight, it was clear to Lesser that it was a futile endeavour. In vain he tried to convince Burroughs to release him from the obligation to employ his son-in-law. Burroughs – who had the feelings of his own daughter to think about – refused, even when Lesser told him that with Pierce in the role his only option would be to make a comedy with Jane as the dominant half of the pair and Tarzan a klutz. Though humourist Corey Ford was commissioned to write such a burlesque, this mocking scenario was not the one Lesser had envisaged when he bought the rights to the character, and eventually he paid Pierce off with $5,000, though not without what seems the deliberate humiliation of ensuring that the screen test for Pierce that was part of the deal was a Shakespeare soliloquy that he was bound to stumble through. Crabbe had been part of the same 1928 Olympics team as Weissmuller and the two were pals, although the media inevitably now portrayed them as cinema rivals. Crabbe had also been screen-tested by MGM for the role of the ape-man in 1931, if somewhat perfunctorily. His performance as the lion-raised Kaspa, incidentally, had seen him even more skimpily clothed than Weissmuller had been in *Tarzan the Ape Man*, with his buttocks on prominent display.

Lesser hired Robert F Hill – veteran of the Elmo Lincoln *Adventures of Tarzan* serial – to direct. Walter Anthony (dialogue), Basil Dickey and George H Plympton provided a screenplay centring around Tarzan agreeing to help Mary find her scientist father, who has been captured by the people of Zar, a treasure-bedecked lost city with a villainous high priest. A thousand-dollar bounty on Tarzan's head and a scheme to rob him of the Greystoke birthright he doesn't know is his add to the intrigue.

Lesser attempted to have his cake and eat it by making both a 71-minute movie (released in August 1933) and a serial. His plans for maximisation of profits came unstuck when some theatres declined his two proffered options of running either 12 weekly two-reel chapters or an opening chapter of an hour's length plus eight weekly two-reel chapters. Many instead ran just the 60-minute opener as though it was a feature, even though it dribbled to a close with no proper resolution. However, the horrific reviews to which the feature was subjected were not just down to this confusion. Right from the get-go, it seems almost as though Lesser is making the burlesque he once threatened: shots of Crabbe swinging somewhat uncertainly on vines to tear at fruit with his teeth seem too silly to be meant seriously. Crabbe's floppy mop of dyed black hair and toothy smile seem more appropriate to a Marx Brothers movie, his thong-effect leopardskin loincloth looks painful – and what are we to make of his mock-spanking of his chimpanzee friend? In having Tarzan speak little more than two dozen words in the feature film version, Lesser takes Weissmuller's verbal minimalism to absurd levels. Despite his innocence and taciturnity, Weissmuller's Tarzan had a semblance of an edge to him, but Crabbe plays the ape-man as an aw-shucks simpleton. Not only does he commit the cardinal sin of laughing – Burroughs' Tarzan might smile grimly but did not laugh, and he made sure that Tarzan radio scripts depicting him doing so were amended – but he does so as gormlessly as an animated Disney character. Tarzan's battle with a rubber croc is as lame as his tussle with an uninterested lion, even if it did institute a tradition in Tarzan pictures.

As with the MGM Tarzan, the deliberate annexation from the source novels creates problems. We are told Tarzan was kidnapped by a great ape when his parents were exploring these parts, but not why his name is Tarzan.

Crabbe never played the ape-man again but did carve out a successful career in serials, becoming particularly well-known for his roles as Flash Gordon and Buck Rogers. Meanwhile, despite his initial poor relations with

Burroughs and such a substandard franchise entrée, Sol Lesser would become a lifelong friend of the author and eventually have a lengthy involvement with the Tarzan character.

From the ridiculous to the fairly sublime. *Tarzan and the Lion Man* was the first and indeed only Burroughs Tarzan tale to break out of the pulp ghetto and be published in a slick. That *Liberty* magazine – which serialised the story in eight weekly parts from the issue cover-dated 11 November 1933 – was an unusually prestigious outlet for the ape-man was reflected in the fact that for the first time a magazine carrying a Tarzan story did not trumpet it on any of its covers. Perhaps it was *Liberty*'s classiness that made it willing to run this of all Tarzan stories, for in several senses it seems a mickey-take of a Tarzan industry that it might have felt to be below its readers.

When an author gets bored with a character, it becomes tempting to start being playful with him, and this seems to have happened with ERB here. Burroughs' flirtation with post-modernism in *The Tarzan Twins* could be dismissed as not really counting on the grounds that in a children's book the rules are different; and the fame possessed by the ape-man referred to in *Tarzan at the Earth's Core* is not explicitly stated as art-related. In this story, however, Tarzan is discussed as both a supposed real-life individual whose adventures are recounted in this and other books and as a cultural figure who is known from films.

The comedy parts of the book suggest another motivation on Burroughs' part beyond playfulness: revenge on the Hollywood industry that had turned his noble creation into a fool. Burroughs himself was not in too much of a position to carp about Tinseltown's creative leaden-foot. Herein we are treated – again – to a Tarzan double (the photogenic but cowardly actor playing the ape-man), misanthropy (spirited stuntwoman Rhonda Terry is the only likeable character, while Burroughs' insistence that only man evinces unnecessary brutality is not only repetitive but scientific nonsense), a safari whose constituent parts get separated, and – again squared – a hidden city.

Though Burroughs is not exactly a rapier wit, there is some amusement on offer in his apparent pops at both Buster Crabbe (*The Lion Man* of the title is a Tarzan rip-off movie being shot in Africa – Burroughs can't have been unaware that Crabbe had appeared in a Tarzan knock-off of exactly that title; his fictitious director Thomas Orman pointedly comments 'Sounds familiar' when the premise of *The Lion Man* is explained to him) and Weissmuller (the vaguely similarly-named Stanley Obroski is the star of *The Lion Man*, and it is remarked of him, 'He don't have to act, but he looks great stripped').

Meanwhile, Tarzan himself lets Obroski's friends – unaware that he has succumbed to fever – believe that it is the movie star pulling off the daring deeds he performs to save them from peril. Additionally, Burroughs depicts Hollywood movie types as philistine and clueless. (One of them thinks there are tigers in Africa – imagine!)

Burroughs' latest hidden city rather tickles the funny bone. London, as it is called, was built by a mad scientist who styles himself 'God.' His experiments with transplanting cells from humans to gorillas have created a race of apes capable of talking and utilising tools (though Burroughs sidesteps the issue of how building an entire city is possible in the absence of fully opposable thumbs and the true precision grip). That the cells in question are from bodies interred in Westminster Abbey has led to simians boasting names like Buckingham, Suffolk, King Henry the Eighth and Thomas Wolsey, as well as rather regal airs, who are resident in antediluvian architecture, including a castle. Tarzan gets the shock of his life when addressing one of these ostensible Bolgani in the Mangani tongue: the gorilla, who has no idea what Tarzan is saying, responds in English. God, meanwhile, has gone in the other direction, sprouting hair as a gruesome consequence of planting gorilla cells into his own decaying body.

The final chapter is a sort of comedy coda that takes place a year after the other events and sees Tarzan – in his civilisation persona of John Clayton – visit Los Angeles out of curiosity. With no effort, he ends up being considered for a role in 'a Tarzan picture.' However, the production manager nixes the casting with a curt, 'Not the type, at all.' Tarzan does get a consolation role as a white hunter – and then gets himself fired when a lion goes out of control on set and he deals with it in his customary, blade-flashing fashion.

It's difficult to know how to take this story. On one level, one can't help feel that it slightly spoils the Tarzan series insofar as it deconstructs the boundaries of art. Do those who love Burroughs for his stern-browed and resolutely heroic adventures want a Tarzan that skirts spoof? Certainly, some Burroughs fans hate his Venus series, whose first instalment appeared in the pulps a year previous to *Lion Man*, for the way its bumbling protagonist Carson Napier is almost a parody of the author's usual swashbuckling heroes. On the other hand, though *Tarzan and the Lion Man* is hardly a masterpiece, it is impressive that the author has found yet again another way to relieve the tedium of a rigid formula and keep at bay for an occasionally entertaining couple of hundred pages his bewilderment about where to take the series.

Though Buster Crabbe had been risible in the loincloth, it took Johnny Weissmuller's second appearance as the ape-man for the public to begin to perceive him as the definitive Tarzan.

The first Weissmuller picture had been important in establishing the parameters for the new Tarzan but it had also been a movie that was feeling its way, something exacerbated by the fact that the methods of talking pictures were still being codified. *Tarzan and his Mate* was an altogether more confident enterprise. Though the result would not be palatable to the Burroughs super-purist – and nor would any Weissmuller movie – it is considered by many the greatest Tarzan movie ever made.

Released in April 1934, *Tarzan and his Mate* has a screenplay by James Kevin McGuiness. Howard Emmett Rogers and Leon Gordon are credited with 'adaptation,' although this is certainly no adaptation of anything written by Burroughs. The author could sometimes bring himself to dispense with his torment about such matters: he had recently shruggingly opined in correspondence that the character had 'survived' much traducing. Plus he was being paid in the region of $45,000. Though nothing was shot in Africa itself, the staggering 1.2 million dollar budget thrown at the film showed on-screen in a lush affair awash with extras and animals.

Surprisingly considering the stature *Tarzan and his Mate* now possesses, the shoot was beset with serious problems. Filming was suspended for a fortnight without explanation. When it resumed, Rod LaRocque – originally cast as the character Marlin Arlington – had mysteriously disappeared, replaced by Paul Cavanaugh. The supposition is that LaRocque had become another of those silent screen thespians whose voice didn't cut it in the world of the talkie. With over a third of the picture having been shot, much footage had to be discarded. Though he receives full directorial credit, not long afterwards Cedric Gibbons also disappeared from the set. Gibbons was an MGM art director with directorial ambitions, but the chance Metro gave him to prove his mettle behind the cameras transpired to be a costly indulgence, as 127,000 feet of footage was binned. He was replaced by Jack Conway. (That in his proper field Gibbons was talented is indicated by the fact that he designed the Academy Awards 'Oscar' statuette.) Additionally, an appendectomy for O'Sullivan necessitated her absence for over a month (with a double replacing her for some scenes). Then there was the unfortunate matter of Weissmuller suffering scraped skin in a sensitive place when astride a rhino. Nonetheless, when the shoot wrapped, the result was a picture now officially deemed 'culturally, historically or aesthetically significant' by the United States Library of Congress.

The events of *Tarzan and his Mate* take place nearly a year after those of *Tarzan the Ape Man*. Holt has returned with colleague Arlington to loot the elephant's graveyard discovered in the last (Weissmuller) movie. Unfortunately, Holt can't remember the way to the waterfall entrance and needs Tarzan to help them. Holt has the additional motive of wanting to return Jane – whom he loves – to civilisation, to which purpose he comes loaded down with tempting silk gowns, stockings and perfume.

Tarzan is not even heard until just under 21 minutes (of a 95-minute movie), when his yodel rings out as the safari is attacked. When he does appear, Weissmuller is even more buff than in *Tarzan the Ape Man*. He is living in a Garden of Eden idyll with Jane (who is referred to as his wife in the film, not the sexually suggestive 'mate' of the title). Jane (who is shown as having her own, more feminine yodel) comes into her own in this picture, which marks the point where her name and Tarzan's became synonymous in the popular consciousness. This is partly because she becomes a stronger character (faced with an advancing pride of lions, she quickly rustles up a barrier of flame) and partly because of the allure of Maureen O'Sullivan. The Irish actress's beauty seems to blossom herein, her newly wild tresses tumbling about a chiselled, high-cheeked face into which glittering eyes seem set like jewels. This transcendent beauty is enhanced further by the skimpy two-piece outfit she wears in her new role as jungle housewife: audiences completely unused to screen flesh must have been maddeningly distracted from the plot by the creamy thighs and hips exposed by her high-cut loincloth.

Though MGM were at least conscientious enough to affix large African-style ears to the more manageable Indian elephants they had elected to use, there is no realism involved here. What on earth Tarzan and Jane have in common when they can barely communicate is conveniently never explored. There's also lots of anthropomorphism, such as chimps kissing and holding hands, a hippo ferrying an injured Tarzan to shore and Cheeta navigating hazardous waters on a log in order to fetch the ape-man. Tarzan battles a crocodile underwater but also stabs to death a rhino, an animal more blameless and peaceable than which it's difficult to imagine. Meanwhile, Arlington shoots an elephant on the assumption it will realise it's a goner and instantly make a beeline for the elephant's graveyard – which it does. Despite the occasional bloody death, this is a celluloid comic strip, or even fairytale. However, it's a charming one. It is sweet to see Tarzan's teasing of Jane, Jane's leaps from high places into Tarzan's arms, Jane's excited trying on of the feminine attire brought by Holt, Tarzan's passing on of coffee he finds distasteful to an eager Cheeta, and Tarzan's exhibiting bewilderment at the music emanating from a gramophone. (A similar scene to the last appeared in the Crabbe movie but disagreeably seemed to be inviting us to hold the ape-man in contempt.) The tree-top acrobatics are once more breathtaking, if again reliant on the fact that squinting audiences couldn't be quite sure, between the detail-obscuring monochrome and judicious long-shots, if Weissmuller's double was using a trapeze swing. At the climax, Tarzan calls on chimpanzees and then elephants to arrive *en masse* and save the day as the safari is deliberately exposed by natives to a shedload of lions. It's easy for modern audiences to laugh at such cartoonishness, the wonky understanding of African fauna, the anthropomorphism and the back projection utilised to keep the actors safe in the more dangerous scenes, but this would all have been a mysterious, beautiful and scary spectacle on the pre-TV big screen, particularly the scream- and drums-punctuated mass battle scenes between bearers and cannibals and the big cats in which the film is virtually drowning. Or, as *Time* described it, 'A wild, disgraceful, highly entertaining orgy of comic, sensual and sadistic nonsense ...'

This film could have been even better. In the original cut, Tarzan and Jane engage in a swimming scene in which Jane is nude. Excellent underwater cinematography and graceful, leisurely strokes and patterns by two Olympians – 1932 gold medallist Josephine McKim served as O'Sullivan's double – combine to create something exquisite. Even the notoriously prudish Burroughs adjudged it 'very beautiful and artistic.' Though audiences in more permissive American states and in some foreign territories did get to see it, the scene became the first major victim of the Hays Code, a list of rules designed to bring morality to the silver screen that were first properly enforced that year. The cut was a small tragedy. Happily, it has been restored for DVD releases.

Tarzan and his Mate was quite possibly the first cinema sequel of any description superior to its predecessor, and it did according box office.

In the mid-1930s, the cinema-going public certainly had their pick of Tarzans. In early summer 1935, with the release of *The New Adventures of Tarzan*, Herman Brix became the third actor to portray the ape-man in as many years.

This must have been confusing, but Edgar Rice Burroughs was as little concerned with that as he was with the fact that box office receipts clearly showed that Johnny Weissmuller was the public's favourite. As was his custom with current movie ape-men, he had diplomatically enthused about him to the media. Privately, he felt Weissmuller's Tarzan was a cartoon. Accordingly, in mid-1934, he entered into a deal with businessmen Bennett Cohen, Ashton Dearholt and George Stout to form a company called Burroughs-Tarzan Enterprises, Inc, which would for the first time grant him total control over a celluloid Tarzan project. Added to the attraction of a cinema Tarzan that would for once be faithful to his original vision was the welcome additional revenue stream it would bring to his financially overstretched world.

The project was beset with disaster throughout. Perhaps Burroughs should have foreseen it from his long experience of misfortune befalling his associations with Tarzan cinema, whether it be his embittered departure from the very first Tarzan picture, having to pursue William Parsons for overdue monies or the potentially disastrous breach of contract he had ended up executing in regard to *Tarzan the Fearless*. The first misfortune to befall his own Tarzan cinematic venture was the fact that Messers Cohen, Dearholt and Stout turned out to be the latest in a line of movie entrepreneurs who came up fiscally short: Burroughs had to guarantee a bank loan to them on the eve of shooting. As he had forgone an advance in return for equal profits and choice of leading man, this meant that Burroughs was effectively paying his supposed partners to make the film. The shooting itself was extremely taxing. The main shoot took place in Guatemala because, as independents, the producers had no studio and Dearholt, possessed of some experience of the Central American country, felt he could save a bundle. It ended up costing far more than it would have to film domestically. Guatemala had no film studios or industry, engendering a complete location shoot. The crew and actors had to endure primitive conditions, as well as the funny-tummy afflictions often associated with unsanitary scenarios in tropical climes. They also had to put up with local corruption (the country's President secured a cameo in exchange for co-operation), tropical storms and humidity, the latter of which destroyed film stock. The script was rewritten during the shooting. The budget ran out before the four-month shoot was over and the crew had to literally hide from creditors before they could return home.

That there were supposedly over a hundred candidates considered for the lead role sounds like typical Hollywood hype of the era. The loincloth went to Herman Brix, another man who had made his name in an Olympic sport (shot-putting). He had been in the running to play Tarzan for MGM but was ruled out when – you guessed it – he sustained an injury. Though not as muscular as Weissmuller, Brix was trim, solid, tall and looked good swinging on a vine. In fact, his physique is probably closer than Weissmuller's to what someone with Tarzan's jungle upbringing would realistically possess: it is only the visual shorthand employed by cinema that makes us assume his biceps should bulge. (Of course, *truly* realistic casting would see Tarzan played by a man with freakishly over-developed forearms resulting from tree-swinging.) The handsome Brix additionally wore his hair in a reasonably wild fashion, swept back off his forehead. Unfortunately, with many more lines to deliver than any previous sound-era Tarzan, he showed the drawbacks of casting inexperienced actors on the basis of their physique.

Contrary to some reports, Burroughs did not provide the basic story for what was originally entitled *Tarzan and the Green Goddess*. Correspondence between Burroughs, Dearholt and others involved in this production shows that Charles F Royal conceived the story told in his screenplay, which at some point acquired the new name *Tarzan in Guatemala*. As can be discerned, Guatemala was not serving as a substitute Africa the way that California and other locales had in previous Tarzan pictures. Though Tarzan had been seen in Paris and Algiers in *The Revenge of Tarzan*, this was the first cinematic Tarzan adventure to make a virtue of him visiting a foreign country; something that would in time become a tradition in the series. It was presumably down to Burroughs that the project followed the ill-advised template of recent novels in not featuring or mentioning Jane. The spirited 'feminine lead' Ula Vale (played by Ula Holt) would have been scant consolation to those cinemagoers charmed by the interplay between Weissmuller and O'Sullivan, especially those lucky enough to have seen their *Tarzan and his Mate* swimming scene.

The project ultimately became *The New Adventures of Tarzan* by way of *Tarzan and the Lost Goddess*. The story sees the ape-man travel Guatemala-way in search of the missing Paul D'Arnot. His path crosses with a father-and-daughter team with a dual mission of discovering jewels and a formula for explosives, both suspected to be hidden in the remnants of a Mayan city. A chaotic climax in a Mayan ruin sees Tarzan lift more than one native above his head and fling him to a bloody death.

The film properly explores the possibilities of the sound age. The cinema Tarzan is heard to speak fluently and intelligently for the first time (even if this does begin another movie debate: why does Tarzan have an American accent?) Fidelity to Burroughs' novels is achieved in other ways. The name 'Lord Greystoke' litters the script and there are references to his English estates. Handily, Brix looks as good as a dickey-bowed Greystoke as he does a loinclothed Tarzan. His yodel can't match Weissmuller's, but that can be said of every successor to the swimmer. Brix tries gamely, with a yell that is a variation of (and in one example a possible straight lift from) the Jim Pierce radio Tarzan cry. Tarzan's primate friend is a strange combination of the MGM creation Cheeta and Burroughs' Nkima: though called Nkima in the credits, Tarzan calls him 'Chkima' and the beast is played not by a monkey but a chimp.

Guatemala is depicted as having exactly the same wildlife as Africa. This is certainly ludicrous, but when the ape-man battles a lion, we for perhaps the first time in a Tarzan flick feel that someone has been saved from being eaten. This is because the direction (by Edward Kull) and cinematography (Kull and Ernest F Smith) is the best yet seen in a Tarzan movie. Even what *Variety* termed 'cut-ins' back in 1918 are high-quality, with aerial photography used to impressively capture herds of wildebeest and elephants (if in the act of running away from the noise of aeroplane engines). The parts of Guatemala that are genuine – architecture and landscapes – provide a variation on the now over-familiar Africa backdrops.

Unlike with *Tarzan and his Mate*, the production chaos was not a harbinger of commercial success. Even before the picture was in the theatres, Burroughs had lost faith in the venture, or at least in its capacity to make him money. Had he not, Weissmuller would probably not have become the definitive Tarzan, for MGM's original deal with him had been for just the two pictures already released. Burroughs agreed to extend terms with Metro in order to keep the cash coming in. The Metro deal in turn served to undermine *The New Adventures of Tarzan*, for MGM – far from being grateful to Burroughs for the chance he had provided them to build on the millions they had already made from his character – used underhand tactics to destroy its prospects. Movie theatres were warned that MGM's next Weissmuller Tarzan would not be offered to them if they elected to screen Brix as the ape-man. Consequently, *The New Adventures of Tarzan* was restricted to the smaller American theatre chains. Rumours even persist that the unfavourable tone of the US reviews was down to pressure from MGM, then a mighty force in the land. Proof of both theories is possibly provided by the fact that MGM-immune overseas territories were as receptive to Brix as they had been to anyone else in a loincloth.

Burroughs-Tarzan, Inc responded to the MGM campaign by releasing the movie in three different ways, either undaunted by or unaware of the fact that such a strategy had simply sowed confusion with the Buster Crabbe *Tarzan the Fearless* feature-cum-serial. *The New Adventures of Tarzan* was made available as a 12-chapter serial, a 75-minute feature film and a combination of 75-minute feature film and 11 following serial chapters. No doubt the 'New' part of the title was also intended to add allure, but the corollary of such a designation is that it becomes confusing and dates the release as soon as it is succeeded by another. The poor domestic fortunes enjoyed by the venture may not have been the cause – some journalists had been stating that serials were old-fashioned even as far back as *The Son of Tarzan* in 1920 – but this would be the last Tarzan 'chapter play'. Despite MGM's alleged machinations, in summer 1938 Burroughs-Tarzan Enterprises, Inc edited a new 72-minute feature film from the last ten chapters of *The New Adventures of Tarzan*, inserting some unseen footage and releasing it as *Tarzan and the Green Goddess*. What was really another bite of the cherry was billed as an 'amazing sequel.'

Despite success in other serials, Brix was conscientious enough about his adopted trade to study acting and come back under a different name, Bruce Bennett. He was reasonably successful in his quest for credibility. Much the same could be said of *The New Adventures of Tarzan*. It wasn't anything like the flop MGM were hoping, but even had it been, it would still have served a useful function in notifying cinema audiences that the ape-man had an elevated hinterland not to be gleaned from the Weissmuller interpretation. Unfortunately, the problems encountered in the making and marketing of the project ended Burroughs' direct involvement in Tarzan movies and therefore any possibility, at least in his lifetime, of the ape-man being represented on the big screen as he was depicted in his novels.

When *Tarzan's Quest* was serialised in six parts in *Blue Book* starting from October 1935, it was known as *Tarzan and the Immortal Men*. The bland final title was adopted for book publication. Its working title was more interesting: *Tarzan and Jane*.

Some have surmised that the reappearance of Jane in Burroughs' Tarzan series after an absence of 11 years and nine stories was a result of the author suddenly becoming less disenchanted with the female sex following the departure from his life of Emma Burroughs after 34 years of marriage and several years of domestic torpor. Burroughs divorced Emma while shooting of *The New Adventures of Tarzan* was taking place. By April of 1935, he was married to Florence Dearholt. A friend of his daughter Joan, as well as the recently divorced wife of one of his partners in Burroughs-Tarzan Enterprises, Inc, she was three decades the author's junior. Joan would later make clear to Burroughs biographer Robert W Fenton that she thought Dearholt had married her dad for money, but she seemed to bring him genuine happiness, at least for a while.

However, while the chronology supports the aforementioned theory about Lady Greystoke's revival, it actually seems more closely related to an attempt by Burroughs the previous year to assist his daughter in her career – one that, as with his play *You Lucky Girl!*, had come to naught. When Burroughs had declined to renew American Radio Features' contract for the Tarzan radio series, his three-page synopsis of his first intended story for his own Tarzan wireless venture had included a prominent role for Jane in order to give Joan something into which she could get her thespian teeth. Ultimately, however, she had not come back to the role, and the script had not been recorded. One is tempted to assert that someone whose recent work had shown he was desperately short of ideas for ape-man stories was bound not to let the contents of said script go to waste, but perversely ERB had declined the suggestion that he write a tie-in novel for the *New Adventures of Tarzan* serial. In any event, Burroughs now revived the Joan-inspired storyline for what would be his nineteenth adult Tarzan book.

Burroughs certainly seems ambivalent about Jane's involvement in *Tarzan's Quest*, something that is understandable if one considers that her personality – created long before he met his current wife – must have been informed by or even based on that of his first spouse. Jane greets her husband curiously formally when their parallel paths finally bisect ('Tarzan! Tarzan of the Apes'). Though this meeting occurs in the last chapter, it is still peculiar that Tarzan doesn't speak to his wife once in the narrative. Neither would Jane be seen in anything other than passing in the series again, with Tarzan returning to his equivalent of staying down the pub with his mates: preferring to spend his time with the Waziri, Nkima and Tantor. Bearing in mind the story's origin, it's unclear if the apparent obsession with resisting ageing that forms part of the book's fabric stems from Burroughs' recent marriage to a younger woman with energy levels far in his own past.

The plot of *Tarzan's Quest* revolves around a hunt led by Tarzan for the daughter of his Waziri friend Muviro. She has been abducted by the Kavuru, who are headed by the Greek God-like Kavandavanda. The latter estimates his age at a thousand years, the consequence of his tribe having discovered a formula that when ingested monthly in the form of pills can hold off the Grim Reaper indefinitely. As with everything in life that sounds too good to be true, there's a catch: in addition to pollen, plant roots and the spinal fluid of leopards, the pills' ingredients include 'the glands and blood of women – young women.' Consequently, the Kavuru regularly send out deadly scouting parties for females, having already worked their way through their own. Meanwhile, Jane has travelled over from the Greystokes' English estates both to visit her husband and to join pal Kitty and her friends in a hunt for a witch doctor who has 'an amazing formula for renewing youth and inducing longevity' – a curious, unresolved cul-de-sac in the tale that additionally betrays the frequent Burroughs flaw of a high level of coincidence. Inevitably, their plane crash-lands, inevitably the party includes a wisecracking man of the people (Neal Brown), inevitably Neal falls in love with another of the party (French maid Annette), inevitably Jane ends up in the clutches of Kavandavanda and inevitably Kavandavanda is instantly smitten with her, despite his stated conviction that 'Man may only attain godliness alone. Woman weakens and destroys him.'

The reader doesn't blame him for being smote. Burroughs' *Tarzan and Jane* working title should have been adhered to (*Blue Book* changed it): this is as much Jane's book as her husband's. Burroughs' apparent sometime disdain for Jane/Emma/all womankind is rather ironic, because the character as he draws her is rarely less than likeable and admirable. No swooning damsel in distress, she copes pluckily with being surrounded by a hostile jungle (rendered in all its sweaty, sticky, scary glory, far from the cartoon projection of the wilderness of which Burroughs had sometimes been guilty) and the necessity to hunt for food (she despatches a lion threatening her intended quarry with some well-aimed arrows), and all done with a touchy-feeliness not in the frame of reference of her forest god.

At the end of an adventure that, despite its predictability, zips along smartly and contains a couple of shockers (murder and suicide among the jungle visitors), Tarzan puts paid to the Kavuru village by crashing a plane into it with explosive results.

Though the grotesquely evil Kavuru are white and though the Waziri are as usual depicted as noble, early on in the story the otherwise saintly Jane makes reference to 'smelly natives.' Perhaps we shouldn't be too surprised then that the close of the book sees the adventure's survivors dividing among themselves the life-prolonging but blood-drenched pills with inappropriate jollity.

The artwork of the jacket and plates of the book version of *Tarzan's Quest* marked the end of an era, seeing the last Tarzan illustrations by J Allen St John. Though St John had been shunted aside before when Burroughs switched to Metropolitan and then started self-publishing, it had been because the writer felt he couldn't afford the artist's rates. Now it was more sentimentality that dictated a change as Burroughs' talented son John Coleman ('Jack') became his regular illustrator. As St John had been drawing Tarzan interior plates almost without a break since *The Return of Tarzan* and covers since *The Beasts of Tarzan*, he had moulded the mental image of the ape-man for an entire generation of readers. (He also illustrated other Burroughs works, so had the same effect with John Carter *et al.*) St John may have been inconsistent in dressing Tarzan in a loincloth or a singlet but, perhaps partly due to a conscientiousness that meant he preferred to read a book twice before starting work on illustrations, his art was usually stunning. He tended to favour two vivid figures centre-stage, although also wasn't averse to colourful backdrops. Particularly memorable were his images of a giant eagle carrying off Tarzan for *Jungle Tales of Tarzan*, Tarzan almost forming an inverted comma with a lion he is wrestling on the cover of *Tarzan and the Jewels of Opar* and the heaving wraparound battle panorama he provided for *Tarzan at the Earth's Core*. Many Burroughs fans cite one particular St John image of the ape-man as just as iconic as Clinton Pettee's immortal 1912 *All-Story* painting, even though it was unusually minimalist for him: his cover for the Grosset & Dunlap edition of *Tarzan and the Golden Lion*, on which the ape-man and Jad-bal-ja are seen in profile atop a hillock, a spear-carrying ape-man resting a hand on his wild companion as they both gaze at the horizon, stylishly all rendered in monochrome except for the gold-coloured cat. This striking, elegant image is now used as a logo by ERB, Inc and has even been turned into collectible statuettes.

Tarzan featured in Whitman Publishing's Big Little Books and Better Little Books series from 1933. These were compact, sturdy hardbacks that featured novelisations of contemporaneous Tarzan movies and collections of Tarzan newspaper strips. Big Little Books also served another purpose in providing an avenue into print for the sequel to *The Tarzan Twins* on which Burroughs had precipitously embarked in 1928 and that had long lain in his metaphorical bottom drawer (in reality, probably his safe).

In 1934, with Volland gone to the wall, Whitman reprinted *The Tarzan Twins*. Evidently pleased by the sales, they proved receptive to the idea of a follow-up where Volland had not. *Tarzan and the Tarzan Twins, with Jad-Bal-Ja, The Golden Lion* was published in March 1936 (again, there was no prior magazine publication). As this was nearly a decade after the *The Tarzan Twins'* original publication, the readership would have been of a new generation. The sequel was designated a Big Big Book, and also served as a colouring book. The illustrations to which the readers were invited to apply their pencils were supplied by Juanita Bennett, who had provided the interiors for Whitman's edition of *The Tarzan Twins*. Unlike with that book, she also supplied the cover, and it was babyish even by Whitman's unthreatening standards, possessing that 'blocked' style of much art of the era intended for kids' eyes as well as a technical naiveté (one of the twins has his back to the reader). When Canaveral Press issued the two Tarzan Twins books in one volume in 1963, things had moved on sufficiently for the publisher to commission a stylish cover from Roy G Krenkel that was juvenile-orientated but in no way condescended to the reader.

The story is stated as following on directly from that of *The Tarzan Twins*. A loinclothed and tooled-up (jungle-style) Dick and Doc leave the Greystoke estate in the company of Tarzan and Jad-bal-ja. They get separated from the ape-man when he goes off to investigate something in the jungle that is making his lion nervous. When a storm breaks, they also get separated from the golden lion (whose 'cruel, round, yellow eyes' make them fearful in any case). Trying to make their way back to the Greystoke estate, the 'twins' come across some outcast Oparians who are planning to set up an alternative to that city in which they have decided that 'Kla', a re-christened kidnapped missionary's 12-year-old daughter, will be their new high priestess. The boys decide to rescue her. This seems a presumptuous plan for a pair of tykes until a hidden Dick starts systematically slaughtering Oparian priests with his bow and arrows. Further sadism that it's difficult to imagine in a modern day kids' book occurs when Tarzan arrives in the nick of time to prevent Dick dying on the sacrificial altar: he unleashes Jad-bal-ja on the high priest with deadly effect. The girl – real name Gretchen von Harben – is returned safely to civilisation.

Tarzan and the Tarzan Twins, with Jad-bal-ja, the Golden Lion was an absolute mouthful of a title but possibly not Burroughs' doing: his working title was *Jad-Bal-Ja and the Tarzan Twins*. It was at least not confusion-sowing like the title that Canaveral Press gave their otherwise useful '63 compendium: *Tarzan and the Tarzan Twins*. Though they don't provide any particular problems with chronology, because they are not meant for an adult audience, both Tarzan Twin books are considered by Burroughs fans – to use a contemporary anorak phrase that would have no doubt made the author harrumph in contempt – 'non-canon'.

By the mid-'30s, Burroughs' ape-man-related energy levels were getting so low that he could muster only enough enthusiasm to write Tarzan novellas.

While *Tarzan the Untamed* had itself consisted of two separate magazine serialisations bolted together, that was a fat tome whose two constituent parts could conceivably have been issued as separate books. *Tarzan and the Magic Men* (published in *Argosy* in three parts from September 1936) and its sequel *Tarzan and the Elephant Men* (*Blue Book* in three parts from November 1937) would have been rather slim affairs if issued alone rather than combined in the novel *Tarzan the Magnificent*. Nor did they feature anything like the inspiration that marked the constituent parts of *Untamed*.

Of the two parts, *Magic Men* is the superior, even if it wanders again into the type of science fiction/fantasy and post-modernism that is such a far cry from the ape-man's original quasi-realism. Like several of the Tarzan tales of this period, it is set in Abyssinia (now Ethiopia), where the ape-man has journeyed at the request of an unnamed emperor 'to investigate a rumor that a European power is attempting to cause the defection of a native chief by means of bribery.' Considering the lethargic indifference Tarzan has shown toward the entire world of late, this mission seems a somewhat unconvincing and contrived way to manoeuvre him into a new adventure. Having said that, it is a blessed relief how agreeable Tarzan is in this story.

When Tarzan stumbles upon the Kaji and the Zuli, the author at least injects a couple of additional dimensions into his hoary old device of two white settlements at war with each other, firstly in the form of a pair of magicians who hold great power in their respective communities via a form of telepathy and secondly by a motif of miscegenation – the warrior women of the Kaji have turned themselves Caucasian by kidnapping white men – that surprisingly seems to have an enlightened motive, if also one a little inchoate. American writer Stanley Wood and his two guides are this book's compulsory interlopers from civilisation whom Tarzan has to rescue from danger. When he does – repeatedly – they all engage in discussion about who their bronzed saviour is. 'Say, he flits through the trees like a regular Tarzan,' remarks one, once again placing the ape-man in a world in which his life and character have been represented in books and movies.

Wood and his guides reappear in *Tarzan and the Elephant Men*, as does Gonfala, the Kaji Queen with whom Wood falls in love in *Tarzan and the Magic Men*. That this story is less inspired than its predecessor is demonstrated by the fact that Burroughs can't even be bothered inventing a new lost city but instead has the ape-man return to Cathne and Athne from *Tarzan and the City of Gold* for an adventure that in some respects is just a miniature rehash of that novel. A nice scene in which Tarzan generates good karma for himself via his good-natured rescue of a trapped Tantor provides one of the few moments of pleasure.

Jack Byrne, editor of *Argosy*, refused to publish *Tarzan and the Elephant Men* even though the novella to which it was a sequel had appeared in his magazine. He wrote Burroughs a long letter that constituted a polite but passionate critique of where the author was going wrong in his writing, condemning Tarzan's recent lack of motivation and the fact that when he uninterestedly wandered into the affairs of others, those people were themselves uninteresting. He also suggested that Burroughs was descending into a stultifying style because he was too isolated from other authors and literary trends. Though Burroughs responded by selling the story to *Blue Book* and pointing out to Byrne that many publishers had been wrong about *Tarzan of the Apes*, he also conceded in this correspondence, 'I am rather fed up on the type of stories I have been writing for over a quarter of a century. I have said everything that I can think of saying about Tarzan, and said it over and over again.' Perhaps it was the weariness Burroughs revealed in this letter that explained why he had latterly been allowing editors to make the sort of changes to his writing that he would once not have permitted. Perhaps it was also because he felt he couldn't afford to make a fuss, with the rates paid by pulps continuing the downwards spiral into which they had been tipped by the Great Depression. Certainly, without the ancillary Tarzan profits – especially the $40,000 per picture he was being paid by MGM – it's difficult to imagine that Burroughs would have been able to support his lifestyle purely with writing at this point in his life.

As with *Tarzan and the Leopard Men*, *Tarzan the Magnificent* was published out of sequence, collated and issued by Burroughs only after his next Tarzan story, *Tarzan and the Forbidden City*, had made it into book form.

Just when MGM were on a roll with Weissmuller – two strong films, two box office hits, an extension of their contract opening up the path to more bounty – they almost threw it away with the third movie.

The origins of *Tarzan Escape*'s failure lie in the same sort of squeamishness that had seen the naked underwater ballet removed from its predecessor. It wasn't the bare flesh that exercised the guardians of morality this time (O'Sullivan's no-way-is-she-wearing-knickers outfit had been replaced by a decorous raggedy dress), but gore and horror. In July 1935, MGM put into production a movie called *The Capture of Tarzan* written by *Tarzan the Ape Man* screenwriter Cyril Hume that was a tough and sinewy proposition. It saw white hunter Captain Fry arriving in Tarzan's patch with the objective of capturing the ape-man and taking him back to civilisation to exhibit him like a beast in a cage. Jane's cousins are with him, though their aim is to help Tarzan's mate claim a fortune she doesn't know she has been bequeathed. Mass ritualistic slaughter by natives, bloodthirsty pygmies, vampire bats and gargantuan lizards were some of the perils faced by the interlopers and/or the ape-man against sometimes gothic, fog-wreathed backdrops. At the end, Tarzan despatched Fry with extreme sadism. No copy of the original edit completed in late 1935 seems to have survived, but it sounds like the best ape-man picture yet from any studio.

The satisfaction MGM must have felt at what appears to have been its second incremental improvement of the Tarzan franchise was short-lived. Preview audiences turned out to be hostile. One wonders how seriously to take the reports that children were terrified by such things as giant bats swooping out of the sky to carry off screaming porters: the fact that various leagues of decency formed the protesting parties suggests that adults were presuming to take umbrage on behalf of children secretly thrilled as they watched through their fingers. On the other hand, the Frankenstein and Dracula pictures of the same period that seem so tame to us today were never seen by the young then, so depictions of terror and bloodshed may have been genuinely unsettling to those of tender years.

The film's director Jim McKay was unenthusiastic about the cuts and reshoots ordered by the studio and replaced by John Farrow, but the latter's changes were still not enough to please Metro. (Though Farrow, like McKay, received no formal credit, some proof of the fact that he was on set at some point is the seven children he proceeded to have with Maureen O'Sullivan.) Richard Thorpe replaced Farrow, and indeed directed every other MGM Tarzan flick of that era. It's difficult to know which director was responsible for which changes but the family-orientated end-product saw the vampire bats excised, the ritualistic slaughter scenes toned down, much anthropomorphic chimpanzee behaviour introduced, jolly character actor Herbert Mundin brought in as a comedy foil and a somewhat overfamiliar climax added featuring Tarzan rustling up an elephant herd to save the day. Also in the spirit of 'Well, it worked before' was the inclusion of the crocodile fight from *Tarzan and his Mate* (yes, the exact same one). Even the title was made less hard-hitting, *Tarzan Escapes* being limp and puzzling.

It wasn't until November 1936, two years after the start of production in an era when a movie would generally be in the theatres only months after filming began, that the 89-minute finished film made the screens. MGM tried to brazen out the public knowledge of its troubled gestation by trumpeting '2 years to produce!' on the posters, but decades before the likes of *Ishtar* and *Waterworld*, *Tarzan Escapes* was a movie that had a pre-release bad smell hanging over it. Its jinxed reputation went beyond the production problems: producer Irving Thalberg died a week after completion and John Buckler (Captain Fry) perished in a road accident a week before release. Whether or not the bad portents worked to prejudice reviewers, the movie was panned, although *Variety*, for instance, could hardly be blamed for the 'derisive laughter' its reporter heard around him in the theatre.

It's an indictment of this picture's quality that the biggest impact it had on the culture is its apparent legacy in *The Flintstones*. A woolly mammoth whose trunk serves as a vacuum cleaner, a woodpecker whose beak doubles as a record player's stylus and lifts elevated by pulleys around brontosaurus necks were appropriate in the context of that '60s television comedy cartoon, but a rope-and-pulley lift to Tarzan's treehouse operated by a docile elephant, an ape-powered fan, a baking oven constructed of mud and washing basins made of upturned tortoiseshells serve to remove Tarzan almost completely from his bloody, savage origins.

Though Sol Lesser had sold three of his remaining Tarzan options to MGM, he had astutely hung onto one. Seeing the ill fortunes of *Tarzan Escapes*, he decided the time was right to re-enter the game.

He was profoundly less astute in the man he chose to fill the loincloth. There was nothing particularly fatuous about his decision to pay attention to the sports fields in a quest for a new Tarzan: all previous Tarzans had been cast mainly for their physiques and most had had no acting experience. Moreover, though they had enjoyed mixed fortunes in the role, the last three men cast as Tarzan had been Olympic competitors. His plumping for Glenn Morris – gold medallist in the decathlon in Munich in 1936 – was therefore on the surface not a bad choice, especially as he was trim, muscular, 6' 2" and (a little-reported prerequisite for a movie Tarzan) smooth-chested. To those in the know – which didn't include the general public at a time when such things weren't widely reported – Morris's behaviour at those Olympics, when he ripped off the blouse of Nazi documentary filmmaker Leni Riefenstahl and kissed her breasts in front of 100,000 astonished spectators, made him even more natural for a role associated with animalism. Lesser's Jane-equivalent was also pretty wild: Eleanor Holm was well-known for a dissolute lifestyle, and not just as a result of having been kicked off the 1936 US Olympic swimming team for drinking and gambling. Possibly to capitalise on her wild-child image, Lesser gave her character the same Christian name as her.

Though the Elmo Lincoln picture *The Revenge of Tarzan* was now nearly two decades in the past and marooned in the already antiquated silent era, calling the new picture *Tarzan's Revenge* seems a little lazy. However, that was in keeping with an enterprise that Lesser himself later admitted was a 'cheap quickie.' The script by Robert Lee Johnson and Jay Vann depicted the Reeds, a couple of big game hunters (one of whom was played in another piece of gimmick casting by famous gossip columnist Hedda Hopper) arriving in Africa with their grown daughter Eleanor and her fiancé. A turbaned, pipe-inhaling nawab takes umbrage when Eleanor declines to become the hundredth wife in his harem, and she spends the rest of the picture evading his clutches. Tarzan saves the day, and whisks Holm off her feet, speaking a total of four words in the process ('Tarzan' twice, 'Eleanor' and 'Good'), not counting his yodel, which as usual for a rival movie Tarzan's sounds pitiful next to Weissmuller's. There are some good moments. The by-now *de rigueur* interludes featuring a chimpanzee engaging in play are undeniably cute. The picture has an equivalent of the Weissmuller-O'Sullivan underwater ballet, with the two leads engaged in exciting synchronised water-cutting (clothed). Additionally, the warlike natives – all facepaint, feathers and nose-rings – are fearsome, while the photography captures nicely the nabob's opulence. However, D Ross Lederman's direction is plodding and the fact that three of the main actors are not trained thespians inevitably shows, no matter how likeable the spirited Holm.

Although the scriptwriters find room in a rather short picture (70 minutes) to provide another ostentatious display of Holm's swimming prowess, Tarzan is on screen for just ten minutes. Maybe this is because Lesser realised he had made a terrible casting mistake. Pictures of Morris hurling javelins in his previous life show his muscles straining impressively against his skin, but such sights apparently blinded Lesser to the drawback with his face. Morris looked like Harpo Marx, the silent lunatic of the four film brothers, something exacerbated by his hills-and-dales hair. When he didn't look silly, he simply looked too nice. Having said that, there was no call for Weissmuller's wife Lupe Velez to kick him in the shins at a Hollywood party with the cry, 'You are not heem!'

Neither Morris nor Holm ever acted again (many unkind critics disputed they had done so in *Tarzan's Revenge*) and the film was a flop upon its January 1938 release. Having emerged from the jungle in a mauled state twice in a row, one might imagine Lesser would have left well enough alone, but he would be back in that vicinity again.

Controversy and confusion has raged about the Burroughs book that was published as *Tarzan and the Forbidden City* in late 1938 but serialised in *Argosy Weekly* in six parts starting in March 1938 as *The Red Star of Tarzan*.

Well before that serialisation, its storyline had formed the basis of the 1934 radio serial *Tarzan and the Diamond of Asher*, whose writing was credited to Rob Thompson. Also before the magazine serialisation, Burroughs wrote a continuity storyline of it for the Tarzan newspaper strip that, deemed unacceptable, was rewritten by one Don Garden. Derivation wasn't the only issue. When the *Argosy* serialisation started, the fact that Paul D'Arnot was referred to as 'Pierre' and that several Mangani language terms were incorrect led some to assume that it was a ghost-written work. The fact that it contained slapdash and stereotyped writing that was of a parodic level only strengthened this impression. In fact, the reality was less sinister and perhaps more depressing: overzealous sub-editing by *Argosy*'s Ben Nelson and Burroughs Mitchell was responsible for the mistakes and inconsistencies, while Burroughs' complete lack of interest accounted for how awful was the writing.

The book version follows closely Burroughs' semi-rejected script continuity. It features a Tarzan lookalike yet again in the shape of adventurer Brian Gregory, although even Burroughs seems bored with the hackneyed and implausible device, because he ceases to make play with it a short while in. Gregory has gone missing while on a quest to find the lost city of Ashair, which reputedly hosts the legendary Father of Diamonds. D'Arnot, in his last appearance in a Burroughs Tarzan tale, is assisting Gregory's father in his search for his son. (In a parallel of Burroughs' real-life infatuation with a woman 30 years his junior, D'Arnot has the hots for Brian Gregory's 19-year-old sister Helen.) Tarzan displays no inclination to remove himself from the back of Tantor, where he is found lolling, until he is informed his old friend is in the vicinity. Ashair is one of a pair of warring cities, the other named Thobo, located in an extinct volcano. We are left to infer from sketchy details that they are descended from ancient Egypt: unlike with his previous lost settlements, Burroughs can't be bothered devising a detailed backstory. Nor, with the exception of the appearance of some giant sea horses, can he be roused enough to make anything special of the potentially intriguing fact that parts of the plot are set underwater. Burroughs throws in a baby Tyrannosaurus Rex, but its presence is not explained. The contrast between such authorial lethargy and the incredible enthusiasm and inventiveness behind that dinosaur-bedecked lost city Pal-ul-don is painful.

One of the few moments of inspiration comes when Tarzan is confronted not by the customary single lion but by a pair of Numas: he escapes from the predicament by lifting one above his head and hurling it at the other. The lions fight, leaving Tarzan to vanquish the tired victor. Meanwhile a twist in the tail that seems a nice touch falls apart when one starts to think about it. Atan Thome, Brian Gregory's rival in the hunt for the King of Diamonds, opens the casket containing his object of desire only to find it contains – a lump of coal. Er, but how would the primitive Ashairians have acquired the geological knowledge of how diamonds are formed? By now it was obvious that Burroughs couldn't give a toss about such internal contradictions.

Perhaps allowances should be made for the fact that the story originated as a radio script (which itself may not even have originated with Burroughs): radio action series predicated on the belief that they will be heard, not read or seen, don't lend themselves to the nuances of a novel. However, an author of Burroughs' vast experience could surely have made good such inherent problems. The argument could even be made that his work was made easier by an existing plot.

Not that Burroughs was completely without authorial pride. When he published the magazine story as a novel, he reinstated his original manuscript, jettisoning all the changes that correspondence shows he acquiesced to *Argosy* making. *The Red Star of Tarzan*'s title derives from a Tarzan-less prologue in which a witch doctor babbles about a red star that will lead to unimaginable riches. The fact that the prologue was not included in the book and that *Argosy* was part of the Munsey 'Red Star' line suggests the prologue was contrived self-promotion written by Burroughs at the behest of *Argosy*. Incidentally, by means not easily fathomable, the magazine version did leak out into book form: it was printed in the UK New English Library paperback of *Tarzan and the Forbidden City* in the 1970s, for instance.

The trajectory of diminishing enthusiasm marked by two novellas followed by a novel based on an already broadcast radio series continued. From here, Burroughs' Tarzan work slowed to a crawl.

Though *Tarzan Escapes* had had its problems, a proposition as strong as the Weissmuller Tarzan franchise was not to be thrown away on the basis of one flop, nor even the bombshell dropped by Maureen O'Sullivan that she wanted out. Accordingly, in June 1939, after a gap of two-and-a-half years, MGM came back with a Tarzan movie that reinvigorated the series.

Weissmuller's contract with MGM forbade him from taking other roles between Tarzan pictures. The happy-go-lucky Weissmuller filled his days by throwing himself into a glamorous lifestyle and taking part in aquacades, a then-popular form of entertainment in which people who had made their name in competitive swimming, such as Weissmuller, Eleanor Holm and Buster Crabbe, would wow the crowds with water-based feats. O'Sullivan, however, was a serious actress for whom the Tarzan franchise was a limited and increasingly limiting quadrant of her career. She was also beginning an epic series of pregnancies. Added to that was her hatred of the chimp playing Cheeta, which for some reason insisted on trying to tear chunks out of her. Accordingly, she asked to be given the traditional no-way-back exit. The studio acquiesced to her character's death, and shooting started in January 1939 on what was originally called *Tarzan in Exile*.

MGM – perhaps mindful that one of the reasons that rival Tarzan pictures almost always failed was that a lone ape-man had no-one to play off or provide smooth counterpoint to his charming primitivism – cannily decided to fill the hole O'Sullivan's departure would leave in the Tarzan family. Just as the fourth Tarzan novel had resorted to the device of providing the ape-man a son – as had the fourth Tarzan cinema venture – so the fourth Weissmuller film gave the ape-man male progeny. However, 'Boy' was no Korak, although he was a Greystoke. The screenplay by Cyril Hume depicted a crashing in Tarzan and Jane's territory of a plane carrying the nephew of one Lord Greystoke, his wife and his infant son. The latter is the only survivor in the wreck and Jane is keen to adopt him, over Tarzan's initial objections. This set-up was deemed necessary in light of the fact that, unlike in the books, the MGM Tarzan and Jane had never been shown to be formally married and the Hays Code banned either depiction or overt suggestion of pre-marital intercourse.

Tarzan quickly comes to love the child he and his mate have prosaically named Boy, even running down female antelope to provide him with milk. This was mirrored by the real-life affection between Weissmuller and Johnny Sheffield, the seven-year-old from Pasadena over whose casting as Boy he had had final say. Their chemistry shines through in the traditional scene showing off Weissmuller's swimming prowess wherein the two perform their own lengthy underwater ballet, one that culminates in Tarzan grabbing hold of a giant turtle while Boy clings to Tarzan's ankle. This and other examples of a loinclothed-but-happy nuclear family can't help but be sweet. Jane, incidentally, is sometimes seen behind baskets of fruit, furniture and other handy means of masking O'Sullivan's swelling belly.

After a gap of several years, the inevitable snake enters the Garden of Eden when a search party comes looking for the heir to the Greystoke fortune. Most of their number – particularly the slimy Austin Lancing (Ian Hunter) – do not have noble intentions but are out to reap the benefits that go with power of attorney. Jane doesn't know this and is persuaded that Boy will be better off brought up in London. She has to cruelly deceive Tarzan to enable Boy's whisking away to civilisation.

As originally scripted, Tarzan's hurt at that was to be nothing compared with his devastation when Jane received a fatal spear injury from the Zambeli tribe who captured the departing safari. Ironically considering the way he had neglected the character (she had already made her last appearance in his novels), Edgar Rice Burroughs was furious when he heard that Jane was for the chop. MGM responded to his I'll-sue telegram by pointing out that their contract banned them from compromising Tarzan's character, not anyone else's. However, though Jane's creator might not have been able to stay the studio's hand, public opinion was. The outcry that erupted when details of Jane's intended fate appeared in newspapers motivated Metro to ask O'Sullivan to shoot an alternate ending wherein she recovered and she, Tarzan, Boy and their chimpanzee allies made for home atop a trio of elephants.

There is a sense of *déjà vu* attending some of the 82-minute film: Tarzan once more calls upon a herd of elephants at the climax to enable a rescue from a hostile village, while the footage of him killing that poor rhino is resurrected from *Tarzan and his Mate*. *Trader Horn* wildlife and scenery stock is also poured in (the only location shooting done for this picture was in Florida, so as to take advantage of its crystal clear waters). However, *Tarzan Finds a Son!* provided a Tarzan picture with a very different, warm tone, and furthermore increased the appeal of the series to kids, who now saw one of their own number up there on the screen. Those who didn't like the new direction – the American suburban family set-up transplanted to a forest treehouse – would have to get used to it: Boy would appear in all but one of the remaining eight Weissmuller Tarzans.

Though he expressed in letters that he was 'rather fed up' with his writing and implicitly in particular with Tarzan, about whom he had long ago opined he had said everything 'over and over again', Burroughs seemed to feel no fatigue when it came to promoting the ape-man and widening his markets. In mid-1939, he was busily trying to stoke up interest in his new idea, the Tarzan Clans of America.

Burroughs wrote privately of an aim of two million members. A project that sought almost to turn every boy in the United States into a miniature Tarzan and even to rival the Boy Scouts wasn't as presumptuous or over-ambitious as it might seem. When at this juncture a leading American magazine declared Tarzan to be 'the best-known literary character of the 20th Century', it was not exaggerating. Who at that point in history had not been exposed, probably repeatedly, to Tarzan via books, magazines, cinema, stage, radio, comic strip or a combination thereof? What child had not fantasised that he was the ape-man? (And indeed what adult had not fantasised something else about Johnny Weissmuller or Maureen O'Sullivan?) Though Burroughs had taken a genuine pleasure in the Tarzan Tribes movement kicked off a quarter-century before by young Herman Newman, and though the stated ideals of the Tarzan Clans were very similar, the Clans could be viewed as in the Burroughs tradition of cutting out the middle man: just as he had become involved in making Tarzan films and radio programmes and had begun publishing his own novels, so he was now seeking to oversee personally an equivalent of Signal Oil's Tarzan Club, which itself of course had been a commercialised variant of the Tribes.

For a membership fee of one dollar, kids (girls were allowed to join at the discretion of the Clan members and with the permission of their parents) would get a membership card, the latest Burroughs novel and the Clans' Official Guide. Though Burroughs made a big mistake in putting an illustration of a Waziri, not Tarzan, on the cover, thus rendering it instantly less covetable, the Guide was quite substantial: Burroughs was responsible for all of its 32 pages of text, which was like a version of the minutely detailed notes he habitually wrote on the planets and lost cities traversed by his novels' protagonists. It contained instructions on Clan formation, ranks (chief, sub-chief, medicine man, scribe, high priest, etc), conduct of meetings, initiation, Clan songs, Clan dances, construction of weapons and dismissal and demotion of members. It was rounded off with an ape-English dictionary.

Yet for all the energy this man approaching his sixty-fifth birthday put into it, for all the value-for-money of the membership fee (sending members his latest novel would have resulted in a net loss for the author) and for all the success of the movies of Weissmuller – whom Burroughs obtained MGM's permission to name 'Chief of Chiefs' – the Clan project got nowhere. Some have posited the reason for it grinding to a halt not long after it was set up to be the same one that caused the retraction of many other enterprises at that point in history, but America's entry into the Second World War was over two years into the future. The real reason seems to be that Burroughs did not have a large organisation like Signal Oil behind him with its easy access to vast numbers of potential recruits. He had envisaged MGM as fulfilling this role, hoping they would distribute leaflets and information about the Clans in the lobbies of theatres showing *Tarzan Finds a Son!*. (This was in the pre-anti-trust ruling days when movie studios owned venues in which their products were screened.) When MGM disappointingly requested only 60 copies of the Official Guide, it was clear that they were not planning on providing the huge promotional springboard Burroughs had thought they might.

That their booklet is now an incredibly rare collector's item is a stark measure of the Clans' failure. Whereas Signal Oil had 415,000 members at its peak, it is estimated that only around 200 copies of the Official Guide of the Tarzan Clans of America were ever distributed. Teenager Herman Newman had done far better back in 1916.

At the end of the 1930s, Burroughs wrote to magazine editors about a new idea he had for Tarzan: to turn him into 'a jungle Sherlock Holmes' in a series of short stories.

On the surface, this notion of the character using his wilderness nous to solve mysteries like the murder of a colonial official, the kidnapping of a woman by white slavers or the disappearance of a big game hunter was intriguing and suggested a fresh impetus for the ape-man. The format ERB proposed also seemed wise: after all, the author had previously employed the short story form to work his way out of a narrative impasse to fine effect with *Jungle Tales of Tarzan*. Perhaps the latter is why Burroughs embarked on his project of writing four 15,000- to 20,000-word Tarzan stories across the course of 1939 despite the fact that the response his idea received from editors was not exactly overwhelming enthusiasm and in the face of warnings from at least two editors of the low remuneration he could expect per story. When he did submit the results of his endeavours, Burroughs sometimes allowed extensive rewriting by his unimpressed clients. Humility is always an admirable quality but it still seems rather sad that a man presiding over a million-dollar industry like Tarzan whose track record as a successful author was unassailable should so readily acquiesce to his art being tampered with by anonymous sub-editors for the sake of pitiful sums like $250.

Following the first story, Burroughs abandoned his jungle detective plan, if not the short story format. 'Tarzan and the Jungle Murders' (published in *Thrilling Adventures* in June 1940) apparently quickly apprised him of the fact that his hero being able to follow spoor with his keen sense of smell hardly rivalled the dazzling deductive armoury of the man at 221b Baker Street, and that his own particular narrative strength did not lie in the incremental reveal. Following the second story, 'Tarzan and the Champion' (actually the first of the stories to be published, appearing in *Blue Book* in April 1940), Burroughs abandoned the idea of short ape-man fiction. In the first two months of 1940, he wrote a new novel (*Tarzan and the Madman*), then turned his attention to his other franchises until the following November when he embarked on a novella he called 'Tarzan and the Castaways' (serialised in three parts in *Argosy Weekly* starting in August 1941 with the second-hand and nonsensical title 'The Quest of Tarzan'). The two short stories and the novella were somewhat ghettoised in Burroughs' lifetime, with the author not bothering to collate them into a book. They saw the light of day again only in 1965 via the compendium *Tarzan and the Castaways*, when – a decade-and-a-half after his creator had passed away – the world was suddenly hungry for literary Tarzan once more.

It's difficult to assess the only version of 'Tarzan and the Jungle Murders' that has seen print, as according to Irwin Porges it is just as much a *Thrilling Adventures*' sub-editor's work as Burroughs'. (Had he still been alive, Burroughs would never have allowed the magazine version to be printed in the *Castaways* compendium, always publishing in book form his own, not the pulps', versions.) It's a mixture of Poirot and Tarzan, with the ape-man solving a murder mystery by his jungle wits but gathering everybody together to unmask the culprit in classic drawing room whodunit style. Unfortunately, Burroughs' can't write in the whodunit style. Not only is the mystery a no-brainer, he fails to drop any hints along the way and engages in the ultimate cheat by referring to a crucial clue for the first time right at the end. 'Tarzan and the Champion' sees Tarzan's jungle invaded by a heavyweight boxer, 'One-Punch' Mullargan, who has come with his manager to hunt game, if hunting is what one calls machine-gunning zebra. Mullargan and the ape-man engage in a bout of formalised fisticuffs that Tarzan inevitably wins easily, although the two then join forces to rescue the boxer's manager from a tribe of genuinely scary cannibals. The story culminates in Mullargan responding to the suggestion that Tarzan could take his championship away from him, 'Who? Dat bum?' This brief story is amusing and serviceable.

Tarzan and the Madman, Burroughs' return to ape-man novels, was written over the first three months of 1940. It was a groan-inducingly bad Tarzan *reductio ad absurdum* featuring the nth Tarzan double, the nth sinister safari that serves to keep Tarzan offstage and the nth warring lost city (this one a Portuguese settlement that is chocolate-coloured through inter-breeding with natives), containing the nth high priest keen on human sacrifice. Colin T Randolph Jr (or 'Rand', also known – slightly confusingly for those who had read *Tarzan and the Lion Man* – as 'God') doesn't actually possess Tarzan's looks, but the very fact that he is mistaken for the ape-man and – due to the amnesia and delusion hinted at in the title – believes he is him is risible enough: Tarzan's identity is one not possible to step into without exceedingly uncommon strength and heroism. Apart from the evocative or powerful scene or two to be found in every Burroughs book, the only thing to be said for *Tarzan and the Madman* is that it's short.

Magazine editors had put up with a lot of sub-standard plotting and unlikely scenarios from Burroughs over the years. However, in 1940, 28 years after *All-Story* had bitten his hand off to publish *Tarzan of the Apes*, the pulps had finally had enough. Despite the allure of Tarzan's name and his continuing popularity in the media of the comic strip and film, *Tarzan and the Madman* was the first adult Tarzan story that Burroughs failed to place with a magazine. In their replies to Michael S Mill – Burroughs' rep-cum-agent, eight years in his employ – some magazine editors added biting criticism to their rejections, one lamenting, 'Tarzan doesn't seem to be Tarzan anymore.' ERB clearly knew the work wasn't up to much. Significantly, he didn't bother putting it out as a book, unlike a subsequent Tarzan story also rejected by magazines.

'Tarzan and the Castaways'/'The Quest of Tarzan', written at the end of 1940, actually indicates that Burroughs was on the right path in reducing the word count. Though it contains absolutely nothing new, the fact that it is about half the length of an average novel leads Burroughs to dispense with the sort of disjointed capture-chase-recapture and safari in-fighting scenarios to which he had increasingly begun resorting. Instead he distils everything to its essence. The brisk pace and lean prose mean that our patience isn't tried, even despite us being presented yet again with such staples as an ape-man who has lost his memory through a blow to the head, a young couple who fall in love, a lost city that practices human sacrifice and a fight to the death with a lion. Something else that assists the energised feeling is a change in backdrop. The action takes place on the uncharted Pacific island of Uxmal after a shipwreck, although the fact that the ship has a cargo of African animals that Tarzan compassionately frees helps give the wildlife a familiar look. The lost city this time is of Mayan descent, which again enables Burroughs to indulge his wont of providing an interesting historical factoid or two. One doesn't even have to buy into Burroughs' love of societal hierarchy to delight in a passage in the story wherein a snooty woman is bad-mouthing Tarzan only to be astounded when another character icily puts her right with the comment, 'Madam, "that creature", as you call him, is John Clayton, Lord Greystoke, an English viscount.' The chief villains of the story, incidentally, are Germans. With the Second World War now raging beyond America's shores, Burroughs seems to be insisting 'I was right after all' about the furore over his depiction of the Hun in *Tarzan the Untamed*.

In fact, America's entry into the War in December 1941 was the main reason Tarzan – and indeed most other writing – disappeared off Burroughs' agenda. Once the United States entered the conflict, aside from his war correspondence Burroughs wrote nothing except two unpublished (non-Tarzan) scraps until June 1944. Paper rationing also brought to a halt the printing schedules of Edgar Rice Burroughs, Inc. Considering the unproductive and rejection-strewn nature of Burroughs' Tarzan writing recently, the intervention of the war may have come as a welcome event to him.

Despite Burroughs' recent artistic failings, America's oldest war correspondent found that Tarzan's impact on the culture was inescapable and positive. Burroughs rarely had to carry his own bags in his new role, but this deference wasn't completely age-related: as ERB proceeded to travel the world, he found himself surrounded by journalists half his age and younger who had been weaned on Tarzan films and in some cases learnt some of their writing chops from his ape-man novels.

Tarzan made his debut on phonograph records in 1941 in the form of two record sets produced by ERB, Inc that utilised the same production crew as the radio show. Elliott Lewis was the man picked to play the ape-man in sound adventures licensed for release by Decca.

Meanwhile, should they have been left in any doubt despite the way he had seen off all pretenders so far, the public would be caused no more confusion during Weissmuller's remaining occupancy of the loincloth about who was the real movie ape-man. Film studios, producers and Janes were subject to change, but all eight Tarzan pictures released between 1941 and 1948 featured Johnny. His position was further underscored by a doubling of the rate of new releases. In contrast to its impact on Burroughs' Tarzan writing, the Second World War was a period in which the cinematic Tarzan industry was cranked up, seeing the release of no fewer than five Tarzan flicks, even if the production of the first of these technically predated America's entry into the conflict.

Tarzan's Secret Treasure was a minor and short (81 minutes) entry in the series. Despite MGM trotting out the 'two-years-in-the-making' spiel again, shooting wrapped two months after its June 1941 start. It was released in December 1941, the very month of the Pearl Harbor attack. (John Coleman Burroughs' comic strip *John Carter of Mars* debuted on that historic 7 December itself.) An early script outline by veteran Tarzan screenwriter Cyril Hume had revived the idea of Jane being killed off, this time to enable the ape-man to take up with a glamorous big-game hunter. However, MGM had only recently agreed to a salary hike to retain Maureen O'Sullivan. Myles Connolly and Paul Gangelin subsequently devised a concoction with less of a sizzle factor. Their story involved the revelation that Tarzan's area of the jungle is awash with gold, which of course is of no use or interest to Tarzan, his mate and son, but of vast intrigue to some nefarious elements of a group of scientific explorers whom Tarzan saves from hostile natives. The explorers end up kidnapping Boy in order to get Tarzan to lead them to the gold, but they all wind up in peril in a native village before – what else? – Tarzan calls an elephant herd to the rescue. In other words, nothing new whatsoever – unless Tarzan being introduced to whiskey counts. The second-hand feel was aggravated by budget cuts that took place after the death of producer Irving Thalberg that necessitated the re-use yet again of the crocodile fight from *Tarzan and his Mate* and further airing of *Trader Horn* travelogue.

There are plenty of the now expected underwater scenes, for which Florida was utilised once more. Boy – already more articulate than Tarzan, albeit with an inexplicable American accent – gets his own interludes in which he is seen going off exploring on his own and playing with his native pal Tumbo (Cordell Hickman). Comic Cheeta passages are featured more heavily. This and the ever more ludicrous treehouse all-mod-cons – this time we see an egg-timer (Cheeta holding an hour glass) and a fridge (a bamboo trough that constantly pours water on perishables, which include caviar) – make it unmistakable that the studio is aiming if not exclusively at kids then at a family demographic. Burroughs put his foot down when he became aware of a scene in which Tarzan laughed uproariously, and it was excised. The author's thoughts on the way that Weissmuller was noticeably thickening are not recorded. It's an indicator of just how popular Weissmuller was that he would appear in seven more Tarzan movies when his best days, physique-wise, were already behind him.

Coming up to the next Tarzan picture, MGM apprehended a problem that Burroughs had encountered a long time back: that a jungle backdrop provides limited opportunities for fresh storylines. With *Tarzan's New York Adventure*, released in April '42, the studio decided to address this difficulty by making the ape-man's jungle a concrete one.

Burroughs had put Tarzan in the developed world as far back as the close of the first novel and for much of *The Return of Tarzan*, but MGM avoided the mistakes he had made by creating an intriguing and amusing juxtaposition. The author had occasionally shown his hero startling 'civilised' people with a reversion to his savage instincts, but generally he had been too eager to depict a Tarzan conversant with society's customs and mores, which was not only implausible but a wasted dramatic opportunity. *Tarzan's New York Adventure* explored more fully and entertainingly how difficult a man raised in the jungle would find it to negotiate a big metropolis.

In the screenplay by Myles Connolly and William R Lipman from Connolly's original story, the action starts with the underwater jungle swimming scene featuring Tarzan, Jane and Boy from *Tarzan's Secret Treasure* and the crocodile fight from *Tarzan and his Mate*. This however is where the familiarity – if not the re-use of old clips – ends. When Tarzan and Jane are attacked and left for dead in a forest fire, it is assumed by some visiting circus-owning trappers that Boy has been orphaned. The youngster is taken back to civilisation – if that is what one can call New York. In fact, the ape-man and his mate are alive and well and follow the trail back to the Big Apple, paying their way with gold ingots. There, Tarzan has to deal with new experiences like cantankerous cab drivers, pompous hotel desk clerks, shower stalls, telephones, radios, smoke-filled nightclubs and court cross-examinations as he and Jane seek to wrest legal custody of Boy from circus owners Rand and Sargent. The latter have had a lucrative foreign offer to buy the child and the animal act he has developed under their care and are therefore reluctant to let him go (though hardly enthusiastic about admitting this as their reason). Though Cheeta gets plenty of his usual light-hearted screen-time, the comedy potential of Tarzan's bewilderment at what he calls the 'stone jungle' ensures he has his own scenes of a not dissimilar tone. However, though the ape-man is seen yodelling fully clothed in the shower and remarking of a wailing singer on a radio 'Woman sick! Cry for witch doctor!', he is never ridiculed by the filmmakers. In court, the fact that Tarzan continues to have trouble with conjunctions proves less important than the power of his homespun wisdom ('Teach Boy where to find water when thirsty, where to find food when hungry. Tarzan teach Boy to be strong like lion and happy like bird … Wise man need little … Boy grow up to be brother of sun and friend of rain. Hurt nobody, want nothing people have. Grow old like cedar tree. Boy will be good man. Happy man'). It impresses the judge and amuses the public gallery, but a legal setback when it is exposed that he and Jane are not Boy's natural parents sees Tarzan, as it were, go ape. After assaulting the defending attorney, he escapes by climbing up the outside of the building and making his way across the rooftops by means of flagpole ropes and ladders, the chase culminating in a spectacular 200-foot dive off the Brooklyn Bridge. The climax provides a new spin on the elephants-to-the-rescue plot device when Tarzan calls upon circus animals to come to his aid. When the eagerness of Rand and Sargent to retain their money-spinner ends in murder, Tarzan and Jane are awarded guardianship of Boy in court.

It doesn't seem to have been a production motivation, but that Weissmuller is clothed in a double-breasted cream suit for much of the proceedings is a handy diversion from the fact that he is getting out of shape. It's rumoured that the chance to be a clothes-horse was a reason for O'Sullivan agreeing to make the movie. She certainly cuts a dash in the fashions of the day topped by an elaborate hair-do. Original movie ape-man Elmo Lincoln makes a cameo as a circus roustabout.

This brief movie was the shortest of all MGM Tarzans so far – not much more than an hour and ten minutes – but the best since *Tarzan and his Mate.*

The main reason that the rate of Tarzan movie releases stepped up in the early '40s would seem to be that the production baton was wrested from MGM – who had demonstrated a penchant for two-year gaps – and handed instead to Sol Lesser, whose career had revealed a philosophy of striking while the iron was hot.

That Metro had given Weissmuller a new seven-year contract (albeit with option caveats) after *Tarzan Finds a Son!* at a point where they had no guarantee of making more than two further ape-man pictures suggests that their decision to pull out of the market was not voluntary. *Tarzan of the Movies* author Gabe Essoe has theorised that the war's decimation of the foreign markets so crucial to the franchise's bottom line prompted MGM to revaluate its financial worth to them; but, in apparent contradiction, he has also said that Burroughs determined not to renew the studio's right to the character after those aforesaid two pictures were made.

If the latter is true, it may have been because Burroughs knew that Sol Lesser was waiting in the wings. The man who had bludgeoned his way into the Tarzan movie business by buying out that dangling Walter Shumway/Jack Nelson/Jim Pierce film contract had somehow endeared himself to the author, possibly because he was, like Burroughs, a man with his eye permanently on the main chance. When in 1943 Lesser finally became the independent producer of the Tarzan series proper, as opposed to a man occasionally putting out pictures in competition with the 'official' ones, few of the public understood or cared about the reasons for Tarzan movies being attached to a new three-letter movie studio acronym – RKO financed and distributed Lesser's productions – but it marked a new era in cinematic Tarzans lasting 15 years. That period saw the release of 15 movies featuring a total of three different leading men and straddled the transition to colour stock. Lesser, incidentally, later claimed that during his time as Tarzan producer, a healthy proportion of the grosses continued to come from foreign countries (75% in his estimation).

At first, though, not much visibly changed, as Weissmuller and Sheffield were retained for the black-and-white *Tarzan Triumphs*, released in the first two months of 1943. Cheeta was also present and correct. Even the absence of Jane precipitated by O'Sullivan finally bowing out lasted only a couple of pictures. In the meantime, the insurance policy MGM had sought against O'Sullivan's departure was now cashed in as the series temporarily became a Tarzan and Boy double act.

The picture opens with Boy – having presumably been taught literacy by his unseen step-mother – reading a letter from Jane, who is visiting her own mother in London. Jane imparts the news of the World War. Tarzan is no more interested in this than in the beseeching of the beautiful princess Zandra (Frances Gifford) who wants him to come to the aid of her Palandryan people, whose lost city has been invaded by brutal Nazis intent on looting its valuable oil and tin. In a quite transparent geo-political metaphor, when the war impacts directly on his own world in the form of Boy being kidnapped by the Nazis in pursuit of a stolen radio, Tarzan concludes that he cannot continue to pursue a policy of isolationism. The co-opting of Tarzan for wartime propaganda – the fate of many pop culture characters of the day and requested of Lesser by the US State Department – was handy for Tarzan's new producer in one sense. Not only did it give Tarzan a fresh foe and a variation on the usual jungle intrigue, but it provided another way for the ape-man to endear himself to the public. When Tarzan shrugs off his neutral stance with the furious declaration, 'Now Tarzan make war!', audiences are reported to have erupted into cheers. The picture was so enormously successful that Lesser never managed to replicate its commercial impact in his long production tenure.

Despite the Hays Code, the ape-man's pursuit of Germans is almost as bloodthirsty as that seen in the book *Tarzan the Untamed*. However, this no doubt did not provoke the sort of moral qualms that would have been felt by some over the fact that back in 1916 Tarzan Tribes were helping to sell so-called Liberty Bonds. With their death skull insignia and wholesale slaughter, the Nazis genuinely were the sort of cartoon villains that few would object to the ape-man despatching by – as he did herein – tricking them into a lake filled with flesh-eating fish, instructing an elephant to push them off a cliff or (in a scene similar to one in *Tarzan the Untamed*) leaving them to be eaten by a lion in a pit. In a body-strewn 78 minutes, even Boy and Cheeta get in on the bloodshed. The chimpanzee emits one of his characteristic shrill laughs after having filled a Nazi full of lead with a machine gun. Still, makes a change from rustling up a herd of elephants to storm to the rescue. As with so many Weissmuller Tarzan films, the ending features a comic Cheeta scene, this one involving him accidentally reaching Germany on a radio and being mistaken for the Führer.

With the switch in producers and studios, Richard Thorpe was absent from the director's chair for the first time in four (MGM) pictures, replaced by William Thiele. Also changed slightly was Tarzan's yodel, Lesser/RKO not owning the MGM recording of it. Higher production values were evinced by a Tarzan picture being provided a proper musical score for the first time. Roy Chanslor and Carroll Young contributed the screenplay from a story by Young. Burroughs had cause to be incredibly grateful to the latter two men. As if the enforced cessation of his publishing activities wasn't enough, the war had cut off his royalties from many foreign territories and even reduced his income from the Tarzan comic strip, as their lowered pagination had caused some newspapers to cease licensing it. Only six months after its premiere, *Tarzan Triumphs* had earned Burroughs $100,000 in royalties on top of his $25,000 advance.

The fact that he had helmed a successful Tarzan picture for the first time seemed to go to Sol Lesser's head. Within months of the release of *Tarzan Triumphs*, he put into production *Tarzan's Desert Mystery*, another Jane-less affair in which the ape-man took on the Nazis. Not only was the formula the same but its appearance in December 1943 marked an inordinately short gap between two cinematic Tarzan ventures from the same studio. Though not a flop, it was almost predictably far less successful than its predecessor, both commercially and artistically.

Thiele directed again, while the script was by Edward T Lowe from a story by Carroll Young. The sand dunes of Olancha, near Lone Pine, doubled as the Sahara. Jane's absence is explained this time as the result of her tending to wounded soldiers in England. A missive from her requests that Tarzan send a malaria serum for jungle-stationed troops she is nursing. The letter-home-to-the-treehouse device was used again partly because Lesser was still holding out hope that O'Sullivan could be persuaded to change her mind about retiring. However, as with princess Zandra in *Tarzan Triumphs*, he ensured that the distaff side was represented prominently. In fact, perhaps too much so, as Connie Bryce (Nancy Kelly) occupies a disproportionate amount of screen time in contrast with Tarzan, who languishes unseen in a prison cell for long stretches of a picture that is itself only 70 minutes long. Even when he is on screen, Tarzan speaks only about 40 words, a pronounced taciturnity that would be a feature of Lesser's term, with the resolutely commercial producer determined to make things as uncomplicated as possible for non-English speaking markets.

Connie is a jive-talking American magician whom Tarzan saves on his cross-desert journey with Boy and Cheeta to find the plants needed for the vaccine. (Her breasts, incidentally, aren't that much bigger than an out-of-shape Weissmuller's.) She is also not what she at first seems, having a secret mission to expose one Hendrix as a Nazi called Heinrich when the party reach the Arab city of Bir Herari. There are lots of swirling sands, Arab and Nazi villainy and frenetic horse-riding, and no lions or crocodiles in sight (nor, indeed, any of the mystery promised by the title). This could be seen as a worthy attempt to vary the jungle formula, yet the film was panned partly because of the un-Tarzan-like environs. The scenario becomes even more unfamiliar in the film's final act, where Tarzan, who has finally reached the location of the plants he seeks, is pitted against dinosaurs. Well, is shown stepping away from back-projected footage of dinosaurs filched from the 1940 picture *One Million B.C.*. If studio audiences who would not live to experience computer-generated imagery (CGI) didn't know enough to find this comical, nor the inclusion of an oversize man-eating plant, the reports are that they did crease up at the sight of a giant spider that munched on a Nazi on Tarzan's trail.

The latter science fiction-type scenes were clearly added in the reshoots and re-jigs that Lesser authorised when he adjudged the first cut unacceptable: they are not mentioned in early press briefs. There is nothing necessarily wrong with the idea. After all, Burroughs had successfully deployed such fantastical elements in his work, and the technical know-how existed for it to be done right, like in 1933's dinosaur-bedecked *King Kong*. This material could have made a decent Tarzan picture on its own. What results here however is somewhat higgledy-piggledy, and by common consensus the poorest of the dozen Weissmuller Tarzans.

In 1944, Lesser finally bit the bullet and recast the role of Jane. He picked Brenda Joyce to be O'Sullivan's successor. Joyce was a former model who had made a transition to actress in pictures like *The Rains Came* and *Little Tokyo, U.S.A.* Though Joyce was blonde and spoke with an American accent, audiences accepted her readily enough, and in fact she outlasted Weissmuller in the franchise.

Joyce made her debut in *Tarzan and the Amazons* in Spring 1945. Kurt Neumann was appointed to direct a screenplay by John Jacoby and Marjorie L Pfaelzer. By the time the movie was in production, World War II was clearly in its endgame and the impetus for a propaganda picture was no longer present, especially because the public were heartily sick of war. Accordingly, the third RKO/Lesser Tarzan dispensed with the quasi-realism of much of the previous brace of ape-man pictures and went for a story more in keeping with Burroughs' own lost-city bent.

On their way to pick up a returning Jane, Tarzan and Boy rescue a young Amazon woman from a panther. Of course, the Amazons were, as the name implies, from South America, but mis-locating animals by a continent was a Tarzan movie tradition so there was no reason to stop at humans. The ape-man returns the girl to her home city of Palmeria – which with its occasional human sacrifices and immensely plunderable reserves of gold is rather Opar-like – and promises to her queen that he will not divulge the city's hidden location to anyone who might for some reason have cause to ask. Cue the entry of a safari of scientists who, by an amazing coincidence, have heard of this forbidden paradise ruled by beautiful women and recognise jewellery stolen from it by Cheeta as bearing its hallmarks. Though Tarzan keeps mum, Boy is fooled into thinking the scientists have good intentions and takes them where they want to go. Boy is sentenced to death by the Palmerians for his troubles but luckily Cheeta alerts the ape-man to his peril.

Despite having hit 40, Weissmuller has noticeably lost a few pounds since the previous picture and demonstrates the probable way how with an impressive blurred swimming segment that culminates in a crocodile battle that shows the benefits of switching studios: unable to re-run the MGM-owned musty croc fight from *Tarzan and his Mate*, Lesser authorised the filming of a new, superior one. Another memorable scene involves Tarzan allowing two of the villains to die in terror in quicksand, illustrating that, though often cartoonish, the Weissmuller Tarzans were not exclusively kid-stuff.

Tarzan movie titles were beginning to resemble Tarzan book titles again, but just as *Tarzan Triumphs* had nothing to do with Burroughs' *Tarzan Triumphant*, so *Tarzan and the Leopard Woman*, a 72-minute feature released in February 1946, did not comprise an adaptation of the author's *Tarzan and the Leopard Men*.

However, a Burroughs flavour definitely infused this new venture, written by Carroll Young and directed by Kurt Neumann. High Priestess Lea (played by an actress with an even more exotic name, Acquanetta) is not only one letter away from La but similar to the Opar *femme fatale* in her homicidal sultriness. The cult she leads is reminiscent of the Leopard Men of Burroughs' book – and indeed some sources state that *Tarzan and the Leopard Men* was a working title for this picture – though their motives for slaughter while dressed in ceremonial skins and claws are a cross between a form of Satanism and anti-colonialism. Tarzan ends up tangling with them when a young boy from the leopard cult named Kimba (Tommy Cook) infiltrates his household. The brother of Lea, he has been sent to spy on Tarzan, who has been looking into the cult's activities at the behest of a local commissioner, but the boy has his own mission in mind: bringing back Jane's heart to prove his manhood. This all makes for a rather sinister, brooding Tarzan picture, especially as the leopard cult are given their own throbbing dance numbers.

Weissmuller rather peels back the years, looking impressively trim as he defeats Tongolo the Terrible in a wrestling bout, tussles with big cats and simultaneously fends off leopard worshippers and crocodiles. Almost symbolic of his revived physique is the fact that he destroys the leopard cult by bringing the roof down on them, toppling pillars in a Samson-like finale. Not that he doesn't receive some help: once again Cheeta makes a crucial intervention when doom seems inevitable, an inclusion with which Lesser seems to have been as obsessed as his predecessors were with getting Tarzan to yodel for the intervention of Tantor. The growing Johnny Sheffield meanwhile is beginning to rival Weissmuller himself, even if he is not yet quite as tall as his screen father. Accordingly, he is given a fight scene with Kimba.

This feature received unusually extensive advance publicity. Little wonder when Lesser was in the franchise for the long haul: the previous January he had issued an announcement that he had a 20-year exclusive deal to make Tarzan movies.

Though Tarzan had been a pioneer in several media, including adventure newspaper strips, he was a Johnny-come-lately to the new field of what the British call 'comics' and the Americans 'comic books'.

By 1937, comic books had been established in America as artefacts separate from newspaper supplements, but it wasn't until February 1947 that an original Tarzan comic book hit the stands. Indeed, the ape-man had been beaten to that format by adaptations of considerably less popular Burroughs creations John Carter (who became a feature in Dell Comics' *Funnies* in April 1939) and even the Inner World (*Pellucidar* appeared as a one-off strip in Hawley's *Hi-Spot Comics* in 1949, drawn by John Coleman Burroughs, as was John Carter from his fifth Dell appearance).

The hardcover reprints of Tarzan newspaper strips that appeared in *The Illustrated Tarzan Book* and Whitman books don't of course count. *Tip Top Comics* – in which Tarzan appeared from April 1936 off and on through to 1954 – and *Comics on Parade* – which saw ape-man appearances from April 1938 to August 1940 – were recognisably comics, but the Tarzan material consisted of reprints of the newspaper strips owned by United Features Syndicate, the titles' publisher. Though Dell were famous as a comic book publisher, Tarzan's appearances in the late '30s in the likes of their *Famous Feature Stories*, *Popular Comics* and *Crackajack Funnies* were text stories with accompanying illustrations. Dell's *Large Feature Comic, Series 1* #5 (1939) again featured reprints of the Foster strips, but its card/paperback covers and the fact that all of its 76 pages were devoted to the ape-man, makes it arguably the first proper Tarzan comic book. However, for the purists, still not quite the real deal.

The fact that, unlike *Large Feature Comic*, its original material wasn't restricted to a few splash pages of artwork gives *4-Color* #134, cover-dated February 1947, the accolade of first Tarzan comic book proper. It was Western who had secured the American comic book rights to Tarzan. Slightly confusingly, though Western produced the comics, it was Dell who licensed them, issuing them with their own logo. Despite mixed artistic results, Western would hang on to those rights for exactly a quarter of a century and therefore define the comic book Tarzan for more than one generation of children.

APE-MAN

'Tarzan and the Devil Ogre', the all-new story featured in *4-Color* #134, demonstrated many of the problems that would become associated with the Western Tarzan. The cover of the publication is simply embarrassing, a smiling Tarzan waving from atop an elephant with only the fact that he is wearing leopard-skin briefs denoting anything remotely savage. The artist responsible was Jesse Marsh, who also provided the interior illustrations. It would be unfair to judge Marsh's abilities on this comic or any other published over the next few years: this was an era characterised – presumably because comic books were such a new medium – by child-like, scratchy art by young men who had been given their chance before they were quite ready for it. Many of them – including Marsh, Batman's illustrator Bob Kane and Superman's original artist Joe Shuster – grew up in public, blossoming in technique in front of their readerships. Yet Marsh – a long-term Disney artist but unfamiliar with comics – had a skill rudimentary in 1947 and laughable by today's standards. Particularly risible are Tarzan's expressionless face and page-boy hair.

The writing is of far greater interest. This comic, in common with all the films (presumably by contract), states this to be 'Edgar Rice Burroughs' Tarzan'; but in this case it is the truth. The story was written by Rob Thompson, based on his unbroadcast radio scripts for *Tarzan and the Tower of Ho*. That it provides an explanation of the name 'Tarzan', includes Paul D'Arnot, mentions the Waziri, utilises the Mangani language and depicts the ape-man as a cultured, articulate and occasionally imperious individual suggests a writer steeped in the original novels. (As with the radio Tarzan, the victory cry of the bull ape is 'Taar … maan … gah … nie … i … i!!') The 50-page story takes in a lion fight, a beautiful female explorer on a search for her missing father, a wrestle with a white gorilla, a treacherous safari member and a cache of gold. A limp ending notwithstanding, it's not half bad and certainly doesn't condescend to the readership. Few adults read comics in those days, but those who did and who were also familiar with Burroughs' work must have been heartened. Their happy state would not last long.

August 1947 – six months after 'Tarzan and the Devil Ogre' – saw the appearance of the second all-new Tarzan comic book when *4-Color* #161 ran a Thompson-written adaptation of his radio serial *Tarzan and the Fires of Tohr*. With what seems to have been their ape-man experiment adjudged a success, Western then inaugurated a Tarzan comic book with a regular schedule, the 36-page *Tarzan* appearing bi-monthly after its cover-dated January-February 1948 debut. The story in the first issue borrowed elements from Burroughs' *Tarzan the Magnificent*, while the one in the second issue was entirely new. In both cases, it was still Burroughs' Tarzan being portrayed. As early as issue three, however, Dell capitulated to the ape-man as defined by Johnny Weissmuller – treehouse, Boy and all – stopping only at making Tarzan speak in the films' staccato style. By issue 13, the comic was regularly featuring a photograph of the latest screen Tarzan on the cover (admittedly to striking effect).

The decision to create a Tarzan that was a conflation of the movie and novel versions would seem to have been made by the publisher. Though like Marsh he was not formally credited, the writer of Western's Tarzan comic from its second issue, with few exceptions for its entire life, was a man named Gaylord DuBois. He told a Burroughs fanzine that he had been a Burroughs reader and fan since the 1920s and added: 'If I'd consulted my personal taste alone, I would have held faithfully to ERB in all my Tarzan comic scripts – but if I'd done that, I'd have been promptly fired.' Perhaps that gave DuBois a get-out for the rather stolid writing style of which many have complained, although it should be pointed out that however maligned, the Western Tarzan title was popular enough not only to survive for more than two decades but also to step up to a monthly frequency with the issue cover-dated July 1951.

As he had in every other medium, Tarzan crossed the Atlantic in the comic book form. The UK's *Tarzan Monthly* made its debut in 1950 and lasted for 19 issues by publishing reprints of American Sunday newspaper strips. In September 1951 came a Westworld title variously called *Tarzan: The Grand Adventure Comic* and *Tarzan Adventures* that originally appeared fortnightly before switching to a more traditional UK comics weekly schedule. Those stats aside, of somewhat more historical importance is the involvement of a young man named Michael Moorcock. He started out as a contributor (features and short stories) before taking on editorship. Later, he would become a major and very much Burroughs-influenced science fiction author. The phrase 'young man' is not used loosely here: incredibly, Moorcock was just 16 years old when he became assistant editor and 17 when he assumed the editor's position.

Moorcock says, 'I learned to read long before I went to school and my father, who had left my mother, left a few books behind, two of which were ERB titles – *The Son of Tarzan* and *The Master Mind of Mars* – which I loved. I could get the others from a little commercial lending library near where I lived, so it's fair to say I was reading Burroughs since the time I could read … I produced an ERB fanzine from the age of 14 and continued to produce it at 15 when I left school. I worked as a messenger for a shipping company, then as a junior consultant for a firm of management consultants. While there I produced a vast number of fanzines, because they gave me permission to use their printing facilities. I interviewed the then editor of *Tarzan Adventures*, who didn't like the published piece but his colleagues did. It turned out he wasn't popular. He was fired and his assistant wrote to me suggesting I write some features and maybe some text stories *a la* John Carter. I started doing those and a bit later he suggested I apply for the job of assistant editor – letting me know that he was leaving shortly and that I would then get his job. That's what happened. Full-time job.'

Moorcock took over *Tarzan Adventures* with Volume 7, No 25 (21 September 1957). 'It had been running for years, always featuring some text pages,' he says. 'It began as an offshoot of the Mondadori Italian/French large-size comic, which simply reprinted the Sunday pages … The Mondadori company, who published rafts of magazines, had eventually stopped doing it, so Donald Peters, my boss, had changed the format to US comic-book size, so that it would get better display on the racks, and added text features and stories, because in those days schools didn't ban comics which had some "educational" content … Alastair Graham, the previous editor, had wanted to take it in a different direction, which was why he commissioned so much stuff from me. I went further because I had writers and artists standing by, all of whom were ERB fans. The mag became a sort of junior science fantasy pulp, with departments etc … I had an 80-year-old assistant who wasn't up to much. Sammy Samuels came in twice a week to help on press days.' Moorcock describes his editorship role as, 'Normal duties. Commissioning pieces, getting everything together on time … There's a bit more about this routine in my new novel *The Whispering Swarm*, which is semi-autobiographical … I commissioned a lot of John Carter-style stuff, white hunter stuff and so on.' Although Moorcock wrote 'frequently' for *Tarzan Adventures*, including many serials, he says: 'I didn't ever feel the urge to write Tarzan and so never asked ERB, Inc.' It has been stated that amongst its reprints of US newspaper strips, *Tarzan Adventures* occasionally featured British-originated Tarzan strips, the first of their kind. However, Moorcock says, 'All our Tarzan stuff came from UFS, from whom we leased the strip.' However, 'I rewrote some of the Hogarth strips when we couldn't find plates in English. They had all been burnt up in a big [German bombing] raid on London, which destroyed so many books and publications in 1941.'

Moorcock says his adult colleagues were able to take him seriously despite his tender years because, 'sales figures rose sharply; they went from around 7,500 to 25,000.' Westworld ran a Tarzan Club through the publication. Joining entitled members to a large plastic badge, a membership card and the ability via the decoder on the back of that card to read a message printed in the magazine every week. Though members didn't seem to be getting much for their shilling dues above and beyond the thrill of being in the exclusive ranks of a notional club, the venture appears to have been quite successful. When Burroughs bibliophile Vern Coriell joined (even though he was a middle-aged man), his membership card stated that he was member number 8,522.

Though he would continue to be an occasional contributor, Moorcock's editorship of *Tarzan Adventures* ended with Volume 8, No 17 (26 July 1958). 'I went to work for *Sexton Blake Library*,' says Moorcock. 'When I left, Sammy took over, but the circulation began dropping badly and it didn't last much longer.' The publication died right at the end of the '50s.

Moorcock says editing *Tarzan Adventures* was not instrumental in his becoming a novelist ('I was already writing fiction long before'). In 1975, he co-wrote the screenplay of the movie adaptation of *The Land that Time Forgot*, but some are surprised that he did not follow in (or even precede) the footsteps of the six authors who have been licensed to continue Tarzan's adventures in print. 'It never occurred to me,' he says. 'I felt the first three Tarzan novels said all there was to say, and while I read and enjoyed all the others, up to *Tarzan and 'The Foreign Legion'*, I didn't want to add to sequels.' If he were offered the chance now, would he take it? Perhaps answering with the nonchalance that can come only from having himself created iconic characters like Jerry Cornelius and Elric, he says, 'I wouldn't write a Tarzan book. I generally don't use others' characters.' However, he also says that if he did write a Tarzan novel, 'I'd leave out the racism. I noticed how well the books lived without it when BBC radio read *Tarzan of the Apes* as a serial. They abridged it slightly and omitted the racial prejudices of ERB's day. When I came to reread the novel, the racism jarred as it had not when I first read it.' However, Moorcock also observes that *Tarzan Adventures* 'had quite a few black African subscribers from most parts of Africa, so perhaps we're over-sensitive to the [racism] issue.'

Tarzan returned to British comics in the Swinging '60s in *TV Tornado*, published by City. The Tarzan strip illustrated by Harry Bishop that started in its first issue on 14 January 1967 was given justification for the gogglebox-themed weekly by the first Tarzan television series, then on the airwaves. In two milestones for UK Tarzan comics, the strip was all-new and of a continuing nature. It survived when the comic merged with *TV Century 21*. *TV 21 & Joe 90* featured new Tarzan stories by Don Lawrence from its 27 September 1969 debut. Another TV-themed British weekly, *TV Comic*, and its associated annuals, featured both Tarzan strips and text stories in the 1970s.

There were also UK reprints of Western comics material, starting in May 1967 via World Distributors. Top Sellers and Williams also got a turn at presenting Western material for UK eyes in varying formats. A fondly remembered Williams product from the early '70s is *Tarzan – Giant Book*, which lived up to its title in its nigh-A3 dimensions, card covers and thick spine. Originally shrink-wrapped with five free Western reprints, it featured articles on Edgar Rice Burroughs, the movie Tarzan, the Mangani language and African flora and fauna. The three stories it extracted from *Jungle Tales* of *Tarzan* would have been many young people's introduction to ape-man prose. The heart of the book, though, was four wonderful Gaylord DuBois-Russ Manning adaptations of Burroughs Tarzan novels. These were Western reprints (blown up to colossal size) dating from the 1960s when an earthquake in the world of ERB in general and Tarzan in particular caused DuBois to be granted his wish of being able to stick more closely to the Burroughs boilerplate.

Tarzan and the Huntress, the third ape-man movie in a row with a dominatrix allusion in its title, appeared in Spring 1947. Despite his youth, the sprouting Johnny Sheffield was beginning to look far more the part of Tarzan than Weissmuller, who could now only be said to be trim for his vintage.

Kurt Neumann directed the 72-minute picture, which was a surprisingly strong entry in the series. The script was provided by Jerry Gruskin and Rowland Leigh, although the Saint's creator Leslie Charteris gets an enigmatic 'Screenplay Constructor' credit. The plot exploits the fact of the shortage of wildlife in zoos following World War II, with freelance hunters – one of whom is female – coming to the kingdom of Tarzan and Jane's monarch friend Farrod to bag some lucrative wildlife. They are given royal permission to capture just two of each species, but against a backdrop of palace intrigue they renege on that agreement, much to the displeasure of Tarzan, who despite hitherto being always ready to kill a lion or even a rhino in movies is posited as a defender of jungle animals. The plot gives more opportunity than usual to show off wildlife footage, which is sweeping and beautiful and – in the case of the crocodile-infested pool seen at one point – chilling. As is Tarzan's cold-blooded despatch of three of the invasive hunters. They may have been collectively complicit in the death of Farrod in pursuit of their plan, but the ape-man's vigilantism is not so palatable when directed against villains somewhat less diabolical than the Nazis.

Lesser wasn't big on sentimentality in Tarzan pictures but he authorised some extended kissy-kissy stuff between Weissmuller and Brenda Joyce and a lovely new underwater ballet with Tarzan, Jane and Boy, almost enough to put Olympic synchronised swimmers to shame. However, the sentimentality was purely for the screen. Tarzan's comment to his step-son 'Boy man now' turned out to be bad news for Sheffield, as did a general view summed up by the

Hollywood Reporter reviewer's comment, 'It is no longer possible for him to do cute things.' After eight films and eight years' service, Sheffield was dispensed with by Lesser on the grounds that he had outgrown the role.

Edgar Rice Burroughs seems to have enjoyed his time as a war correspondent, despite a lot of his field stories not seeing print. However, such adventures as climbing aboard ships via cargo nets and coming under ack-ack fire on bombing missions were not the ideal prescription for a man who had suffered more than one heart attack before taking up his role. In early 1945, he confided in a letter to a friend that he felt so weak that he didn't think he would ever regain full strength.

He had, though, one last Tarzan-related triumph ahead of him, and it emerged from his war correspondent days. Burroughs wrote *Tarzan and 'The Foreign Legion'* from 10 June to 11 September 1944 in a period during which he was formally stationed on Hawaii, his home since April 1940. By then, paper restrictions were easing sufficiently to enable him to reactivate his publishing house. *Land of Terror* – a Pellucidar novel dating from 1938 and rejected by all of the magazines to which it had been offered – appeared in April of that year. His first post-war publication was *Escape on Venus*, a quartet of stories that had previously appeared in *Fantastic Adventures* in 1940 and 1941. *Tarzan and 'The Foreign Legion'* was published by Burroughs in August 1947. Not only was it the first Tarzan story for six years and the first Tarzan novel for eight years, it would transpire to be the last Burroughs Tarzan tale of the author's lifetime. It ended things on a high note.

That is, if you can ignore the vicious racism-as-propaganda-tool. Having had his fingers burnt over *Tarzan the Untamed*, Burroughs had held off involving the ape-man in the Second World War. He changed his mind at the prompting of George Carlin of United Features Syndicate, who suggested his hero take on the Japanese. The face-off was in some ways illogical for an English peer. Though the British did confront their forces in that conflict, the Japanese were always far more of an enemy to the country in which Pearl Harbor was based. Having made the decision, Burroughs proceeded to make the Japanese in the resultant book every bit as one-dimensional and unambiguously evil as he had the Germans in *Untamed*. He also portrayed them as cowardly, which might surprise any Allied soldier or seaman who had to endure the Japanese armed services' remarkable capacity for self-sacrifice, up to and including suicide.

Yet just as World War I and its literary child *Tarzan the Untamed* reinvigorated the Tarzan franchise, so the Second World War was a blessing in the way it provided the means both to convey fierce drama and to open out the ape-man's world. That was all a writer of Burroughs' abilities needed to produce a fine novel. The stultifying situation that Jack Byrne had suggested existed in Burroughs' life and writing back in the mid-'30s had ended with Pearl Harbor. Burroughs had gone out into the world, seen a lot, learned a lot and no doubt read a lot. Possibly just as importantly, he had taken a break from the Tarzan treadmill he had seriously begun to resent. He returned to the Tarzan series older, wiser and refreshed. Testament to this is the fact that, its absolutism about the enemy notwithstanding, *Tarzan and 'The Foreign Legion'* is a surprisingly understated affair. The persona of Tarzan, for instance, is not referred to until nearly a quarter of the way into the book, up to which point we get instead more than a hundred references to Col John Clayton, who is working quietly as a humble observer on a reconnaissance and photographic mission over the island of Sumatra in the Japanese-occupied Dutch East Indies. In similarly unexpected subdued tone for an adventure novel, Burroughs has the supporting characters debate with each other the nature and validity of hatred.

It is only when Clayton's plane is shot down over Sumatra and his downed party is threatened by a tiger that we are back in familiar territory. The colonel places a foot on his vanquished striped adversary and unleashes the victory cry of the bull ape, at which point his companions apprehend that this is none other than Tarzan of the Apes. (It's rather amusing, even sweet, that in his last Tarzan story, Burroughs finally finds a way to give the ape-man a legitimate encounter with a tiger.) Although once again Burroughs seems to confuse fiction and reality – 'Is dat Johnny Weismuller [sic]?' one of the crew asks – there's a touching valedictory subtext to a post-modern scene when one of the characters observes, 'And there's the scar on his forehead that he got in his fight with the gorilla when he was a boy.'

Being stranded in Sumatra creates a set-up similar to that of 'Tarzan and the Castaways'/'The Quest of Tarzan' insofar as the ape-man has to act as protector of a group cut off in a non-African wilderness. However, the differences begin with the fact that the land is teeming with hostile Japs (as they are almost uniformly called). The island also turns out to play host to a young woman called Corrie van der Meer, last survivor of a Dutch family slaughtered by the invading Japanese who has been living on her considerable wits. Dutch guerrilla fighter Tak van der Bos is also waiting to join the narrative, as is Sarina, a Eurasian female pirate. The three American soldiers with whom Tarzan was flying are of mixed racial parentage – leading to various ethnic bantering – but also possessed of a salt-of-the-earth quality that is no less effective and touching for it being slightly cinematically clichéd. This motley crew are dubbed 'the Foreign Legion' by the local guerrillas. (Note the inverted commas in the title to denote that it's a nickname, not always reproduced by publishers, some of whom seemed to think Tarzan had somehow become a new Beau Geste.) The action is somewhat back-and-forth, full of captures and rescues. However, this is more in the order of an exciting and suspenseful rather than disjointed story and it all culminates in an impressive ocean chase as the party head for the safety of Australia.

Burroughs doesn't stop short at demonising the Japanese. He goes so far as to have Tarzan and his friends threatened by the indigenous (and it turns out Mangani-speaking) orangutan, a gentle simian as undeserving of such a malevolent portrayal as that poor old rhinoceros that Weissmuller slaughtered. Another misstep is Burroughs portraying Tarzan as fashioning a loincloth from a parachute. The drama of a scene meant to convey a reversion to the savage persona in which John Clayton always feels more comfortable is somewhat undermined by folk memories of British women in World War II procuring their frilly undies in the same way. The faults are easily outweighed by the plusses, though. It's not just the change from the African backdrop and the undeniably interesting/exciting situation of war that give the book its power. Burroughs turns back time to the '10s and '20s when his writing was at its keenest, shrugging off that it's-my-job torpor and cynicism that had afflicted his output in recent decades. The characters are believable and, most significantly, the dialogue – Burroughs' perennial weak spot – consistently feels real.

For all of that, this was another adult Tarzan story that Burroughs failed to place with a magazine. *Tarzan and the Madman* was one thing, but the fact that editors were now turning down even a high-quality Tarzan showed how the world was changing: the pulp industry was becoming a thing of history. Still, at least we consequently know – unlike with 'Tarzan and the Jungle Murders' – that this is unadulterated Burroughs and not the amended version of a sub-editor.

During the book's narrative, the 'Legion' begin discussing a people who are reputed to have discovered the secret of eternal youth. Tarzan weighs into the debate. 'I have twice seen absolute proof that perpetual youth can be achieved,' he says. One of those occasions we know about from *Tarzan's Quest*: the longevity pills with a grisly secret behind them manufactured by the Kavuru and shared out by the principals at the end of that novel. The other is something to which Burroughs has not previously referred. Tarzan explains, 'When I was a young man ... I saved a black from a man-eating lion. He was very grateful, and wished to repay me in some way. He offered me perpetual youth.' Tarzan was sceptical but was told by the man's elderly chief that he has known this man – visually in his twenties – all his life, '...so I let the witch doctor go to work on me.' Tarzan himself – who it was established in *Tarzan of the Apes* was born in approximately 1888 and who of course had fought in the last World War – seems to be in his twenties to his companions. It is implied that the witchdoctor is the reason for this, because from what Tarzan says he did not partake of the Kavuru immortality pills as we had previously been led to believe. Cue another breaking of the fourth wall and another note of valediction when a character says, 'I never gave a thought to your age, Colonel … but I remember now that my father said that he read about you when he was a boy. And I was brought up on you.'

The whole passage is rather peculiar. Why did Tarzan fail to bring up during the course of *Tarzan's Quest* that he had no need of the longevity pills? Burroughs seems to have decided to revise the ape-man's past after suddenly realising that if Tarzan stories occurred in real time, the ape-man would have been in his mid-forties when the events in *Tarzan's Quest* occurred, and the pills' benefits commensurately smaller. But why would his thoughts stray in this direction when the general public – especially in an era well before anorak fandom – barely spent a second wondering why popular culture icons were ageless? Was it perhaps a reflex of discomfiture of a near-septuagenarian at the thought of his own mortality?

Tarzan and the Mermaids, released in March 1948, made it four Weissmuller ape-man pictures in a row in which his character shared billing with an exotic female.

However, 'mermaid' is a misleading description of Mara (Linda Christian), a young woman whom Tarzan literally catches in his fishing net. She transpires to be from the isolated island of Aquatania, from which she has fled because the high priest of her homeland is trying to force her into a marriage she doesn't want. Tarzan and Jane – who it has been established have sent the absent Boy to be educated in England – attempt to help Mara in differing ways when she is forcibly taken back to her homeland. In returning Mara to the arms of her true love, Tarzan demolishes the superstitious religion of the Aquatanians based around their imposter god Baloo, whom he hurls to a grisly death. Along the way Tarzan performs an astonishing dive off the Acapulco cliffs – stuntman Angel Garcia died in the execution – and battles an octopus.

The 68-minute movie – written by old trouper Carroll Young – is not top-notch ape-man fare but is unusual. The lush scenery results from the fact that this is only the second Tarzan cinema venture shot on location in a foreign country. Said country is not Africa – though that is where the movie is set – but Mexico. Acapulco, the Aztec ruins of San Juan de Teotihuacán and the studios of Churubusco and Mexico City provide a pleasantly unusual texture, even if director Robert Florey is sometimes too anxious to present a travelogue. Also unusual in an exotic way is the score from Dimitri Tiomkin, which enables some quasi-spiritual temple singing and includes a solo spot for minstrel postman character Benji (John Laurenz).

Weissmuller's comical full figure is not helped in any way here by the bizarre decision to put him in sandals. Though he might have been more sleek than most men in their mid-forties, a useful comparison is Jock Mahoney, who was in his mid-forties when he stepped into the loincloth yet – whatever his deficiencies in the role – had zero body fat. The fact that he was aware of how he had thickened was demonstrated by Weissmuller sucking in his stomach in publicity photos.

Weissmuller had repeatedly complained that he wanted a share of the Tarzan films' grosses. The promise he alleged Lesser made that he would receive this when his contract was renewed after *Mermaids* seems the stalling action of a producer who knew the actor's time was up. (Burroughs had mocked Weissmuller as a 'poor old soul' to Lesser as far back as 1944.) The film sees Weissmuller one last time effortlessly lifting an adversary above his head before hurling him to the ground, the method by which he had always implicitly insisted that great strength continued to underlie his increasing bulk. This consummate aquatic Olympian also gets a final opportunity to show off his prowess in the water at the end of his 16-year reign as Tarzan.

Both Sheffield and Weissmuller immediately found gainful employment after their (separate) exits by playing characters inconceivable without the existence of Tarzan, thereby providing another example of the way the ape-man had fanned out into society. Sheffield assumed the role of Bomba, the Jungle Boy. Bomba was a corporate creation by the Stratemeyer Syndicate dating back to 1926. The company used their in-house pseudonym Roy Rockwood for the tales they sold to publishers Cupples & Leon. There were 20 Bomba novels through to 1938, split evenly in location between the Amazonian jungles and Africa. The series relocated to the latter continent as though the parties concerned could no longer be bothered with a fig-leaf denial of Tarzan imitation. Bomba is white, speaks both English and ape and is a ferocious fighter. He is on a quest to discover his origins, to which clues are discovered in each book. Bomba being an adolescent like Sheffield, the latter was perfect for the role when the character made the transition to the silver screen. He appeared as Bomba 12 times up to 1955. The fact that the last of the Bomba films was titled *Lord of the Jungle* rather seems to be taking the piss, as indeed does the television pilot Sheffield's father then produced for him about a 'new' character called *Bantu the Zebra Boy*. After that show was not commissioned, Sheffield obtained a business degree, armed with which he subsequently pursued a variety of professions.

Weissmuller, meanwhile, played Jungle Jim 20 times between 1948 and 1956. This character was based on a comic strip that debuted in 1934. Illustrator Alex Raymond – co-creator of the character with writer Don Moore – had something of a history of taking his cue from Burroughs, having re-tooled John Carter of Mars as Flash Gordon. As with Bomba's anonymous creators, Raymond and Moore did what was requisite to evade a plagiarism suit, locating their action in Asia rather than Africa and clothing their hero in khaki. Jim was a hunter (cum adventurer) but had both a rapport with the beasts of the jungle and a pet simian. He was popular enough to jump media, appearing on radio and in comic books (some written by Gaylord DuBois) as well as in films. His move to TV in the mid-'50s – where Weissmuller again took the role – bizarrely saw the films drop the Jungle Jim name its producers no longer held the rights to, with Weissmuller there instead portraying (supposedly) himself. Already on $50,000 per film by the end of his Tarzan run, Weissmuller became even more wealthy via Jungle Jim, where he got that percentage he had unsuccessfully sought from Lesser. In between latter-day Tarzan pictures, he had tried to expand his horizons as an actor with scant success. The fact that he was associated with nothing but jungle-related action put paid to his acting career when the Jungle Jim TV series finished. After that, Weissmuller traded both on his swimming career in public relations work and on his name in commercials work in the gleefully unembarrassed way that American celebrities tend to do when their time in the spotlight is over but they retain affection amongst the public. An illustration of this is the fact that, as per Weissmuller's wishes, his Tarzan yodel was played at his funeral in 1984.

It should be noted that in Burroughs' lifetime the author himself showed little inclination toward litigation regarding either parody or rip-off. Though he had misgivings about a wrestler calling himself Tarzan and a murderer being nicknamed Tarzan by the media, neither Buster Crabbe's *King of the Jungle* nor Bomba nor Jungle Jim nor Sheena, Queen of the Jungle (a distaff, glamorous Tarzan who starred in comics, pulps, films and TV starting from 1937) nor a single one of the veritable 101 Tarzan pulp and movie intimations – as opposed to passing-offs – inspired a writ from him. Ditto the plainly John Carter-inspired Flash Gordon strip. The most logical inference from the fact that the author didn't take action even when one of his creations was the obvious inspiration is a fear that witness stand cross-examination might have led to questions about Burroughs' own debts to predecessors. For instance, some claim he got a lot of his Barsoom ideas from obscure novels *Journey to Mars* (1894) by Gustavus W Pope and *Lieutenant Gullivar Jones: His Vacation* (1905) by Edwin Lester Arnold.

Separate from but adjacent to the issue of media characters who would not have existed without Tarzan is that of piracy and plagiarism. Over the course of more than a decade straddling the Second World War, an Argentinian publishing house issued 30-odd Tarzan books credited to J C Bovirio. In Cold War Russia, Burroughs' Tarzan novels were immensely popular, but he did not receive a penny from their huge sales because the Soviet government viewed the concept of royalties as a capitalist irrelevance. Though the author lost – or at least failed to gain – a fortune because of such matters, it was the movie Tarzan that was subject to the most piracy and plagiarism. This process was assisted by the fact that in a more fragmented world than we have today, the Berne Convention on copyright was easier to circumnavigate even where ideology didn't prohibit governmental goodwill on the issue. When for instance news of the 1940 production *The Adventures of Chinese Tarzan* by the Hsin Hwa Motion Picture Company of Singapore attracted the (no doubt belated) attention of Burroughs, the prospect of litigation in an unknown legal system in a foreign language to invoke a law that might not have had an exact equivalent in that then-mysterious land would have been a daunting one. India, another vast and densely populated country with a then-casual attitude toward intellectual property, was responsible for a trio of illegal Tarzan movies in the 1950s – bizarrely, for distribution in Nigeria. In a rare act of competence, ERB, Inc's Cyril Ralph Rothmund obtained an injunction against their continuation. Back in 1944, Sol Lesser's task in stopping the dissemination of a similarly unauthorised Turkish Tarzan film was made somewhat easier when the distributors informed him they wanted to sell him the rights to it. Already aware that they were infringing his live-action privileges, at a screening he found himself looking at his own production *Tarzan's Revenge* with close-ups of a Turkish actor spliced in. He exercised his legal prerogative to confiscate the print.

PART FIVE: EXIT WEISSMULLER

At the end of the 1940s, it must have seemed inconceivable to some that anybody could portray Tarzan on screen other than Johnny Weissmuller. The part having been his for more than a decade and a half, any new actor risked looking presumptuous by taking it. The world, however, moves on. Sol Lesser wasn't going to neglect his lucrative franchise because of some airy-fairy notion of definitiveness, nor was any ambitious would-be movie star about to spurn the opportunity of a lifetime because there was a chance the public would not warm to him quite as much as it had to dear old Johnny. Enter Lex Barker. Though he had a hinterland of American football and track excellence, his summer stock and contract work meant that Barker was arguably the first real thespian to be cast as the ape-man. According to RKO director Lee Sholem, he had interviewed over a thousand actors and athletes after Lesser had set him the task of re-casting the ape-man, but gave the job to Barker without an audition when the latter came up to his office to make enquiries about it. The story has that old smack of Hollywood myth-making about it, but the idea of Fate being involved is in some ways true: Tarzan was just about the only major role Barker *could* play. The actor later claimed his prior contract status with Fox and then Warner Brothers had yielded little work because he would physically outshine the leading man, which status he was considered to be too unknown to be granted himself. Handsome, six foot four and possessed of a barrel chest and a rippling, toned physique, he looked every inch the part except for one thing. Though deriving from refined stock was a fundamental aspect of Burroughs' noble savage, the all-American pucker of Barker's face that betrayed his prep-school-and-Princeton background was incompatible with the general image of Tarzan. Meanwhile, the way his hair was swept up and back raised questions about out-of-place grooming that Weissmuller's increasingly unkempt mane hadn't for a long while.

Tarzan's Magic Fountain, Barker's entrée, directed by Sholem, was released in January 1949. Barker was one of those young American men who had been weaned on Tarzan, and he was so thrilled to be given the role that the 29-year-old was to be heard publicly chattering about playing it until he was 50. Perhaps Elmo Lincoln – given a bit-part in the film in a blaze of publicity by the canny Lesser – had thought the same thing back in the second decade of the century. Presumably on Lesser's instructions, Barker rang the changes insofar as his Tarzan was taciturn rather than incapable of fluent English. He was also different in that he seemed to be versed in martial arts. Familiar elements included Jane (Brenda Joyce becoming the second – and to date last – actress to play opposite two different Tarzans) and Cheeta. The glossy locales of the last Tarzan picture were missing, replaced by the old make-do venues of the LA Arboretum and Encino Ranch.

The film's title was incongruously feminine and an unwise switch from its no-nonsense original *Tarzan and the Arrow of Death*. Scriptwriters Harry Chandlee and Curt Siodmak would seem to have read the latest Tarzan novel, for the fulcrum of the movie is the secret of immortality, in this case one obtained from the titular fountain, located in the hidden Blue Valley, which has kept downed female aviator Gloria James (Evelyn Ankers) the same age for 20 years. When she emerges from the valley, Gloria experiences a transformation more to be expected in a horror movie, as the effects of the fountain are not permanent, prompting her eventual return to the refreshing waters. Naturally, she is accompanied by avaricious interlopers intent on profiting from this phenomenon of nature regardless of the disruption it will cause the natives who call the Blue Valley home; and naturally Tarzan is having none of it. In the grand set-to that follows, people meet grisly ends through rolled boulders, flaming arrows and an avalanche. Gloria and her new husband stay in the now fully sealed Blue Valley, there to remain permanently young.

The 73-minute film was nothing spectacular and Barker would never have a unique yodel – Weissmuller's RKO-era one would be overdubbed – but it was a decent enough effort to set the newcomer on course for, if not portraying the ape-man 'til he was 50, a respectable tally of five movies.

Barker's second outing was originally announced as *Tarzan and the Golden Lion*. Though the 74-minute movie written by Arnold Belgard and Hans Jacobyit was ultimately given the non-Burroughs title *Tarzan and the Slave Girl* upon its May 1950 release, there was a strong strain of the ape-man creator's style in the story.

A lost white tribe descended from ancient Egyptians who worship lions and who come to Tarzan's attention because they abduct young women is a set-up clearly derived by mixing together elements from two or three of Burroughs' latter-day Tarzan novels. The Lionians bring not just terror but a deadly disease, the fatal effects of which motivate their abductions: they seek to repopulate. Tarzan fetches a doctor who has a cure for the disease. Said doctor has an attractive nurse named Lola (Denise Darcel), who becomes the slave girl of the title when she, along with Jane, falls into the Lionians' clutches. When the serum is lost, it imperils all and sundry. Tarzan calls up elephants for help when he isn't breaking open crypt prisons with brute force or fighting the Lionian kidnapper Sengo to the death. That Barker's type of youth and power hadn't been seen in Tarzan films for several years is made explicitly clear in a physical and frenetic film, directed again by Lee Sholem.

Brenda Joyce had bowed out of the series to raise a family, and the problem with Jane that this created would never really be resolved in Lesser's time. If she had never become embedded in the public's mind as Tarzan's mate in the way O'Sullivan had, Joyce had done well enough in the role to last five pictures that straddled two different leading men. Now, however, there would be a bewildering succession of Mrs Tarzans, as Lesser – who reputedly turned down a young Marilyn Monroe for the part at this juncture – chopped and changed with every single picture to find a suitable replacement. That is, when the actress herself didn't jump ship. The ridicule of what she called her 'intellectual friends' put paid to Vanessa Brown, the brunette who took the role in *Tarzan and the Slave Girl*. Not that she was exactly done a service by the script: depicting a jealous Jane engaging in a catfight with a Lola who has ambitions to burrow beneath Tarzan's loincloth may have been in the spirit of increasingly informal times but was surely undignified and out of character. The suspicion that the catfight might have been designed to entice an older demographic was strengthened by a curious publicity picture for *Tarzan and the Slave Girl*: the sight of the ape-man standing with feet planted apart and knife ready to take on adversaries was expected enough, but not Lola kneeling beside him clinging fearfully to his leg, her head pressed against his hip.

According to *Tarzan – Giant Book*, Burroughs approved of Barker, adjudging him 'the real Tarzan,' and adding, 'Of all those hundreds of men whom I've met who have wished to play Tarzan, he is the only one who has had something more than muscles between his ears.' Burroughs' last public appearance was on the set of *Tarzan and the Slave Girl*, where he and Barker posed with the author's daughter, grandson, daughter-in-law and Vern Coriell, who three years earlier had started the first of what would become multitudinous Burroughs fanzines. In the resultant photographs, it is notable that Burroughs is the only one seated. The author had become increasingly debilitated by heart attacks and the onset of Parkinson's Disease. Before he had started losing his physical capabilities, he had effectively admitted that his mental capacities were less than they had been. In January 1941, he wrote to his son Jack, 'I can't squeeze out a single new plot,' surmising that a writer 'is born with just so many.' He recovered from this lack of confidence sufficiently to turn out some Venus and Mars novelettes, the scraps mentioned previously and two above-average novels, *I Am a Barbarian* and *Tarzan and 'The Foreign Legion'*. His final published volume was *Llana of Gathol*, a compendium of four previously-published Mars novelettes issued in March 1948. Writing-wise, *Tarzan and 'The Foreign Legion'* was his swansong. For the remaining six-and-a-half years of his life after its September 1944 completion, he simply never found the energy or interest to complete anything but letters. He roused himself enough to write 83 pages of a new Tarzan novel in September 1946 before abandoning it. The following year, he had another go at chronicling the ape-man, with even less successful results.

By now, Burroughs was living frugally, having bought a two-bedroomed house in Encino, Los Angeles at the end of 1945, around the corner from ERB, Inc and in the shadow of the mansion he had forfeited during the Depression over the border in Tarzana. His letters suggest he settled happily enough into the role of retiree and old man in these final years. In the last year of his life, he re-read his *oeuvre* to, as he put it, 'see what I had said and how I'd said it.'

It has been reported that Burroughs died reading the Tarzan Sunday newspaper strip. More accurate would be to say that the funnies were before him when he was discovered dead in bed by his housekeeper on 19 March 1950. Journalistic penchant for myth, symmetry and sentimentality seem to have done the rest.

Whatever the exact circumstances, this brought to a close a life that, it has to be said, appears to have been for most of its 74½ years unhappy, unfulfilled or both. Burroughs never seemed to like or be satisfied by his pre-writing employment, and suffered extreme financial hardship when his family were young. There was a glorious period in the '10s and '20s of the 20th Century when he was charged up with the new thrill of being a famous author and a wealthy man at a point where he still had good relations with his wife and had a young family on which he doted. Though it would be absurd to suggest he experienced no happiness from thereon, that which he did seemed almost predestined to be followed by disillusion. It is striking how quickly writing became just another job to him, an increasingly resented means to finance the economic folly of the Tarzana ranch. Then came disillusion with his marriage. While his second marriage did seem to provide him genuine domestic bliss for a short while (like a love-struck teenager, he planted a secret message to Florence Dearholt in the mid-'30s Barsoom novel *Swords of Mars*), that union formally ended after just seven years in May 1942 when the couple had been living apart for more than a year, and its termination created yet more financial burdens. He also had to endure the humiliation of increasingly frequent rejection letters from magazines and the ever-dwindling financial returns from those that did deign to publish his writing, which in any case he privately admitted he was tired of.

Yet Burroughs had triumphed on many levels, with three adored and adoring children, massive success in his chosen field and, despite many artistic failures, continued inventiveness in his Mars books and writing that increasingly evinced greater powers of discipline in general. Above and beyond all that was something that few writers in the history of literature could boast: the creation of a character so iconic and enduring that his name has entered both the language and the dictionary.

The early 1950s saw the beginnings of a new domestic American phenomenon called television. In 1951, though, radio still dominated the hearth, and the return of Tarzan to that medium was therefore a big deal for the ape-man.

The idea was that of Walter White Jr, who operated Commodore Productions and Artists, Inc. Having achieved considerable wireless success with *Hopalong Cassidy* and *The Clyde Beatty Show*, in the second half of 1950 White contacted Cyril Ralph Rothmund, General Manager of Edgar Rice Burroughs, Inc, to broach the idea of licensing Tarzan. With a go-ahead from Rothmund secured, White commissioned some scripts. Budd Lesser, David Chandler and the team of Robert Schaeffer and Eric Freewall are known to have written some of them, although poor documentation by Commodore – a very small outfit – means that it can't be said for certain that they were the only scriptwriters. The show was titled *Tarzan, Lord of the Jungle*. Though each episode had an introduction that included the line, 'Transcribed from the immortal pen of Edgar Rice Burroughs,' with the exception of two episodes partly based on latter-day Burroughs novels, all the scripts featured original plots.

Considering the proprietorial care he had shown over the previous radio programmes, it's doubtful that Burroughs, had he lived, would have allowed the producers to take some of the liberties with his character that they did in the new series. Though he would have approved of the fact that Tarzan spoke fluent English, he would have raised an eyebrow at the fact that as an adult he for some reason lived in the log cabin built by his doomed parents, that he laughed loudly, that he hung around with local Gomangani (who somehow knew Mangani terms for animals) and that his frequent aloofness was replaced by something approaching gregariousness.

Having said which, in one sense the series recalls the idea Burroughs had back in the late-1930s to reinvent Tarzan as a jungle detective. The episodes are kicked off by a visit to the hut by a native or one Captain Stanley Lawrence, who present the ape-man with a jungle-based mystery or problem that he then sets off to solve like a one-man, loinclothed FBI. Tarzan is played by Lamont Johnson, who possesses a stentorian all-American voice that no Burroughs fan would have found *bona fide* but had the sort of authoritativeness that the average listener would have associated with Tarzan's physical strength and power. Dramatic-toned narrator Charles Arlington links well-written and evocative scenes, which feature incidental music and, where appropriate, animal background noise. Each weekly half-hour episode begins with a fairly respectable yodel.

Though decent stuff, the show started slowly, making its debut on a single Los Angeles station – KHJ – on 4 January 1951. However, before long it occupied a spot on 45 Western state stations. From 22 March 1952, it made the jump to national broadcasting, having been picked up by the CBS network. It performed creditably, managing to break into the ratings top ten to nestle alongside the likes of *Amos 'n' Andy*, *Lux Radio Theatre* and *Gene Autry*. Yet this apparently highly promising situation evaporated quickly. CBS stopped broadcasting the show after 27 June, supposedly for a summer break of 13 weeks. It never broadcast any further editions. After that, it was back to local radio, plus a few foreign sales. White produced 75 episodes in total.

Around this time, Artransa in Sydney, Australia began producing a daily 15-minute Tarzan show. Transmitted Monday to Friday at 6 pm, *Tarzan, King of the Apes* saw the ape-man played first by future Hollywood star Rod Taylor then later by Ray Barrett and Lloyd Berrell. Jane was also played by three different actresses: Marcia Hathaway, Pamela Page and Joan Landor. It is estimated that over 1,000 episodes were broadcast. The few that remain are high quality and more faithful to Burroughs than the Commodore series. The royalties from the Australian show had to be given by ERB, Inc to Walter White when he pointed out that he held the rights to Australian Tarzan radio broadcasts. This act of incompetence by Rothmund was not untypical: in the early '40s he had publishers who wanted to issue cheap editions of Burroughs books virtually tearing their corporate hair out with his penchant for simply not responding to letters or, when he did, engaging in counterproductive brinkmanship, as a consequence of which three Tarzan books – including, insanely, *Tarzan of the Apes* – were out of print even before Burroughs died.

The glossy locales of Weissmuller's last outing *Tarzan and the Mermaids* had been missing from his successor's first two films, where it had been back to the dependable old domestic venues. With Lex Barker's third flick, Sol Lesser finally decided to take the plunge and make the first Tarzan film shot in Africa. He didn't intend to do it by halves either: possibly mindful of those who had noted what a waste it had been shooting the spectacular Mexican landscape in black-and-white in Weissmuller's swansong, he also determined that this would be the first colour Tarzan film. Almost all of his efforts went to waste.

Shooting began at Mount Kenya and its surrounds in July of 1950, the height of summer – in the States. In Africa it was winter, and Barker found his bronzed tone fading. This was only the start of a series of calamities. Cheeta did not appear in a Tarzan picture for the first time since 1932 (competing Tarzan films excepted) as a consequence of the chimps that had been brought along playing up and Kenya transpiring to be short on simian acting talent. Half of the footage was lost in an accident. The weather got so bad that in late August, cast and crew retreated to the safety of California locations, at which point the production lost its director Phil Brandon. His replacement Bryon Haskin had scriptwriters Samuel Newman and Francis Swann (John Cousins is credited with additional dialogue) rework the story. Just as the crew had retreated from Africa, so the producers retreated from the concept of a colour film. The monochrome picture made it to the cinemas in March 1951 as *Tarzan's Peril*, although the tradition of Tarzan sharing the billing with a glamorous female continued in the UK where American working title *Tarzan and the Jungle Goddess* was retained. Despite Lesser's ambitious intention of widening the scope of Tarzan pictures, what emerged was merely a serviceable ape-man flick, although it could be argued that even this was an achievement in the circumstances.

The story revolves around Ashuban Queen Melmendi (Dorothy Dandridge) who declines the offer of marriage to Yorango tribe king Bulam. The latter joins forces with a thoroughly nasty gun-runner called Radijeck (George Macready), who provides Bulam with the weaponry to take Melmendi's village. Radijeck also slaughters police commissioners, leaves one partner-in-crime to die in the jungle and murders the other before turning up at the treehouse to demand Jane lead him to civilisation. Jane is saved in the nick of time by her returning mate, who has already turned in a good afternoon's work by freeing Melmendi's people and despatching Bulam. Radijeck gets a deserved death-plunge. Jane is here played by Virginia Huston, although the soon-to-be renowned actress doesn't get much of a chance to shine in the role. In the few sections of the 79-minute film in which she is present, she is done no favours by either a strangely luxurious white pelt costume or a functional housewifely hairdo that is quite a contrast to the memory of O'Sullivan's tumbling curls.

The history of Tarzan reveals a creative tendency to turn to the concept of a junior ape-man to reinvigorate the franchise. This is what Sol Lesser did with *Tarzan's Savage Fury*, released in April 1952.

To this purpose, Lesser even went to the extent of hiring Cyril Hume, the scriptwriter who had introduced Boy in *Tarzan Finds a Son!*. Hume collaborated with Hans Jacoby and Shirley White. The trio's script saw an attempt to incorporate some of Burroughs' books into the movie Tarzan landscape, although the results are compromised by the requirement to stay within the parameters already set for the celluloid ape-man. We learn that Tarzan is a Greystoke heir and was raised in the jungle by his father and are introduced to a tribe called the Waziri, although they are not under Tarzan's command. Continuing the garbled translation of Burroughsonia is the fact that there is a villain called not Rokoff but Rokov (Charles Korvin). (The scene in which Rokov bewilders the Waziri with magic tricks even suggests the writers have read *The Tarzan Twins*, although it is probably actually down to the fact that director Cy Endfield was a trained magician.)

Rokov and companion Edwards (Patric Knowles) are seeking valuable industrial diamonds to which they know Tarzan can lead them. Rokov murders Tarzan's cousin Oliver, Lord Greystoke, and Edwards assumes the dead man's identity. Oblivious of their machinations, the ape-man is busy being a father to Joey (Tommy Carlton), a white boy made an orphan by lions whom he recues from the fate of becoming native crocodile bait. Jane enjoys playing mother to Joey, who naturally is loinclothed up to become a miniature of his new step-father. Dorothy Hart becomes the first redheaded Jane herein, although only people who read the more luxurious fan magazines could see this for themselves, as the film was in monochrome again. She is, though, by no means the first Jane to persuade Tarzan to do something against his better judgment for visitors who she belatedly learns are up to no good. In this case, she persuades her mate to lead his supposed cousin and Rokov to the diamonds they say are necessary for British national security. Enraged hippos and hungry cannibals bar their path. When Rokov steals the diamonds and murders a Waziri witchdoctor, Jane is marked by the tribe for execution. Joey, meanwhile, gets over his understandable lion-phobia the hard way. Tarzan fights Rokov and flings him into a lion pit before dashing to the Waziri village to make an eleventh-hour intervention in Jane's sacrificial ceremony.

Some of the location footage from the ill-fated African excursion for *Tarzan's Peril* is deployed in the picture. Endfield's direction is strong in a pacy 80 minutes whose action is leavened with nice sentimentality.

Barker got to speak an unusually high number of lines – 137 – in *Tarzan's Savage Fury*, but this upward dialogue gradient – for which the actor had agitated – was considered by Lesser to be the reason for the picture's lacklustre box office performance, and he determined to reverse it with the next one. (He presumably also adjudged the experiment with Joey a failure: the boy promptly disappeared from the series as though he had never been.) Around the same time Lesser made this decision – it's unknown whether it was before or after – Barker informed him he would not be signing a new long-term contract once the current one – which had one more movie on it – expired. Barker was too much of a Princeton gentleman to say anything publicly other than, 'It's time for a change … although I have nothing against playing the part.'

Lex Barker had done well in his tenure in the loincloth, looking the part in films that were mainly high quality. Though he still looked a million dollars in his June 1953 swansong *Tarzan and the She-Devil*, he was not, as he had previously been, furnished with a good script, nor many lines (a record low for him of 83), nor much action. Consequently, he departed the series not with a triumphant yodel but with a whimper.

Not only did Joey disappear from the franchise as soon as introduced, but Dorothy Hart – whose pre-Raphaelite beauty would have been ideal for the forthcoming colour age – also failed to return. Barker's fifth Jane in five movies was Joyce MacKenzie. In shades of the book *Tarzan the Untamed*, Tarzan spends much of this movie in a distraught state when he discovers the burnt-out remains of his home and believes his beloved to be dead. However, where that dramatic set-up gave *Untamed* its impetus and power, here it drags the proceedings down, as the ape-man spends a large chunk of the 76 minutes moping apathetically in the cell to which he has been consigned by Lyra – she-devil of the title – and Vargo, her accomplice in ivory poaching. Future Perry Mason Raymond Burr plays Vargo, while Monique Van Vooren as Lyra convinces us that she is indeed deadlier than the male. There is a little twist on the Tantor-to-the-rescue set-piece of so many Tarzan films when the ape-man is forced upon pain of Jane's death to call up an elephant herd by the villains, who desire their tusks. Naturally, Tarzan turns the tables on the khaki-clad ne'er-do-wells. Kurt Neumann directed the Karl Kamb and Carroll Young script. The Arboretum and RKO Encino Ranch were the backdrops not provided by footage from 1934 movie *Wild Cargo*.

Barker was actually prepared to make more Tarzan pictures, but only on an *ad hoc* basis. Lesser wanted a long-term commitment. Though he was typecast a little for a while, Barker had more acting chops on which to fall back than Weissmuller. He also had a more refined intellect. Subsequently, he became a multi-linguist thespian who made movies all over the world but was particularly successful in West Germany. That success bought him homes in Geneva, Rome and Barcelona and a 50-foot yacht, but not a long life. As if to prove that a magnificent physique is a guarantor of nothing, Barker died in 1973 at the shockingly young age of 54, the cause of death being a heart attack.

In the 1930s, Burroughs had suggested to Tarzan movie producers that they make an ape-man picture a dependable annual event. In the following decade, his dream came true, to such an extent that it was noteworthy when 1954 marked the first year without a new Tarzan feature in the theatres since 1944.

Part of the reason for that hiatus was the necessity to find another man to fit the loincloth. As with Lex Barker, the official story, which might even be true, is that serendipity provided the actor where auditions hadn't. Despite the testing of many prospective Tarzans – 200 was the customarily implausible figure quoted – 27-year-old Gordon Werschkul was found working as a lifeguard in a Las Vegas hotel by a holidaying Hollywood agent. Six foot three and good-looking, he had a torso shaped like a 'V' and a chest that was, amazingly, even broader than Barker's, and if his bodybuilder's physique was technically not the type that would be created by a life in the trees, only the fanboys – as they then weren't called – were going to cavil. Ditto for his elaborate pompadour – although there was a hint of wild man in the fact that his hair was almost shockingly abundant for the time. That long hair may have been a sign of changing times, likewise the fact that the new Tarzan's loincloth was the skimpiest yet. As was common in showbusiness in those days, Werschkul's name was de-ethnicised and he became Gordon Scott.

Yet with *Tarzan and the She-Devil* not having done appreciably better than *Tarzan's Savage Fury*, Lesser decided to debut his new ape-man as cheaply as possible rather than make an investment in him. Scott's entrée, *Tarzan's Hidden Jungle*, was released in February 1955. With movie audiences becoming ever more sophisticated, its extensive use of mismatching stock footage held the franchise up to ridicule. Complicating matters was the fact that distributor RKO was in severe trouble. In fact, so strapped for cash were the studio that a married couple turned out to have more wherewithal, even if that couple were Lucille Ball and Desi Arnaz, who bought them out in 1956.

Though Cheeta is present, Jane does not appear. This seems to have been less to do with Lesser wearying of casting a new woman in the role each time than with a desire to inject spice into the proceedings, or as much as was possible in the era: there is a sexual frisson attending Tarzan flinging the beautiful United Nations nurse Jill Hardy (Vera Miles) into a pool after she notes that she needs a wash, and in the way he watches her nude bathing. However, the ape-man remains as chaste as he does in Burroughs' Jane-less novels. Instead, his passions are channelled into saving his beloved jungle from Burger (Jack Elam) and DeGroot (Charles Fredericks), big game hunters who care not a fig for the fact that they are trampling all over the sacred animal-exalting beliefs of the local Sukulu tribe and are not above fooling a United

Nations doctor (Dr Celliers, played by Peter Van Eyck) into helping them in their quest for ivory, hides and animal fat. Because of their trail of havoc and mischief, Tarzan has to nurse a baby elephant back to health and rescue Jill from a python. Additionally, he is sentenced to death by a witch doctor. Burger and DeGroot meet a grisly end beneath the feet of elephants stampeding at the ape-man's behest. Tarzan then saves Jill and Celliers from lions. Presumably, the limp way he does this – a few 'Umgawas' making the animals back down – is because a tussle to the death was deemed inappropriate at the climax of a movie in which he is posited as the friend and protector of wildlife.

Harold D Schuster directed the 73-minute film, whose script was furnished by William Lively. The Sukulu chief was played by Rex Ingram, who had had a bit part in 1918's *Tarzan of the Apes*, 37 years and ten Tarzan actors previously.

Inevitably after the death of an author of a long-running and popular series of books, the issue of succession starts being raised among some of his fans. This fact was illustrated by Stuart J Byrne's *Tarzan on Mars*.

Pulp author Byrne, who often wrote under the *nom de guerre* John Bloodstone, was flattered by the suggestions of admirers of his work that he might be a successor to Burroughs and overcame his initial scepticism to write as a sort of exercise a novel in which the ape-man travelled to the red planet to rescue both Jane and La. The text showed how steeped in Burroughs Byrne was by tying the high priestess of Opar into a loose thread of the author's recorded Barsoomian history. Ray Plamer, editor of *Other Worlds Science Stories*, loved what he read so much that he wrote an article in the November 1955 edition of that publication enthusing over Byrne's manuscript – whose author's name he did not reveal – and encouraging people to write to him with the vague pledge 'I'll back you up on Tarzan!' With an ambition that wasn't too outlandish in the days of mass circulation print products, he aimed for '100,000 names on my desk within the next 60 days.' Byrne later claimed that Hollywood began sniffing around, that famous science fiction author and Burroughs devotee Ray Bradbury gave his blessing and that Palmer had a potential 20,000 orders for the published book worldwide. Street & Smith Publications, Inc then made a formal overture to Edgar Rice Burroughs, Inc, guaranteeing a 25% royalty upon a go-ahead to publish. However, Cyril Ralph Rothmund, acting for the corporation, said no, instantly turning the mini-tsunami of hope and intrigue that had suddenly sprung up in Burroughs-world into a body of stagnant water. Byrne was convinced that the pitch was wrong: his agent and Street & Smith had tried to sell him as a successor to the recently deceased Burroughs rather than promote the manuscript on its own terms. From there on, *Tarzan on Mars* existed only in a twilight world of mimeographed copies circulated through the post amongst intrigued Burroughs fans. (It was joined there in 1972 by *Tarzan at Mars' Core*, a spiral-bound book by one Edward Hirschman whose alleged private print run of 2,000 was high for such enterprises.) In the modern age, of course, it is easily available, whizzing around the world in e-mail attachments and even available in full online, where the threat of legal action that prevented its publication before seems not to be a factor because nobody is making money from it. It was also serialised in a hard copy fanzine over three years in the 1990s.

Yet Byrne may have been wrong about ERB, Inc's reasons for blocking publication. He had a vested interest in not perceiving his manuscript as over-long (at well over 100,000 words, it is longer than all Burroughs Tarzan novels except *Tarzan the Untamed*), his action plodding, his character motivation impenetrable (Tarzan literally waits years before setting off in search of the missing Jane), his exposition interminable and his knowledge of previous encounters between Tarzan and La surprisingly sketchy (especially considering his attempts elsewhere to show off his familiarity with Burroughs with obscure references to minor characters from each series). For all these reasons, *Tarzan on Mars* is really little more than a grand precursor to the 'fan fiction' with which it nowadays shares space online.

Following *Tarzan's Hidden Jungle* there was once again a two-year gap between ape-man pictures. However, when *Tarzan and the Lost Safari* was released in March 1957, it inaugurated the new era that Scott's first film might logically have been expected to.

In need of a new distributor, Lesser approached MGM. The studio that had had such great success with the character in the 1930s was understandably amenable to renewing its association with the ape-man. With Metro's big bucks behind him, Lesser was finally able to fulfil his ambitions relating to widescreen and colour that dated back to the beginning of the '50s. Colour film – generated by various means – was technically around at the dawn of cinema, but it had truly taken off in the 1930s. Though even by the mid-'50s plenty of cinema releases were still in monochrome, if any film series was ideally suited to colour it was Tarzan. MGM cranked up the lustre by approving filming in British East African locations. Furthermore, for the first time, African location shooting consisted not just of establishing shots but of primary action sequences. Even the non-jungle shooting was far-flung: the cast and crew decamped to Elstree Studios in England. Just as importantly, a high-quality script was procured from Montgomery Pittman and Lillie Hayward.

The action starts when Tarzan spots a 'sky-bird' crashing in the jungle. Having rescued the passengers just prior to their aircraft sliding over a cliff, he agrees to lead them to the coast. Lost safaris of around half-a-dozen people were a speciality of Edgar Rice Burroughs, and the crashed crew are reminiscent of his writing in their disparateness: wealthy couple Dick and Diana Penrod, gossip columnist 'Doodles' Fletcher, blonde bombshell Gamage Dean and bored playboy Carl Kraski. Another ERB trait emerges in the way that romance blossoms between a pair of them, even if they are a former couple who begin to regret their split. The fly in the ointment that provides the film's drama beyond Tarzan protecting the safari from the dangers of the jungle is the fact that Diana is captured by inhabitants of the village of Opar. Though Tarzan rescues her from the prospect of the sacrificial altar, the Oparians are on the party's trail for the remainder of the proceedings, assisted by hunter 'Tusker' Hawkins, who desires both Diana and the ivory bounty that is the Tusks of Opar.

H Bruce Humberstone's pacy direction of the dramatic set-pieces and the lustrous colour are almost enough across the 84 minutes to make us not miss Jane. (Once again, the ape-man shows no interest in the beautiful women he encounters, although they certainly take an explicitly stated interest in him.) Cheeta, who for once isn't deployed to overly comic effect, plays a crucial role in setting Opar on fire with Doodles' lighter. The climax occurs on a burning rope bridge, on which Tarzan battles Hawkins while dodging Oparian arrows.

Though the Opar village here bears little resemblance to Burroughs' city of that name, there are more elements of the author's original ape-man than usual, including Tarzan explaining a backstory that involves being raised by apes after his parents perished in the jungle. (The scriptwriters get Kerchak and Kala mixed up in this recounting.)

Reviews of the picture were good and the path was set for a new Tarzan era: there would never be another black-and-white Tarzan movie.

Lesser was clearly feeling confident about Tarzan's viability. *Tarzan and the Lost Safari* hadn't even wrapped before he turned his attention to bringing the ape-man to the small screen.

The rise of television had been rapid indeed. From virtually a standing start in the late 1940s when the networks began broadcasting, by the mid-'50s half of all American homes had a TV set. It was presumably the fact that it was already clear that cinema had a huge rival – one that at the time nobody had any way of knowing would not be the death knell for movies – that caused Lesser to exercise his Tarzan rights in that direction.

Or, rather, try to exercise what he imagined to be his rights. Walter White

Jr had already been granted such rights by the incompetent Cyril Ralph Rothmund in December 1950. A brace of legal tussles followed. ERB, Inc – who understandably wanted Sol Lesser to apply his considerable live-action expertise to an ape-man TV show in preference to the shoestring operation of Commodore Productions and Artists – instituted a suit against Commodore to get them out of their obligations. When ERB, Inc lost, White issued proceedings against Lesser, who during the shooting of *Lost Safari* had formed a Tarzan TV company and then publicised an agreement he had reached with NBC. The latter network promptly pulled out of the deal until the dispute with White was resolved. Lesser opted for the ploy of conceding the first-refusal of which White's rights consisted – he knew White did not have the wherewithal to mount an expensive TV production – and the predictable outcome of him buying White out eventually occurred.

When Lesser was finally in a position to authorise production of the ape-man's TV debut, he did it as a job lot with the next Tarzan cinematic venture. Three Tarzan TV pilots were filmed back-to-back alongside the movie *Tarzan's Fight for Life*. All four projects featured Scott in the lead role, the wholesome, blonde Eve Brent as Jane and another reincarnation of Boy in the shape of Tartu, the couple's ten-year-old adopted son, played by Rickie Sorenson. Incongruous with the ambition Lesser had lately poured into the ape-man, all four projects betrayed a pedestrianism largely responsible for their failure, which itself was ultimately responsible for Lesser bowing out of the Tarzan industry completely.

That *Tarzan's Fight for Life* was not shot in Africa – or even Elstree – but at MGM's Culver City studios was a clear and puzzling step backwards. The intercutting of African footage garnered on the location trip for *Tarzan and the Lost Safari* was not compensation, not least because the screenplay left much to be desired. Perhaps Thomas Hal Phillips was genuinely trying to do something refreshing by spurning the time-tested device of white interlopers with sinister plans, but he failed to come up with anything of comparable inherent dramatic possibility: the film could actually have been titled *Tarzan's Fight to Get Jane an Appendectomy*. Aside from Mrs Tarzan's burst appendix, the action – directed by Bruce Humberstone – revolves around the difficulties encountered by Dr Sturdy (Carl Benton Reid) in bringing modern medicine to a jungle where witchdoctors and their potions hold sway. Tarzan – an unlikely champion of medicinal enlightenment – is on more comfortable territory when he battles an 18-foot python. When the film was released in July 1958, much was made in publicity of the fact that the year marked the fortieth anniversary of Tarzan cinema. The reviews however concentrated on the film's dullness – something not helped by its unusually extended length of 86 minutes – and it did relatively poorly at the box office.

At least, however, it saw the light of day. The first of the Tarzan TV pilots revolved around a battle between the ape-man and a trapper, the next two a hunter with Tarzan in his sights and a treasure-oozing lost city. With the character having proved his on-screen popularity with the public via what was already the longest-running franchise in cinema history, it might be assumed that Lesser and NBC would readily obtain a sponsor for the show. In fact, none proved interested – the kiss of death for a prospective American TV series with a high budget. Apart from footage included in two travelogue TV shows called *Bold Journey* that aired in 1956 and 1957, the public did not get to see any of the Gordon Scott Tarzan TV series until 1966 when a 74-minute TV movie was compiled from the three pilots and broadcast as *Tarzan and the Trappers*. Technically, this made it the first Tarzan television programme, even if it was by only a matter of four months and even though it was a one-off. It's palpably different from big-screen Tarzan, not just in the fact of it being shot in black-and-white but also in its family-orientated tone that sees Tarzan sporting a very modest loincloth hoisted right up over Scott's navel and the provision of separate, sex-thoughts-banishing treehouses for each member of Tarzan's family. Charles F Haas and Sandy Howard are the credited directors and Frederick Schlick and Robert Leach the writers of the telefeature, which being an artificial construct is doomed to be episodic, as well as difficult to assess aesthetically. Its backdrop would have made it exotic fare for mid-1950s TV (what den would not have resounded with joy at such sights as Tarzan chasing villains on the back of a commandeered giraffe?). Additionally, its nuclear family set-up – a sort of Jungle Family Robinson – would have chimed well with the cornball tone of the broadcast drama of the era.

With *Tarzan's Fight for Life* bringing in disappointing returns and the TV episodes sitting uselessly on a shelf (their monochrome would have made them seem somewhat old-fashioned if they had been released in the cinemas), Lesser was disillusioned. Producers Sy Weintraub and Harvey Hayutin found him when he was vulnerable (he'd also recently suffered a heart attack) and he accepted their offer of two million dollars for his production company, which of course included the rights he held to the Tarzan character.

Lesser had started as an interloper in the franchise and an irritant of Burroughs but had become the dominant force in the screen Tarzan, which in terms of exposure was – for better or worse – the most culturally important manifestation of the ape-man. His departure from the stage after 15 features and a serial was truly the end of a Tarzan era.

PART SIX: THE WEINTRAUB ERA

Though Harvey Hayutin was originally his business partner, Sy Weintraub bought him out after two pictures and it was he who became the public face of the new Tarzan movie franchise's production company. Weintraub was a TV man whose career included devising *The Late Show* and becoming vice-president of the largest supplier of films to American television. He had decided to buy out Lesser because he felt that he could modernise Tarzan and return the movie series to the spirit of the books. Through his run was not as long cumulatively or even consecutively as Lesser's, he turned out high-grade films while updating the character for people weaned on James Dean, Elvis Presley and Marilyn Monroe, a generation whose values were not as conventional as those of Lesser, Edgar Rice Burroughs or, come to that, Lord Greystoke.

No sooner had Sy Weintraub assumed control of the Tarzan franchise than he found himself facing competition from an 'unofficial' picture when MGM announced that they were to embark on a remake of Weissmuller's entrée *Tarzan the Ape Man*. Weintraub naturally protested, but MGM had every legal right to shoot the movie, as at the relevant time remake options were written into their contracts as standard. Metro paid a heavy price for their remake that would not even have been compensated for had it been a box office hit: Weintraub initially did not allow his ape-man productions to be distributed by them.

Had he been of an immediate mind to replace Gordon Scott, buying out his contract at this point would probably have been prohibitively expensive for Weintraub. He did though make some immediate changes to the nature of the character and to the flavour of the series, starting with his first effort, *Tarzan's Greatest Adventure*, released in July 1959. Weintraub decreed his Tarzan would speak intelligently, conjugations and all. He also ordered some spice, dispensing with Jane to this purpose. In 1960, he would explain, 'The kids of today want action and adventure, and a bachelor figure is more exciting than a jungle suburbanite swinging home every night to tell his little woman what happened during the day.' Jane would not appear in another Tarzan film until 1981. More realistic – and sometimes harrowing – violence was to be allowed in the series. Weintraub also paid close attention to quality. Key to that was production values: the combination of Kenyan location shooting and British technicians that was deemed to be behind the success of *Tarzan and the Lost Safari* was replicated for *Tarzan's Greatest Adventure*. On top of that, the script by Berne Giler and John Guillermin from a story by Les Crutchfield is mean and lean – something probably inadvertently helped by the minimal presence of Cheeta due to the imported American chimps being frightened by jungle noises. Tarzan himself is also mean and lean, with nary a trace of playfulness or humour. Guillermin maintained the tautness with quickstep direction of the 90-minute feature. He also beautifully photographed the lush, teeming landscapes, often with imaginative camera angles. It's presumably on this picture that Weintraub learnt of the sound problems inherent in Tarzan pictures: he developed a *modus operandi* of silent shooting because post-dubbing (usually in London) was the best way to get around the issues created by passing aeroplanes, noisy natives, the cries of indigenous fauna and the commands of animal wranglers.

The plot is propelled by the deeds of a party of white villains led by an old adversary of Tarzan's named Slade (Anthony Quayle) and including a man named O'Bannion (a young Sean Connery). Slade's sassy blonde aviatrix girlfriend Angie (Sara Shane) starts out as a member of said crew but defects to the side of light when she sees the extent of her companions' ruthless venality. *En route* to a diamond mine they intend to plunder, the group murder hospital staff in their quest for dynamite. Tarzan follows their trail, enduring the attentions of a crocodile and a poisonous spider in between attacks from Slade's party, though is helped by the members of the latter turning on each other. When villain Dino is trapped in quicksand, his mauling by a panther when helpless epitomises the new edginess of the franchise. The exciting movie climaxes with Tarzan and Slade fighting to the death on top of a cliff. Even the poster art is powerful: a long shot of Tarzan unleashing a victory cry, fist clenched, from the precipice from which Slade has just fatally plummeted. The only black mark is the way Weintraub chickens out of fully sexualising Tarzan: a scene wherein the ape-man and Angie sucked face was excised, even though audiences were left in little doubt as to what happened immediately after the cut.

After all that care, and despite glowing reviews, the picture ended up a relative flop due to half-hearted promotion and poor distribution on the part of Paramount: this film was not designed to be playing two-fers with the Jerry Lewis comedy *Don't Give Up the Ship*.

Tarzan's Greatest Adventure was the sort of superlative-packed title common in Hollywood at the time, but on this occasion it was more than hype. Not even just a superior Tarzan picture, it for some remains the best even to this day. More remarkably, it's difficult to see Burroughs doing anything other than unequivocally approving of it.

The man MGM chose as their competition for Gordon Scott in the new *Tarzan the Ape Man* was a 24-year-old contract player named Denny Miller.

He was an unusual Tarzan, but – he points out – not unique: 'They keep saying I was the first blond, but Buster Crabbe was a blond.' (In fact, the first was technically Jim Pierce.) In respect of physique, Miller was like every other man who had played Burroughs' forest god. Miller explains, 'My father was a physical educator. He was on President Kennedy's and President Eisenhower's Council for Youth Fitness. He bought me a set of weights when I was in eighth grade, because I was so skinny at one time I was 5' 11" and weighed 121. I didn't have a shadow until I was 22 years old. I got into [bodybuilding] because I wanted to improve my athletic ability of playing football, baseball and basketball. It paid for my education at UCLA – I was on a scholarship there because I could play a sport.' Miller was in charge of the gymnasium in his army days. 'For about six months I spent my evenings with the weights,' he recalls. 'I put on about 20, 25 pounds of muscle mass.' It was this and his Greek god looks that attracted the attention of movie talent-scout Bob Raison.

Miller recalls, 'My first job was in *Life of Riley* with William Bendix. I was in *Some Came Running* with Shirley MacLaine and Dean Martin and Frank Sinatra and a couple of others.' Miller didn't consider being cast as Tarzan his big break, having a rather matter-of-fact approach to his roles. 'I took the work that they told me to take,' he shrugs. 'I've heard of people with more whatever-it-takes than I did to turn down things, but I was a misplaced basketball player so I didn't particularly care to do any of that.' That notwithstanding, he originally told the studio that they might be looking in the wrong direction for Tarzan: 'I recommended Bill Smith, the actor, because I had worked out at the same gym and knew that he had a better build than I did. However, they screen-tested I think Bill and [me] and several others, and for some reason or other I got the part.'

Of his screen test, Miller recalls, 'Believe it or not I walk out of the jungle and Jane is sitting on a log and I'm soaking wet – obviously it's either rained or I've been in the water – and I sit down with her and recite the 23rd Psalm. They kept telling me that they were going to make this version of Tarzan a much more educated and more intelligent variety than they had before. I said more in that screen test than I did in the whole movie.' Regarding the issue of his movie being frowned upon by Weintraub, Miller says, 'I was happily ignorant of all that going on.'

Miller took the trouble to sit down and watch several of the previous Tarzan movies: 'I enjoyed Elmo Lincoln very much. I'd seen most of the Johnny Weissmuller ones and a couple of the Gordon Scotts.' Miller also boned up on the yodel. 'They gave me a recording of one of the yells,' he says. 'I don't know which one it was, but it was the one that they used in the film. They gave it to me way before the shooting started, and I was living at the beach and at night I would go down and yell at the waves so as not to be arrested. I did never come close. I sounded like a wounded yak when I yelled. I did a yell and then they just snipped it out in the sound department and laid in the other sound. Carol Burnett does it much better. I officiated at some Tarzan yell contests. Usually little girls and women [win].'

Miller had to go through the bizarre-sounding process of attending a loincloth fitting. 'As a matter of fact, I have one of them,' he reveals. 'They had two of them as far as I know, because when one was wet and they wanted it dry, it was better to have one waiting instead of trying to take a hairdryer and dry the one off. I don't think I ever had to change, so I don't think that happened due to scheduling.'

Miller received instruction on how to swing on a vine from a stuntman. He was told to '… start off with your arms extended and not in a right angle so that you didn't panic when you get to the upside of the swing. Some people panic when they can't hold their arms at a right-angle because of the added gravity.' His training didn't prevent mishaps when swinging: 'My stunt double was a very good stunt double [but once] he was on another job and I did a swing that he would have normally taken that was quite a long one,' he explains. 'I swung out from a tree house. They had erected a stand for two guys to stand on about 30 feet high to catch me when I got there. The person that tried the swing before me was considerably less weight than I and he was much shorter. He got there just fine. When I went out on my swing I knew that my chest was going to hit the top of the thing and I curled up and took the collision with the bottom of my feet. That kind of tipped the thing and the two guys that were supposed to catch me were reaching for something to hold on so they wouldn't fall off of the stand, so I just went backwards and bounced off the side of the bamboo house, which cut my leg a little bit. I got in smaller and smaller arcs until I was still and I was holding onto the vine – it's a rubber-coated rope with a leaf here and there sticking out so it looks somewhat real – and they got a ladder and came up and let me down. But I didn't ever fall off of a vine.' This was fortunate, for in the days before workplace health and safety regulations, there was no trampoline to break a fall. Not that there was no protection at all for the actor. Miller: 'If it was a very high swing, they usually gave you a leather loop that was attached to the rope and covered with leaves so it wouldn't be seen, so I could have hung there for quite a while before they came and got me.'

Tarzan the Ape Man was written by Robert Hill, who had a long association with the movie Tarzan. MGM's conscientiousness in preparation for the 82-minute film, shot over six weeks on their backlot in Culver City, West Los Angeles, makes it all the more curious that the studio in most other respects treated the new *Tarzan the Ape Man* – and its audiences – almost with contempt. 'MGM had done other low-budget films but I don't think ever that low,' says Miller. A case in point was a scene shot with Joanna Barnes, this movie's Jane, on a cement-bedded river on which some of Johnny Weissmuller's swimming scenes had been filmed. The budget didn't extend to heating the set. 'Her teeth were chattering so much they couldn't understand what she was saying,' says Miller. 'So they gave her several drinks of brandy and that warmed her up enough to be able to say the lines.' It was understandable that a remake should follow the plot of the original Weissmuller movie fairly closely, but not so much that the footage should include parts of that and other Weissmuller movies. Also featured were sections of *King Solomon's Mines* (1950). Miller notes, 'I was amazed that they had so many wildebeest charging across the screen. It was a piece of stock footage so we didn't do that scene for sure on the backlot.' The crowning piece of the farce is the fact that nowhere in the movie is Miller's character referred to as Tarzan.

The tone of the production was set, albeit inadvertently, with the first scene Miller filmed. 'Sound stages and outdoor stages are full of hazards for people who are running around barefoot,' he explains. 'Nails and what-have-you, splinters and twigs and glass. So they took an impression of my feet, then they made me rubber or Styrofoam soles for my feet and glued them on. The first shot of the show was me swinging on a vine from behind the camera, over the camera, letting go and dropping with my back to the camera and stopping and putting my hands up and telling Jane and her father that we got to go hide because there's going to be a stampede. Well, they rolled the camera, I swung out, I dropped where I should have been and hopped just a little bit. Those soles were right where I'd landed – they came off. I never saw them again.'

Though it would be unfair to suggest that this film was cursed – filming a Tarzan picture is hazardous almost by definition – the shoot does seem to have been afflicted by pratfalls and misfortunes. Miller: 'When I showed up that morning there [was] a 30-foot wire fence around the indoor set. They had a little old lady there and a guy with a shotgun. I found out later my stunt double wasn't there; a new guy was there. They asked me to go in there. It would be an easy thing: "You just wrestle around with this house pet." It's a cheetah. A little old lady had hold of him by a leash and they had [a] painted-over … muzzle on his mouth so he couldn't open [it]. I said – very wisely afterwards, I thought – "I'd like to see the stuntman do it first." So they got the stuntman up on a tree limb, and he was supposed to drop down when the cheetah went under him. Well, they got a live goose and they held the goose by the neck and showed the goose to the cheetah and they held the cheetah behind a bush. They let the cheetah go and the cheetah crouched down like he was going to get that goose for lunch, and as soon as he was under the branch, the stuntman just moved about an inch and the cheetah heard him and now they can't get the cheetah to go under the limb. So they asked the stuntman to just stand in front of the cheetah and they unleashed him and they started to film it and the cheetah lay down on its back and rolled over like a big kitten and wanted to play. They tried slapping the cheetah in the face – and there was a blur. The stuntman stood there. The cheetah was off in a corner of the sound stage. They got the little old lady to go get him. The stuntman was bleeding from his shoulder, down his chest, along his left side, down his thigh. After that happened, I said, "I won't go in there." So they got this stuffed animal. And it looks like a stuffed animal.'

Not that this prevented Miller from having teeth sunk into him. 'A chimp bit me on the hand once,' he says. 'The trainer had told me, "If he bites you, hit him, because he'll take a part of you with him." It wasn't the chimp's fault, really. He was a nice little chimp. Marvellous. They're so intelligent. They had a shot where the camera shows me walking away and the chimp has come to get me to go back to help Jane. He is instructed by his trainer to run up to me and reach out for my hand, and he wants to pull me back. Well, after I get ahold of his hand, the trainer is behind the camera and yells to the chimp to come his way, and I won't let him go. Naturally the chimp is going to go where he gets his food and his instructions, so I felt his teeth on the meaty part of the outside of my left hand. I lifted up my hand and the chimp came with it. I punched him in the nose and he let go and he went up in the rafters, and it took us half an hour and a BB gun to get him back down.'

Meanwhile, the crocodile Miller was supposed to fight to the death was in no fit state to bite anything. Miller: 'They tried to use the same mechanised 20- or 30-foot alligator that Johnny had fought in one or two or more of his films. It turned into a fiasco. I jumped on its head as they were pulling it by wire because the mechanism didn't work anymore. It'd been sitting out in the sun for 20 years or more. When I jumped on it from the water, I went down to the bottom and came out, I thrashed around and I got up, and when I was tired I stood up, and everyone was on their hands and knees on the shoreline, laughing. The camera had been on a boom and the operator had laughed himself right out of the chair. They told me that the tail went up and it sunk like a submarine. They never could use it.' Instead, the crocodile fight from *Tarzan and his Mate* was used yet again. This recycling had been risible enough the first few times, but now it was little short of desperate: *Tarzan and his Mate* had been in black-and-white whereas the new *Tarzan the Ape Man* was in colour. Miller: 'They tinted it, and it looks like tinted black-and-white film. It's kind of a terrible green.' To add to the farce, Weissmuller's face is clearly visible in the scene in places.

The several times Miller rode elephants – real ones – were a happier experience: 'It was fun.' However: 'They don't like chimpanzees on their back so it took us all about half an hour to get up there. They handed the chimp from behind the elephant so he couldn't see.'

As for his Jane, Miller says, 'Joanna Barnes was very pretty.' He states, 'We got along fine', despite revealing a painful piece of improvisation on her part: 'In one scene where we were fighting and she's frightened to death, she tried to bite me on the knee, which wasn't in the script, but it made the fight look realistic.' Barnes has gone on to become a successful novelist.

MGM's bizarre decision to give the film a low budget was exposed as the archetypal false economy when *Tarzan the Ape Man* was derided for its shoddiness upon release. Inevitably, there were no more unofficial Tarzans made by MGM, at least in that era. 'I heard at the time that they had the rights to do two more, and I was not against having to do those,' says Miller. 'But I never heard again it mentioned.' Not that he was waiting around to hear anything: 'I was off on many other projects. I've been very lucky. A long career in Hollywood is ten years. A career of over 50 years [like mine] is not unique, but it's very [rare] … I've never brooded overmuch and certainly not [over] whether I get a job.'

Miller didn't take in *Tarzan the Ape Man* until two or three years after its October 1959 premiere. 'I didn't see anything that I did for a very long time because it made me so nervous,' he explains. 'I would say that there are more than half of [my roles] I haven't seen ever.' His reaction when he did see the film? 'Like I always did with other roles, I would get involved with thinking, "Oh my goodness, I don't walk that way." It was all physical – there was no mental piece to it: "I wish I had done this" or "I wish I had done that".'

Although Miller has the distinction of being the oldest surviving movie Tarzan, his film boasts a more dubious accolade: 'It's listed in *Tarzan of the [Movies]* by a friend of mine under a chapter heading "Tarzan the Worst".' Miller is philosophical: 'I laughed at that and I've talked to [the author] Gabe Essoe since. He says, "It was not you, it was the production".'

Miller has embraced his place in history as one of the select few to don the loincloth far more enthusiastically than many actors who are better regarded or had longer reigns as the ape-man. 'I've been to at least ten or 15 Dum-Dums,' he says of the conventions of Burroughs devotees. 'Only on two occasions did I ever see another Tarzan attend. Ron Ely has never been at one I've been to. I've spoken at several of them. My licence plate is "X-Tarzan" ... I know of people who consider playing the role of Tarzan to have ruined their acting career. Bruce Bennett changed his name. His autobiography, written by a friend of mine, the title of it is *Please Don't Call Me Tarzan*. I know Mike Henry thought that whatever career he had being a second banana to Jackie Gleason, he thought Tarzan didn't help him out. I have never had the feeling that I didn't get a part because I had played the role of Tarzan. On the contrary. I played one called Tongo of the Jungle on *Gilligan's Island*. It was one of the most fun. When I go to film festivals, people ask for pictures of Tongo more than any other part that I've played, and I've played hundreds of parts ... I did enjoy everything in the film. I've enjoyed it ever since. It's fun being a cartoon.' Miller even goes so far as to say, 'There's been no negative aspect of playing the role of Tarzan. I've had it described as one of the longest-living hero figures in fiction, at least in the United States, that has entertained more little kids ... It's grouped together with Superman, Batman and Mickey Mouse all over the world ... It was a unique job. It was not like going to a circus, it was like being in a circus: go ride that elephant, play with that monkey, swing on that vine, jump from that right into the water ... What's more fun than that?'

The consequence of the *Tarzan the Ape Man* film for Miller's career as a physical instructor has been 'delightful.' He says, 'It's helped me get into offices of doctors at hospitals and places to talk to fourth graders about too much violence on television.' Messianic about physical education, Miller is the author of the fitness book *Toxic Waist? Get to Know Sweat!*, as well as the autobiography *Didn't You Used To Be ... What's His Name?*

'Having played Tarzan is probably one of the biggest joys of my life,' summarises Miller.

Weintraub may have been trying to improve Tarzan films, but on one level he was just as much the cliché of a movie mogul as Sol Lesser: for his second venture, he tried to repeat the formula of his previous film, seeking to re-recruit *en masse* the actors who played the four villains in *Tarzan's Greatest Adventure*, even though their characters had all met a grisly fate therein. Perhaps luckily for the growing integrity of the series, only Al Mulock was available to come back to portray a different interloper.

Tarzan the Magnificent, released in July 1960, was 88 minutes long and, as with the previous film, distributed by Paramount. It's not related to the

Burroughs novel of the same name, though does share something with his writing style in the shape of a narrative that alternates Tarzan's escapades with the adventures of a safari comprised of disparate types: a black engineer, a pompous ass (played by British character actor Lionel Jeffries), the latter's bored high society wife, a doctor and a smouldering sexpot. The safari members are passengers on a boat until it is blown up by the family of Coy Banton, a villain whom Tarzan is transporting to Kairobi [sic] to be punished for a number of murders, including that of a policeman friend of his. As the ape-man is indirectly responsible for their plight, he reluctantly allows the group to accompany him. Banton's brothers remain on his trail, led by their father Abel (John Carradine).

Tarzan fans could live with the absence of Jane and the reduced role of Cheeta but a refinement too far for some was the absence for the first time since talkies began of a Tarzan yodel. Robert Day's able direction, the Kenyan location shooting and the reversed chase element of the screenplay by Day and Berne Giler all make for an evocative, taut and exciting picture similar to its (Weintraub) predecessor, if not quite as good – with one exception. Just as *Tarzan's Greatest Adventure* had a set-piece mano-a-mano battle between the ape-man and the chief villain atop a cliff, so this picture culminates in Tarzan and Banton fighting to the finish. The scrap is a corker, starting on a bluff adjacent to a waterfall, descending into a river and winding up on rocky shore. It's a rumble in the jungle that is a vicious, grimacing, spiteful affair for its entire five-minute duration. Scott had always prided himself on doing his own stunts and the fact that his adversary was played by top Hollywood stuntman Jock Mahoney only added to the scene's power.

And Scott's reward for this? To lose his job to the actor who played the man whom in the film he subdues and drags off to state justice. Though Scott's technique had blossomed as his character's vocabulary had widened, the producer had decided he wanted a leaner, more agile man in the lead role. Scott subsequently made some sword-and-sandals pictures in Europe before his career sputtered to a halt in the mid-'60s. Though Weintraub must have paid off the remaining two years on his contract and though he was able to milk the convention and signing-booth circuits, his death in 2007, aged 80, found Scott penniless and – having left a trail of wives, children and debts behind him – pretty much friendless.

Scott not only made two of history's best Tarzan pictures, but is unique on a couple of counts: he straddled monochrome and colour Tarzan movies and portrayed the ape-man as both a pidgin English speaker and an articulate individual.

With both Harvey Hayutin and Gordon Scott dispensed with, Weintraub – having already made significant changes to the franchise – pursued a new vision for Tarzan.

He explained in an interview, '...50 percent of our profits are made aboard ... I want to stress the international aspect, make Tarzan somewhat of a world traveller ... I'd like to do something in Peru, or India, perhaps ... He's international; every country thinks he belongs to them.'

As for the leaner, more agile man Weintraub recruited for the lead role, Denny Miller says, 'Jock Mahoney was one of the best stuntmen in the history of stuntmen in Hollywood. He was an athlete. I've heard people say he could vault over three horses from the side and not touch them other than the middle one and just the saddle. He could stand in the saddle and ride at full speed. He had all those wonderful attributes because he had a strong, agile, coordinated body.' Mahoney wasn't merely a stuntman though. Graduating to *bona fide* actor, he appeared in many action films and became world famous by playing the title character in the early-'50s TV Western series *The Range Rider*. Weintraub of course had become cognisant of Mahoney's physical qualities when he saw the rushes of *Tarzan the Magnificent*. Having lost out to Lex Barker over a dozen years previously, Mahoney was in a fairly long tradition in Tarzan movies of actors who got the ape-man role second-time-around. Six-foot-four and devoid of body fat, he was ostensibly perfect for the role.

Weintraub plumped for India as his first exotic location, recruiting John Guillermin to direct Robert Hardy Andrews' script. *Tarzan Goes to India* sees Tarzan requested to come to the sub-continent by his friend the Maharajah (played by Murad) and his beautiful daughter Princess Kamara (Simi) because they are very concerned about the construction timeframe of a power plant and dam: it is so tight that it will not enable the shipping to safety of a herd of 300 elephants whose home ground the plant is to be built upon. Bryce (Leo Gordon), the man tasked with erecting the plant, is an old adversary of the ape-man, having run into him on Tarzan's home turf when he was poaching ivory. Naturally, he is left cold by Tarzan's pleas to postpone the construction long enough for him to save the elephants by driving them through a mountain pass. Tarzan joins forces with a young boy named Jai (played by an actor of the same name), a Mowgli variant who travels around aback an elephant. Jai is a crucial buddy-figure for Tarzan in the absence not just of Jane but also of Cheeta, as well as a point of identification for a great wedge of the intended audience. Everything ape-man-related Weintraub did from hereon would feature a character similar to Jai. Not only does Tarzan save the elephants, he then uses his pachyderm friends to assist in the finishing of the power plant.

The fruits of a two month location shoot in places like Bangalore, Bombay and Madras are evident on screen. They are enrichened by this being the first Tarzan film shot in CinemaScope widescreen and underlined by noted Indian musician Ravi Shankar contributing to the exotic soundtrack.

It seems a shame that though he sanctioned Tarzan tussling with a rogue elephant, a leopard and a cobra, Weintraub neglected to take advantage of the perfect opportunity afforded by the location to depict the ape-man battling a tiger. At least Tarzan's yodel is reinstated. Having evidently forgiven them for the Denny Miller picture, Weintraub granted *Tarzan Goes to India*'s distribution rights to MGM, who released the 86-minute film in March 1962. They responded by giving him the highest Tarzan grosses to date. Even if no doubt greatly assisted by the vast audiences receptive to this particular picture in India itself, this was quite a feat.

So what's not to love? Well, both Mahoney's casting and the international aspect create problems. The internationalism is a perfectly valid idea and a good way to inject variety, but when Burroughs had Tarzan visiting far-flung locales in 'Tarzan and the Castaways'/'The Quest of Tarzan' and *Tarzan and the 'Foreign Legion'*, he set up the relocation properly. Robert Hardy Andrews does not. We are mystified as to how Tarzan and the Maharajah are friends, and why the ape-man is well-known on a different continent, and – because the screenplay does not explain the character's Lord Greystoke hinterland – how he has the wherewithal to charter a plane. (The film begins with the ape-man dropping into a lake in the titular country, having needed only to dispense with his flying helmet and goggles to be in traditional Tarzan costume.)

As for Mahoney himself, he is in great condition for a man of his age – but that age is 42, only one year younger than Weissmuller when he was belatedly pensioned off. In many scenes, his vintage is painfully apparent, especially ones involving that beneath-the-chin angle that is so unforgiving for the over-forties no matter how well-preserved. His lank, swept-back hair only adds to the impression of looking at your uncle. His non-chiselled features are also incongruously, almost farcically, ordinary. And fat-free though his body is, it also teaches us the value of the cinema shorthand that the muscular physiques of previous Tarzan actors had constituted. Yes, our brains tell us that a man brought up in the treetops would more likely have a body like Mahoney's than Gordon Scott's, but our eyes insist that he is a big long streak. Cruel as it may sound, Mahoney as Tarzan is a joke.

Though Tarzan movies had always been popular, *Tarzan Goes to India* was released into a world that was unexpectedly newly receptive to Tarzan books, a surge of interest that of course fed back into the cinema incarnation.

A school employee in Los Angeles suburb Downey was the reason. Her profession was librarian, a breed with which Edgar Rice Burroughs had an edgy relationship while he was alive. In March 1922, for instance, the *Wisconsin Library Bulletin* featured an article by one Professor Noble that condemned his books on grounds of both their allegedly harmful moral effects on children and the unlikeliness of their plot devices. Burroughs later stiffly declined a request from a library in Tarzana for a set of his books on the grounds that the main Los Angeles Public Library had banned his works because they supposedly had no literary value. Not that he didn't have nice comments from library staff: an English librarian copied him in on a letter he had written in rebuttal to Professor North, while a Syracuse, New York librarian, in denying to the author a rumour that had reached his ears that a ban was about to be enacted, pointed out that his books were so popular that they had problems keeping 'them from being stolen from the shelves.' However, Burroughs' hurt and hostile feelings on librarians in general can be gleaned from this passage of a letter from 1928: 'I, too, have noticed how my name is always ignored by literary writers, librarians and other members of the intelligentsia … I wonder why they dislike me so much.' The Los Angeles ban outlasted Burroughs himself by two decades.

The issue relating to the Downey school librarian was of a nature that Burroughs had actually encountered while he was alive. A priest had once contacted Sol Lesser threatening to denounce Tarzan from the pulpit over the fact that the ape-man and Jane were living in sin. As he was clearly talking about the films, the holy man was actually on firm ground, but when Lesser passed on Burroughs' message that he should check out the wedding ceremony in the book *The Return of Tarzan*, he was placated. In removing from the shelves two donated Tarzan books on similar moral grounds, the Downey librarian – who perhaps mercifully remained anonymous – found herself referred to in terms like 'spoilsport.' She was acting on a complaint by a parent, but of course there was no reason why she should have meekly surrendered in the face of that complaint.

A scandal of minuscule proportions ensued. The Downey ban became public knowledge on 27 December 1961 when newspapers across America picked up an Associated Press story about it. That the district's imposition of a similar ban on Zane Grey titles was mentioned only in a footnote indicates that editors were printing the story not because they were taking it seriously but because they were rejoicing in the opportunity to run headlines like 'Librarian Trees Tarzan On Morals Rap' and humorous references to the jungle drums beating out the rumour that Tarzan and Jane had been living in sin in their treehouse, et groan cetera. As Supt Bruce Moore of the Downey Unified Schools District said that he and his colleagues were opposed to any ban, and as Sol Lesser was responding to reporters' phone calls with the line about *The Return of Tarzan* he had trotted out to the clergyman several years previously – and as the inevitable Burroughs fans, ostensibly outraged but secretly pleased to be able to show off their knowledge, were sending corrections into newspapers – this hardly had the potential to develop into a media storm. Two days after the story broke, papers were running headlines like, 'Are Tarzan and Jane Wed? South of NC Nobody Cares', and in a turn of events that would no doubt have infuriated Burroughs, a (different) librarian canvassed for his opinion said he only objected to ERB's books on literary grounds. The story was dead before the year was.

Fate, though, works in peculiar ways. With the subject of Tarzan books suddenly all over the newspapers, it reminded people of an almost forgotten pleasure. It also prompted some weaned on them to consider the possibility of passing on their childhood addiction to the kids they themselves now had. Additionally, it alerted fans of the Tarzan movies of ape-man adventures to which they had paid little attention or even of which they had not been previously cognisant. Demand for Tarzan novels shot through the roof, and continued to do so into 1962, a publicity boon marking Tarzan's half-century that could not have been more advantageous if it had been planned. The only problem was, that demand could not be met.

Here was where the haughty incompetence of Cyril Ralph Rothmund had categorically backfired. The general manager of ERB, Inc had in the dozen years since Burroughs' death presided over a shocking decay in the business with whose profitability he was charged. Not only had he allowed every single one of the books published by ERB, Inc – which included nine Tarzan titles – to fall out of print, but he had refused to license their release as paperbacks by other publishers. That format had existed as far back as the 1930s but in recent years had begun a big growth in popularity. The fact that it was later estimated that worldwide paperback sales of Burroughs books between 1962 and 1968 totalled 50 million – more sales than all the previous years combined in all editions – gives an indication of how costly this was. In 1961/62, the only Burroughs ape-man adventures still orderable at bookstores and libraries were the Grosset & Dunlap budget editions licensed from McClurg. Grosset & Dunlap's sales now increased by 25%. In his usual style, Rothmund didn't bother affording New York booksellers Jack Biblo and Jack Tannen the courtesy of an answer when they wrote to ERB, Inc – they estimated 'several times' – about the publishing situation with Tarzan books, requests for which they found themselves swamped by in the wake of the newspaper reports. This latter discourtesy cost the company even more money.

Biblo and Tannen evidently made the assumption that ERB, Inc's apparent indifference indicated that they no longer had a financial interest in the character's prose adventures. They instigated a copyright search at the Library of Congress. US copyright law at that time dictated that copyright on works expired after 28 years unless renewed. The pair found to their amazement that ERB, Inc had not renewed the copyright on approximately half of Burroughs' published books. This meant that they could, if so they so wished, re-publish these books themselves and – as would be the situation with any other public domain work – pocket all the profits. They quickly set up Canaveral Press, and by April of 1962 were soliciting orders for 21 Burroughs books, three of them Tarzan titles. Even so, they were actually beaten to the punch by Dover Publications, who released ten Tarzan novels in four paperback compendiums. Paperback publisher Ace also joined in the ERB free-for-all. Ballantine Books, meanwhile, struck a deal with ERB, Inc for an official paperback line. Chaotic and confusing though the situation was, it at least meant that the demand for prose Tarzan could now be fulfilled. By November 1963, *Life* magazine was reporting that the ERB re-releases had 'sold something more than 10 million copies, almost one thirtieth the total annual sales of all paperbacks in the US.' Ace and Ballantine had ordered second printings of 300,000 and 110,000 per title respectively of their Tarzan books, of which Ballantine had already issued a dozen and planned the remaining ten. The 'Tarzan of the Paperbacks' special report in which that statistic appeared in one of the country's most iconic magazines was, of course, itself a boost to the tsunami of publicity on which the books' sales were riding.

Playwright, screenwriter, journalist and soon-to-be novelist Gore Vidal – a boyhood ERB fan – was prompted by the boom to re-read several Burroughs books. He delivered his verdict in the December 1963 edition of men's glossy *Esquire*: 'Though Burroughs is innocent of literature and cannot reproduce human speech, he does have a gift very few writers of any kind possess: he can describe action vividly.' He concluded on a note of intellectualism of which the concurrent Burroughs retrospectives were innocent: 'James Bond, Mike Hammer and Tarzan are all dream-selves, and the aim of each is to establish personal primacy in a world which in reality diminishes the individual. Among adults, increasing popularity of these lively inferior fictions strikes me as a most significant (and unbearably sad) phenomenon.'

The Wall Street Journal and *The New York Times* had previously reported on the Burroughs revival too. That revival was massively assisted by Rothmund's retirement that year. (Robert Barrett: 'He was asked to retire.') Almost symbolically, when the three Burroughs children assumed control of the company and investigated its safe, they found within it half a million words of unpublished Burroughs prose that nobody had known existed, including many complete novels. Needless to say, a wave of brand new ERB books shortly began appearing.

The free-for-all didn't last long. Lawyers working for ERB, Inc discovered that the copyright on the magazine versions of the Burroughs books had in fact been renewed. The subsequent book versions were therefore automatically protected. (As it's difficult to imagine anyone but the magazine publishers themselves renewing those copyrights, it would seem that ERB, Inc were an unintended beneficiary of their conscientiousness regarding their own periodicals.) The fact that Canaveral were allowed to continue publishing Burroughs hardbacks of which Ace and Ballantine took the paperback rights suggests that the corporation may have felt obliged to come to an accommodation with the 'unofficial' domestic publishers in light of uncertainty over the copyright issue within the United States itself. However, publishers all around the world were now advised to cease and desist.

The Ballantine paperbacks came with the pointed banner slogan 'Authorised Edition,' but their dull typography and boring cover illustrations made them somewhat less covetable than the Ace books, which had dynamic cover layouts and exciting art by Roy Krenkel and Frank Frazetta. Because Frazetta was also used for covers and spot illustrations by Canaveral, and because he provided some new Ace covers in the early 1970s, his vision of the ape-man became by default as important and defining for a certain group as St John's had been for the readers of his era. Most Frazetta fans think the artist was not working at the top of his game when rendering Tarzan. His pictures certainly weren't as lushly erotic and vibrant as either his own celebrated Conan paperback cover paintings or Boris Vallejo's Tarzan paperback covers of the 1970s. (The beautiful Vallejo cover painting gracing this book first appeared on Ballantine's 1977 edition of *Tarzan the Magnificent*.) Nor were they as dynamic as Neal Adams' covers for the same Ballantine series that Vallejo's pictures graced. The possible exception, not intended for book publication, was a watercolour (date unknown, but judging by its explicitness, much later than the '60s) called *Tarzan meets La of Opar*, in which a bound ape-man is being presented to the High Priestess by two naked women. La is herself proffering her naked pudenda to the captive. At the insistence of the gallery buying the piece, Frazetta painted out the erection he had given Tarzan.

There were also 'new' Tarzan books on the back of the Burroughs boom. Back in 1950, *The New York Times* had claimed that the just-passed Burroughs had left behind 'approximately 15 incompleted Tarzan tales.' This intriguing figure has been scaled back by subsequent archive research to two, plus two humorous playlets, *Tarzan & Jane: A Jungleogue* (1933, a 16-page distillation of *Tarzan of the Apes*) and *Tarzan's Good Deed Today* (circa 1940s, a three-page play for children). However, there was some complete Tarzan material that had never been published in book form and one complete novel that had never been published in any form. In the new atmosphere of hunger for Tarzan prose, *Tarzan and the Madman* was transformed from a Tarzan self-parody considered unfit to print by both magazines and ultimately Burroughs himself into a myth-shrouded 'lost' ape-man novel. Either that or ERB, Inc sanctioned its release because they thought at that point that it might well be one of the only Tarzan works to which they had exclusive publication rights. Its appearance in June 1964 from Canaveral rather spoiled the dignified end to the series that *Tarzan and the 'Foreign Legion'* had constituted. Things were redeemed a little when in December 1964 the only other completed Tarzan prose material that had not appeared in book form – the pulps-published Tarzan short stories 'Tarzan and the Jungle Murders' and 'Tarzan and the Champion' and novella 'The Quest of Tarzan' – were mopped up and issued together by Canaveral as the reasonably solid *Tarzan and the Castaways*. It was still a slightly flimsy coda, though.

In a sense, most of the Tarzan books published from the Burroughs boom onwards were new. In 1962, the '60s may not yet have been a swinging proposition but it was already clear that times and values had changed profoundly since the ape-man's entrée. Burroughs fans will swear blind that the author was not as racist as some make out. They have some ammunition insofar as many Negros – as society was then beginning to feel uncomfortable about calling them – were depicted by him as noble, intelligent and brave. But more were depicted as brutish, stupid and vicious. This in itself was not completely damning – it would be absurd to have white baddies but ban the depiction of black villainy – but there is no getting around the fact that some of Burroughs' lines portray the very state of being black in pejorative terms. In the era of JFK and Martin Luther King, much of the public would be repulsed – and no doubt many publishers were – by this in a way they would not have only a decade before. (It's interesting that no parent seems to have been recorded as demanding Tarzan books be removed from library shelves on the grounds of racism over those 50 years.) Ballantine's versions of the Tarzan books cut out many of the racial epithets and toned down colloquial speech that might be interpreted as insulting such as Esmeralda's 'Lawd-a-mighty' dialogue in *Tarzan of the Apes*. Even innocuous references to skin colour were sometimes altered. Canaveral meanwhile completely removed anti-black comments from their compendium *Tarzan and the Tarzan Twins* on the grounds that the book's child demographic did not know enough to be able to recognise and reject bigotry. Both the Ballantine and Canaveral alterations were made with the blessing and in some cases encouragement of ERB, Inc. Inevitably, over the years the situation became one wherein many readers – and one suspects some reprint publishers – didn't even know that the books in their hands were bowdlerised.

There were also new ape-man tales Burroughs had nothing to do with. 'Today's great interest in the adventures of Tarzan and some of the many other exciting characters created by the master storyteller Edgar Rice Burroughs has brought a demand for new, fresh Tarzan stories.' So read a blurb on the second page of a series of five Tarzan novels published in 1964/65 credited to Barton Werper. The name was a pseudonym (derived from a character in *Tarzan and the Jewels of Opar*) for married couple Peter and Peggy Scott, who along with their publishers Gold Star were taking advantage of the confusion over whether or not Tarzan was in the public domain. This was arguably a reasonable enough pursuit, and the assertion of an interest in new Tarzan stories would transpire to be demonstrably true, but the execution was more questionable. *Tarzan and the Silver Globe, Tarzan and the Cave City, Tarzan and the Snake People, Tarzan and the Abominable Snowmen* and *Tarzan and the Winged Invader* reveal the Scotts to be not Burroughs aficionados like Stuart J Byrne (*Tarzan on Mars*) but merely jobbing writers. It shows in their lack of knowledge not so much of names but of established details and modes of behaviour: Kala is portrayed as a mother of many when in fact she bore only one child; the Mangani – stupid and easily distracted in Burroughs' books – are given almost human-level intelligence and powers of mental retention; Tarzan, Jane and La are unrecognisable as the characters we know: the first immature where we had always known him as noble, the second stuck-up where Burroughs' version exuded warmth and the third crudely strumpet-like in comparison with the subtly sensual template. The Scotts take it upon themselves to create a new backstory for La, which would be a bloody cheek even if it were not ludicrous (she's now a 300-year-old Venusian). Over and above the unfamiliarity with the territory, their writing is sloppy, full of inconsistencies and repetition and guilty of such bad pacing that they throw away what could be entire chapters in a page or two of blurred action. The Scotts also directly lift passages from Burroughs books, and if we can forgive that legally – at the time it appeared it was safe to do so –

we can hardly extend the same understanding on aesthetic or moral grounds. Burroughs was mocked by many for his formulaic style but it is pastiche as bad as this that makes one see just how nuanced – and therefore difficult to emulate – that style was. Not that readers seemed to care overmuch: that Tarzan was once again a licence to print money was demonstrated by the fact that Gold Star only refrained from issuing further books in the series because of legal action by ERB, Inc.

The number of pirated and plagiarised Tarzan – and other – films had diminished in recent years as reliable and quick global communication had made it more difficult to put on show unauthorised work without it coming to the attention of legally interested parties in the First World, and as Third World countries anxious to avail themselves of the benefits of cooperation with the developed world began submitting to their standards regarding policing copyright. However, the confusion over the issue of his copyright status created a new rush to make Tarzan pictures, all of which – whether the makers knew it or not – were illicit. Early-to-mid 1960s Italian, French, Russian, Jamaican, Czechoslovakian and Indian Tarzan productions were either planned or finished before ERB, Inc and/or Sy Weintraub put the relevant people right. Most of these productions were the usual laughable, tacky and lost-in-translation Third World fare. (One Indian production even had Christine Keeler of the Profumo sex scandal taking a role.) An American production (possibly with some West German involvement) was to have featured Brick Bardo in an adaptation of *Jungle Tales of Tarzan*. What on the surface sounds reasonably intriguing becomes anything but when it is discovered that the scriptwriter was one Ron Haydock, who had just started on a literary career as Vin Saxon studded with books rejoicing in titles like *Perverted Lust*, *Sex-a-Reenos* and *Pagan Lesbians*. Some projects however sound like they could have been fairly worthy. The impressively-built Joe Robinson took the lead in the Italian production *Tarzan Roi de la Force Brutale*. After the legal manoeuvres, it was released with Tarzan's name changed to 'Thaur'. The Jamaican production – *Tarzan and the Jewels of Opar* – had an imported New York crew and, playing the ape-man, Olympic pole-vaulter Don Bragg.

More legal action from ERB, Inc caused Charlton Comics to cease publishing the Tarzan title they had started in December 1964, but this story was one that involved more love than avarice and furthermore had a positive outcome. In 1962, Western had parted company with their former client Dell and begun publishing a Tarzan title in their new Gold Key line, although the fact that they continued the numbering and employed the creative staff from the Dell publication meant that for readers it was the same comic, even if it changed its title to *Tarzan of the Apes* from November '63. Apart from its beautiful painted covers, it was certainly the same staid proposition it had always been. Western's comfortable world, however, was shaken up by the appearance of the first issue of Charlton's *Jungle Tales of Tarzan*. The comic publisher had decided to adapt that particular book because it was one of those whose copyright status was then in question. Editor Pat Masulli stated inside that 'the true flavour of Tarzan as created by Mr Burroughs has rarely been tasted in comic books. We intend to change that.' The four issues of the title published through to July 1965 – written by Joe Gill and drawn by Sam Glanzman – certainly succeeded in that objective of authenticity and were surely the best Tarzan comics published to that date. ERB, Inc managed to get them off the shelves on the grounds that, public domain questions aside, Tarzan was a registered trademark; a tactic that would stand them in good stead.

Nonetheless, the artistic gauntlet had been thrown down, and Western were prompted to (ahem) ape Charlton's strategy of being faithful to the original. Enter the third famous Tarzan artist, Russ Manning, who had already been responsible for Western's Burroughs-faithful *Korak, Son of Tarzan* title and who now set about illustrating, in an elegant style a universe away from Jesse Marsh's scratchy naïveté, a series of Gaylord Dubois-written adaptations of the original Burroughs novels that for many provide the definitive comics depiction of Lord Greystoke to this very day. The only element of Manning's beautiful work to which anyone could object was the colour he gave Tarzan's loincloth: what jungle animal gives rise to a crimson pelt?

That jump in quality of Western's Tarzan comics – though high – was probably the least significant of the massive changes that had been wrought in the Tarzan landscape since December '61. History no more records the name of the Downey parent who demanded that the supposedly immoral Tarzan books be removed from the shelves than it does the librarian to whom s/he made that demand. Said parent, however, had an effect akin to a publishing earthquake – proving, some might suggest, that history is written by the whiners.

While the Tarzan publishing business was going through its turmoil, Sy Weintraub was preparing the follow-up to *Tarzan Goes to India*.

With his choice of actor and his concept of a globe-trotting Tarzan apparently vindicated by box office returns, he now decided to send Mahoney to Thailand. Although the country depicted in the resultant 92-minute film *Tarzan's Three Challenges* was a nameless generic Oriental kingdom, full use was made of Thailand's breathtaking backdrops, including jungles, temples, giant Buddha statues, elaborately decorated elephants and an army of exotic dancing girls. In fact it's rather unfortunate that the man playing Tarzan didn't match up to such splendour.

Once again, the ape-man's presence is requested in a faraway land in which he inexplicably has contacts. He arrives by parachute, observed by a child who runs to him with an excited cry of recognition. His mission is to protect a young spiritual heir named Kashi (Ricky Der) from the machinations of one Khan, brother of the dying spiritual leader Tarim, both latter roles played by Der's real-life uncle Woody Strode. In order to prove his worthiness to be Kashi's protector in the dangerous jungles that form the path to the Crown City where the succession ceremony will occur, Tarzan must face Khan in three trials, two physical, one cerebral. Though Cheeta is again absent, anthropomorphic comic relief is provided by a baby elephant named Hungry.

The script by Berne Giler and Robert Day is reasonably good and Day's direction also fine, but Mahoney is once again a problem. That he was now the oldest Tarzan ever is painfully apparent in places, especially during the challenge in which he has to endure buffalos pulling on his arms from opposite directions: as he grimaces in agony, there seems no end to his chins. Matters were further complicated by a dramatic drop in Mahoney's weight when he picked up amoebic dysentery, dengue fever and pneumonia. Never powerful-looking in the first place, by the end of the film he seems farcically tired, frail and aged. Accepting that he has bested Strode in a hand-to-hand battle, engendered by Khan exercising his right to challenge the succession, is simply impossible.

This would be Mahoney's last Tarzan film. The talk afterwards was of a contract dissolved by mutual agreement, but the realities of Hollywood are such that Weintraub almost certainly paid the actor off, even if an exhausted Mahoney – who took 18 months to regain his lost weight – was probably glad of the respite. Weintraub doesn't seem to have concluded that he had made a mistake. Even before *Tarzan Goes to India*, he had been talking about taking the Tarzan franchise to the small screen, and with these plans now lain, and with them being by definition long-terms ones involving arduous week-in, week-out shooting, he needed somebody of a younger age than the 44 that Mahoney was upon the June 1963 release of *Tarzan's Three Challenges*.

Mahoney does have his fans. Al Bohl enthuses, 'Jock Mahoney in my opinion was the best Tarzan. He played him as a very intelligent man who was intuitive with social graces, had a pretty solid world view of culture and also at the same time was very physical. His interaction with animals showed him as being one that was very engaged with the animals. A snake, he respected it but at the same time it didn't shock him. Even the way he would interact with monkeys and stuff showed that he understood how to play the character.' It's doubtful though that Bohl would find many who agree with him – even amongst those Burroughs aficionados who had always thought rippling, bulging muscles were not the likely outcome of a simian rearing. With Mahoney, such Burroughs fans learned the wisdom of the adage, 'Be careful what you wish for – it may come true.'

The two years and 11 months between *Tarzan's Three Challenges* and the next entry in the series in May 1966 was the longest gap between Tarzan flicks since 1927, but it did not indicate a lack of activity.

The hiatus is partly explained by the fact that a new Tarzan actor had to be chosen, partly by the fact that Weintraub was working out an elaborate plan to use the film series to piggy-back the new actor into a TV show and partly by the fact that Weintraub was stockpiling productions shot back-to-back. Partly, also, it was because he was busy shaking up the concept, or, for younger readers, rebooting the franchise.

The usual stratospherically high number of candidates interviewed to be the new Tarzan was given out (400 this time), but as is common, possibly even standard, in the cinema Tarzan story, the lucky man was actually approached by the producers rather than vice versa. Mike Henry was a 28-year-old footballer (American variety) of seven years' standing. In addition to thrilling the fans of the Los Angeles Rams with his exploits as a line-backer, he had a smattering of acting experience, having performed some small TV and film parts in the early '60s. He also had a brain: though Weintraub was a Rams fan, he got the idea of trying out Henry when he watched a TV documentary that the latter had produced about the team. After Henry passed his screen-test, Weintraub signed him up, though stipulated he lose 20 pounds. Henry made another sacrifice of his own volition, retiring from football. He may have been a little stiff as an actor, but Mike Henry was probably the best-looking Tarzan so far. His six-foot-four frame was a study in physical perfection, packed with rippling muscles where Weissmuller had been merely trim and toned, yet not tending towards the over-solidity of Scott, while his handsome face not only seemed to have come straight from the pencil of Hal Foster but was devoid of Barker's rich-boy softness.

This well-'ard Michelangelo's David was to appear in Tarzan movies like none before, even if they were on the update-and-toughen gradient Weintraub had begun seven years previously. His entrée was *Tarzan and the Valley Of Gold*. That the picture – distributed by American International – was originally named *Tarzan '66* (posters with that title were prepared) indicates how anxious Weintraub was to make Henry a Tarzan for a new age. Though the original title was abandoned, the content of the movie screams out the zeitgeist and asserts that, jungle lord though he might be, Tarzan inhabits the same world that has recently been transformed by the Beatles, James Bond and sexual liberation. There is some wacky opening title credit lettering and modishly jazzy soundtrack music. Meanwhile, 007 (then defined by Sean Connery's portrayal) is poured on by the bucketload: Tarzan is seen with short, neat hair, wearing a suit, carrying a briefcase and boarding planes and helicopters. That Henry is the first film Tarzan allowed a hairy chest seems another nod to the hirsute Connery. As per usual, Tarzan doesn't get up to hanky panky with the film's *de riguer* smouldering sex bomb, but there is a deliberate frisson of eroticism in the record skimpiness of his loincloth. There's even a little Bondian humour, such as when Tarzan kills a baddie by toppling a giant Coca Cola bottle on him, or when he cracks when preparing to turn from civilised man to ape-man, 'I'll need a good rope, a hunting knife and a soft piece of leather.' Weintraub himself said of the new Tarzan in a press statement, '…he is the embodiment of culture, suavity and style, who is equally at home in a posh night club or the densest jungle.'

The ape-man's adversary Augustus Vinaro (David Optashu) is slavishly in Bond-movie-villain tradition: a rich madman, he blows people up with elaborate time-bombs and employs a hulking, Oddjob-like goon (Don MeGowan) whose very name – Mr Train – is of Ian Fleming-esque parodic formality. Even Vinaro's death – being buried under an avalanche of the gold he craves – is tangentially reminiscent of the gold paint-sprayed demise of Jill Masterson in *Goldfinger*. Though script writer Clair Huffaker had a grounding in Western material rather than espionage pictures – not many were versed in the latter young medium – he had clearly been employed because of the vast knowledge of pacy adventure he had gained on TV shows like *Rawhide*, *Bonanza*, *Lawman* and *The Virginian* and movies like *Seven Ways from Sundown* and *The Comancheros*.

Tarzan also got nasty under Henry. His extraordinarily bloodthirsty trio of films saw Weintraub take full advantage of the relaxing of rules on movie violence in recent years. However, though the grown men in the theatre audience had plenty of realistic bloodshed to entertain them and the grown women plenty of Henry's body to occupy them, Weintraub's estimation of the age group and gender of a large proportion of the demographic was made clear by the fact that he again included a young boy character, in this case ten-year-old Ramel (Manuel Padilla Jr). Meanwhile, should hilariously lugubrious and wizened old Incas need someone with whom to identify, Francisco Riquerio as Manco does the honours. His crown looks like it weighs more than him, although not more than his bottom lip. Despite the changes, Weintraub perseveres with his Tarzan-as-globetrotter strategy. The action takes place in Mexico, with Weintraub's Banner production company showing off the splendour of the Acapulco-adjacent jungles, Chapultepec castle, Plaza de Toros bullring and Aztec ruins in the full colour in which many felt the Weissmuller film *Tarzan and the Mermaids* should have depicted its Acapulco settings.

The ape-man is summoned to the country by Ruiz, an old friend. When he gets there, he finds himself tasked with the objective of preventing Vinaro – who has slaughtered Ruiz – looting the ancient treasures of the Incan people of Ramel, whom he has abducted. Tarzan is assisted by Vinaro's ex Sophia (played by Nancy Kovack, but originally intended to be portrayed by Sharon Tate before, it's rumoured, the latter's agent decided she was too good for such material), a chimpanzee (Dinky, not Cheeta), a lion and a leopard. Though Tarzan has the expected hand-to-hand fights, he is also shown in more high tech combat: grounding a helicopter with bolas (the crash immolating the crew) and commanding a tank. Like all the Henry Tarzans, the 90-minute, Robert Day-directed film is entertaining without being great, and perhaps more interesting (especially from this distance of time) for its commercial objectives than its artistic achievements.

Many viewers unfamiliar with the more cosmopolitan ape-man of Burroughs' books must have felt that Tarzan as a global adventurer was a totally contrived device unmoored to logic. Had they read the film's Ballantine paperback novelisation by Fritz Leiber – which joined the dots between the prose and screen Tarzans – it would have made more sense to them.

'It was Ballantine Books who contacted Hulbert Burroughs, Ed's son, about continuing the Tarzan series, because they were reprinting the Tarzan books,' says Robert R Barrett. Whitman had published a 282-page novelisation for young readers of the *Tarzan and the Lost Safari* film, believed to have been written by Frank Castle (Burroughs' is the only name on the cover), but a brand new Tarzan novel for adults was the type of eventuality about which many 'ERBivores' had long fantasised. That Leiber was a celebrated author in a field adjacent to Burroughs', and an ERB fan to boot, was additionally exciting. However, even *Tarzan and the Valley of Gold* being conferred canon status by the '25' on its cover – continuing the number sequence from *Tarzan and the Castaways* – couldn't hide the curiousness of the fact that, the very first time ERB, Inc had authorised a non-Burroughs Tarzan novel for adults, it was not a new adventure but an adaptation of a film.

Though the movie Tarzan had moved back toward the prose Tarzan in recent years, a novelisation of a Tarzan picture written in a Burroughs vein is something of a contradiction: the two are different and often conflicting beasts. Then there is the fact that novelisations are even more the bastard offspring of literature than pulps. Leiber – an award-winning author in the fields of science fiction and sword and sorcery – would have understood the latter point. It was presumably eagerness to fulfil a longstanding ambition to follow in his author hero's footsteps that led him to agree to take on the job.

Leiber approaches the task at hand seriously. The book is a solid 300-plus pages. Moreover, he doggedly strives to maintain continuity with Burroughs' books via numerous footnotes that refer to previous Tarzan adventures, and to reconcile the traduced/simplified screen version of Tarzan with the prose original where he can. On the debit side, he is also anxious to show off his research in other areas: his wodges of Brazilian history and travelogue are the kind of action-interrupting waffle Burroughs would never have included in his fiction, even if he wasn't averse to going into mildly boring detail about the customs and landscapes of imaginary places. Meanwhile, as it's inconceivable that he hasn't read *Tarzan's Quest* and *Tarzan and 'The Foreign Legion'*, one is not quite sure what point Leiber is making by portraying the ape-man as puzzled by his own agelessness.

Throughout, Leiber enriches the material he has been given by the movie studio, providing additional backstory, motivation and symbolism without contradicting or obstructing the narrative derived from the Huffaker screenplay. He also impressively displays discipline in dispensing with his usual postmodern style for a straight-ahead adventure yarn in Burroughs' spirit.

Sales of the book were not encouraging, although some have suggested that this might have been because Ballantine confused potential purchasers by utilising a cover illustration that had already been seen on their edition of *Tarzan and the Golden Lion*. Because of those poor sales, whatever hopes fans were harbouring for Tarzan books – more Leiber stories, perhaps even original ones, or Leiber being authorised to finish the unpublished Burroughs Tarzan tales whose existence was publicly known of if not their correct number, or even John Coleman Burroughs, now a published science fiction author himself, taking on the task of continuing his dad's character's adventures – had to remain in the realm of dreams. There would be no new ape-man novels for another two decades. The Burroughs boom, it would seem, had already bumped up against its natural ceiling.

Though Mike Henry's tenure in the loincloth spanned exactly two years in theatrical release date terms, his lifespan as Tarzan was in reality more fleeting. He filmed his three Tarzan movies one after the other – a process lasting about 12 months – and handed in his notice not only before the third was completed but prior to the first's cinema release. The second, *Tarzan and the Great River*, was shot in Brazil while *Valley of Gold* was in the editing suite. There was supposed to be a hiatus between that and the third, *Tarzan and the Jungle Boy*, allowing for a rest period prior to filming commencing on the TV series, but Weintraub instead decided to take advantage of the good weather in Brazil and get the third movie in the can. In addition to the arduousness of shooting in succession three feature-length films whose physicality was by definition greater than that of the average Hollywood production, Henry suffered an endless series of misfortunes: a chimp bite that left him feverish, dysentery, an ear infection and a liver infection. The third movie turned into a nightmare when torrential rain reduced production to a crawl. Emotionally and physically exhausted and – with the imminent shooting of the television series – facing what seemed like eternity far away from home, Henry informed Weintraub that he was finished in the role.

With the Tarzan TV series due to start filming in a month, Weintraub was bereft of a leading man. Worse was to come for him when Henry pursued a $875,000 civil action for maltreatment, abuse and working conditions detrimental to his health. That the legal notion of 'duty of care' was then not fully established and that Henry had indicated that in principle he was game for danger by insisting on doing his own stunts would have raised interesting points of law had the suit proceeded to hearing stage, but as Henry explained to *Filmfax* magazine in 2011, 'We amicably settled the whole thing out of court.'

When forced to dispense with his plan for a parallel TV and cinema Mike Henry Tarzan, Weintraub stumbled upon an actor who embodied possibly the perfect compromise between muscle-bound exaggeration and realistic leanness. Ron Ely was a 28-year-old with just a few scattered acting credits. He had already secured a part in one of the *Tarzan* TV episodes as an ape-man imposter, and Weintraub hurriedly upgraded him. Some reports have posited Ely as yet another actor to have secured the part at the second attempt, but he claimed in a later newspaper interview that he had decided after auditioning for the job Henry eventually obtained that he didn't want the role, because: 'Tarzan was nothing more than a muscle man, which I'm not.' With his good looks and his imposing six-foot-four height, Ely had two of the attributes associated with the ape-man. Though he didn't have the third – a mass of rippling muscles – Weintraub decided that his lean body would work. Unlike in the case of Jock Mahoney, he was right: Ely may not have possessed bulging biceps or a chest like a beer barrel but he was still visibly nobody's pushover.

That *Tarzan* the TV series even made it to the airwaves was a small miracle, for such were the production's travails, the crew became convinced it was jinxed. When filming started in February 1966 not far from Rio, torrential rains washed away specially constructed sets and then washed them away again when they were rebuilt. Mosquitoes, dysentery and fraught misunderstandings with locals were rife. Only five episodes had been filmed after five-and-a-half months, and the show was half a million dollars over budget. Co-producer Jon Epstein bailed. In May '66, filming was relocated to Mexico, where Weintraub spent close to $200,000 building new sets. The productivity went up a little, with five more episodes completed in two months, but lest the demoralised and battered crew think the curse of the programme had evaporated, a panicked elephant killed a trainer on set. Not long afterwards, Epstein's replacement Leon Benson himself left. Weintraub's hair is reported to have gone grey by the eight-month mark, by which time 11 episodes had been completed. There were 20 still to be made for the first season.

Ely had done his own stunts, with the inevitable consequences. A now well-known publicity photo of a heavily bandaged and plastered Ely demonstrated the 17 injuries he accrued during filming of the first season – lion bites, broken shoulder and cracked ribs among them – with numbered indicators. Though this photo was clearly over-the-top – he couldn't have had all the injuries at the same time, and the criss-crossing of some of the plasters was cartoonish – advertising the perils of playing Tarzan was perhaps a rather dangerous move by Weintraub considering the Henry litigation.

1966 was a bonanza year for live-action Tarzan, with three different actors being seen by the public in the role. NBC decided to transmit in part the Sol Lesser TV Tarzan project they had abandoned nearly a decade before. The three Gordon Scott pilots edited into a feature-length movie aired on 5 May 1966, the same month as *Tarzan and the Valley of Gold* reached the big screen. Either that Henry film had prompted NBC's move or else it was the imminent arrival of the Ely series. If the latter, it was a curious way for the network to herald its own show. Not only was the Scott vehicle poor quality, but its monochrome looked dated: the Ron Ely *Tarzan* was one of the first action-adventure television series seen in colour. The latter show made its debut on 8 September, one week earlier than originally planned following some scheduling skirmishes between NBC and ABC. Considering how behind with production Weintraub was, bringing it forward was not a wise move, but even less judicious was NBC's decision to invite all the remaining living movie Tarzans to a reunion in Mexico to arouse interest. Three showed up to meet Ely, and though Jock Mahoney was still in reasonable shape, the resultant publicity photos of him and Ely standing on a branch preparing to swing on vines beside the similarly loinclothed but profoundly out-of-shape Johnny Weissmuller and James Pierce were not a pretty sight.

The *Tarzan* TV series was the most intensive ape-man project ever assembled: the 57 hour-long episodes provided by a team of over a dozen writers across its two seasons equated (minus adverts) to nearly 30 Tarzan cinema features. Even the serials had not come close in screen time. It was also the widest exposure for the ape-man there had ever been: no matter how many millions of books there were in circulation and no matter how many screenings there had been of Tarzan films at the cinema or on TV, nothing could match the regular weekly presence of the character in living rooms across the planet.

Which leaves the question: was the show any good?

American television in the second half of the '60s was a limited medium, squeaky clean-cum-socially-conservative, tending toward morality tales and conforming to a square-jawed Hollywood paradigm of heroism in which the irony, playfulness and ethical doubt common today did not feature. This combined with the severe restrictions that then existed on depictions of violence – especially in a show that had a 7.30 pm transmission time and was destined to be seen by large numbers of children – meant that the Tarzan herein wasn't even going to be as savage as his cinema incarnation let alone the prose original.

The show depicts a Tarzan who is loved by some, feared by others but known by all. Wandering a jungle country never identified by name, he is either called upon for help or else stumbles into difficulties with which he can assist. Princesses, poachers, witch-doctors, diamond smugglers, gun-runners, missionaries and revolutionaries all cross his path, and with a combination of a rather all-American politesse and, where he has to, fisticuffs, he wraps their problems up in a neat little bow by episode's end (except with two-partners). In one episode he even enters a jungle Olympics in order to assist the forces of good. Tarzan's warning cry is Weissmuller's classic MGM yodel, to which the astute Weintraub had clearly somehow secured the rights. Another inheritance from the movies is Cheeta.

By now, Burroughs fans were long used to the trade-off with authenticity that commercial reality, practicality and technical limitations always imposed on live-action depictions of the ape-man. Inevitably, though, there were fundamental tamperings with the source material destined not to go down well with the purists. Perhaps in light of her absence from many of Burroughs' books, the non-appearance of Jane can't be counted as an example of such. However, even the best Tarzan books and films without her had proven a little emotionally arid, and this series is afflicted by the same problem, one for which the presence of an adopted orphan son doesn't compensate. Jai was always a curiosity. The character's name was stolen from the Indian boy actor in *Tarzan Goes to India*, while, for those bothered to think about it, his ethnicity was puzzling: he was played by Manuel Padilla Jr, a Californian of Filipino heritage, who had appeared as an Incan in *Tarzan and the Valley of Gold*. In the TV show, though his character's caste was not specified, it was obvious that he was a geographical anomaly. Tarzan doesn't tangle with wild beasts much: at times he could almost just be a cop without trousers. As for Tarzan's noble lineage, Weintraub commented in December 1967, 'We dropped the English lord business because of Ron Ely's American accent.'

Each episode of the Ely series would start with the spoken précis: 'The dark land of the jungle is the country of the unknown, of savagery, terror and peril beyond the imagination of men. Here in the forbidden tangle of the jungle, a child was found and raised by the great apes. The boy took the name Tarzan and later was educated in civilisation. But then, Tarzan returned to the deadly land he knew so well, and everywhere in the jungle from the great falls, to the huge mountains, to the land of ghost men and the limitless rainforest, the cheetah has grown to know one who is swifter, the lion knows one who is braver: Tarzan. The strength of Tarzan no man can say. Deep in the jungle, Tarzan continues to enforce his law … the law of right. Tarzan's awesome warning cry is known to every living creature in the jungle. Hearing that cry, the antelope knows he is safe, the lion pauses, the crocodile seeks the safety of the water. The elephant comes to his friend … Tarzan of the Apes.' It's an interesting exercise in providing a background that doesn't necessarily chime with Burroughs' original but doesn't quite contradict it either: 'great apes' are mentioned but not Mangani; the genesis of Tarzan's name is not quite explained; the means by which he was both found by apes and educated in civilisation are left opaque.

Many Burroughs fans were relatively happy with the balance struck between lowest common denominator fare and authentic Burroughsonia, especially toward the end of the first season as early aesthetic fumbling gave way to production slickness and more adult-orientated scripts. Of course, the show was designed not for ERBivores but for Mr and Mrs Average and their two-point-five children, who in the main had never heard of Burroughs.

Though ratings started out shaky – it initially didn't break the top 50 – by December *Tarzan* was top 20. The urgent baritone of the announcer and the way that the series logo gradually appeared across the screen in the wake of Tarzan swinging on a vine, as well as its wildlife montage, made for an exciting title sequence, the kind of thing that creates viewer goodwill even before the action starts. It should also not be underestimated just how novel the series was in the way it provided a window on the spectacular natural landscapes of what were then parts of the world little seen on television, especially in glorious colour. *Tarzan* also genuinely seems to have succeeded in its aim of being a family show. While men and kids liked it as much as anticipated, the allure of Ely's scantily clad form also seems to have drawn in the ladies: *Tarzan's* first season had the highest proportion of female viewers aged 18 to 34 of any prime-time show.

Tarzan and the Great River, released in September 1967 and distributed by Paramount, is the weakest of the Mike Henry triptych.

Originally proposed by Weintraub as a feature called *Tarzan, Spain*, it ended up being set in Brazil. As before, the ape-man is summoned by one of the friends he mysteriously has dotted around the globe, and as in the predecessor film, he journeys there looking like a Madison Avenue exec before stripping down to a hardly-there breechcloth. The script by Bob Barbash from a story by Barbash and Lewis Reed sees Tarzan's friend the Professor (Paulo Gracindo) alert him to the activities of the Jaguar Cult, who are led by Barcuma (Rafer Johnson, a former Olympic decathlete) and have as their twisted mission the enslavement of local villagers for work in diamond mines. Those who resist are liable to suffer death by poisoned jaguar claw. The cult predictably make things personal for the ape-man by killing the Professor. Tarzan sets off after them in the company of a lion (Baron) and a chimp (Cheeta) that he had previously given to the Professor for his menagerie. What might seem a reasonably clever way to justify the inclusion of fauna familiar from Tarzan flicks is later completely undermined by Tarzan encountering, with no explanation, lions in the Brazilian jungle and hippos in the Amazon river. On his travels, he runs into the comedic character Captain Sam (professional funnyman Jan Murray), and his cabin boy Pepe (Manuel Padilla Jr again). The now traditional feisty eye candy to whose charms Tarzan is strangely immune is Dr Ann Phillips (Diana Millay), to whom the Captain delivers medical supplies and whose jungle hospital comes under attack by the cult for encroaching on Barcuma's patch.

Robert Day directed an 88-minute film that is an awkward mixture of plodding and frenetic, sweet (there is plenty of levity involving Captain Sam,

Pepe, the lion and the chimpanzee) and sadistic (Tarzan slaughters enemies willy-nilly, including a group he burns alive without bothering to find out if they want to surrender).

There are a couple of blasts from the past: Weissmuller's classic yodel was dubbed in and the ape-man's high dive into a river was spliced from *Tarzan's Greatest Adventure*.

On 15 September 1967, three days after the release of the second Mike Henry film, the NBC Tarzan series returned to the screens. Famous faces like Jock Mahoney, Woody Strode, Don McGowan and Julie Harris (some of whom were of course familiar from Tarzan flicks) had speckled season one, but it was in the second season that the guest stars got really impressive: the Supremes, Ethel Merman and Helen Hayes were among those who put in appearances. Weintraub explained that this was so as to ensure a large adult audience. The ante was also upped with regard to backgrounds: it was planned for episodes to be shot in London, Guatemala and Mozambique. Consequently, ratings continued to be pleasing. Three months into the second season, Weintraub was publicly saying, 'We think – and NBC thinks – the series is good for ten years.'

What on earth happened in the two months between that confident prediction and the announcement on 21 February 1968, with six more episodes of season two still to air, that *Tarzan* did not feature in NBC's plans for the next TV season is not known. However, once the second series ended, the show never came back. Upon the news of the NBC cancellation, Weintraub airily spoke of the show returning, and possibly even to NBC, on the grounds that it was one of the highest-rating shows ever to be dropped from the schedules. Weintraub said, 'We will continue production to meet our present obligations.' That the second season ended up being five episodes shorter than the first suggests that he was told by the network not to bother with those obligations, and that scripted *Tarzan* episodes remained unfilmed. Certainly the London edition (where, according to author Gabe Essoe, the title Lord Greystoke was finally due to be enunciated) didn't materialise.

Though it burned brightly but briefly, Ely's '66-'68 Tarzan show had a long tail. Because it was still being repeated well into the '70s, when the ape-man was not being represented on cinema screens, it defined the character for more than one generation. There have been subsequent live-action Tarzan television shows, but their actors do not linger in the memory of a public who can instantly cite Ron Ely as the lead of the programme from their childhood.

Mike Henry named May 1968's *Tarzan and the Jungle Boy* as his favourite of his three ape-man movies because it was the one that dispensed with the 'Bondage' and moved back toward the character's origins. Though it was filmed in Brazil, the script also moved the character back to his home country. The only thing Bond about the picture is Steve Bond, the youngster who plays 13-year-old Erik Brunik, aka Jukaro, the jungle boy of the title, whom journalist Myrna Claudel (Alizia Gur) and her husband have decided to try to track down after he has been spotted by an aerial photographer.

The boy has survived in the wild by his wits for six years after the death of his father when their canoe tipped over. (Even more impressively, he has managed to retain a mop of hair that looks like it's just been shampooed.) Tarzan decides to look for him, though won't help Myrna in her mercenary pursuit of a story. While on his quest, the ape-man interferes in a battle for succession between the sons of a dying native chief. The bad son Nagambi (a returning Rafer Johnson) bears a grudge against the ape-man for preventing him cold-bloodedly killing his sibling Buhara (played by Johnson's real-life brother Edward), with the inevitable frenetic consequences. Meanwhile, Myrna has defied Tarzan's orders not to follow him, with the inevitable life-threatening consequences. When Tarzan catches up with Erik, he naturally strikes up a rapport with his vine-swinging, loinclothed mini-me. Counterpointing this warmth and the comedy of Cheeta is more of the protracted bloodshed unique to the Henry trilogy.

Steven Lord wrote and Robert Gordon directed the 90-minute film, distributed by Paramount. It was a good way for Henry to bow out. He subsequently had a long acting career that lasted into the 21st Century. At the time of writing, he is sadly stricken with Parkinson's Disease.

A short clip from this production showing Steve Bond walking through the jungle with his character's pet leopard was used to denote Tarzan as a young boy in the opening credits of the Ron Ely series.

In the month before the second season of the Ely series started airing, Sy Weintraub ceased to be the owner of the live-action Tarzan rights when he acquiesced to a buy-out by National General Corporation, although he continued to head the Banner production company they had gobbled up. The business-as-normal airing of the second season disguised it at first, but it was the end of another era for the ape-man, and in more ways than one.

In the same interview in which he predicted the cancelled *Tarzan* show would be back, Weintraub said that there might be Tarzan feature films starring Ely. In the event, though, the only cinema releases featuring Ely as the ape-man were *Tarzan's Deadly Silence* and *Tarzan's Jungle Rebellion*, spliced two-partners from the NBC series given a theatrical outing in 1970. Ersatz though these exercises were, without their respective releases, there would have been no new *bona fide* cinematic Tarzans in the '70s whatsoever.

ABC responded to the cancellation of the Ely show by broadcasting a 60-minute edit of Denny Miller's *Tarzan the Ape Man* two days later as a pilot for a possible new series. It would be unwise to infer too much from the fact that the series didn't happen – the reason could as easily have been that movie's poor quality as a lack of public interest in the ape-man. However, although the Tarzan live-action rights Weintraub had sold ran until 1972, and no doubt could have been easily extended, they were not exercised.

The only person who seemed to be interested in shooting Tarzan pictures was Manuel Caño, who helmed two Spanish-Italian projects, *Tarzan En La Gruta Del Oro* (*Tarzan in the Golden Grotto*), released in 1970, and *Tarzan Y El Arco Iris* (*Tarzan and the Rainbow*, but probably better-known as *Tarzan and the Brown Prince*), released in 1972, both starring former Mr Canada Steve Hawkes as the title character. It's perhaps unfair and patronising to immediately tag as ersatz two movies that were filmed in English and dubbed into Italian and Spanish and that secured no general release in the UK or US. Nevertheless, farce seems to have surrounded both productions, and in discussions of cinematic Tarzans they have tended to be lumped in with the likes of *Tarzan Roi de la Force Brutale*. However, in an interview with the website tarzanmovieguide.com, Hawkes insisted that rights were properly sought and obtained from ERB, Inc – up to a point. Of the first picture, he said, 'The American producers, in the middle of the film, ran out of the money due to the flood in South America. They lost all the equipment and almost all the footage. The company was unable to pay the Edgar Rice Burroughs fees and they negotiated a lesser amount by changing it from Tarzan to Zan … The second movie, *Tarzan and the Brown Prince*, the rights were paid in full. I was present when the contracts were signed. I'm not sure whether the Italians paid their dues or not.'

That the second movie became the 'proper' ape-man film by virtue of being able to use the Tarzan name is somewhat of an irony, as it is considered the weaker of the two, with Tarzan – an impressive crocodile fight aside – taking almost a passive, observer's role. The first picture was well-made, albeit in an over-archetypal Tarzan style. The solidly-built Hawkes is an impressive figure in both films. Also known as Steve Sipek (he was born Stjepan Šipek in Croatia in 1942 before emigrating to Canada), he has since run a big cat sanctuary in Florida, a career direction inspired by his life being saved during the shooting of his second ape-man picture by a lion that dragged him from a fire and ripped off his bonds. He bristles when his films are described as unauthorised. At one point, clicking on his name on his website unleashed a Weissmuller Tarzan yodel.

That the Caño/Hawkes films were all the Tarzan movie franchise could muster at this point in history demonstrates the rather rapid debasement of its currency. Though Weintraub had modernised the live-action Tarzan, he had taken the character as far as it could go in a changed world. The '60s had been a questioning decade, one in which relatively upstanding and conventional characters like Tarzan had begun to lose their attraction to a youth who wanted their heroes cut from more rebellious, less clean-cut cloth. Even Mike Henry's mass-murdering Tarzan would have seemed unhip to fans of *Bonnie and Clyde* and *Easy Rider*, as would the Burroughs Tarzan, which bought into all the assumptions about privilege dear to those at the top of the English class system and loathed by the emerging counter-culture. Moreover, in what were ideologically-charged times, the production of escapist fare seemed to some – especially the young – a political act, one that was conservative and regressive. There was also an ever-increasing trend toward realism in art: jungle escapades couldn't help seem a little florid set against urban grit. There were no doubt other reasons why the ape-man came to be perceived by financiers as a less viable option after *Tarzan and the Jungle Boy*, the decreasing exoticness of Africa in a more connected planet among them. Whatever the precise truth, though Tarzan would continue to be visible in the culture during the '70s in comic books, an animated TV series, merchandise and that never-ending comic strip, as well as in the pastiches and spoofs that had always been intertwined with the character's life, of the crucial, most prestigious, most profitable stuff – i.e. live-action drama – there was none. After more than half a century, the days of Tarzan bestriding popular culture like a colossus were drawing to a close.

PART SEVEN: THE LEAN YEARS

Though historical perspective now enables us to see that 1968 marked the end of the live-action Tarzan franchise in any meaningful sense, Burroughs fans continued to foster grand dreams in that direction. Two mooted Tarzan cinema projects became a combination of a Holy Grail and a running joke.

The first was a Gene Roddenberry picture. Roddenberry had helmed two series of *Star Trek*, the show he had created, but anxious to make the jump into 'features' in 1968 he left the show and signed a contract with National General, current owner of live-action rights to the ape-man. The National General deal – according to his private correspondence – involved 'a Tarzan feature and getting a contract for a second feature of my own choosing by doing so.' If this implies a reluctance to make an ape-man film, Roddenberry seemed to disprove this with his next sentence: 'Actually, the Tarzan thing does interest me since I have long felt the subject has never been handled properly on film and that the only right way to do it is to return as much as possible to the original Burroughs concept.' Roddenberry detailed his thoughts about 'a new approach' to the character to Sy Weintraub in a 14-page letter dated 7 June 1968 in which he spoke of having viewed Tarzan films from different eras and concluded that Tarzan should be presented as an intelligent man in a romantic and mysterious period but departing from Burroughs' template in dispensing with Jane: he felt Tarzan should be a virile free agent.

As the creative brains behind the TV show that, despite its imminent cancellation, was already on its way to overtaking Tarzan in the stakes of world's most popular fantasy franchise, and one that furthermore had a crossover in demographic with Burroughs' SF works, Roddenberry seemed an ideal figure to take hold of the character's flickering cinema flame. The prospect he dangled via newspaper interviews that had headings like 'How I'd Film Tarzan', of a movie true to the source that wasn't rooted in the now comical techniques of a previous era like the 1918 *Tarzan of the Apes* or botched like *The New Adventures of Tarzan*, was mouth-watering. However, the project never got anywhere. Explanations differed. Some sources claimed that the budget Roddenberry was offered by National General was inadequate, some that it would cover only a TV movie when the small screen was a ghetto he sought to escape, and some that the sexual explicitness he planned would have been problematical. Symptomatic of the differing recollections, even Roddenberry's authorised biographer David Alexander wasn't quite sure whether Roddenberry thought he was embarking on a production meant for cinemas or for the small screen. Roddenberry's production colleague Morris

Chapnick told Alexander a few things about the project, among them that Roddenberry wanted to portray Tarzan as racist by having him clinically watch a native being tortured but intervene when the same thing happened to a white man, and as casual about sexual mores to the extent that bedding down for the night with a woman he asked her, 'Do you want to mate?' (He was rebuffed.) Plans were to shoot the picture in Kenya and Italy. An excursion was made to the Olympic Training Camp in Lake Tahoe to find a leading man.

Philip José Farmer had a different perspective on the then-prevailing assumption that Roddenberry was a Tarzan fan and steeped in Burroughs lore. He later disclosed that Roddenberry had given him a copy of the script just after he'd written it and asked him to look it over. 'I didn't think much of it,' Farmer wrote, 'although some parts did have merit. My judgment may have been influenced by some inexcusable errors re names and events in the Tarzan canon.' Farmer claimed that he found out later that Roddenberry didn't really know the books: 'He'd sent out a man named Hank Stein to research Tarzan for him. Stein spent an afternoon in the library and handed in his notes to Roddenberry.' According to Joel Engel, author of *Gene Roddenberry: The Myth and the Man Behind Star Trek*, the suggestion of Roddenberry's lack of familiarity with the source was supported by ERB fan and Roddenberry friend Sam Peeples, whom Engel claimed Roddenberry approached for assistance before embarking on his ape-man script.

Though Roddenberry's script – titled simply *Tarzan* – features La, D'Arnot and the Waziri and presents Tarzan as articulate, in its own way it strays as far from the Burroughs template as MGM and Sol Lesser had and possibly further. Burroughs had injected some science fiction elements into his ape-man stories, but only – *Tarzan at the Earth's Core* excepted – via relatively small exaggerations of reality. Roddenberry's script is closer in tone to a Robert E Howard sword and sorcery tale with its combination of ruined civilisations, a mysterious cylinder that can unleash deadly heat and a revived ancient alien that Roddenberry describes as 'Half-manlike, half some strange animal.' Roddenberry also seeks in the tradition of comics characters to make Lord Greystoke the mild-mannered alter-ego of his superhero secret identity, Tarzan. That Roddenberry unburdens Tarzan to be a fornicating bachelor by having Jane killed in the film, and that he sets the action in 1890 so as to portray an Africa un-demystified by industrialisation, are matters of taste, but had it been made at the time, overall it's difficult to see this movie not being ridiculed as the effort of a man trading on a character he did not understand, whose tenure on *Star Trek* had blinded him to the fact that not every story needs an extraterrestrial.

In 1970, Burne Hogarth retired from teaching comics at the School of Visual Arts that he had co-founded in 1947, one consequence of which was that he returned to illustrating Tarzan after a break of more than two decades.

There are many candidates for first graphic novel but the 1972 Watson-Guptill publication *Tarzan of the Apes*, written and drawn by Hogarth, is definitely one of them. That it was a beautiful, large-format, full-colour hardback of 122 pages at a time when comics were seen as disposable kid-stuff was just the half of it. The book saw Hogarth take full advantage of the fact that he was now free of the restrictive stylistic and size parameters of newspaper strips: his dynamic layouts on his large canvas saw his characters literally bursting through conventional, regular panel shapes. He also exploited his freedom from the Comics Code Authority and the family orientation of newspapers. The boy Tarzan had been seen nude in comic strips and comic books often enough, but here the only concession Hogarth made to decency was convenient obstruction of the view of his genitals. Hogarth added to the classy air by not using speech balloons. Tarzan's popularity and consequent ripeness for adaptation had caused him so many times before to be in the cultural vanguard, and here was another example. This was comics – let alone Tarzan comics – on a whole new level.

As the book adapted only half of *Tarzan of the Apes*, many were hoping Hogarth would finish the job. Some were disappointed, then, when his next Watson-Guptill book was *Jungle Tales of Tarzan* (1976). Even worse, these adaptations of four of the stories in that Burroughs collection were rendered in monochrome only. However, Hogarth rose to the challenge of black-and-white magnificently, layering so much detail into his already pleasantly florid style that the effect was almost dizzying. Furthermore, the philosophical and existential conundrums Burroughs had explored in the stories chosen – 'Tarzan's First Love', 'The Capture of Tarzan', 'The God of Tarzan' and 'The Nightmare' – made for an unusually quiet and thoughtful Tarzan comics experience. In both books, there was symbolism and hidden imagery for those who cared to look. *Jungle Tales of Tarzan* was Hogarth's farewell to the character.

That other great Tarzan artist Russ Manning was also responsible for Tarzan projects that can be termed graphic novels, if not on quite the same deluxe scale. When he ceased work on the daily newspaper strip in 1972, it was to write and draw the comics that ERB, Inc were providing for European publishers. Amongst this work were such large format paperback publications as *Tarzan in the Land that Time Forgot*, *Tarzan and the Beastmaster* and *Tarzan in Savage Pellucidar*. As with Hogarth's material, his beautiful art was equal to his love for the character.

While standard comics could not hope to match the prestige of such enterprises as Hogarth's Watson-Guptill books, that quadrant of the Tarzan universe saw an upgrade in 1972 when the Tarzan franchise was transferred to National Periodical Publications. This company was the home of DC, which if it did not produce the best comics was the biggest name in the business, chiefly because it was the home of the massively iconic Superman, Batman and Wonder Woman.

With the exception of just half a dozen of its 52 issues, the DC Tarzan comic became synonymous with one man. At various points, Joe Kubert handled everything on the title: writing, drawing, cover illustration, editing and even briefly lettering. 'My understanding was that one of the prime reasons the Burroughs people gave the character to DC was [that] they had seen my work and had me set to do it,' says Kubert. However, he does admit, 'I've heard another story to it. My friend Carmine Infantino, who was the boss at the time, tells me that he had to convince them to permit me to do it.' If ERB, Inc were apprehensive about Kubert working on Tarzan, they perhaps had some justification. He was probably best known at this time for his artwork on army character Sgt Rock. He was also only a writer 'off and on.' However, Kubert says of the corporation's reaction to his Tarzan work, 'From the outset the people up at Burroughs were happy with it – more than happy with it.'

'I loved his books,' Kubert says of Burroughs. 'My conscious attempt when I started doing the Tarzan was to perhaps capture that feeling that I had when I first read the books and to try to convey it in the work that I was doing. For that purpose, I re-read all the books again.' As mentioned previously, he had also adored the depiction of the character by Hal Foster. 'One of the reasons I think that I became a cartoonist in the first place was because of the beautiful work that was done originally, especially by Hal Foster when he was doing it through the newspapers,' he says. 'It was a living, believable character. That's what I was trying to do. I re-read all the Foster material.' Though Kubert had also enjoyed Burne Hogarth's work, he was not very familiar with Russ Manning's: 'I really hadn't followed or seen the Tarzan as it was published in other magazines.' As for the movie Tarzan, Kubert says, 'I loved Johnny Weissmuller. He came probably closest to what I envisioned as what Tarzan should look like and Tarzan should be. The others I was not too crazy about. The tendency with a character like a Tarzan – so popular, so successful – is try to twist the damn thing any way to Sunday to try to make it a little different, a little bit more personal, and in the process tear away pieces rather than add to it.'

DC's book premiered in early 1972, the inaugural issue cover-dated April. At first it was titled *Tarzan of the Apes*, but would eventually mostly be just

Tarzan, though for a spell it was *Tarzan, Lord of the Jungle* and it would also change depending on what book adaptation was currently running in its pages. The debut featured the words '1st DC issue' in a prominent yellow circle on the cover, but directly across from that was the information 'NO. 207,' which must have been confusing to some. DC were continuing the numbering from the final Gold Key book, presumably because they thought this would engender the inheritance of its readership.

Spread across the first four DC issues was an adaptation of the novel *Tarzan of the Apes*. A four-part story was unusually long in American comics at the time, especially at DC. 'They gave me complete freedom in what I was doing,' Kubert says of his employers. He notes of the process of adaptation, 'You are definitely encumbered. There are perhaps dramatic effects that might be slightly different, compositions for panels, but essentially you have to follow that story as the story was written. It doesn't mean that it was a chore. I loved it, because I felt that despite the fact that the story was going to be the same, perhaps there was something I could add to it, perhaps something I can do just a little bit differently than was done before … What I concentrated on was to get the sense of the character, the feelings, the credibility that I felt when I was a kid.' Kubert set the beginning of the story in 1888, just as in the Burroughs book, but he adds, 'More important than the timeframe was to get the sense, the feeling of the character, the nuances, the characterisation – not some large muscle-bound guy running around in a loincloth but somebody who was believable and credible.'

Of course, Kubert was by no means the first comics writer to adapt Tarzan books. 'Strangely enough, that didn't intimidate me as much as it did invigorate me,' he says. 'It gave me something to shoot for. I have been influenced by every good piece of work that I've seen. Nevertheless, I've never felt that I was competing with those artists, trying to do a better job than they did. I don't try to emulate them as much as I try to learn from them.'

Tarzan of the Apes, The Return of Tarzan, Jungle Tales of Tarzan and even *Tarzan and the Castaways* were logical choices for adaptation, although *Tarzan and the Lion Man* – one of the later, weaker Tarzan books – is less explicable. DC's *Tarzan* alternated these adaptations with new Tarzan stories. Kubert doesn't recall why but suggests, 'Perhaps it was the tediousness of going through the whole story and then digesting it – there were no more four-parters – into a 30-page or a 32-page magazine.' The science fiction and fantastical elements of some of the newly-written stories – for instance, the snow ape and dinosaurs the ape-man battled in issues 227 and 228 respectively – suggested that Kubert was trying to compete in the sword and sorcery field with Marvel's *Conan the*

Barbarian, which was the darling of comics fandom at the time. Kubert: 'No. I wasn't reading a lot of the other books. I did not have a hell of a lot of time. Just as a change of pace, I would try to vary the stories as much as possible. There are certain directions you can take in doing a jungle story but then you're limited to the jungle and the backgrounds, so trying to get a little magic into a story or histrionics or anything to make it look a little bit different would be a plus.'

Although he divested himself of lettering duties, Kubert continued to write, draw and edit Tarzan, as well as contribute covers. Asked if he should have reined back in some areas, he says, 'Perhaps, but the writing didn't take an incredible length of time because I would have had to lay out the stories anyhow to make sure that they were told the way I envisioned them. And the way I write, I write and do the rough layouts at the same time.' He does concede that editing his own work created a potential conflict of interest: 'That third eye is something that every artist and every writer has to have.'

That first DC issue of *Tarzan* had featured not only the debut instalment of Kubert's *Tarzan and the Apes* adaptation, plus a Hal Foster newspaper strip reprint, but also the start of an adaptation of *A Princess of Mars* – evidence that DC were interested in Edgar Rice Burroughs properties across the board. Two months after the *Tarzan* title started, the company began their own *Korak* book, which also continued the Gold Key numbering. As well as the exploits of the son of Tarzan, *Korak's* first issue boasted strips featuring Carson of Venus and Pellucidar. Three months after the *Korak* title's debut came *Weird Worlds* (or *Tarzan Presents Edgar Rice Burroughs' Weird Worlds*, as the cover rendered it), which featured Barsoom and Pellucidar strips. The Burroughs characters were dropped from the title after seven issues. From November '75, *Korak* morphed into *Tarzan Family*, a reprint-dominated anthology. Kubert drew covers for all of said books, and was editor of *Korak*. He says of Korak, 'Frankly I didn't feel that the character had any kind of personality or background or reason other than it being just another Tarzan.' However, the title was differentiated from its *Tarzan* stablemate a little by the fact that it featured a quest (Korak's search for Meriem) spanning multiple issues.

On the main *Tarzan* title, the ERB butter was spread even thinner from the April-May 1974 issue when it became a 100-page book. 'The responsibility of putting it together was given to me, so I did it,' shrugs Kubert. 'This is above and beyond doing the kind of work, especially with the drawing, that I've continued to love. It is a business besides an artform. I kind of separated myself from involvement or even asking questions.' Kubert adds that there was no difficulty filling those pages, but does acknowledge the tenuousness of the connection of some of the strips – Bomba, Congo Bill and Detective Chimp featured – to the title character: 'As happens very often in my business, it becomes almost a helter-skelter kind of an operation. You just drown the original idea.'

Pragmatic he may have been, but one thing by which Kubert was distressed was his inability to maintain the quality of Tarzan's adventures. 'Despite the fact that I loved doing the character – it was like going back to my childhood – I was editing about half a dozen different books at least, and doing I don't know how many different covers, and I found that I just couldn't maintain the schedule,' he recalls. 'I had to call on other artists to help me with the work. Despite the fact that the artists I had were incredibly good, incredibly talented people, and I laid out all the stories – I would rub them out on 8½ x 11 stationery and send it to them in illustrated form in addition to the text of the script itself – still it wasn't the thing that I had envisioned.'

Almost farcical measures were resorted to in order to help Kubert keep up with the publishing schedules, including an artificial collaboration with his hero Hal Foster on 'The Stone Sphinx' (issue #237). 'I incorporated things that perhaps were printed years and years [before],' explains Kubert. 'I even used a Burne Hogarth story from the daily strips or from the Sunday papers and converted it into the comic books in a vain attempt to meet some sort of schedule with the book. The set-up for the Sunday pages – the grids, the panel sizes themselves – very often did not fit into the design of the page that I was using, so I would add some drawings of my own to pre-existing work in order to make it feasible and complete the illustration. I took great pride in at least making an attempt to keep up with those masters.'

On the front cover of issue 221, Kubert seemed to be paying homage to another master: his illustration of Tarzan astride a lion, about to plunge a knife into its flank, is very reminiscent of Clinton Pettee's classic depiction of the ape-man on the front of *All-Story* in 1912.

The conclusion of his adaptation of 'Tarzan and the Champion' in issue 249, cover-dated May 1976, was Kubert's last original contribution to the DC *Tarzan* book, barring front covers and a pair of 'Balu of the Great Apes' back-ups. He recalls the reason for his ceasing to work on the title as, 'The sales did not warrant continuing to publish it,' although he admits that he has no idea why an adaptation of *Tarzan the Untamed* in the following six issues was contributed by Gerry Conway and Denny O'Neil (scripts) and José Luis Garcia-Lopez and Rudy Florese (art). 'I'd always been a huge fan of Tarzan, and the opportunity to work on the title after Joe left was irresistible,' says Conway. 'But I think we were all aware that the book hadn't been selling well and that in all likelihood it was doomed to be cancelled. So it was a bittersweet experience.' The final two issues were half-hearted, given over to reprints of Kubert work from the first year of the title's existence. The DC *Tarzan* comic book had existed for two months shy of five years. Both Kubert's scratchy and impressionistic artwork and his stories infused with deep knowledge of the characters are fondly remembered by ERB aficionados.

March 1972 saw the publication of a rather bizarre book called *Tarzan Alive*, sub-titled *A Definitive Biography of Lord Greystoke*. Written by science fiction author Philip José Farmer, it posited Tarzan as a real person who had appeared in heavily fictionalised accounts written by Edgar Rice Burroughs.

Of course, Burroughs himself had said as much in his 'I had this story from one who had no business to tell it to me' introduction to *Tarzan of the Apes*, but plenty of novels of the era carried similar tilts at authenticity, and it was understood that they were as much fiction as what followed them. Farmer wasn't actually the first to stake a claim for a real-life Tarzan, above and beyond those who had cited the examples of alleged feral children whose stories had elements of similarity to John Clayton's. In their issue cover-dated March 1959, the New York-based *Man's Adventure Magazine* published a feature by one Thomas Llewellan Jones titled 'The Man Who Really Was … Tarzan'. Though the article of over 3,300 words conceded, 'There never was a Lord "Greystoke". That particular name was made up; pulled right out of the air,' it also baldly stated, 'But the actual character, the person on whom the entire series was based, did live. There really was a man, an English nobleman, who, shipwrecked on the jungle coast of Africa, was cared for by the apes, grew up with them and eventually survived a thousand adventures before returning to London to assume his rightful title and position. The man was William Charles Mildin, 14th Earl of Streatham. For 15 years, between 1868 and 1883, his life was the prototype of Tarzan.'

What strikes one when reading the article is its verisimilitude. It smacks of truth partly because it *doesn't* follow the Burroughs story and its deviations from it are convoluted. Mildin, it is claimed, ran away from home aged 11 in a boyish fit of anger and obtained a berth as a cabin boy on an African-bound vessel called the *Antilla*. He was the only survivor when a storm wrecked his vessel and washed him ashore. He made friends with a hideous but unexpectedly friendly group of apes of an unspecified species and lived with them for six years. Though he did not become king of the tribe of apes – he was far too physically puny – his knowledge of fire and the advantages provided by his greater dexterity with his hands made him a fondly regarded member of the group. Nor did he learn the ape language, but he did pick up the meanings of various simian sounds. His ape name was (phonetically) 'Okhugh'. From there the story departs wildly from that of Burroughs, involving Tildin making friends with first one black tribe and then another, marrying polygamously women of 'coffee-colored skins and high, firm breasts' and having several children. Hearing of a nearby trading post manned by whites, he ultimately made a 22-day trek to civilisation. With him having resumed his seat and inherited his fortune back in Britain, war-fever and English libel law kept his extraordinary tale out of the newspapers until his death in 1919 and beyond. His one (white) son died in 1937 and the latter's will stipulated his papers be sealed for 20 years after his death, upon which time his father's handwritten account of his jungle adventures was discovered and then just as quickly buried lest its revelations of far-flung offspring jeopardise the bequests his son had made to charities or cause legal headaches based around succession.

It's a more plausible story than *Tarzan of the Apes* because it side-steps all of the questions provoked about why a man raised from infancy by simians was so 'normal' and how a child who had never heard English could teach himself to read it. Yet the issues of *The Times* that Jones claims verify the existence of Mildin and the edition of Lloyd's *Register* that he says confirms the wreck of the *Antilla* have proved to contain no such information. The sheer depth and believability of the article begs the question why – aside from money – Jones made up such a story. Or perhaps the fact that within it he confesses to having been a Burroughs fan answers that question. We'll apparently never know: Thomas Llewellan Jones itself seems to have been a pseudonym, for no other article with that by-line readily comes to light. Philip José Farmer was sceptical of the article in an afterword he wrote to it when he reprinted it in his collection of writing on feral children, *Mother Was a Lovely Beast*, but he was clearly being wilfully provocative: *Tarzan Alive* is like a grand version of 'The Man Who Really Was … Tarzan.'

Farmer claims in the introduction to *Tarzan Alive* to have tracked down Lord Greystoke through a 'close study of *Burke's Peerage* and another source I am not free to divulge.' He then takes the reader through each and every published Tarzan novel and explains what happened in the real-life equivalent adventures courtesy of conversation with the ape-man. (Tarzan revealed that a surprising number of the lost civilisations succumbed to dysentery; meanwhile Farmer informs those readers who hadn't already apprehended it that the known scientific facts ruled out the events of *Tarzan at the Earth's Core* as having taken place.) Farmer reproduces what he claims is the Greystoke coat of arms, gives Jane Clayton née Porter's recorded vital statistics (38-19-

36) and includes a bizarre section in which he invents what became known as the Wold Newton Universe. In the latter, fictional characters like Tarzan, Doc Savage and Sherlock Holmes supposedly gained their powers via the fact that their forebears were exposed to genetic code-changing ionisation in 1795 when a meteorite crashed in the Yorkshire village through which they were passing. This all sounds the domain of mimeographed fanzines – the means of distributing fan effusions before the internet cut out the need for paper – but the book ran to over 300 pages and was published by mainstream Doubleday.

In 2001, the present author asked Farmer whether *Tarzan Alive* was a spoof or if he was serious in holding that the ape-man really existed. He replied, 'I get asked that question quite often. I say, "Well, if you can believe in God, you can believe in Tarzan – and vice versa". He then laughed heartily. The conceit of Tarzan being a real person was possibly a ploy to enable Farmer legally to publish a book with 'Tarzan' in the title. The 1970s were littered with Farmer-penned works in which he effectively sought to inherit the mantle of Tarzan scribe without bothering with the permission of the Burroughs estate. He dodged legal bullets via effectively invoking pastiche and not using the actual Tarzan name.

In *A Feast Unknown* (1969), Farmer depicted characters called Lord Grandrith and Doc Caliban, a thinly disguised Tarzan and Doc Savage, who share a common father in the shape of Jack the Ripper. Both men get aroused by engaging in acts of violence. It spanned two sequels – *Lord of the Trees* and *The Mad Goblin* – printed literally back-to-back (in the Ace Double series) in 1970. Each book in the volume told the same story through the eyes of a different one of the pair. It was published in the same year as *Lord Tyger*, which depicted a young boy of noble birth named Ras Tyger growing up in a jungle with ostensible ape parents who repeatedly answer 'because it is written' (or 'not written') when he enquires about aspects of his life that puzzle him. It turns out that the written and unwritten things in question are in Edgar Rice Burroughs' *oeuvre*. Boygur, a mad millionaire ERB fan (i.e. someone like Farmer only with a lot more money) has arranged for young Ras to be given an upbringing as close as possible to that of Boygur's literary ape-man hero. When Tyger learns the truth of his false life, he unleashes hell. In *Time's Last Gift* (1972), a group of people travel back in time from the far future to prehistoric days. Burroughs fans will spot the clues indicating that one of them – John Gribardsun – is another of his disguised Tarzans. It spawned two loosely related sequels, *Hadon of Ancient Opar* (1974) and *Flight to Opar* (1976), both of which, as their titles imply, flesh out the primary lost civilisation of ERB's Tarzan stories. The Farmer Opar books were given approval by ERB,

Inc, but with *The Adventures of the Peerless Peer* (1974), the corporation finally took action against the man who had for so long been writing veiled Tarzan adventures of whose tone Burroughs would most certainly not have approved. As with so many Farmer books of this ilk it was intriguing – positing Tarzan and Sherlock Holmes teaming up to defeat evil, their adventures related as usual with Holmes books by Dr Watson – but the fact that the peerless peer was actually named Greystoke (even if he was never referred to as Tarzan) was clearly considered to be taking the piss. The book disappeared from the shelves, and when the story reappeared as 'The Adventure of the Three Madmen' in the compendium *The Grand Adventure* (1984), Mowgli (from the now public domain *The Jungle Book*) had taken the place of the Tarzan figure. Farmer was again pushing the boundaries of copyright in *Mother Was a Lovely Beast* by including a supposed part of the autobiography of Lord Greystoke. This and a verbatim supposed interview with Tarzan conducted by Farmer for *Esquire* in 1972 were later included in a 2006 Bison Books reissue of *Tarzan Alive*.

Some Burroughs fans were intrigued by Farmer's works but others were literally disgusted, not least because Farmer stayed true to the fascination with bodily functions and naturalism that had made him a groundbreaking SF author, the first of which undermined the glamour of the Tarzan character, the second of which undermined his entire premise. Farmer's love for and expertise on the Burroughs Tarzan books was obvious. (As touched on previously, in one essay, he modestly disavowed one person's claims that he was the world's foremost ERB expert but did concede that if the same person had '… said I was the greatest authority on Tarzan, he'd have been right.') Yet he could not or at the very least did not write like ERB. Burroughs sought at all times to shield the reader from the sexual act and bodily exigencies but Farmer veritably rubbed them in the reader's face. Whereas Burroughs depicted people mesmerised by Tarzan's awesome beauty, in *A Feast Unknown* Farmer showed a smitten man raping him. At the end of the book, the Tarzan character has his erect penis ripped off by the Doc Savage character in a fight (which, unbelievably, is not the most sickening depiction of violence in the narrative). Whereas in *Tarzan Alive* and his parts of *Mother was a Lovely Beast* Farmer displayed signs of obsessive-compulsive disorder in attempting to rationalise internal discrepancies in Burroughs' Tarzan work and explain away facets of it that cannot have stemmed from real life, *Lord Tyger* goes in the opposite direction, seeming to be a cathartic admission that the entire Tarzan series is comic book-level bunkum. Its protagonist behaves in ways far more logical for someone of his extraordinary upbringing: he has no social graces, eats like a pig and is sexually predatory toward local African girls, a visiting

European woman and pet monkeys.

Tarzan Alive includes what is effectively a Tarzan short story, and it is both impressive and rather poignant, with the ape-man wandering through a devastated, deserted Opar forlornly calling out 'La!'. Farmer must have felt at the time that this was the closest he was ever going to get to what was clearly his fantasy of writing a 'proper' Tarzan book, but toward the end of his life fate would transpire to have a trick up its sleeve in that regard.

Farmer got surprisingly good reviews for *Tarzan Alive* from upmarket newspapers, whose reviewers had clearly decided to show they were good sports by being willing to join in the pretence of the ape-man's existence. Meanwhile, the stone that this book dropped into the pool of literature created an altogether unexpected ripple.

The subject matter of his previous books had established J T Edson as the British equivalent of Zane Grey. A Derbyshire man, his Wild West was nothing more than an aggregation of the mythologised versions he had read in print or seen on the screen, and he cheerfully admitted this, but he compensated for it with compelling storytelling that owed much of its power to his meticulous attention to mechanical and geographical detail (though not to internal series continuity). So popular were his tales of the likes of Dusty Fog, Mark Counter and the Ysabel Kid and so prolific was his workrate that by the mid-1970s he was well on his way to the publication of his one hundredth book. Before that 1979 milestone, he embarked on a quite unanticipated Tarzan-esque side-turning in his career.

Edson had read and clearly been tickled by *Tarzan Alive*: little nods to its theory of a genetic link between the world's army of (supposedly) fictional heroes would crop up regularly in his books. He went a stage further, though, in picking up on an assertion in Farmer's work that Korak was not Tarzan's real son but adopted; a typically anal Farmer way of explaining the discrepancies in Burroughs' books regarding Korak's age. To Farmer, Jack Clayton was instead John Drummond-Clayton, the biological brother of pulp hero Bulldog Drummond. Edson approached both ERB, Inc and Farmer for permission to expand upon this nugget of an idea with a second adopted son of Tarzan. Their permission so to do gave him a legal way of getting into print the adventures of a jungle hero on which he had embarked even before his cowboy writing career began. The result was *Bunduki*.

James Allenvale Gunn was orphaned in the Mau Mau uprising (1952-1960) and adopted by the Greystokes at the age of three. He is also the adoptive cousin of Dawn Drummond-Clayton, granddaughter of Korak and Meriem, who – in an example of how Wold Newton universe machinations can easily

skirt incest – becomes his 'mate'. Nicknamed Bunduki after the Swahili word
for firearm, Gunn works as the Chief Warden of the Ambagasali Wild Life
Reserve. One day, both he and Dawn plunge over a gorge in a Land Rover,
but instead of crashing to their deaths awake in a literally alien land. They
have been transported to the planet Zillikian in order that, should he so wish,
Bunduki can become Chief Warden of this jungle world populated by tribes
from other planets and a hodgepodge of Terran wildlife from all continents,
including Mangani (which we are informed Bunduki's 'father' had told him
became extinct back on Earth in the 1950s). When Bunduki and Dawn finally
meet the 'Supplier' who brought them to the planet and ask him why he did so,
they receive the reply, 'It has long been our wish to do so with a pair from your
family. But we are not permitted to remove any life from its natural habitat
unless it is on the point of dying. Every time we saw one of your family in
danger, we computed that … they would contrive to escape.'

It's rumoured that the alien planet conceit was a sop to ERB, Inc because
they were anxious that the series not encroach too much on their intellectual
property (though it's a mystery how that squares with Edson taking it upon
himself to claim that Tarzan and the entire Clayton clan – made homeless
after Kenya gained independence – now live in Pellucidar). The alien planet
premise immediately poses a problem with appreciation of the perils the hero
faces: the author is free to make up his own physiological and geographical
rules rather than adhere to the ones of which the reader is already cognisant.
Moreover, the aliens stripping Bunduki of his warden's outfit and placing him
in a leopardskin loincloth possesses no logic but instead feels like a form of
Tarzan fetishism. In any case, the Suppliers received a bad hand. Neither raised
by apes like his step-father nor even the beneficiary of a Korak-style relocation
to the jungle as a boy, James Allenvale Gunn is merely tall, strong, good with
weaponry, adept with languages (including Mangani) and – because of the
household in which he grew up – trained a little in following trails and spoor
and in possession of pill-assisted longevity. Truly, a second-rate Tarzan.

Another problem is Edson's prose, which reads like he typed it with his lip
bitten. His pages are stuffed with interminable description of weaponry and
his action is repeatedly interrupted for irrelevant conversations and pedantic
footnotes. There are occasions where his obsession with footnotes bisects an
anal mentality as pronounced as Farmer's to insufferable effect: 'At no time
in his 24 biographical books on the life of Lord Greystoke does Edgar Rice
Burroughs suggest that Tarzan made use of vines when travelling through
the trees.' Edson seems to think this is all compensated for – rather than
exacerbated – by his habitual use of exclamation marks. This clunkiness is

emphatically not Burroughsonian, even if his distaste for depicting sex and printing obscenities is. (On a related note we are told that Bunduki chose to attend a Kenyan university because he was 'disenchanted with the so-called permissive society in England.')

However, a combination of Edson's large fanbase, book-starved Tarzan fans and the fact that the era was a boom one for casual purchases of men's action novels clearly made the series viable. As well as *Bunduki* (1975), Britain's Corgi published the sequels *Bunduki and Dawn* and *Sacrifice for the Quagga God* (both 1976), all with the strapline 'Adopted Son of Tarzan'. Edson then hit a snag. Marion Burroughs was the ERB family heir through marriage to Edgar Rice Burroughs' son Hulbert and hitherto an absentee chairman. When she assumed active control of the company in 1976, she adopted a rather hardline approach to ERB, Inc's intellectual property. Not only did she vigorously pursue alleged breaches of it but she also decided to rein back on co-operation with projects that she felt blurred its margins, including Edson's. She became a hate figure among some fans who could understand why she might launch a suit against blue comedy *Jungle Heat* on the grounds that it denigrated the Tarzan character but not why she sought to obstruct Edson, Farmer and John Eric Holmes (author of a Pellucidar novel published with the corporation's blessing), writers who adored Burroughs and his creations and were serving a public hunger that ERB, Inc hadn't seemed inclined to satisfy.

Either way, it left Edson in a bit of a pickle, especially as he would seem to have stockpiled Bunduki novels. He got round it by dropping any reference by name to Tarzan in his next Bunduki book *Fearless Master of the Jungle* (1980) and hoping that the characters, backgrounds and precepts he had established in what was by now a franchise of his own would see him through commercially. However, though he included four Bunduki short stories set on Earth before the character's alien transportation in compendiums published between 1979 and 1990, there would be no further novels featuring the character, and the completed Bunduki book *Amazons of Zillikian* remains unpublished to this day.

What is most peculiar about the whole Bunduki affair is that ERB, Inc were (originally) prepared to authorise this series but apparently not new Tarzan books. If, on the other hand, it was the reluctance of publishers that saw an absence of new ape-man tales on the shelves, one would have imagined that the success of Bunduki might have made them think again. It so happened that the year Bunduki made his debut was also the Burroughs centenary year, which accrued the author's creations some measure of publicity. That there was no new Tarzan novel in 1975 was negligence on the part of someone.

APE-MAN

Michael Heseltine's collar-length, un-parted blond hair had already made the Member of Parliament a bizarre figure in the House of Commons, let alone his own Conservative party, when in 1976 he furiously swung the Commons' ceremonial mace in a heated debate about nationalisation. The combination of that intemperate gesture and his unruly thatch saw him, courtesy of journalists, acquire forever the nickname 'Tarzan'. The bestowing of that title was proof positive that the ape-man's name was still an instantly understood byword for wild and untamed.

Meanwhile, August of that year saw the arrival of a musical titled *T. Zee*, one of what turned out to be many futile attempts by Richard O'Brien to match the success of his *The Rocky Horror Show*. Though the contents were more a general parody of comic book culture than of Tarzan itself, the show featured an out-of-shape monosyllabic muscle man searching for a Jane-esque mate. For anyone unsure about to whom this alluded, the title provided a further clue.

Spoof and parody attend any successful artistic creation. Indeed, both are a litmus test for a work or franchise's societal impact and amongst the greatest compliments that could be paid to that mocked creation's success. Except that the nature of mocking means that it doesn't always come over as a compliment. Hence in part the frequent sensitivity of copyright holders to mickey-takes: to be mocked is bad enough but to be aware that the person doing the mocking is making money from it can be infuriating. In addition, there is sometimes a genuine belief on the part of copyright holders that the parody might cheapen the commercial worth of the original property by making the pubic perceive shortcomings on which they had not hitherto focused.

Since Arthurs Gibbons and Carlton tried to put the kibosh on Dick Mortimer's skit *Warzan and his Apes* back in the 1920s and failed on the grounds of their lack of promptness, various US Supreme Court rulings and equivalent verdicts in other countries have put such ventures beyond the reach of the law by asserting that parody is a legitimate, lawful means of artistic expression distinct from passing off (a form of deception involving tricking the consumer into believing on whatever level that he is purchasing something involving someone else's creation) or plagiarism (blatantly lifting other people's work or concepts). In any case, as society became ever more irreverent, it is difficult to imagine the Burroughs estate, or even Burroughs had he been alive, finding anything but hilarious the early-'60s Peter Cook sketch 'One Leg Too Few' in which a massively optimistic monopedal actor auditions for the role of Tarzan. (The casting director famously observes, 'I've got nothing against your right leg. The trouble is – neither have you.')

However, there arises a question of when parody becomes either damaging or free-riding. ERB, Inc sought to quash the 1975 French-Belgian motion picture *Tarzoon: Shame of the Jungle*. A 15-minute preview of this X-rated animated feature went down a storm at the 1974 Cannes Film Festival but somewhat less well with the Burroughs estate, who tried to prevent the full movie's release. A French court upheld the makers' right to parody. The knife was twisted further by the American distributors who in 1978 cannily commissioned Johnny Weissmuller's son, also called Johnny, to voice one of the parts for its American distribution, as well as a movie poster from Don Martin, whose style was instantly recognisable to that considerable part of the US public who devoured *Mad* magazine. The Burroughs estate in the meantime had alighted upon a US law about degradation of trademark, and a domestic judge ordered that their intellectual property not be further damaged by forcing the producers to remove the 'Tarzoon' part of the title – with measurable financial damage to the picture. As mentioned, ERB, Inc also took action against the '90s movie *Jungle Heat*, another parody whose porn ingredient could be argued to be hazardous to a wholesome franchise. Its occasional presence on cable TV demonstrates that they ultimately failed to do little more than slow down its circulation. They did, though, manage to prevent a comic book called *Hoverboy* published by the independent American publisher Vigilance from continuing its 1978 lurch into a parody of the Tarzan story involving their titular hero becoming as one with the animals when his plane crashes into a jungle. Vigilance might have gotten away with it had they not decided to include a cover sunburst declaring, 'Because you people seem to like Tarzan,' with the ape-man's name rendered as that unmistakable and trademarked double-outlined Tarzan logo. *Tarzan Presley*, a 2004 novel by Nigel Cox, was a literature-reality mash-up featuring the story of a man raised in the forests of Wairarapa, NZ, who becomes rock 'n' roll's first major icon. It was critically acclaimed and a bestseller in the author's native New Zealand. However, ERB, Inc prevented it from being sold in any other country and ensured that all Tarzan references were removed from future editions in the author's homeland, where it is now known as *Jungle Rock Blues*. The disingenuousness and arrogance of the author ('...what was I going to do, write a letter to … whom, I couldn't imagine … saying, "I think I might be going to write a book in which a character from one of your books might appear, though in radically changed form – is that okay?"'), of the publisher Fergus Barrowman ('Tarzan is so much a part of the general culture and discourse that I believe it ought to be part of the public domain') and of sympathetic journalist Steven Price ('Burroughs never asked Kipling's permission to write his Tarzan stories') make one inclined to forgive the corporation for being over-zealous in their fears of the effects of this work and possibly a little too cynical in their knowledge of the fact that parody is less well-defined and protected outside the United States.

When an emotionally and physically shattered Mike Henry handed in his notice to Sy Weintraub, he made an interesting career choice in signing up to play the title character in a TV pilot called *Taygar, King of the Jungle* (1967). Recalls Denny Miller of the character, 'He was a klutz. He was always falling into natives' traps and he was always taking the wrong vine. My ex-wife Kit Smythe was the Jane part, which was Ruthie. The first shot of the pilot is her making a salad in the treehouse and the whole wall caves in and she turns to Mike, who has crushed the side of the house in, and says, "That's the third wrong vine you've taken this week." It was a delightful show. I saw it after it was completed.' Miller was in fact one of the few people who did see the pilot, because Sy Weintraub's Banner Productions instituted legal action to stop it being broadcast and the putative series going into production on the grounds that it was a deliberate attempt to burlesque and ridicule the Tarzan character. Yet the similarly-themed *George of the Jungle* animated TV show made it to the airwaves in 1967 without legal ramifications (and in 1997 became a successful live-action motion picture). Perhaps this dichotomy can be put down to personal issues between Weintraub and Henry, while *Taygar* failing to find a sponsor and hence a buyer can probably be ascribed more to a lack of appetite for legal tussles *per se* than proof of the legitimacy of Weintraub's objections.

Adding to legal cloudiness about when spoof becomes denigration is the conduct of MGM back in the '30s. In 1933, the studio – then owners of Tarzan live-action rights – allowed Charley Chase to portray the ape-man as a wimp with glasses in *Nature in the Wrong*. In 1934, the same studio was responsible for the distribution of *Hollywood Party*, in which Jimmy Durante riffed on a similar theme by playing 'Schnarzan'. This must surely have played a part in making those inclined to parody and mock Tarzan consider they had permission so to do, or a get-out if challenged.

The fact that licensees of Burroughs' work proved more prepared than the author himself to take legal action has its own kind of logic. For all the millions of words Burroughs wrote, the one piece of shorthand that instantly puts people in mind of Tarzan is something that had little if anything to do with him: Johnny Weissmuller's yodel.

Considering his presence at the forefront of so many new media, it's something of a surprise that it wasn't until the late '70s that anybody seems even to have considered adapting Tarzan into the format of animation.

In the 1960s and 1970s, Filmation were the kings of American Saturday morning animated action series. Headed by Norm Prescott and Lou Scheimer, their *modus operandi* was not to create new franchises like competitors Hanna-Barbera but to acquire licences for the adaptation of existing intellectual properties. A whole generation of by-now 40- and 50-somethings were weaned on their cartoon takes on Superman, Aquaman, *Journey to the Center of the Earth*, *The Hardy Boys*, *Sabrina the Teenage Witch*, *Gilligan's Island*, *Star Trek*, et al.

As their offices were virtually within walking distance of those of ERB, Inc in Tarzana it was perhaps inevitable that Filmation would license the ape-man. Yet the very fact that in the mid-'70s the Burroughs estate gave the go-ahead for a Filmation Tarzan cartoon is a measure of the falling stock of their property. Robert Kline, storyboard supervisor and storyboard artist on the Filmation Tarzan show, candidly concedes, 'When Lou finally got the rights to something and was able to put it on the air – and this was often commented on by critics and so forth – it [was] kind of the last gasp of a property. They wouldn't put it on Saturday morning as a limited animation TV series until they figured, "Well, we can't really do much else with this." An awful lot of what Filmation produced were knock-offs of extinct properties. It was rare that they would be able to do a show that had any kind of name recognition if that property was really hot at the time.' Certainly no great cachet was going to attach to 1970s Saturday morning fare. The dazzling allure of the familiar characters and properties Filmation licensed was sometimes necessary to blind kids to the shortcomings of their rather basic product. Their animation was cheap-and-cheerful and its trademark was the overused 'stock' shot. Kline: 'They insisted that we use as much repeat footage or same-as footage as possible.' Kline also reveals, 'It was rare that you were able to test the footage before it went into full colour production, so often a scene would be animated without really knowing how it was going to turn out. The animator would just have to base his decision on previous experience. Even at the time, studios like Disney would look at pencil tests and so forth and re-work [material]. There was no such luxury at Filmation or Hanna-Barbera.'

'We worked with Danton Burroughs,' explains Kline of contact with the ERB estate. 'I don't recall meeting Marion Burroughs. As it was, we did not spend a lot of time interacting with them, although I do recall Danton did the Tarzan call that's used in the Filmation version. I think he had worked on it for years and years and got it down, and Lou Scheimer wanted him to do it.' This certainly tallies with Denny Miller's recollection of ERB's grandson's prowess in that department: 'He was the best at it that I have ever heard … We were on a talk show, six of us together: Gordon Scott, Johnny, Buster Crabbe,

James Pierce … Danton Burroughs hid behind a partition and any [of the six] that wanted to, they'd put their hands up and he'd do the yell so that the live audience didn't know that they were faking it.'

Kline points out that though Filmation did things as cheaply as possible, that doesn't mean they operated inexpensively in a universal sense: 'We had over 350 people working on the shows at different points of what needed to be done: you had storyboard people, layout people, designers. The layout people would draw the scenes in detail: the background and the characters, where they were going to be positioned. Then you'd have the animators that would move the character, the assistant animators, the clean-up people that would do the final lines, background painters. There was a recording studio there, there was editing facility there, everything that was needed to make the film except processing … It was only in terms of re-runs and merchandising and other benefits that the show could even show a profit.'

Filmation titled their show *Tarzan Lord of the Jungle*. Because it was kids' fare, violence was reduced to, er, cartoon level. Says scriptwriter and associate producer Len Janson, 'As writers, we had access to all the Tarzan books, read them all and used what we could. They were great books, but the violent aspects inherent to the stories could not be used because of the hard line of CBS' Broadcast Standards. I remember one fight with the censors that underlines the frustrations of doing that show: they refused to let the ape-man carry a knife despite our promises that he would never use it. There were many battles like this and we lost probably 90 percent of them.' The weaponless Tarzan sent threatening animals packing with an 'Unk!' (Mangani for 'Go'). If he had no option but to engage in physical contact, it would be done via bland methods, for instance, bloodless wrestling or the disablement of a dangerous snake by wrapping it in a knot and depositing it on the ground, with the animators even going to the length of making sure the viewer saw the snake was not left in distress by depicting it untangling itself and slithering to safety. Moreover, says Kline, 'Lou Scheimer was concerned about what he put on the air for kids. He didn't want to put anything on that didn't have a good moral attitude.' That *Tarzan Lord of the Jungle* tended to morality tales might not have made it any different from the Ron Ely live-action series but, considering that several of the episodes were direct adaptations of Burroughs stories, it sometimes required some shoehorning. Then there was the effect of something that had not existed when Burroughs created his character. What the world had not yet dubbed political correctness dictated that black Africans be seen nowhere on the show. Says Kline, 'That would have been too controversial. It would have been too difficult to show them in a way that wouldn't create some kind of critical backlash, so it was just avoided by not having any and dealing with Burroughs' lost cities and those kind of locations.'

Despite having to navigate around all of these potential pitfalls, Filmation actually created a reasonable product that had several worthy components, for they were not a purely mercenary company. Their *Star Trek: The Animated Series*, for instance, used the voices of the actors from the original live-action series and featured mature scripts by well-known SF writers, while their *Fat Albert and the Cosby Kids* had a significant educational content.

Tarzan Lord of the Jungle began airing on the CBS network on Saturday mornings on 11 September 1976. It consisted of episodes of half-an-hour each (including the interludes that followed the 'We will return after these messages' announcements). The series' Tarzan voice belonged to Robert Ridgely, who seemed to have almost a monopoly on heroic voiceover parts at the time as he also vocalised the animated *Flash Gordon* and *Thundar*. That Ridgley's stentorian American voice was most certainly not the kind of thing heard wafting across the benches of the House of Lords mattered less than its combination of authority and drama. Each episode's opening titles featured a Ridgley-voiced introduction: 'The jungle – here I was born, and here my parents died when I was but an infant. I would have soon perished too had I not been found by a kindly she-ape named Kala who adopted me as her own and taught me the ways of the wild. I learned quickly and grew stronger each day, and now I share the friendship and trust of all jungle animals. The jungle is filled with beauty and danger, and lost cities filled with good and evil. This is my domain, and I protect those who come here. *For I am Tarzan – Lord of the Jungle!*' The opening credits ended with an in-profile Tarzan delivering a facsimile of the Weissmuller yodel, which froze into a title card, emblazoned naturally with the double-outlined Tarzan logo.

Quite unexpectedly, this show was amongst the closest movie or TV adaptations of the Burroughs books there had yet been. Kline's recollection is that the relevant creative staff were reasonably steeped in Burroughs: 'It was only a few years before that there had been the big paperback renaissance of the Tarzan books and the John Carter books, so for those of us who were in our twenties or early thirties, we'd gotten familiar with Burroughs through that renaissance.' The main credit here seems to be due to Len Janson and his fellow associate producer Chuck Menville, who co-wrote all of the first two seasons. None of the seven other writers brought in for the third and fourth seasons managed to write more than four episodes each, either singly or in combination, and the credits show that Janson and Menville were still masterminding the series and sometimes still contributing odd scripts or turning other writers' storylines into teleplays even at that point. The first season of 16 episodes and assorted episodes thereafter reveal an astonishingly detailed knowledge of the original books: portraying Jad-bal-ja, Pal-ul-don and Pellucidar was one thing, but Pal-ul-don, Mangani and Opar references and words are used in incredibly layered and sometimes almost mischievous detail.

The animation is actually a cut above the usual Filmation done-cheap-and-looks-it fare. The studio continued its money-saving use of the same scene-shifting shots over and over again, while their curiously quasi-slow-motion action sequences were no doubt a symptom of their policy of employing as few frames per second as feasible. However, their decision to use rotoscoping – the tracing over of live-action footage – added a slightly more realistic feel. ERB, Inc loaned Filmation copies of the early Weissmuller films *Tarzan the Ape Man* and *Tarzan and his Mate* for this purpose. Kline: 'We rotoscoped live-action footage for some of the scenes in the series that were used over and over again where Tarzan is swinging or landing on a branch or where a lion runs at the camera and jumps over it – those kinds of things. In those cases the timing is right off of live-action footage.' Also helpful in achieving a degree of class was Tarzan's resemblance to Burne Hogarth's handsome, noble vision of the ape-man. Kline: 'Herb Hazelton was responsible for designing the Tarzan character. He did the original model sheets from which other people drew the character. It was Hogarth's way of drawing Tarzan that was being emulated on purpose.' Dramatic music and atmospheric jungle noises added to the rich feel.

Though Filmation's Tarzan endured for four seasons in total, only the first was in its own dedicated series. Kline, though, denies that this was because the studio lost their nerve about the character's appeal. 'If you track any of the other shows, the same thing happened with all of them,' he reasons. 'Very rarely was a show in its initial form allowed to do new episodes season after season after season. Even with *The Flintstones*, they still had to re-think how they were presenting [it] – it couldn't just be another season of *The Flintstones*. The kids would have to feel like they were watching something that they hadn't seen before.' Thus, when the ape-man serial returned for its second season in 1977, it was as part of *The Batman/Tarzan Adventure Hour*, not a team-up between the pair as might be assumed but merely a shared billing. Six new Tarzan episodes alternated with repeats of first season episodes, a somewhat unwise juxtaposition considering that the quality was now on a downward gradient. The Burroughs content was also diminishing. There was additionally an increased science fiction element, with the ape-man having adventures with a whale in Atlantis and winged men, one of whom – Argus – was a refugee from a Dell comic for copyright and motivational reasons unknown. Then there was the giant robot... 'This wasn't my idea of the right way to approach it, of course,' says Kline, 'and yet it was so common to the thinking then that it seemed like it was perfectly safe to proceed in that way. When you talk about the absence of any authentic Burroughs-style conflict involving action and violence, you've got to replace it with something.'

For the third season in 1978, the ape-man was part of a show billed as *Tarzan and the Super 7* and his segments were now just 15 minutes long, which meant that the repeats that alternated with the six new episodes were severely edited. Burroughsonia was again in short supply. Additionally, the moral messages were now being laid on with a trowel.

Just when the show seemed to be in an unstoppable tailspin, the fourth season, incorporated in the second run of *Tarzan and the Super 7* in 1979, saw the ape-man's sections brought back up to the level of quality of the first season. Tarzan's episodes were of 30 minutes' duration once more, Burroughs' world was again represented by more than scattered Mangani speech, and the African wildlife that had been curiously absent lately began reappearing. Making an appearance after a complete absence hitherto was Jane ('Look Nkima – it is three men and ... a young lady! How beautiful she is!'). The opening credits had always shown a smouldering cabin prior to Kala picking up a helpless human babe, but that was as far as an explanation of Tarzan's origins went. The episode *Tarzan and Jane* was a loose (and naturally seriously telescoped) adaptation of *Tarzan of the Apes* in which the ape-man filled in a few more details when talking to Professor Porter and his daughter in the log cabin: 'This house was built by my parents, who were marooned on these shores much like yourselves. When my parents died, I was adopted among the great apes, but I later returned to this house, rebuilt it and from these books taught myself the language of men ...' The ape-man goes with a giggly Jane on a rather suggestive sight-seeing tour of his 'strange' but 'not forsaken' wilderness home. Following an adventure in a lost city, Miss Porter and her father decide to defer their return to civilisation. Tarzan promises he will visit them often.

That fourth season was the last hurrah for the Tarzan cartoon, which when it re-emerged in 1981 consisted only of heavily edited repeats in the *Tarzan/Lone Ranger/Zorro Adventure Hour*. A brief afterlife was provided by 1984 re-runs.

Kline has misgivings about the quality of the *Tarzan Lord of the Jungle* episodes he has revisited on YouTube: 'It's pretty dull by today's standards ... The original [Burroughs] stories have such a different quality to them, they're so exciting from an action standpoint. That had to be cut back so much. You can see the results of that creative handicap. Plus there was so little time to accomplish whatever had to be done for it. The best way to demonstrate that variance is to compare the Filmation Tarzan TV series with the Disney feature film … It was just so infuriating to us as kids in our twenties that we had to work under those economic and time restrictions, because we really wanted to do great things. Our biggest influence at that time were the Superman cartoons that the Fleisher studios did back in the '40s. We were never able to even get close.' Janson has equally harsh memories about what was his first-ever writing job: 'We felt that the show was watered down to the point it had little to do with the original vision. But that was and still is the reality of kids' TV and one reason most of it is so bad.' However, asked if *Tarzan Lord of the Jungle* was considered a success and an endeavour with which Filmation were pleased, Kline at least says, 'Oh yeah. Absolutely. I do believe it was quite popular. I remember one of the major creative people at Hanna-Barbera, Bob Singer, going out of his way to compliment us on what a good job we had done. He was very impressed with how well we had put that together. If you go back and you look at what was on television at the time, it's a bit of a stand-out in terms of the quality.'

Joe Kubert and Gerry Conway may have got the impression that the DC Comics Tarzan title had been cancelled due simply to poor sales, but that was not the story circulating elsewhere.

In *Eerie* magazine #79 cover-dated November 1976, journalist Joe Brancatelli told a very different tale. Quoting what he termed a reliable source within ERB, Inc, he claimed, 'ERB, Inc was displeased with National's stories and artwork on Burroughs' characters and disappointed that the company had not lived up to an apparently unwritten agreement to promote the lesser-known Pellucidar and John Carter features. ERB, Inc subsequently chose not to renew NPP's contract when it expired earlier this year.'

ERB, Inc president Robert Hodes was instead planning to start a comic book publishing company of the corporation's own. Hodes figured that the editorial costs would be funded by the fact that ERB, Inc was already producing comics material for sale to foreign publishers. Mark Evanier was appointed managing editor of the comic book division in April '76, by which point production on the new material had already begun. Pre-contract agreements were made with a printer and a distributor. It was a scenario almost designed to make comics-reading Burroughs fans drool at the mouth. Here was their Holy Grail: comic adaptations administered by people who would not be allowed to deviate from the principles established in the canon in the way that many DC stories – to

ERBivores' fury – had done.

However, the corporation seemed to have jumped the gun. Foreign publishers who owned the comic book rights to Burroughs characters proved uninterested in the Evanier material, which posed a potential problem because their contracts gave them the right to generate their own material should they wish. (Brancatelli also reported of foreign publishers that 'they had been unimpressed with National's material including Joe Kubert's Tarzan.') Nevertheless, Evanier was authorised to continue and to backlog material. Enter Marion Burroughs. Two of the first things she did when she decided to take up the reins of her inheritance were to cancel the comics publishing company and to cease in-house comics material production.

This left ERB, Inc with only the option of casting around for a new comics publisher for their characters in the States. To some extent they were in a seller's market. Such was the pulling power of Tarzan and Korak at least that Western/Gold Key would almost certainly have welcomed them back, while National Periodical Publications' president Sol Harrison had actually indicated he would even be prepared to have DC publish stories produced by ERB, Inc. Charlton Comics would no doubt also have been interested, although there would have been severe psychological obstacles to ERB, Inc working with a publisher that had provoked legal action from the corporation in 1964 after falling victim to the then-prevailing mass delusion that Tarzan was a public domain character. Brancatelli didn't mention in his article any possibility that ERB, Inc might be considering offering their properties to Warren Comics, publisher of the magazine in which he was writing. Warren published A4-sized comic books with glossy covers and black-and-white content aimed at a slightly older market. (Periodicals with magazine formats were not bound by the Comics Code Authority and were able to be slightly more daring.) An adult-orientated Tarzan title to stand alongside Warren publications like *Vampirella*, *Eerie* and *The Spirit* might well have been the greatest Tarzan comic of them all.

In the end, the corporation plumped for the obvious choice. An eager Marvel Comics had produced sample Tarzan material in 1972 when it was known that Western were being forced to relinquish the licence. However, they had lost out to what they wryly termed their Distinguished Competition. In some senses it was logical and even desirable that Marvel should now be given their chance. At this point in history, Marvel were considered the hippest of the American comic book companies, their storylines on a higher intellectual plane than most DC fare even if their sales figures were generally lower. Moreover, they were more associated with comics based on licensed properties than DC. In that field, they were just entering their pomp: their adaptation of new movie *Star Wars* was about to become one of the biggest-selling American comics of all time.

Marvel's adaptation of *Star Wars* was written by Roy Thomas, although that was less a reason for his being picked to script the new Tarzan title than his celebrated work on another of Marvel's licensed properties, *Conan the Barbarian*. The latter adaptation of the pulp sword and sorcery works of Robert E Howard (a Burroughs devotee, of course) had taken the comics world by storm since its introduction in 1970, and it seems it was the fact that Tarzan was another loinclothed non-superhero that prompted Marvel supremo Stan Lee to give Thomas the gig. Thomas admits he was not overjoyed. 'I got a call from Stan personally,' he says. 'He said they were going to do that and the John Carter comic. I wanted to do John Carter [but] Marv [Wolfman] had already put in dibs on that.' However he does concede, 'I always kind of wanted to do Tarzan even though I wanted to do John Carter more.' As with apparently just about anybody who has written Tarzan comic books, Thomas was steeped in the character and the works of his author: 'Stan had read Burroughs when he was young. Marv and I were both Burroughs fans … I was fairly familiar with Burroughs … It's not so much that you remain a fan exactly of the writing but you have to admire that imagination if you're into heroic science fiction or even just superheroes.' So impressive was Thomas's knowledge that Marion Burroughs was, he says, 'very enamoured of me for a short time.' He explains, 'Stan had me write a thing about how to exploit the other Edgar Rice Burroughs characters if it did well.' He wrote a 'long memo' about 'all the various series we could make out of it.'

Thomas had followed the DC book. 'Joe [Kubert] didn't keep enough of the dialogue and certain things like that for my particular taste,' he says, 'but [he's] my favourite comic book artist and I think he did a wonderful job on it in terms of the art. Probably the writing was pretty good too. It just was a little more spare than I was interested [in].'

John Buscema was chosen to be Marvel's Tarzan artist because, Thomas admits, he had been his long-term collaborator on *Conan the Barbarian*, though Thomas adds, 'And because John was one of the best artists around. John wasn't that eager to do Tarzan. He liked the character. He loved Joe Kubert's version. He felt like he had nothing to add to the character, but I think he did a pretty good job anyway. After the first couple of issues, though, he only did layouts. He wasn't very involved emotionally. He just adapted the books with a few notes from me and then I would do the dialogue.' In contrast to Kubert's 'snatched' style, Buscema was renowned for clean lines and chiselled features. Asked if he gave Buscema any suggestions about how Tarzan should look, Thomas says, 'Not too much. I just left it to him, and he drew it to look rather like the character had looked in some of the earliest pictures by J Allen St John and by Foster in the comic strips. I may have suggested a leopard skin rather than the lion's hide [loincloth] that [you] saw in some of these comic books drawn by Jesse Marsh and others.'

Thomas set his Tarzan world in the era of biplanes, not monoplanes. He reasons, 'When you modernise Tarzan too much ... you're messing up that character every bit as much as Johnny Weissmuller and the guttural, non-verbal approach that they had.'

The 'Fury-filled first issue' of Marvel's *Tarzan* was cover-dated June 1977 and, unlike the DC title, began its sequencing at #1. It featured a Buscema cover with a by-now very familiar image of Tarzan, knife unsheathed, astride a lion. Thomas readily admits the homage to the Clinton Pettee *All-Story* picture: 'I especially wanted that. I just had him add a woman on the cover. I felt like that would be a good addition.'

The Filmation *Tarzan Lord of the Jungle* series was now playing on television, but although Marvel's book was subtitled 'Lord of the Jungle' throughout its run, Thomas says of the TV show, 'I'm not even aware of [having been] aware of it, and if I was, I wouldn't have paid any attention unless they'd absolutely told me I had to. I wanted nothing to do with anything except the original work of Burroughs. And I really wasn't interested in making up new Tarzan stories right away, although I would have done some. I wanted to just adapt the novels, to pick up where basically DC had left off.' He adds, 'There [are] elements in the first couple of issues that are original simply because he's telling a story to somebody, but except for those minor incidents and a couple of things here and there in the first couple of stories, I didn't do anything original.' In the second issue, Thomas became the umpteenth comics writer to tell Tarzan's 'origin' story. He 'ignored' the antecedents and took a lateral approach by having Jane recount Tarzan's backstory in a sequence in which just one speech balloon was employed.

Impressive as dealing with that origin story in seven pages might be, Thomas displayed even greater condensation powers in Marvel's youth magazine *Pizzazz* that Autumn. Thomas explains, 'I wanted to do something different, so I thought, let's do the Young Tarzan and we'll make up little stories.' This series of brief peeks into Tarzan's formative years – an equivalent in a way of *Jungle Tales of Tarzan* – logically kicked off with an origin story. This time, Thomas managed to reduce the *Tarzan of the Apes* novel to one page of six panels. 'That was fun,' says Thomas. It would be his last contribution to this *Pizzazz* series, with David Kraft taking over from him, as he did on the *Tarzan* title itself.

The fact that American comics were cover-dated months in advance of their actual newsstand appearance means that Marvel's *Tarzan* would have first gone on sale well before the stated June, but it's still an interesting coincidence that it was in that month that Britain got a new Tarzan publication in the shape of *Tarzan Weekly*. Published by the little-known Byblos and co-edited by Russ Manning, it was a fine title, dripping with specialist knowledge, both in its strips and in its text articles. It even featured a strip devoted to Akut, Tarzan's Mangani friend in *The Beasts of Tarzan*. It deserved to last longer than the 20 issues it managed before becoming a monthly (a reduction in status, as this was and is a much less common publishing schedule for comics in Britain), which in turn dribbled away into irregular specials that staggered on into the early '80s.

In his stint on the Marvel Tarzan title, Thomas tackled *Tarzan and the Jewels of Opar*, *Tarzan Lord of the Jungle* and *Jungle Tales of Tarzan*. The book lurched back and forth haphazardly between those Burroughs tales on occasion, but Thomas raises a different demerit when he notes, 'I'm not wild about certain things I did. I think I kept too much of Burroughs' description in the captions, probably because I had been able to do that more with Robert E Howard because he had used a purple prose that lent itself to comic book adaptations. But Burroughs' prose really just told what was going on, so therefore you needed less of it. I wish I had done those adaptations a little differently, but it was still a nice book, especially the first two issues.'

There was one original Tarzan story the adaptation-orientated Thomas would have definitely countenanced writing. Given that he was more interested in John Carter than John Clayton, it would have been logical for him to engineer a team-up between the two characters: Marvel's *John Carter, Warlord of Mars* had made its debut at the same time as the *Tarzan* title. Thomas: 'I wanted to do it. I remember reading the early science fiction fanzines in the early '60s about this book *Tarzan on Mars*, which I was very eager to see. When I finally did see it and read a little of it, it wasn't anything to write home about. It was a great idea. I've hated the fact that since then Dark Horse did it and I wasn't in on it.'

However, neither that encounter between Burroughs' two greatest heroes nor any other Tarzan story was feasible from Thomas's point of view after he took a call from Marion Burroughs in, he estimates, late 1977. Thomas: 'Up to that time we'd had an excellent relationship. I knew her reputation for being difficult, but somehow or other I had managed to avoid any problems with her. They kind of left me alone, because I wouldn't have taken any guff from her earlier ... Basically, she got unhappy because I adapted two or three of the stories from *Jungle Tales of Tarzan*, which I was told by our lawyers and so forth that had looked at the contracts that we could do. I don't know if they were wrong, but Marion called me up one day to complain about this. She said, "You can't do that." I said, "Well, they told me I can. Your beef is with the people back in New York, not with me. I obviously won't do it if they tell me I can't do it." Then she kind of accused me and even Buscema of plagiarising – didn't use that word, but that's what it amounted to – the work of Burne Hogarth, because he had earlier adapted one of the same *Jungle Tales of Tarzan* in one of his hardcover books ... She was afraid of trouble with him, but she didn't say he had complained ... She said, "Even some of the wording is similar." I said, "Well of course it is. We were both adapting an Edgar Rice Burroughs story." She was a stupid, foolishly flawed woman. I knew Buscema didn't have the book and didn't even like Burne Hogarth. He was very much a Hal Foster/Allen St John fan. I really got upset at the veiled accusations, and I just hung up on her. I called Marvel and I quit the book effective immediately. The book lasted some months longer. I didn't mind quitting that much, but I wasn't going to deal with that idiot woman anymore ... Around the same time, I quit doing *Star Wars*. I wasn't interested in having somebody tell me what to do in the comics. Maybe if Stan told me I could take it, but I wasn't going to take it from Marion Burroughs [or] even from George Lucas ... Danton Burroughs apologised to me once or twice years later for her behaviour. I don't think she was good for that company, but she was there and at that stage there was nothing Danton or anybody else could do. She was the widow of the son of Edgar Rice Burroughs and that took precedence over him as the grandson. I don't think she was ever the fan that Danton was.'

As well as David Kraft, Bill Mantlo succeeded Thomas in the writing duties on Marvel's *Tarzan* book. 'I guess they did fine,' shrugs Thomas. 'I never read any of the issues all the way through. I know Dave was assigned to rewrite one of my *Jungle Tales* near the end, made it look like he wrote it rather than me because they were trying to appease Marion Burroughs by changing the wording.' Thomas blames neither those writers nor the introduction of original, as opposed to adapted, storylines after his departure for the fact that Marvel's *Tarzan* title was cancelled after 29 issues. (There were also three annuals. The *John Carter* title lasted 28 issues and three annuals.) Thomas: 'Neither the DC nor later the Marvel book sold particularly well, though I don't recall any sales figures. They weren't disastrously bad but they weren't good enough. I was told this was true with Marvel – and perhaps it was with DC as well – that Edgar

Rice Burroughs, Inc insisted on a high enough payment for it that made it more difficult for it to make a profit if it didn't sell exceptionally well … We got *Star Wars* free. Conan was almost free – two or three hundred dollars an issue.' DC's Gerry Conway agrees. He says, 'The cost of the license and the weak sales made it a poor prospect for either company economically. The only reason to do the book – at that time – was fan nostalgia on the part of the publishers and professionals who got a chance to participate.' Marvel did put out another Tarzan title in 1983, but whether or not the world needed yet another version of his origin story, as presented in *Marvel Super Special* and reprinted in two issues titled *Tarzan of the Apes* the following year, is a debatable point.

Thomas says, 'I remember Stan telling me he sat down with Marion Burroughs, and I don't know who else was there at the meeting, in New York and they thought they had everything all [sorted] out, and then they got a contract from Tarzana which almost [made it seem] like the whole conversation didn't happen, all the agreements weren't there. I always said that Marion Burroughs was the person who woke up in the night in a deep sweat fearful that somewhere in the world somebody besides her and the estate was making money out of Tarzan.'

Pretty soon, few would be making money out of Tarzan. Though Tarzan movies had been scarce in this decade, what with the Filmation series and the comics titles either side of the Atlantic, the years 1976 to 1978 had been good ones for the ape-man. The fact that he was now visible mainly in an animated series and in comics confirmed Tarzan's complete transmogrification down the decades from a character for adults to a children's icon, but he was at least still prominent. From this point, after an almost unbroken half-century, there would be no regular American Tarzan comic books for a generation. Meanwhile, though Ballantine continued to publish Tarzan paperbacks in the States, ape-man novels were becoming hard to find in the UK. New English Library and Flamingo – who had inherited UK paperback rights from Four Square – had passed the reins over to Panther, who published the first few books and then lost interest. It was all symptomatic of Tarzan's eclipse as a major cultural figure.

Aside from the Roddenberry film, the other Holy Grail/running joke Tarzan project drooled over by Burroughs fans was a film both written and directed by Robert Towne – celebrated screenwriter of the likes of *Chinatown* and *Shampoo* – that was intended to adapt the *Tarzan of the Apes* novel faithfully for the first time in the modern era.

Talk of that project first began appearing in print in the mid-'70s. In 1976,

Danton Burroughs excitedly announced, 'Towne says he's going to give my grandfather's Tarzan to the people. I've liked some of the screen Tarzans, but none of them has been like the man my grandfather created. If you've read the books, you know that Tarzan was actually an English lord who was well educated and didn't use "me" in the nominative case.' It was indeed exciting news, if made less exciting by Danton's simultaneous declaration that he would be interested in taking the lead role. (He said he worked out a lot.)

The movie was subject to such delays and switchbacks in fortune that for several years it seemed destined for the same fate as the Roddenberry film. It was beaten to the screens by a picture that went in completely the opposite direction as regards its fealty to the source, *Tarzan the Ape Man* starring Bo Derek. It may even be the case that the reason the late-'70s saw Tarzan's last gasp as a major cultural figure is this latter 107-minute 1981 venture.

Many a Tarzan/Burroughs fan would have been ecstatic at the news that the character who had – Ron Ely pseudo-movies and Steve Hawkes ersatz movies excepted – sat out the '70s cinematically was making a big screen comeback in what was the second remake of the exalted 1932 Weissmuller flick. Their ecstasy was to turn to horror. Though the first remake – the 1959 Denny Miller film – had been dubbed by Gabe Essoe 'Tarzan the Worst', remarkably this film stole that dubious crown.

The 1981 *Tarzan the Ape Man* is referred to in some sources as *Tarzan, the Ape Man* based on the fact that the comma appears in the closing frame of the film, though it is not visible on either the movie poster or the opening credits' rendition of the title. 'No comma on my script title page,' says Gary Goddard, writer of the film's screenplay with Tom Rowe. That, however, does not begin to address the contentious issues surrounding the project.

The movie was produced by Bo Derek and directed by the actress's husband John. An allusion to the perceived power balance within that professional relationship is made by the Frank Frazetta-drawn title card for their production company Svengali that precedes the picture: it shows a smiling, naked Bo dangling her husband on puppet strings. Goddard says, however, 'It was really John's vision. Bo sometimes would sit in the meetings and would contribute some things. She was very much into creating her role, but in terms of the writing and directing she really let John do his thing.' Though that title card may be a joke, there is no doubting that an unusual pecking order is revealed in the credits: Bo Derek (Jane) is given star billing, Richard Harris (Jane's father) second billing and Miles O'Keeffe – who happened to play the title character – receives an 'Introducing' at the credits' end. Additionally, the movie poster depicted Bo Derek swinging alone on a vine. It may be difficult to remember

215

now, but at the time, Mrs Derek had a status in popular culture that justified the part of said poster's strapline that read, 'The most beautiful woman of our time …' With her riding high on the fame created by her chiselled beauty, incongruous cornrows and perfectly formed breasts in *10* (1979), it didn't seem too outlandish an idea to build a new Tarzan movie around her. The result was ostensibly a film that made up big-time for the 22-year absence of Jane from the cinema franchise. It also effectively destroyed Bo Derek's career, even though, despite an 'R' rating unprecedented for a Tarzan flick, it pulled in $30m more than its budget.

Though Burroughs fans (and indeed ERB, Inc) were infuriated by Jane's elevated position, the film was actually a dilution of the Dereks' original intentions. Explains Goddard, 'After Bo had done *10* and was a huge sensation, John had a concept for a movie that he called *Me, Jane*. It was the Tarzan story from a Jane perspective, which when you look back on it, was ahead of its time, because it was before *Wicked*, it was before all of these other [projects] where you take existing fairytales and you turn them around, tell them from a different vantage point. The idea of *Me, Jane* was a great idea. However, they went to MGM to do this, and MGM found they only had very narrow rights. They had the rights to do a remake of *Tarzan the Ape Man*. So the trick was to create a story that fulfilled John's desire to tell it from [Jane's] perspective without veering from the essential structure from *Tarzan the Ape Man*.'

An opening voiceover conversation taking place in (we infer) a stuffy English gentlemen's club promises a 'bizarre adventure,' and that at least can't be disputed. A clue as to the overall lack of judgment for which we are in has already come via the famous two-part growl of the MGM title card lion being buffoonishly replaced by a Tarzan yodel. The story is set in 1910, i.e. one year after the concluding (African) events of the *Tarzan of the Apes* book, although we don't get too much of an impression of the Edwardian era. The '80s hairstyle and moustache of supporting character Mr Holt (John Phillip Law) in particular seem anachronistic. Derek plays Jane Parker (as in the first film version, not Porter). Here, she is journeying to Africa to find the father she has never known. Jane shoots an intruder dead before the title credits are finished and is an independently wealthy adventurer, but this feminism is later undercut by her unutterable lip-bitten coyness in scenes with Tarzan.

Richard Harris plays James Parker as an Irishman who left Jane's now deceased mother in the year after his daughter was born for reasons never adequately explained. In their soap opera reunion, Jane suggests to her dad that he is 'a first-class bastard.' The viewer is left thinking, 'She came all the way to Africa to tell him that?' Despite her contempt for him, Jane insists on accompanying her old man on his quest to find the fabled elephant's graveyard. This is implicitly because she fancies Holt, although that sub-plot is not pursued. While on this trip, she hears a strange yodel and thereby learns of Tarzan, a legendary name – if one of varying pronunciations by the cast – that strikes fear into the native bearers.

The party conquer a huge rock barring their path – unexcitingly. When they lose one of their men due to a frayed rope, Harris is seen screaming at the sky, 'Why did you *do* that?' According to Bo, this was the Dereks' moralistic replacement of the chillingly racist 'What was in that pack?' line in the equivalent scene in the original, but the fact of a celestial and impassive shaft of light shining down beside Harris, coupled with the actor's rather unemotional delivery, creates a guffaw-provoking tableau.

The party come upon an inland sea, where Jane elects to take a bath. Cue some nude aquatic frolicking befitting the sex symbol of the age. Though Derek is beautiful, there is no getting around the fact that when Miles O'Keeffe appears chasing his pet lion along the sand, he is even more appetising. O'Keeffe was actually far from first choice. A late replacement, he had been the stand-in double for ex-boxer Lee Canalito, the man intended to be Tarzan until reputedly Bo Derek decided he wasn't trim enough. Goddard even remembers another actor being in the running in the person of Klinton Spilsbury, who played the title role in the 1981 release *The Legend of the Lone Ranger*, but a previously enthused John Derek came back from a meeting with him with a changed mind. Goddard: 'I don't think he ever said why. John wasn't like that. He goes by the gut.' Bo Derek thought a lot more of O'Keeffe's physique than she allegedly did of Canalito's, describing it in her autobiography as 'the most beautiful body' she had ever seen. O'Keeffe's physical perfection – rippling, toned, muscular but not thickset – is topped off by both a buttock-revealing loincloth and the fact that he carries himself like he's strutting down a Parisian catwalk. After calling off his oversized moggy, Tarzan wades into the surf and grabs Jane none too gently, but he is scared off by the report of a rifle as Jane's father and Mr Holt appear. Yet Jane goes from terror of Tarzan to fierce loyalty toward him for no reason in the blink of an eye: in the very next scene, she objects to her father's stated view of him as an animal.

The absurd is piled upon the ridiculous when the party sets off again and – as though this is a 1930s B-movie – James Parker vaguely remarks 'Something's not right' as unseen hostile natives in menacing paint masks gaze at them. The attacks these natives mount on the party are assumed to be the work of Tarzan. Though Tarzan is innocent on that score, he shortly materialises again with apparently dubious motives, erupting from a river at which Jane is filling her flask and swimming off with her. On dry land again, Jane produces a gun and its report sends Tarzan packing – at which point Jane unaccountably pleads, 'Don't go!' The bad acting, incomprehensible motivation and maladroit direction continue in a scene in which a python coils itself around Jane. Tarzan swings in on a vine and rescues her in an atrocious, confusing, repetitive, unexciting, overlong scene shot in the slow-motion that for no apparent reason keeps recurring. Tarzan falls ill from a snake bite, at which point his animal friends miraculously appear to help him, one of which is inexplicably an orangutan. At least in the 1920s when orangutan star Joe Martin featured in silent screen Tarzan fare like *The Revenge of Tarzan* and *Adventures of Tarzan* the excuse could be made that audiences weren't sufficiently worldly to understand or care that his was a type of ape indigenous to Asia. An elephant scoops the unconscious Tarzan up in its tusks and carries him off. This scene makes sense in the original, but here all the pachyderm is doing is taking Tarzan to a river different from the one in which he has just wrestled the python. This problem of a scene transplanted so arbitrarily from the predecessor film as to be perplexing or idiotic afflicts the entire remake.

Jane then becomes the predator. She strokes Tarzan's prone, unconscious body, the virgin revelling in this never-before experienced sensation; and when he awakes and moves away from her, she pursues him and sits beneath a tree in which he takes refuge. Eventually, the two spend a chaste night in a tree nest. The next day, they achieve some sort of rapport, although a primitive one: Tarzan is mute throughout the movie (which at least gives a quasi-excuse for his backstory being unexplained). Notes Goddard, 'That is a decision that John made. I would have liked him to speak. He liked the idea of the silent, brooding embodiment of the male machismo … He wanted him to be this presence … In John's mind, he was making *Me, Jane*.' The pair engage in some idyllic frolicking and splashing, with Jane keeping up a commentary of babbling nonsense. In another snort-inducing passage, Jane bites her lip in delight as Tarzan inspects the contents of her blouse. It is the crassly adolescent polar opposite of the mature, beautiful sensuality of the nude swimming scene in *Tarzan and his Mate*.

Tarzan delivers Jane back to her father's party but is frightened away by their hostility. Cue the re-entry of the hostile natives, who slaughter some of the party and take the remainder, including the Parkers, back to their village. The fearsome, gargantuan and curiously punk rocker-like chief of the tribe almost idly impales James Parker on an elephant tusk before advancing menacingly on Jane, who has just featured in an extended scene in which her naked body is ritualistically washed, with her on all fours. Alerted by a chimp friend to Jane's situation, Tarzan rides to the rescue aback an elephant. He swings in on a vine to confront the tribal leader. In another ineptly shot and totally unengaging slo-mo action scene, Tarzan triumphs by snapping his enemy's neck. The tribe conveniently don't interfere as the pair fight, and then evaporate when the tussle is over. Tarzan throws his head back and yodels – as elsewhere, clearly an overdub of Weissmuller vintage. Despite the elephant tusk through his guts, Harris delivers an interminable death speech to his daughter. Even had that speech contained any trace of pathos, it would have been washed away by the scene immediately following, in which another opportunity is taken to put Derek's chest on display as Tarzan washes Jane of the ceremonial paint in which she has been forcibly daubed. A subsequent quite pretty *From Here to Eternity*-esque prone beach sequence with Tarzan and Jane is then undermined by a lengthy closing credits sequence wherein a topless Jane is seen engaging in horseplay with orangutan and ape-man.

'I had the vision of, "I'm going to write the greatest Tarzan script ever, because I know Tarzan, I love the material",' says Goddard. So where did it all go wrong?

The original script – filtered as with all its drafts, of course, through the original MGM *Tarzan the Ape Man* and then John Derek's sensibilities – was by Tom Rowe. Goddard: 'He had done at least two drafts before me. I thought it was decent. The essential difference is I believe he was an older guy, I was a younger guy. He wrote from a different life experience.' He adds, 'We're credited together but we never met each other. The Writers Guild determined that we had a shared credit.' The 24-year-old Goddard was just starting his screenwriting career. He had been working for John and Bo Derek on a Marvel Comics-related project called *Dazzler*. Goddard recalls, 'One day John says, "We're working on this project at MGM, *Tarzan the Ape Man*. We really like your writing and we're not that happy with the script that we just got and we'd like you to do a dialogue polish." So I started doing a dialogue polish only of the entire script and I got about 70 percent through it, and by then MGM were anxious to get the movie into production. They said, "We really like your writing but we don't like what it's based on. We want you to do a whole new script from page one; start over, but you got to do it fast, and we want you to go with us to the Seychelles islands." I lived in the Seychelles islands with Bo and John in a villa for almost a month, and in the course of that month did almost three full rewrites of the script … The MGM head of production told me, "When you're done writing it and John approves it, our legal department has to vet it." It's tough enough to write a screenplay, but you have to write a screenplay with all these rules.'

Nonetheless, Goddard was ecstatic at the position in which he found himself, and it wasn't just the exotic surroundings that overawed the young writer. Not only was he working for the biggest female star in the world at that time but he was 'a huge fan' of Richard Harris: 'I wrote that character with his voice in mind and with his bombastic personality.' Additionally, 'If I didn't read all the Tarzan books growing up, I read most of them, so it was a big thrill for me to be able to write this Tarzan script.' Goddard watched neither the Weissmuller nor Denny Miller *Tarzan the Ape Man* movies in preparation: 'I did read the original script that we were basing it on, 'cause I had to know that script, but I was really trying to create this world that John wanted.' Of the latter he says, 'John had very specific ideas.' He adds, 'I think in my enthusiasm and excitement to make what I felt would be a great Tarzan film, I brought a lot of unique things to it.' However, Goddard had a shock in store. He says, 'I got the lesson you always hear from writers. I learned the writer is the most important person on the job until the day shooting starts, at which point he is now almost a non-entity.' Goddard did not attend the eight-week shoot in Sri Lanka and the Seychelles, where ex-movie Tarzan Jock Mahoney (credited as Jack O'Mahoney) was stunt coordinator. He got to find out what had been done to his script only when he attended a preview. Goddard: 'I was all excited. It starts unfolding and I'm like, "Did I write that? I don't think I wrote that".' At the end of the screening, he was 'stunned.' He recalls, 'I'm realising all my friends and peers are going to watch this and go "God, Gary wrote that, could you believe it?"' Yet he faced a dilemma: 'If you take your name off, you also don't get your residuals. Everything's tied to your screen credit. I just had to bite the bullet.'

He elaborates on the changes that had been made: 'John did have a penchant to improvise a little bit on a theme. While the basic structure remains pretty much as written, in some of the scenes a lot of the dialogue was improvised based upon what I wrote.' Other elements were wholly new. Of the risible celestial shaft of light and boobs-groping scenes, Goddard says, 'Neither of those are in the script! John considers himself an artist. He's a photographer by nature so everything in his films is visual first.' Like many, Goddard was puzzled by John Derek's insistence on slow motion. He feels he came to understand it when he subsequently worked with the director on a picture called *Pirate Annie* that didn't get produced. He offers, 'John was afraid of action sequences, 'cause he didn't know how to shoot them, and the artistic part of him that believed a director must shoot every frame prevented him from [being] willing to hire a second unit director [to shoot them].'

Of course, for all anyone knows, Goddard's script as originally envisioned would have made an equally terrible movie. However, perhaps a yardstick for the way that he feels his vision was traduced is the section in which Jane is painted. In the finished product, the white paint is puzzling where it doesn't seem an excuse to show off Bo's bod. Goddard's original idea had a sophisticated hinterland, being based on the elaborate religious paintings rendered on elephants in India. Goddard also says, 'You wouldn't even realise [initially] she was naked: it would look like she's in this very elegant, embroidered, form-fitting gown, then when the camera moved in on it, only then you would realise that she's been decorated. It's a very beautiful thing. I was a little surprised when I saw the film that it was just all that white paint going on her. John said, "Oh my God, I was on such a tight schedule".'

Though one prominent critic – Gene Shalit – lauded it as an enjoyable, fun movie, the reviews of *Tarzan the Ape Man* were generally savage. Goddard doesn't blame Bo Derek's widely-derided acting: 'If you look at Bo in *10*, she's very charismatic. I think she had a lot of innate ability. Everyone in Hollywood wanted to work with her.' However, Goddard admits he was not surprised by the reviews. He says of John Derek's intentions, 'I think he went into it thinking he would somehow get his vision in there, and he somehow did, except not really, because the structure's the structure. Maybe that movie done by John in his own artistic way would have been very cool, but trying to bend the plot of *Tarzan the Ape Man* into that really couldn't work, so he wound up with this hybrid that certainly didn't make the Tarzan fans happy, and I'm not sure that it made the Bo Derek fans happy.'

John Derek admitted that before the film opened he had had to edit out two minutes and four seconds of material that a federal judge had decided violated the clause of Burroughs' original contract with MGM. Though that contract had allowed – even insisted – on a certain distance from the books, it had also stated the original story could not be drastically changed. There was further legal action. The fact that Tarzan didn't appear until over half-way through the picture as well as the 'R' rating led ERB, Inc to sue MGM over derogatory treatment of their character. Danton Burroughs: 'MGM had the rights to remake *Tarzan the Ape Man* in perpetuity given to them from a contract that my granddad wrote. It was just a bad wording, so we took them to court to try to stop the movie in the 1980s. We stopped them. They can never do another re-make of *Tarzan the Ape Man*, but that one got out.' With a mixture of horror and admiration, Danton said, 'It was so unique. It's a cult classic.'

Danton also said, 'Miles O'Keeffe was just excellent, but he didn't talk.' Indeed. The film is a failure on almost every level imaginable, yet there is one shining exception to the overall ghastliness. No-one – not Kamuela Searle, not Johnny Weissmuller, not Gordon Scott, not Mike Henry – had ever looked as good as O'Keeffe in a loincloth. Everybody questioned about him for this book enthuses over O'Keeffe. Denny Miller, star of the previous *Tarzan the Ape Man* as well as an expert on physical fitness, says of him, 'He looked better than any of us. He was really ripped.'

How ironic that the finest ever visual representation of the ape-man should feature in the worst Tarzan movie of all time.

The Holy Grail Robert Towne-helmed movie meanwhile continued its long, tortuous journey to fruition, but when it finally reached the cinemas Towne was out of the equation.

'What happened was, Bob Towne got into a fight with Warner Brothers so he stopped doing the rest of the screenplay, so that Warner Brothers only used half of it,' explained Danton Burroughs. 'Then Hugh Hudson had to finish the rest.' Hudson himself recalls things slightly differently: 'Robert Towne sold his rights back to Warner Brothers because he was making a film called *Personal Best* and he needed another million dollars I think. Warner Brothers agreed to give it to him if he gave up his rights in doing *Greystoke*.'

Offering the director's job to Hudson – whose work on 1981's *Chariots of Fire* helped win that production an Oscar for Best Picture – demonstrated a goodwill and serious commitment to the property on the part of the studio. At one point, *Chariots of Fire* producer David Puttnam was even set to come aboard the project. Hudson: 'He pulled away from it. We tried to find a producer. In the end they said, "Well *you* do it." I produced it and directed it, but out of London where I had the Warner operation supporting me, so really it was produced by Warner Brothers.' Stanley S Canter was credited as co-producer with Hudson, but the latter says, 'I never met him. He wasn't involved in the film as far as I'm concerned. He got a credit because he was involved from the past.'

'All my life I've read them,' says Hudson of Burroughs' books. 'I liked them. They were great. Certainly the first one or two. So many films had been made and television things and they always changed things … I liked the concept of it, of going back and doing it for real. As real as you could do it … It was a very interesting story about all sorts of things. I tried to deepen it as much as I could, make it about nature and nurture and all those things. He's an interesting invention, Tarzan. It's become a myth of the 20th Century. Although it's an invented character, it's like a mythic character.'

Hudson says of the script he inherited from Towne, 'It had the germ of a very interesting [film]. Half the film was silent: people speaking animal talk. There was no dialogue until they meet the white people, very little. I liked that concept. It's quite faithful to the original story ... He'd written half of the script ... He hadn't taken it back to England. He'd sketched out various ideas for going back to England and we followed some of them, and they were much in the style of what we finally did.'

Hudson brought in Michael Austin to finish Towne's semi-screenplay. Austin had previously written the Alan Bates movie *The Shout* (1978) and the Sean Connery vehicle *Five Days One Summer* (1982). He was not steeped in Burroughs like Hudson but the director explains he was a 'very witty man. Very witty dialogue ... We did it together, we structured and decided how to do it and we produced a screenplay which Warner Brothers liked.' Hudson says that simply in order to remain faithful to the book there was no thought given to setting the film in the present day. When it is pointed out that the ending of the film doesn't retain faithfulness (Danton Burroughs: 'The second half had nothing to do with my granddad's story'), Hudson shrugs, 'We had to make it into a film.'

Leaving aside instances when budget limitations and zoological ignorance had seen them rendered as of indeterminate species, for the first time on film, Tarzan's tribe are depicted as the undiscovered Mangani species of the books. Moreover, the production techniques of that time enabled their realisation to be frequently convincing. Notes Hudson, 'If you look at something like [*Rise of the*] *Planet of the Apes* [2011] today, everything is constructed in a computer, but we were making our film before any of that was a current form of film effect, and we had to do it for real. We couldn't use midgets. We had to use small people, dancers, mainly female. So we managed to create a species of ape which was about five foot four maximum, and we trained them for three months in a studio somewhere. They created a primate tribe with a hierarchy, an alpha male, children.' The sole exception was that the crew 'used chimpanzee babies.' Hudson says of his apes, 'We did a very good job considering the period. They're not quite right, but even today they're pretty good. They're a little bit more primate than Stanley Kubrick's apes in *2001*, 'cause he had them slightly further advanced.' Hudson is not jealous that the film was made pre-CGI: 'I think what we did is totally acceptable now, and it's actually better than ... [*Rise of the*] *Planet of the Apes*. It's very successful, but ... there's something too perfect about it, something slightly mechanical.'

The fidelity to the source in this aspect goes only so far, though: the heart rather sinks when the apes' – and therefore the hero's – mode of arboreal transit is shown to be swinging on a succession of conveniently placed vines as though this is just another Johnny Weissmuller flick. In response to the suggestion that he could have shown the ape-man swinging from bough to bough instead, Hudson says: 'I didn't want to do it. We could have done it. He managed to do it once, and it wasn't necessary to do it all the time.'

Hudson 'saw many' actors hoping to be the new screen Tarzan. (He was not aware of Danton Burroughs' interest in screen-testing.) He says, 'We finally tested four ... An American dancing as a lead with the Dutch Royal Ballet ... I think the name was Fahy ... Julian Sands, Christopher Lambert and Viggo Mortensen. We did proper tests. We built an area and we tested them all, and we picked Christopher Lambert. He had a wonderful way of looking; he had a gaze beyond the camera into the distance. It's only because he's myopic, actually. It was a very interesting look. And he was a complete loner ... He's not a bodybuilder – I absolutely specifically didn't want that. Johnny Weissmuller was a most magnificent-looking man and he wasn't overbuilt: he didn't have enormous pectoral muscles or six-pack stomach muscles.' Whatever qualities Hudson may have seen in him, 26-year-old Frenchman Lambert was a controversial choice, because he was unlike any previous screen Tarzan in possessing no discernible biceps. Because of his apparent physical unsuitability for the role, some might suspect that Lambert's French accent played a small part in him being cast as a man who learns his English from D'Arnot, but Hudson says, 'No. It just was by chance.' He says he did not have cause to regret his choice, either because of Lambert's lack of physique or his screen experience: 'His body was pretty good by the time we'd trained him and built it up. It was fine ... I think he was very good. He works very well. And of course he's supported by the magnificent Ian Holm and Ralph Richardson, another superb actor.'

In fact, far more problems were caused the director by Andie MacDowell, the woman cast as Jane. Hudson: 'She was a model and she didn't know how to use her voice to portray the emotions ... We were in the middle of the shooting and we started to try things out. It didn't work, so I just let it go and did what I could ... So we overdubbed her with a very good actress ... It was a terrible blow for her no doubt when she realised that was happening ... However, she went immediately to acting and vocal school and she became a pretty good actress.'

Hudson was to encounter more problems after the wrap. The audience reaction at previews motivated Warner Brothers to order the chopping out of large chunks of the completed film. The studio's nervousness was understandable: they had spent a then-massive $46m on production, nearly a sixth of which had gone on Rick Baker's ape makeup and costumes. Hudson denies rumours about the length of that first cut: 'It was never three hours. Two hours 40 minutes … The demand from the studio was it should be made, maximum, two hours ten minutes, and [they said that] it was too violent.'

The makers of the first Tarzan picture had distastefully boasted in publicity about their star killing a lion on set, but Hudson – who shot only simulated wildlife death – encountered a problem that perhaps indicates the pendulum had since swung too far in the other direction: 'It was tested and people were turned away and said, "It's too violent, it's awful, the animals killing each other." And then they watch it quite happily [in] David Attenborough shows … You can't kill animals [in movies]. They don't mind *people* killing each other.' Hudson admits that as he set about re-editing the picture with his non-violence remit, he wondered if his cuts were removing the entre point of the picture, but in the end he was happy with the compromise: 'We have to find another way of doing it. You finally believe he is the king of the animals' kingdom. He gives a panther to them, he's proven to be a provider of meat.'

The film was finally released in March 1984. In being named *Greystoke* it cleaved to the current fashion in cinema for single-word, myth-draped titles. However, the subtitle *The Legend of Tarzan, Lord of the Apes* was understandably appended lest its subject matter escape the vast majority of the public who had no idea that Tarzan went by another name. Just to fully cover themselves, the studio authorised a movie poster containing a précis eight words shy of a hundred.

That this is a very different Tarzan movie is apparent right at the beginning, which consists of a still shot of a tree captioned 'OVERTURE', which lasts for one-and-a-half minutes to the accompaniment of classical music. However, cinemagoers not already apprised of it by the reviews would have to wait until the end credits to apprehend another arresting departure from all previous versions except for the silent-era movies and the Denny Miller film: nowhere herein is the word 'Tarzan' uttered – presumably the reason for the 'legend' in the title, an apparent attempt to give the name the quality of a handed-down myth. Was the non-use a matter of dispensing with the difficulty of explaining such a non-simian sounding word? Hudson: 'I don't think we thought of it like that.' Hudson says he can't remember now what the exact reason was, but from his comments it rather sounds as if he felt the name had acquired a 'cheese-factor': 'We were trying to make a realistic story.'

Another caption tells us that the opening scene proper – the death of the baby of the character we know from the books as Kala – occurs in Equatorial West Africa in 1885. Many Burroughs fans would doubtless welcome the film being set in the era of the *Tarzan of the Apes* novel, though why all filmmakers without exception have stubbornly resisted the 1888 Burroughs date for the sailing of the *Fuwalda* is a small mystery. The way the Mangani (who are never called that) are depicted is a mixture of excellent – very good faces, especially the yellowed fangs of the elders – and laughable – sometimes they are as obviously men in hairy suits as the trapeze artists in the 1918 *Tarzan of the Apes*; Kala's dead baby looks like the doll it is.

We are then taken back in time and across to Scotland where Lord Jack (sic) Clayton is preparing to leave the Greystoke family seat for a trip to Africa. That no less a celebrated actor than Sir Ralph Richardson plays the kindly old duffer grandfather of the unborn hero is not incongruous. The cast is positively studded with renowned British thesps, James Fox, Ian Holm, David Suchet and Richard Griffiths among them. The Americans meanwhile are superstars in waiting: not only is Jane played by Andie MacDowell but she is voiced by Glenn Close. What seems the first of many places where it is obvious that a huge chunk of the film has been excised follows, when we are witness to the aftermath of a shipwreck whose cause is not explained. However, Hudson reveals that the easy assumption that the book's mutiny was shot and then dumped is incorrect: 'We didn't bother to do that. We were going too high in the budget.'

The Claytons build a cabin in their new jungle home while sole fellow survivor Captain Billings sails off (we are told but not shown) to seek help, never to be heard from again. From the 14-minute mark when a newly widowed Clayton cries out when being killed by a bull ape to gone the 31-minute mark, there is no human dialogue whatsoever in a succession of generally touching scenes in which we see baby John Clayton being raised by Kala. That times have changed since that first filmed Tarzan origin story in 1918 is evident in content that inaugural production would never have been allowed to include: full-frontal nudity, portrayals of lactation and a scene in which a teenage Clayton urinates on the chief of his tribe. The teenage Clayton is played by Eric Langlois, who for some reason presumably related to confused notions of decency has his buttocks literally glued together. (Daniel Potts – the five-year-old version of the character – is afforded no such dignity in his manifold bending and crouching motions.) It is established in this section (if not quite convincingly) that the young jungle boy has an uncanny ability for mimicry of wildlife from birds to big cats. The panoramas (shot in the Cameroons, whose Mount Cameroon was handily in the process of photogenically becoming an active volcano) are sumptuous sights made all the richer by the Royal Philharmonic Orchestra-played John Scott score. However, the scenes beneath the jungle canopy look like studio shoots and have the sort of acoustics associated with swimming baths.

The boy Clayton is left grief-stricken when natives kill Kala. Wholesale editing presumably accounts for the natives' apparent lack of motive, but it's difficult to know where to lay the blame for the fact that the scene is so limp. When the accomplices of Kala's killer turn and run after seeing Clayton dispense with him with a single back-breaking manoeuvre, this is not the stuff of the naturalism that this movie claims as its currency but instead the corny coinage of old black and white Tarzan pictures.

Up to this point, the narrative has been fairly close to that of the *Tarzan of the Apes* novel. Though Ian Holm is very good in his tetchy but noble interpretation of D'Arnot, it is with this character's arrival that the Burroughs influence begins to drain from the picture, starting with the fact that he is Belgian rather than French and his first name is Philippe rather than Paul. D'Arnot is heading a steamboat expedition whose task is an inventory of fauna for the British Museum, though one of his fellow passengers has a more bloody idea of inventory. The party is slaughtered by cannibals in a powerful and distressing sequence shortly after discovering the late Lord Greystoke's decaying log cabin. D'Arnot flees and hides. One of the picture's most memorable scenes occurs here as he faints in disbelief when Clayton looms over his feverish form with a curious Mangani in turn peering over his shoulder.

This is the first time we have seen the adult Clayton (Christopher Lambert). He wears a headband, his mother's locket and a loincloth. Said clothing – aside from the headband – was of course explained by Burroughs in his novel, as was the fact that the protagonist was clean-shaven at this age. Neither are clarified here, though ludicrously, D'Arnot later teaches Clayton to shave and we are supposed not to notice that he looks no different following the application of the razor. Leaving aside these illogicalities, Lambert is miscast. He's not bad as such – and occasionally conveys well the man/ape duality of his character by simian grunts and a propensity for hopping and bounding where a man would walk – but one can see absolutely no reason why Hudson was so smitten. Not only is he not quite handsome, there is a semi-moronic slackness to his lower lip. Physique-wise, he is completely unimpressive. That a genuine ape/jungle upbringing would not necessarily result in bulging biceps has been touched on here before, but so has the fact that cinema requires a visual shorthand for power, strength and bravery. There again, it is never quite established in this film that Clayton is possessed of those attributes. We see him holding a dead panther around his shoulders but not him slaying it. Not long afterwards, there is a battle between him and this movie's equivalent of Kerchak. The action is un-ferocious and clunky, and the fact that Clayton achieves his victory while out of sight underwater feels a total cop-put: he is now king of his tribe and we are still being asked to take his fighting prowess on trust. His bull ape victory cry, incidentally, is also un-ferocious.

Clayton nurses D'Arnot back to health, starting by – in a nicely realistic touch – forcing on him live grubs. During their six months together in the jungle, D'Arnot starts teaching Clayton the English language. That Clayton's capacity for mimicry enables him to learn quickly and accurately we can accept, but hardly his rapidly attained smooth sentence construction. Tarzan initially resists D'Arnot's insistence that Kala was not his mother ('How many other white apes have you seen!') but ultimately elects to follow him on his trek back to where his own kind can be found. In another jarring jump-cut clearly brought about by imposed editing, Clayton and D'Arnot arrive at a decadent white settlement with Tarzan now somehow fully clothed. Here, Clayton's rescue of D'Arnot from a menacing gang involves another action scene whose toothlessness is down not to cutting but poor scriptwriting: instead of laying into them Mangani-style with fingers and teeth, he hurls a paraffin lamp and sets the place ablaze like some '30s matinee idol.

Another huge leap in narrative takes us to the Greystokes' Scottish castle where his Lordship is being informed that his grandson – whom he seems to confuse with his son, though that's never quite made clear – is on his way to the family seat. 'It's an extraordinary example of man's superiority over beast,' a servant tells him. 'Not only did he survive, he made himself their master. Their lord, as it were.' When his carriage pulls into the Greystoke driveway, in a sweet touch Clayton leans and peers out of the door at his new surroundings just like a wary animal might. Lord Greystoke is delighted at the 'return' to the vast family estate of the man he calls 'Johnny' and tickled pink by his childlike unfamiliarity with civilised ways that leaves him without pretension, malice, or understanding of the fact that porridge doesn't go with kippers. Clayton takes to his Lordship too, but is even more intrigued by Jane Porter, who in this narrative is his step-sister. Jane deepens his knowledge of civilisation and language and is eventually seduced by him. She then rejects the marriage proposal of pompous Lord Esker (Fox). The latter takes out his frustration on a retarded member of the clan whose part has clearly been whittled drastically down. When Clayton rescues this man from a whipping by Esker, we are by now not surprised that a warning growl is the limp extent of the action.

The grandfather – intoxicated with joy by the continuation of his line – decides to replicate a childhood joy of cruising down his castle stairs on a serving tray, with fatal consequences. Clayton – whose ambivalence about being in civilisation has already been shown – is distraught that he has come all this way to suffer a bereavement that mirrors his traumatic loss of Kala. Nonetheless, he becomes engaged to Jane.

The new Lord Greystoke – now short-haired – opens a section of the British Museum. Queasy at being surrounded by dead animals and animal parts, he ducks into a corridor, where he gravitates toward a familiar animal cry. To his astonishment, he finds his ape step-father – Tublat in the books – cooped up in a small cage in a state of distress. In a powerful scene, the two jabber at each other before Clayton releases the Mangani. The pair flee the building and make their way to the nearest jungle-like environment, a local park, Clayton snarling at encroaching parties. They climb a tree together, Clayton now fully reverted to his ape personality. Suddenly, the Mangani topples from the tree, shot by officialdom.

It is the final straw. Clayton wants to go back to what he considers home. His declaration of this to D'Arnot and a family member is convincing enough but ends with a ridiculous vista in which lights go out across the castle in quick succession – a massive edifice put on the same footing as the Waltons' family home. Clayton, D'Arnot and Jane travel to Africa, where Clayton spots a Mangani who, though unsure of him at first, welcomes him. Without a word to his human companions, Clayton strips off and runs into the jungle fastness in pursuit.

It's the end of a film that would be confused and compromised even without the imposed editing that has reduced it to a still overlong 131 minutes. Burroughs fans were infuriated by the tampering with the source, much of it unnecessary, and by the failure to fulfil that promise of fully capturing the spirit of the ERB books. For the general cinemagoer without such purist concerns, it would probably have been more enjoyable, if befuddlingly different from their previous experience of the character. Though the film might lay on too earnestly the who-is-really-the-uncivilised-one message, the ending does possess a pathos and, though it takes a different form, is consistent in tone with the tragic finale of the *Tarzan of the Apes* novel. However, the moral of the story proffered by Hudson/Austin is diametrically opposed to Burroughs' premise. 'He has a noble image and he returns to the head of his tribe in the jungle,' says Hudson. 'He's noble to the end but he doesn't want to deal with the rubbish that's tried to push down his throat by the society that they say he is among the elite of.' Burroughs' original story was predicated on an opposing belief in nature over nurture: that, in other words, Tarzan's real tribe is in civilisation and his fine breeding means that despite his savage rearing he is a Lord to the last.

The first modern Tarzan film to attempt to be faithful to the source material ends up rather suggesting something that many Burroughs fans dare not admit to themselves: that maybe Tarzan as a concept doesn't lend itself to a naturalistic film adaptation. The paradoxically unconvincing nature of a realistically skinny Tarzan is just the start. Hudson lazily opting to show vine-swinging is another problem: the character swinging from bough to bough would probably have been too labour-intensive to achieve. Then there is the thorny issue of sex that the naturalism makes one's mind stray to. (An adolescent boy who knew no better would surely have mated with a Mangani.) The difficulty of explaining the non-simian sounding name 'Tarzan' had it been used is yet another of the many possibly insurmountable obstacles to ape-man cinematic realism.

Praise for *Greystoke* amongst even Tarzan and Burroughs fans is never unequivocal. Says Bill Hillman, 'Most dedicated fans agree that the first half of that movie was excellent and then they changed the script and directors and then they turned it into more of a PC thing after that: the angst of Tarzan. As soon as they took him to England it seemed to collapse. He wasn't the heroic savage and he was little more of a weak joke.' Al Bohl offers, 'As long as he's in the jungle I thought *Greystoke* was really good. But when he went to England … I think Lambert was a very fine version of Tarzan. I just wished they'd stayed more in Africa with that character.' DC comics Tarzan writer Joe Kubert: 'I liked it very much. I liked the actor who played the part, despite the fact that he was kind of small, physically, for the part.' Marvel comics Tarzan writer Roy Thomas says, 'I thought that had a nice feel up to a certain point, but Tarzan wasn't nearly strong enough. Tarzan was a guy who could fight a gorilla and have a chance of winning. They never did anything like that with the character in that movie. I thought it was a step in the right direction despite that ridiculously long title.' Denny Miller: 'The money they spent on that production really showed up on the screen … That's one of my favourite if not my favourite production of Tarzan. I've always regretted that I didn't have as long hair as he did in playing the role. I think it's more fitting to have shoulder-length hair playing Tarzan. If I had cast *Greystoke*, I would have cast a physically bigger man. A more imposing, statuesque, more athletic looking [person] than Christopher was. But I loved what he did with the role. I loved him disrupting people in the castle, by acting more like what he was than what they wanted him to be.'

For all the many misgivings about it, the substantiality of this film was demonstrated by the fact that for the first time ever a Tarzan picture acquired Academy Award nominations: Best Supporting Actor (Richardson), Best Adapted Screenplay and Best Make-up. The middle one is the most remarkable, considering the compromises, changes and editing savagery. It also made Danton Burroughs smile, because Towne had exercised his right to remove his name from the credits: 'The first half of *Greystoke* was excellent because Bob Towne did the screenplay, but he was so pissed at Warner Brothers he [had his work credited to] his dog, P H Vazak. So [the dog] was nominated for an Academy Award.' Had Richardson won, his Oscar would have been posthumous: he died before the release of the film, which was dedicated to his memory. Hudson says, 'It should have won for visual effects. Rick Baker, who's a masterful man, he should have won.' Hudson feels that the re-editing that saw the film's scheduled late-1983 release postponed cost the studio something more than the lucrative Yuletide market: 'If it had come out at Christmas I think it would have been more accoladed, but the whole nine months, ten months waiting and people had to remember it.'

'I talked [of] sequels later on but I never got very far with it,' Hudson says. 'I was onto something else. I don't think the film made enough money to warrant a sequel, actually.' The film did reasonable box office, grossing $42m in the United States in its first nine weeks on release and ending up the fifteenth highest-grossing movie in America that year. However, those figures are less impressive set against its unusually high production costs.

Asked if *Greystoke* fulfilled all his artistic hopes for it, Hudson responds, 'Yeah. I think it did. Absolutely.' Those Tarzan fans less convinced of the movie's aesthetic merits might be interested in seeing a director's cut that presumably would not be blighted by so many of the structural weaknesses of the theatrical release. 'Hundredth anniversary may generate it,' says Hudson. 'It is being proposed.' Surprisingly, he reveals that there is no extant copy of the original cut, but he says, 'The material of the cut will be in the vaults somewhere … It's all there to be got out and redone. It would be quite a job 20 or 30 years later, but it's possible. People are still around who would remember what to do.'

Flawed though it is, its quality, renown, ambition, production values and degree of faithfulness make *Greystoke* one of the four most important Tarzan films alongside the first Elmo Lincoln picture, the second Weissmuller film and a movie yet to come, Disney's 1999 animated feature *Tarzan*.

Following the big splash of *Greystoke*, things were quiet on the Tarzan motion picture front for 14 years. However, said film would seem to have worked to revitalise the commercial worth of the ape-man judging by the plentiful activity surrounding the character during that nigh decade-and-a-half in books, comics, live-action television and another, newer medium that would have been beyond even the imagination of the mad scientists encountered by John Carter on Mars.

The ape-man's image and double-outlined logo had long been seen on pinball machines, and naturally they began to be observed on what were to a large extent their successors, the arcade games that acquired popularity in the early 1980s. (There had also been unofficial items involving generic white jungle men in loincloths, at least one of which – arcade game *Jungle Boy* aka *Jungle King* – attracted a successful legal action by ERB, Inc.) In 1984 came the first officially sanctioned ape-man home computer game. Called simply *Tarzan*, it was released for the Commodore 64, BBC Micro and Colecovision platforms. Its sideways-scrolling gameplay, involving the ape-man collecting points by punching human and arachnid antagonists against jungle and lost city-ish backdrops to the accompaniment of bubbling synth music, was cutting-edge. However, this new entertainment medium boasted the most ferociously rapid development pace in human history, and less than a decade later, graphics so fuzzy that a sprite was recognisable as Tarzan only via his bare legs and chest would seem comically primitive.

This quick-fire development of the medium could be followed through *Tarzan Goes Ape* (1991, platforms: Commodore 64, Sinclair ZX81/Spectrum), *Jungle no Ouja: Tarzan* (1994, Super Nintendo, Japan only) and *Tarzan: Lord of the Jungle* (1994, Gameboy). By the time Disney issued a game to tie in with their 1999 *Tarzan* movie on PlayStation, Game Boy Color and Nintendo 64, home computer games were unrecognisable from the mid-'80s: players could take a Tarzan sprite visually indistinguishable from how he appeared in the movie through 14 levels on the journey from child to adult, collecting points by bulldozing through fruit and tokens and throwing objects at monkeys that promptly exploded into butterfly swarms. The lustrous backdrops across which the sprite moved were also identical to those seen in the film, something that could be verified by comparing them with the scenes from the film interspersed throughout the gameplay.

In the '80s, there was still space in this soon-to-be digital world for games on the printed page. 1985 saw the publication of *Tarzan and the Well of Slaves* by Douglas Niles, an instalment of the Endless Quest gamebooks published by TSR, famous for Dungeons & Dragons. As well as the usual interactivity that allowed the reader/player to choose the story's ending, this new series had an educational element. *Tarzan and the Tower of Diamonds* by Richard Reinsmith followed in the same series in 1986.

PART EIGHT: THE KELLER ERA

It's not widely recognised, but the period during which husband-and-wife production team Max and Micheline Keller held the live-action ape-man rights is as indisputably a distinct and significant Tarzan era as that of Sol Lesser or Sy Weintraub. The two TV movies and two TV series they produced over the course of a decade make them responsible for more screen hours featuring the ape-man than anybody in history excepting Weintraub.

They began somewhat inauspiciously with *Tarzan in Manhattan* (for which Gina Scheerer was co-producer). Recalls Micheline Keller, 'My husband woke up with the idea about bringing Tarzan to New York. We actually lived in Encino ... only ... about ten minutes away from the Burroughs offices in Tarzana. He spoke with the president. Her name was Sandra Galfas. She said they were very particular who they licensed the rights to. They weren't sure they wanted to do it with an independent. Marion [Burroughs] was still alive and she said, "Well let me see some of their work," and we sent over one or two of our TV movies. She liked the quality of our work so she agreed to grant us a license for a television series ... It was on the expensive side of what the licensing rights were for television products but it was within the realm of what we could do.' Says Keller of the long relationship her company had with the Burroughs estate, 'They had the right to read every script, [but] after the first few scripts they felt comfortable so they didn't bother. I think we still sent them over every script, but we never got any notes from them. They really let us do our thing.' However, there were limits to the corporation's *lassiez faire* attitude: 'Edgar Rice Burroughs, Inc had a series of rules that they gave us about what things Tarzan could do or could not do, and they were kind of interesting: no bad language, no sexual relations with Jane, no smoking, no alcohol ...'

The *Tarzan in Manhattan* project went in completely the opposite direction to the period-piece nature of the last two live-action Tarzan projects, recasting the franchise in a contemporary and even urban form. Some Burroughs fans might seethe at the very idea, but juxtaposing the ape-man's savagery and directness with the softness and cant of civilisation is something that Burroughs himself had done as far back as 1913's *The Return of Tarzan* (and even part of *Tarzan of the Apes* before that), while of course it had also formed part of the drama in *Greystoke*. Dispensing with *Greystoke*'s (broad) adherence to Burroughsonia, however, was another matter.

Keller explains of the casting process: 'Agents were sending us actors and we just didn't find anyone we liked, so we had an open audition call in

233

Hollywood and Joe Lara was at that open audition call. Interestingly enough, as was Wolf Larson, who we later used. Joe Lara, we just felt he had that animal magnetism.' Lara, a 26-year-old former model, is reasonably well-cast as Tarzan. With his flowing locks, chiselled face and toned body he looks the part in a way that Lambert didn't, without conveying the impression of a body that could only have been honed in a gym in civilisation.

The Kellers commissioned a script by Canadian husband-and-wife team Anna Sandor and William Gough. Though this decision was based on their satisfaction with work the couple had done previously for them, Keller adds, 'William Gough I believe was a Tarzan fan.' Their work is a curious mixture of prose Tarzan and film Tarzan: Kala features, if briefly, but so does Cheeta. No explanation is provided for Tarzan's fluency in English, his upbringing or his name.

Tarzan is traumatised when hunters kill Kala and abduct Cheeta. His only clue to the perpetrators' identities is a matchbook from a New York nightclub. 'How do I get to New York?' he demands of an African friend in a scene that would have greater impact were he not drawling in an accent that suggests he's never been beyond American borders. Tarzan by a financial means not explained pursues the killers to civilisation, where he is initially dressed in jeans and T-shirt before switching to a loincloth. (He is later seen in a smart suit.) Setting off the loincloth is a pair of knee boots, which might sound unspeakable but actually doesn't look too bad, nor unreasonable considering the fact that the streets of Manhattan are strewn with more hazards than the average jungle floor. As is traditional, the ape-man runs into Jane Porter, but she is not the delicate young lady of the *Tarzan of the Apes* novel but updated to become a ballsy cab-driver.

Jane is played by Kim Crosby, but more interesting is who didn't get the role. 'Our first Jane was almost Sharon Stone,' reveals Keller. Having made a TV movie featuring the unknown Stone, the Kellers 'thought she would be a great Jane, the kind of sharp-talking, taxi-driving Jane. She was willing to do it but [said] "I don't want to go audition for CBS because they know me now." The head of casting at CBS said, "What? If she's not coming to audition, she can't have the part".' The network also nixed auditionee Teri Hatcher, soon to be famous as Superman's girlfriend Lois Lane. Jane's father is played by screen legend Tony Curtis. He is not a Professor of science here but an ex-cop-turned-private-eye who nonetheless insists on being called by his full name 'Archimedes' not 'Archie'. Curtis hams up his boorish/endearing part – he calls Cheeta 'Chiquita' and treats Jane like a 12-year-old – with a twinkle in his eye

The potentially interesting and amusing savage-in-civilisation premise is spoilt by the execution. Although we see Tarzan breaking out of his customs cell by pulling apart steel bars and later hoisting a man above his head, they are amongst the few hints of a preternatural strength. We see examples of Tarzan's archery ability and Lara placing a foot on the defeated (though emphatically not killed) form of an enemy and emitting a (not very impressive) bull ape victory cry. In all other respects, though, the action – directed by Michael Schultz – is as anodyne as that of the average chase movie, and the fisticuffs marked by a markedly un-feral blandness. Not that grit seems to have been uppermost in the producers' minds: scenes such as Cheeta driving a car indicate that this is 'family' fare. Keller: 'A gentleman that owned that company once said to my company, "CBS, we are *broad*casting, so we are creating products for the masses." So we were really looking for a family audience, [making] something that the kids could watch with their parents and an elder adult might enjoy because they knew the Tarzan legacy.' In other words, not too dissimilar to Weissmuller's *Tarzan's New York Adventure*, aside from the inclusion of a mild science fiction element in the shape of the discovery that the pseudo-philanthropic Brightmore Foundation that gets Cheeta in its clutches is conducting illegal experiments designed to transfer thoughts between animals. Altogether, hardly the enterprise the world was expecting after the adult-orientation and extravagance of *Greystoke*.

The 94-minute (*sans* commercials) *Tarzan in Manhattan* was first broadcast by CBS on 15 April 1989. That Tarzan elects to stay in the Big Apple to work for Archimedes' security firm for minimum wage and all the bananas Cheeta can eat is not exactly logical, but this ending was intended to set up a regular series. 'What we did discover out of that was that people really would prefer to see Tarzan in the jungle, so after we did the two-hour movie CBS did not pick it up as a series,' says Keller. 'That was a big, big, big disappointment. And I think it was a mistake on CBS's part, because a couple of years later [came] *Lois & Clark*, which was a similar action series, and that [was] very successful on another network for many years.'

While Keller's disappointment is understandable, it's probably for the best that *Tarzan in Manhattan* did not progress to a full-blown series, not only because it was a step backwards for Tarzan's live-action incarnation after recent progress but also because its innocent-abroad premise was done better before by the likes of *Catweazle* and *Man from Atlantis*.

The Kellers went back to the drawing board to decide what to do with the live-action ape-man rights they held.

Micheline Keller: 'We had worked really hard, spent a lot of money in producing this pilot, much more than the network paid us, so it was quite heartbreaking, 'cause we were a small company. My husband just decided he was going to get it on the air by hook or by crook somehow.' In their reboot, they gave Tarzan ideals that were the preserve of the peculiar when Burroughs brought him into a world where people with lion heads mounted on their walls and zebra pelts spread on their floors were more admired than despised. Keller: 'We decided to go with [a] Tarzan that would be helping to save the environment, and along the way we felt the show could also have a lot of nice comments about ecology and protecting animals and protecting rainforests and conservation and not polluting our rivers.'

Perhaps more important than the concept though was the successful marketing of the programme. Keller says of her husband's by-hook-or-by-crook efforts, 'He actually ended up doing a series as an international co-production. I had a cousin that was French, and we asked him to form a French production company, which he did, and then my husband sold [the series] to TF1 to come in as a partner. TF1 is the largest French station, government-owned. Tarzan is very popular in France. They even have a Tarzan museum. They were the first country to come in. We did it as a French-Canadian co-production, and then it became a three-way co-production ... because neither of those countries had the kind of terrain that you needed ... We shot it in Mexico, so we had a Mexican producer come on board ... Officially, we were the developers of that series and not producers because we were Americans and Max set it up as a three country co-production for the financing, which did not allow for American producers.'

The resultant series was called simply *Tarzan*. The French money presumably accounts for why some sources render an accent over the second 'a,' but it is not apparent in the title sequence logo of the show. It also accounts for the non-American main casting. 'We had to switch our Tarzan because as an international co-production, neither of [the leads] could be American,' says Keller. 'Joe Lara was very American, so even though we would have loved to have kept him, we had to look for a Canadian actor or a French actor for Tarzan, and Wolf Larson was Canadian.' The apparently splendid poetry of the name of this 32-year-old graduate of *Dynasty*, who paid the bills when 'resting' by taking a multitude of calendar modelling gigs, is somewhat less impressive when it is revealed that Wolf is an apparently artful diminutive for Wolfgang while his real surname is von Wyszeck. His physique was similarly less impressive than it at first sight appeared: though he was statuesque, buff and handsome, his mane of hair was clearly the product of one of civilisation's styling salons (thus compounding his blondness), while for UK viewers he bore a distracting resemblance to well-known DJ Pat Sharp. Keller laughingly admits, 'He was not as rugged and wild as Joe Lara looked, so it was a different look.' Jane Porter might have a very Anglo surname but as presented here is a Gallic zoologist played by Frenchwoman Lydie Denier. The show's location dictated a geographical change, or at least fudging. 'We were shooting in Mexico so we made a decision that it would be generic jungle,' Keller says.

Rather rarely for an action-orientated drama series, each episode was only half-an-hour in length, making for screen time minus commercials of just 22 minutes, including the opening titles. Once again, this is attributable to the exigencies of juggling the specific demands of investors. Keller: 'That's what TF1 wanted and they were the first ones to come on board.' Complicating matters was the fact that Italian television – which had also purchased the programme before shooting started – insisted on an hour-long show. The Kellers addressed this by a device that made splicing easier: 'Every episode [had] a little tag at the end that ran it into another episode, talking about, "Now, we're going to go on to look for the poisonous egg", [or] whatever the next show was about.'

Many a Burroughs fan no doubt groaned when they saw that, like his predecessor, Larson sported knee-high boots. The actor revealed to *People* magazine that he changed his mind about going barefoot when he became cognisant of the poisonous snakes abounding in Cuernavaca, Mexico, where the first series was shot. Nonetheless, the Kellers had started this tradition and would continue it. Keller: 'The jungles are full of animals and very dangerous insects and we had people that were bitten by tarantulas. We just felt we would be putting him too much at risk to have him run around barefoot. We did take that license just to protect the actor.' That instance of wimpiness aside, Larson showed he was game by doing his own stunts. The series swings back toward the movie Tarzan, featuring as it does a pidgin-speaking ape-man, Cheeta and the Weissmuller yodel. (Keller says of the latter, 'It was public domain. I think it might have even been mixed with a tiny bit of Joe Lara. Joe Lara did an amazing job too. Oh my gosh, we spent a lot of time on that yell.') However, there was at least one nod to the Burroughs hinterland: 'We did one episode where he got [out] a locket of his parents and he talked about having crashed and all of that. We did it as a plane crash as opposed to the shipwreck that was in *Greystoke*.'

Despite all the changes from *Tarzan in Manhattan*, the new production had something in common with its predecessor in the form of wholesome storylines geared toward the family audience. Eyebrows might be raised by the fact that Tarzan lives with a young man. However, his relationship with Roger

Taft (Sean Roberge) seems as chaste as the one he has with Jane. The gauche Roger shares comic relief status with Cheeta, who usually closes episodes with some endearing action. Tarzan, who is teaching Roger his jungle lore, hangs around with a man from whom he learnt much of his, Simon (Malick Bowens). The latter character provides a framing device via voiceover readings from his journal. He is also the only black person in sight. The show's credits carried the pointed line, 'Based on the copyrighted Tarzan stories written by Edgar Rice Burroughs.' Ron Ely guest-starred in a first-season episode.

The show began syndicated daytime Sunday transmissions in the US on 6 October 1991. However, those American broadcast dates are pretty much irrelevant for this show, whose commercial achievements, though substantial, were in non-English speaking territories. Keller describes the programme as 'Tremendously successful' around the world: 'In France they put it on Christmas week around six o'clock and it just broke all records for TF1. Sixty percent of the televisions were tuned on to Tarzan every night, 'cause they ran it every night for the first ten nights. In Canada it did well too. In Canada it grew, so it got more and more popular every year. Unfortunately, in America we had gone with a Spelling [distribution] company called Worldvision the first year and it just didn't work out financially. They wanted to lower the price so much for the second year. It was a shame because I think it would have done the same as it did in Canada.' The show failed to find a buyer in the UK until Disney launched their cable/satellite channel there in 1995.

Larson didn't want to return to Cuernavaca for the second season (Keller: 'It was very remote') so shooting was relocated to the larger if less beautiful Puerto Escondido. Keller: 'The third one we shot in Acapulco because we were [also] going to be shooting a series called *Acapulco Heat* ... We felt that we could be preparing the other series while we were shooting *Tarzan*, so we shot that about an hour outside of Acapulco.' As with the first season, the second and third seasons of *Tarzan* each consisted of 25 episodes of 30 minutes' duration (including commercials). Simon disappeared from the series, replaced in the second season by Jack Benton (Errol Slue) and in the third by Dan Miller (William S Taylor). Though again both seasons found receptive audiences across the globe, there was a five-year gap before the Kellers found anyone interested in following up the first season in the United States. By the time season two began its American airings on 28 September 1997 (season three was broadcast from 15 March 1998), the show was dead. 'I think the cost had just gone up and we might have lost one of the countries,' says Keller. 'It was really a financial decision. We just couldn't go into deficit on it. France and Canada both very much wanted to continue with the show.' However, the

Kellers were not finished with the ape-man.

March 1992 marked the return of Tarzan comics to the American newsstands (not counting some '80s Blackthorne reprints of newspaper strips in comic book format).

'You've never seen Tarzan like *this* before!' declared the front cover of the first issue of Malibu's *Tarzan the Warrior*, a five-part series. Burroughs fans wearily familiar with 're-imaginings' of the character in recent years could be forgiven for not being excited by this promise. Sure enough, writer Mark Wheatley and penciller Neil Vokes proffered a story involving Bigfoot, a siren-punctuated car chase and shape-shifting aliens. The company's next mini-series in August – the three-part *Tarzan: Love, Lies and the Lost City* – did at least feature an adaptation of *Jungle Tales* story 'Tarzan's First Love' amongst the furiously self-conscious updating. Malibu's final ape-man offering before they relinquished the comic book rights was *Tarzan: The Beckoning*, a six-parter that begun with an issue cover-dated November 1992.

Dark Horse was a publishing company established in 1986 with the twin objectives of treating comic books as being as valid as all other forms of entertainment and recognising the concept of the rights of comics creators, the latter a policy that in theory led to higher creativity. It seemed good news therefore that in 1995 the American Tarzan comic book rights passed over to these hip new kids on the block.

Dark Horse's first Tarzan project was incongruous. They were awarded the accolade of publishing the first previously unseen Burroughs Tarzan prose since *Tarzan and the Madman* in 1964. The story was issued across four paperbacks adhering to the months of the first quarter of 1995. This was of course in the tradition of the serialisations that with a few exceptions had preceded the book publication of other Burroughs Tarzan tales. The illustrations by Arthur Suydam and Tom Yeate were deliberately designed to echo the style of the pulps. Subsequently, the work appeared as a deluxe Dark Horse hardback and a Ballantine paperback. All three editions appeared with the title *Tarzan: The Lost Adventure*. This of course was not the name given it by its author, but the very fact that it had lain in a safe since 1946 demanded a mythos be attached to this untitled story.

As Burroughs' manuscript was a mere 83 pages, even had it possessed an ending it would have amounted only to a novella. Spurning the option of just issuing it unfinished *a la* F Scott Fitzgerald's *The Last Tycoon*, Dark Horse contracted a writer to expand it to 200 pages and resolve its plot. Considering his ape-man-rich history and his familiarity with the comic book demographic, it might be assumed that Dark Horse would have offered the job to Philip José Farmer. Burroughs scholar and chronicler Robert R Barrett reveals that in fact this was his suggestion when in 1994 Danton Burroughs – with whom he was friendly and who that year took over the running of ERB, Inc following Marion Burroughs' death – called him to discuss the matter. 'I began to heavily lobby Dan to get Dark Horse to hire Phil,' says Barrett. Barrett was not the only person to suggest that Dark Horse engage the services of Farmer. Another was author and comic book writer Joe R Lansdale. Recalls the latter, 'I was on the phone with Jerry Prosser who was at that time working at Dark Horse. We were just talking about the project that we were doing at that time, which was a comic project. I don't know exactly how it came up but I was talking about how much I liked *Princess of Mars* and the Tarzan books etc and he said, "D'you know, we have the rights to the Tarzan book. We're looking for someone to do it." I said, "Oh my God, you got to get Philip José Farmer".' Dark Horse disagreed. Barrett: 'Finally Dan told me that Dark Horse on their own initiative had hired Joe Lansdale to rewrite Ed's portion of the novel and then to complete it. Both Dan and I were very disappointed that Phil wasn't chosen and, to my knowledge, Dark Horse never gave Dan an explanation as to why they had not chosen Phil.'

It's possible that the hatred of Farmer among some sections of the Burroughs fanbase for his realistically sexual and vicious Tarzan pastiches may have turned off Dark Horse. However, the choice of Lansdale instead was a somewhat baffling one. Though he estimates he had by that point published – including under pen-names – 12 to 15 novels, they had been in the fields of mystery, horror and Western. However, there was some sort of logic to the decision. 'I'm a Tarzan and Edgar Rice Burroughs fan from day one,' says Lansdale. 'I was born in '51 and I started probably when I was about 11 or 12 … I wouldn't be a writer had it not been for Edgar Rice Burroughs.' Though Farmer might have been his first choice to continue Tarzan's adventures, when told by Dark Horse that he was their preference, Lansdale was hardly going to turn the job down, even though big bucks were not on offer: 'My deal was a one-time payment. It was work-for-hire, which because it was Tarzan I was willing to do. It was way under my pay-scale.' He was also not afforded much in terms of time. 'I had to turn it around almost immediately,' he recalls. 'It might have been six weeks, two months at the most … I didn't have any time at all to prep outside of re-reading some of the Tarzan books.'

Lansdale was sent a hard copy of the unfinished Burroughs manuscript. 'Frankly, I don't think it was something Burroughs planned to publish,' he says. 'It was not outstanding. He whacked a lion on just about every page, or some kind of cat. I was very disappointed when I got it, to some extent, but then there were stretches in there when it just had the old Burroughs magic. It was difficult, 'cause you were obligated to continue as was and stay in that tone, so it was harder than it seemed. It would have been easier to write something from scratch, but it would not have been as wonderful as to have been someone who actually collaborated with Edgar Rice Burroughs.' Of his development and plot resolution, Lansdale says, 'I didn't work it out at all. I don't outline any of my books particularly, because I get bored: by the time I outline it, I no longer want to write it. I followed what I thought was his lead, but as far as the stuff that was not in his manuscript, I just let it happen as I went.' That Lansdale's remit was not just to tie up Burroughs' dangling story threads but rewrite what was already written was something that he says was always the plan: 'They didn't think it stood up very well. It had a tired feeling. That's why it was in the safe. This comes from a fanatic Burroughs fan with me saying this, but you find that it's very repetitious. A lot of the stuff though, I just moved it around. There were also parts of it that were extraordinarily racist. Some of that dialogue was a little too "step-and-fetch-it," even worse. That was worth updating without losing that aspect of it …'

Though Lansdale's Tarzan was a little more vicious than Burroughs' (something he disputes, saying, 'There's some pretty nasty stuff in the Tarzan novels'), he was prevented from moving the ape-man into the modern world: 'I really would have wished I could have updated [it] more. That was the one thing I was asked: to keep it in that tone … I wasn't trying to copy Burroughs absolutely, because then if you did that people would say, "Well you tried to imitate him and you can't do that", which I agree with. I tried to capture the spirit of the Tarzan books as much as possible and yet somewhat bring my own brand to it without letting it override what the original was.' Asked in what year he considered the tale to be set, he says, 'I thought it was just a mythical year, because Africa had changed a lot, but in my mind it happened sometime in the past.'

The joint Burroughs-Lansdale story sees Tarzan getting involved in the adventures of multiple safaris comprised of villains and explorers. Jane is absent but Nkima and Jad-bal-ja appear. Rewriting of even an inchoate and bitty manuscript inevitably aroused controversy (especially when ERB's original pages were subsequently privately published). Perhaps the viciousness of Lansdale's Tarzan can be posited as simply the way Burroughs would have liked to present him had not the mores of the time inhibited him. However, some of the objections to elements introduced by Lansdale seem justified. Tarzan's fings-ain't-what-they-used-to-be musings on the modern world and how things might be better if he emigrated to Pellucidar are simply not within the ape-man's established frame-of-reference. That Tarzan is shown as being familiar with a fighting style learnt from a former Shaolin priest suggests Lansdale is trying to shoehorn one of his interests (kung fu) into another. The repartee between Tarzan and heroine Jean in which the ape-man's flirty banter drips with self-regard suggests the author is attempting to cram some James Bond in too. And would Burroughs have ever done anything so ludicrous as include a giant praying mantis versed in martial arts? Or refer to the jungle animal the 'croc'? As for him opting to exile Tarzan to Pellucidar at the end, it's almost as if Lansdale is seeking to block off the possibility of other writers having the chance to continue the ape-man's prose adventures.

'I felt that it's hard for people to believe in that Africa anymore, which was always an alternate universe really,' says Lansdale. 'There was a time when those books were written, and even into the '60s when I was a kid, that we still didn't know that much about Africa and still thought there was no telling what you might find. You might find a dinosaur somewhere there in the Congo. Then by the time that book was written we all knew that wasn't true and we all knew that that Africa didn't exist. So what I wanted to do was give the option of sending Tarzan to a place that was eternally that way, which was Pellucidar, an option for the readers to have the opportunity to believe that there was a world he could exist in that Tarzan would prefer … I didn't think of it as exile. I thought [of] it as [offering] the possibility of a sequel where he could have more adventures, and if there was no sequel, at least we could all think, "Here is a world that would be full of adventures forever".' As for the Bond-ish flirty banter, he says, 'I was trying to update it a little bit.' The praying mantis he justifies by citing the ant-men, the Ho-don/Waz-don and other science fiction elements of Burroughs' Tarzan books. Certainly ERB, Inc had no problem with what he wrote. 'I never heard from the Burroughs estate,' he says. 'They had final approval and they approved it.'

As for his own evaluation of *Tarzan: The Lost Adventure*, Lansdale offers, 'I didn't think it was [Burroughs'] best work, therefore I was limited for it to be my best work. I tried to do the best I could at the time. I wasn't trying to do it for old glory. I'm certainly not ashamed of it. It's certainly got its fans.' Some, of course, consider it blasphemy for Lansdale or anyone to presume to rewrite Burroughs. He responds, 'I didn't feel it was a sacrilege in the fact that it was unfinished, and Burroughs' work was often used to be filmed or to be made into comics, there were children's books of it, so he always designed his books as a product.' Was he in a no-win situation? 'Yeah, I think I was.' However, Lansdale adds, 'I won better than I thought.'

After they had delivered Burroughs' fans their fantasy of unpublished Tarzan prose, Dark Horse followed it with a series of comic books featuring another staple of fan fantasy: team-ups and crossovers.

In the 1990s, the comics industry began to be taken over by a new generation of writers and artists with a very different attitude from their predecessors. Whereas previously comics had – especially at senior level – been the preserve of people who did not themselves read comics in their free time, now positions in the industry were being filled by people who were also consumers. Them not being indifferent to the product they were purveying was ostensibly creatively ideal. However, it transpired that hand in hand with their love and respect for the medium, the new generation possessed an unfortunate propensity to disappear up their own backsides via an over-earnestness that hadn't been in the uncomplicated narrative vocabulary of the old school.

Though the first Dark Horse product in June 1995 was straightforward enough, that would seem to be because *Tarzan: A Tale of Mugambi* – a one-off written by Darko Macan and illustrated by Igor Korde – was originally intended for publication by Malibu. The following month, the Dark Horse style of – and the current general comics penchant for – what-ifs and parallel realities kicked in. *Tarzan vs. Predator at the Earth's Core* was a four-parter with scripts by Walter Simonson and art by Lee Weeks. That this mini-series saw Tarzan travelling to Pellucidar was reasonable enough in light of the fact that Burroughs had once engineered such a crossover in his own work. However, as if the perils of the Mahars were not enough, Dark Horse decided to throw in a monster from another creator's franchise entirely, namely the man-eating alien Predator that had first become famous in the 1987 Arnold Schwarzenegger movie, to which they held the comic book rights. There's no denying that such team-ups are fleetingly intriguing, in the same way that fantasising about a football team line-up whose inclusions are not inhibited by era or nationality can be. However, whereas such fantasy league schemes are impossible by definition, comic creatives have the ability to put their dreams into action. The results are almost always proof that such dreams are best left to pub debate. *Tarzan vs. Predator at the Earth's Core* was followed in January 1996 by another crossover four-parter, *Tarzan/John Carter: Warlords of Mars*, this one written by Bruce Jones and illustrated by Bret Blevins.

July of that year saw Dark Horse begin a monthly Tarzan title, the first American Tarzan comic book with a regular schedule since the days of Marvel's late-'70s effort. This publication, however, must have seemed boringly conventional to readers whom Dark Horse regularly treated to crossover special events, and it lasted only 20 issues. Though they did issue a conventional adaptation of *The Return of Tarzan* as a 1997 three-parter, and though they handily reprinted European Russ Manning strips and long out-of-print Dell/Gold Key stories, Dark Horse generally seemed either unable or unwilling to refrain from indulging their tell-you-what-would-be-really-cool fanboy whims. Tarzan met Carson Napier of Venus in a 1998 four-parter; re-visited Pellucidar in their anthology title *Dark Horse Presents* the same year; and in 1999 was in Pellucidar yet again in Mike Grell's four-part *The Savage Heart*. By the time of the four-part *Batman/Tarzan: Claws of the Cat-Woman* at the end of '99, there was a suspicion that inebriation and/or dare-you games lay behind story and team-up decisions. Overlapping with that book was Igor Kordey's *The Rivers of Blood*, a four-parter that ostensibly displayed discipline in not shipping in characters from another franchise or medium but had guest-starring roles for Jung and Freud. A two-part adaptation of Disney's concurrent animated Tarzan film the same year was unusual in being conventional and brief.

It was back to chicken-dare in 2001 for the last Dark Horse Tarzan publication for a decade, the three-part *Superman/Tarzan, Sons of the Jungle*. Writer Chuck Dixon posited an alternate reality (i.e. an alternate fiction) wherein young Kal-El crash-lands not in Smallville but Africa, disrupting the mutiny that in Burroughs' book stranded John Clayton in the jungle and handing that fate of being raised in the wilds by apes to the last son of Krypton. In a climax in Opar, a Clayton who has grown up decadent encounters an ape-man even more superhumanly powerful than Burroughs envisaged. As with so much of Dark Horse's Tarzan output, great talent, high production values and undeniable love for the source were invested in an enterprise that ultimately begged the question, 'What for?'

This remained the last official Tarzan US or UK comic until January 2012 when the ape-man returned to Dark Horse. First came a post-apocalyptic three-part *Dark Horse Presents* story 'The Once and Future Tarzan,' written by Alan Gordon and illustrated by Thomas Yeates, who also provided the original concept. This was followed by the graphic novel *Tarzan at the Earth's Core* by Martin Powell and Tim Burgard.

In 1996, Max and Micheline Keller returned to the ape-man character with whom they had thus far had mixed TV success.

Following the savage-in-the-city angle of *Tarzan in Manhattan* and the eco-warrior approach of the Wolf Larson series, they now put a new spin on the character with *Tarzan: The Epic Adventures*. Micheline Keller: 'We maintained the rights, and our partner came to us with the idea of doing a [series of] one-hour [episodes]. The idea was to go back to the Edgar Rice Burroughs vision of a much more sci-fi Tarzan. Our first series was more the fantasy Tarzan that Hollywood had really created.' In fact, this series, preceded a month before by a two-hour telemovie, leaned toward a mysticism that was a half-way house between the Burroughs Tarzan novels of lost cities and quasi-SF and the sword and sorcery domain of Conan. Keller denies assumptions that it took its cue from recent sword, sandals and supernaturalism series like *Xena: Warrior Princess* and – similar in title construction too – *Hercules: The Legendary Journeys*. She also reveals that the Kellers' production partners – the Siegel brothers – were in the creative driving seat: 'Since we had done Tarzan so much, and I was doing another series called *Acapulco Heat*, I thought, "Well, let them be in charge of this one".' Keller was not happy with the Siegels' decision to dispense with African wildlife: 'Everybody loves the animals.' As a fan of family-orientated fare, she also didn't agree with the tenor of the series: 'It's a more grown-up show. It's got a bit more violence in it.'

In casting, the Kellers returned to their first Tarzan actor: 'We took Joe Lara back because it was not an international co-production, so we could have an American.' Not that the *Tarzan in Manhattan* star didn't have to audition like everyone else nor beat out competition. Keller: 'There was a wonderful Australian that actually auditioned that I considered very much. His name was Ingo [Rademacher]. He did a brilliant audition.' However, an ape-man with an Aussie accent was mercifully not brought about (even if this absurdity was only deferred). Lara, now 33, donned the loincloth for a show that couldn't have been more different from his failed pilot of 1989. His flowing locks were immediately an improvement on Larson's in being both dark and alien to a hairdryer. Also making a return appearance from a previous Keller Tarzan project was Lydie Denier, the Wolf Larson series' Jane, who was the Countess de Coude in the *Epic Adventures* pilot.

Said pilot was titled *Tarzan's Return*, directed by Brian Yuzna and broadcast on 28 August 1996. The script by Burton Armus featured the ape-man and his friend Mugambi (first seen in the novel *The Beasts of Tarzan*) pursuing Russian villains Rokoff and Paulvitch to Pellucidar in pursuit of a crystal amulet stolen from Collette de Coude. In the world at the Earth's core (entered not via mechanised burrowing or a polar hole but through a portal opened by the amulet), the ape-man encounters the reptilian winged Mahars (here an all-women race) and their enemy Jana, a beautiful blonde savage.

The pilot set up the series well. However, its relatively high production values held out false hope: once into the weekly grind, a certain formulaicness and patchiness set in. There was, despite the whiff of it being a Conan wannabe, at least more fidelity to Burroughs in *Tarzan: The Epic Adventures* than in any other modern live-action production outside of *Greystoke,* as can be gleaned from the opening voiceover for each episode: 'Tarzan. Orphaned at birth in darkest Africa, raised by the great apes, he grew up in the primitive world of the jungle until fate brought him face to face with his past. Taking his rightful place as Earl of Greystoke, Tarzan soon became disenchanted with civilisation. He returned home to Africa. Tarzan, Lord of the Jungle!' The silver-effect series logo is even based on a famous J Allen St John Tarzan-with-lion illustration. Yet it is Burroughs' Tarzan seen through a distorting lens created either by lack of complete familiarity with his books on the part of the team of approaching 20 writers or by production exigencies, or both. Paul D'Arnot, La of Opar and Amtorans also appear, but as with the Mahars, not in the exact configurations and circumstances originally penned by Burroughs. Joe Lara, the stated Earl of Greystoke, drawls in the traditional Tarzan actor's Americanese. Black marks, too, to the producers for giving the ape-man a fear of enclosed spaces in the episode 'Tarzan and the Demon Within', something emphatically not in the prose ape-man's stoical psychological make-up. The same can be said of the way he is habitually depicted as wrestling with his man/ape dual nature. To be fair, such inner dilemmas do at least underline the adult orientation of the show: other producers wouldn't have bothered with such stuff in their pursuit of an excuse for fight scenes. (Another example of the older demographic tilted at is the thong sported by bad girl Mora in the pilot.) Also admirable is their decision to make this a period piece, even if the dialogue often conveys in no way whatsoever the early 20th Century.

Though such leaps from even Burroughs' fantastical Tarzan stories as spell-casting, power-thrumming crystals, a villainess shooting lasers from her eyes and a portal to another dimension are a little too much, the entire premise is on the whole intrinsically more interesting than that of the Ron Ely series (debuted only 11 days amiss of exactly 30 years earlier), which looks earthbound and hidebound in comparison. With his creepy monsters and sweeping exotic sets, special effects supervisor John Buechler rises well to the challenge of the greatest degree of effects yet required by a Tarzan project on a consistent basis, especially considering the low budgets with which he clearly had to work. Complementing his endeavours are some nicely exotic music and sound effects. The location shooting creates an additional layer of lushness. Keller: 'We initially shot the first two-hour at the Disney studios in Orlando, Florida, but that ended up being quite too expensive. We had to rethink it, so we moved it to Johannesburg and the series was shot in Sun City.'

'Ballantine/Del Rey received permission from ERB, Inc to have R A

Salvatore write a novel based on the new Tarzan TV series, hoping to generate interest in the show,' says Robert R Barrett. Salvatore had been a published author for less than a decade but was already responsible for 20 books. His was a writing genre unmistakably in the same line that Burroughs had created, but one that adhered to rules of science fantasy now codified to an almost absurd and anal degree, exemplified by an obsession with chronicling mystical quests in almost *de rigueur* trilogy or quartet format, with attention drawn to the number of each individual part as though it denoted a sociological milestone. Accomplished in his field then, Salvatore has gone on to achieve a plateau of success and influence within it for which there possibly is no suitable superlative. It was logical therefore that such a marquee name should be chosen to continue the prose exploits of the ape-man and ensnare a new generation of readers.

Not so logical is the fact that his novel – only the second ever adult non-Burroughs Tarzan novel authorised by ERB, Inc – was nothing but a novelisation of the pilot of *Tarzan: The Epic Adventures*. The estate had waited 16 years after Burroughs' death before giving a go-ahead to an acclaimed writer – Fritz Leiber – to continue Tarzan's print adventures but had obliged that writer to work within extreme restrictions. It is almost beyond belief that Burroughs fans had been made to wait fully 30 years simply for another fleshed out screenplay.

Salvatore was a Burroughs fan, though he points out, 'I was always most interested in Pellucidar.' He explains of the way he got the gig, 'I was working with Del Rey at the time, both for my DemonWars novels and some *Star Wars* opportunities, and one of the editors, Steve Saffel, thought I'd be good for the job. I had never done a novelisation to that point, so I thought it might be fun.' As an established writer of original novels, did he not consider a novelisation a step down? 'No, not really. I look at it this way: when I write my own books, I'm driving the race car, but for this project, I was just running the pit crew. It's hard to consider doing anything with the work of someone like Burroughs a step down. Don't get me wrong, I'm not big on novelisations and don't plan on doing any more unless the perfect project [falls] my way. But when it's a giant like Burroughs, or Lucas, well, it might be worth looking at the offer more closely.'

Salvatore had read neither the Fritz Leiber nor the Joe Lansdale Tarzan books, and he did not try to resolve *The Epic Adventures*' inconsistencies with the Burroughs books: 'I knew that this was being done with the blessing of the Burroughs' estate (his grandchildren, I was told). In that context, it's not really my place to come into a project half-way through and presume such things … There were a couple of things that bothered me about the script and the director's cut, and I brought them up, but I was told that much of it would be fixed in production, and really, that was above my pay grade.' Salvatore states that he wasn't aiming his book at Burroughs fans: 'Since I expected that most of the people who watched the show would have no idea of Burroughs' original work, or even who he was (sad, but true), I was just trying to take that script and make it as fun a read as I could manage.'

'Not very well, from what I can tell,' is Salvatore's response when asked how the book sold. 'I don't recall the numbers off-hand, but they were far lower than for anything else I've ever done.' However, this was not his main disappointment over the project. 'The biggest draw for me to take the job was the proposition of meeting [Burroughs'] grandchildren and discussing his work with them,' he says. 'It never happened.'

Like Leiber before him, Salvatore did the best he could with the material he was given. His 280-page *Tarzan: The Epic Adventures*, published by Ballantine imprint Del Rey in 1996, follows the trajectory of Burton Armus's teleplay, but whereas Armus – a writing veteran of the likes of *Kojak*, *The Fall Guy* and *Knight Rider* – had to dance between anodyne American TV conventions on the screen, Salvatore was free to demolish them on the page. His transposition of the narrative saw him inject into it something for which he was and is celebrated: mass, bloody and quasi-balletic fight scenes. 'Writing action sequences is my forte and my love,' he says. 'I want readers to experience a battle as if they're in it. I do this all the time. Other than that expansion, though, I really wasn't given much latitude. I took the script and reworked it into a book form.'

As well as the tie-in book, there was a range of *Tarzan: The Epic Adventures* action figures from Trendmasters, Inc. 'We really did try to do a big push,' says Keller. However, ratings for *The Epic Adventures* were disappointing. 'Worldwide, the show did not perform as well as the half-hours,' says Keller. 'I think it was because of lack of animals and that warmth there was in the half-hours.'

Says Robert R Barrett of its performance in the home US market, 'It was not a show that was developed by any network. It was developed to be syndicated and purchased by any TV station that wished to run it on their station – whether it was first-run or re-run … There weren't many stations that purchased it.'

It was time to go back to the drawing board. The Kellers lined up Xavier DeClie to play Tarzan in a new project and planned the re-introduction of Jane – not seen in *The Epic Adventures* and referred to within it only as the ape-man's ex. Jane's role, it was announced, was to be given to a competition winner. Keller says of DeClie, 'We were going to use him if we were going to do another Tarzan, and then it just didn't happen. It was going to be a whole reboot again … He was going to be back in the jungle, maybe a little bit more wild, more naturally animalistic.' However: 'We just didn't have the financing for it at the time.' The Kellers thought of other ways of exploiting their knowledge of the character. 'We had almost reached an agreement with Sandra Galfas to do a Tarzan half-hour animated series,' says Keller, 'and then all of a sudden she said, "No, I'm sorry, we're going to go with Disney and they want to hold back on any other Tarzan projects." Can't blame them. [We were] very disappointed, because we actually had a company that wanted to do 65 half-hours.'

Thus came to an end the Kellers' association with the ape-man. Asked if their penchant for family fare sometimes worked against the Tarzan character, Keller admits, 'Yes. We did not portray him that savagely. We had a big discussion about whether or not he should eat [raw] meat and we felt that he should not. In the Burroughs books he was chomping down all the time on animals. We never did the really rough, tough Tarzan.'

It could be argued that *Greystoke* should have brought an end to the Tarzan movie franchise. After the Tarzan story had been depicted in that film as realistically as was possible, the reasoning runs, any follow-up would degrade its achievement by diluting that realism in the same way that Burroughs had so often done by coming up with contrived ways to continue the franchise.

Stanley S Canter clearly wasn't of that opinion. The nominal co-producer of *Greystoke* was the brains behind its nominal 1998 follow-up *Tarzan and the Lost City*. He had reputedly envisioned it back in the mid-'80s and had worked on it from when he acquired the rights in 1991, co-producing with Dieter Geissler and Michael Lakewith. However, while *Greystoke* was a multi-Oscar-nominated movie, *Tarzan and the Lost City* is largely unknown to the general public.

On the surface, it was a promisingly Burroughsonian production. The film is again a period piece, taking place in 1913. Tarzan's alter-ego John Clayton is represented. Opar forms a crucial part of the story. However, the bad news starts with that generic title, which could have served for any of half a dozen substandard Burroughs Tarzan books. Then there is the way scriptwriters Bayard Johnson and J Anderson Black engineer the ape-man's return to Africa on the eve of his wedding to Jane in the Greystoke family castle: a vision of something amiss back 'home' projected across the ocean by an Oparian shaman friend – here given the name Mugambi – via a lion's sight-line. This ridiculous device instantly betrays the film's grand visions and intended faithfulness to Burroughs. Additionally, there is a disconnect between this movie and the one to which it affects to be a sequel: Tarzan had renounced both civilisation and Jane at the end of *Greystoke*. He had also not been portrayed as having had any dealings with Oparians. Nor does *Tarzan and the Lost City* possess *Greystoke's* lushness. A theatrical release that can't attract Hollywood investors is almost always destined to look tatty. The South African location shots provide some beautiful scenery, but this German-Australian enterprise otherwise reveals its poverty in such things as Germans playing characters supposed to be British, risible ape costumes and a depiction of Opar that looks like an oil painting (and this despite this Opar being merely a pyramid here rather than a city). The most heart-sinking aspect is the choice of leading man. Christopher Lambert may have lacked a lot, but we are instantly reminded by Casper Van Dien (Johnny Rico in the previous year's *Starship Troopers*) of at least what he mercifully wasn't: a square-jawed, brown-haired, collegiate type. Van Dien's often reedy voice is also not appropriate for a man of preternatural poise like Tarzan. The actor is at least buff and – mercifully – boots-free.

Tarzan arrives in the Dark Continent where Nigel Ravens (Steven Waddington) is intent on plundering Opar. The ape-man – who in this version is friendly with the city's inhabitants, whose domicile is not a bestial dump but the cradle of civilisation – resolves to stop him. Matters though are complicated by his intended (Jane March) following him and needing to be rescued from peril herself. Not that Englishwoman Miss Porter is a helpless damsel: she sports a gun, slugs whiskey and puffs cigars, a feisty modernistic view of womanhood that rather undermines the period setting. Also anachronistic is an eco-warrior strain involving Tarzan freeing caged animals and flinging elephant tusks into a river. Tarzan has a Cheeta-like chimp friend who engages in Weissmuller-era-type funny-endearing stunts like putting on Jane's dress. The yodel Van Dien produces is not Weissmuller's but his own variant, albeit pretty good. Where the film isn't mimicking *Raiders of the Lost Ark*, it descends into *Xena/Tarzan: The Epic Adventures* territory: Mugambi weaves magic spells that do such things as make skeletons grow flesh and become fighting warriors. He even magically gifts Tarzan a loincloth as if he is his Ken doll. His powers beg the question why he needs the purely earthly help Tarzan is able to offer.

Adding to the overall perturbing aura of second-rate is the fact that Swiss director Carl Schenkel is hardly a name with which to conjure. His direction – actors looking directly at camera, a dizzying perpetual motion effect when Tarzan and Jane are arguing about his departure, endless quick cutting – is almost laughably self-conscious. Similarly, while everyone has to start somewhere, this inaugural screen credit for scriptwriter J Anderson Black did not lead to better things – which would hardly have been a difficult achievement.

Initial reports suggested that *Tarzan and the Lost City* would be 102 minutes long, but upon its release in April 1998 it mustered only 83. Some critics suggested that, sub-standard though it was, it would suffice as family fare. Canter seemed to indicate that this was his intention ('I structured the story on the action serials of the past, as I wanted to make a high adventure film with a really interesting love story'). However, that objective was undermined by a PG rating engendered by male nudity, profanities and explicit violence.

For Burroughs diehards, the film had one saving grace: Casper Van Dien was the first actor in the 80-year history of the franchise to attempt an English accent.

PART NINE: ENTER DISNEY

The '90s had already been a good decade for the ape-man profile-wise, but 1999 was truly a Tarzan bumper year.

The digital games *Disney's Tarzan* and *Tarzan Action Game* (platform: IBM-compatible PC) were just a fraction of it. A new Tarzan animated feature was released on video, a blockbuster Tarzan film hit the cinemas and, best of all for Burroughs diehards, a brand new Tarzan novel for adults made it to the bookshelves. Moreover, though none was perfect, each had its merits, some considerable.

The least impressive of the bunch was *Tarzan of the Apes*, released on home video as part of the Sony Wonder *Enchanted Tales* series in March. (When DVD superseded the video medium, it was reissued as a double-set with, of all things, Moses story *A Tale of Egypt*.) Produced by Diane Eskenazi, its 1997 derivation and 48-minute length (i.e. about one hour if it had been interspersed with commercials) lead to the suspicion that it was a made-for-TV film that no television channel wanted and was put out three months before the June '99 release of the Disney Tarzan movie when the makers realised that they could ride the back of the latter's publicity and maybe even confuse some people into thinking that theirs *was* the Disney movie. Though it's no Disney production, one can't quite see why it found no broadcasting takers. The animation is cheap but perfectly adequate, as is the soundtrack, which mixes public domain classical anthems like 'Ride of the Valkyries' with three specially-commissioned songs (including a title theme song for the ape-man) in the mould of Disney's *The Lion King* set-piece numbers. Though it is aimed at pre-pubescents, there is even something in it for the grey-haired Burroughs fan in its faithfulness to source. Everything in Mark Young's script is much as it is in the novel *Tarzan of the Apes*, with what changes there are almost all due to the exigencies brought about by the unsophisticated young target audience (Mangani become brown apes, Tarzan's father dies of natural causes, bloodshed is minimal), plot compression (the cabin is not built by Tarzan's father but discovered by him), political correctness (black maid Esmeralda becomes a cockney sparrer) and the need for a tidy resolution (Tarzan doesn't have to wait 'til the next instalment to get his title and the girl). The Samsonite Tarzan herein looks fine, although one wonders why yet again the ape-man is given an American accent (voice actor uncredited).

A Disney Tarzan movie – the first animated ape-man story to be released in cinemas – was a somewhat different proposition. ERB fans might have blanched at the idea of a Tarzan cartoon on the grounds that it would continue a shunting of the character into a juvenile market that his creator had never intended. However, way back in 1936 Burroughs had been all for an animated feature with plenty of humorous content, with the only caveat – expressed in a letter to one of his sons – that the 'cartoon must be good. It must approximate Disney excellence.' Then, as in 1999, Disney was a by-word for the best in animation.

The Jungle Book – that work with which *Tarzan of the Apes* had so much in common and from which it partly took its cue – had of course been the subject of a charming Disney adaptation back in 1967, so a version of the Tarzan story by the same studio seems so much a logical step that it's surprising that it didn't happen sooner. No doubt if Disney did make an approach to the Burroughs estate around the time of *The Jungle Book* regarding licensing, it is lost in the mists of time and the recesses of whatever impenetrable filing system Cyril Ralph Rothmund operated.

The screenplay for Disney's 85-minute film *Tarzan* was written by Tab Murphy and Bob Tzudiker and Noni White. The opening is very clipped; almost a shorthand of the *Fuwalda* mutiny story. An unnamed couple flee a burning ship with their baby. They build a treehouse that would be implausibly elaborate even without their apparent lack of luggage and tools. Kala, meanwhile, loses her baby to a leopard (here given the generic Burroughs lioness name Sabor). Kala's tribe are neither Mangani, nor chimpanzee nor an indeterminate species: for the first time ever, a Tarzan adaptation depicts the apes who raise him as gorillas. In the best scene in the movie, Kala tentatively opens the door of the eerily quiet cabin and finds another scene of devastation left by Sabor: bloody paw prints indicate the fate of the shipwrecked couple. However, their baby is still alive and the instantly smitten Kala takes it back to her tribe. Her mate here is not Tublat but Kerchak. Though he is not the raging brute of Burroughs' original, Kerchak is uninterested in raising the human who he feels can never take the place of the child he and Kala have lost. When Kala decides to call the babe 'Tarzan', it is merely a conjunction of syllables carrying no meaning. 'Tarzan? Okay – he's your baby,' exclaims Terk, a sassy female youngster in the baby's adoptive tribe.

We see Tarzan growing up in an Africa with no visible black people. He graduates from the nappy in which he was found to a loincloth with no explanation. 'Why don't you just come up with your own sound?' Kala says to her skilled mimic step-son, and he does in the form of a Weissmuller-like yodel that doubles as his victory cry later on in life. Terk is one of Tarzan's two lifelong friends, the other being an elephant named Tantor, who like the rest of the depicted pachyderms is red. Despite his superficial assimilation, Tarzan is aware of being different, not least because of the non-acceptance of the stern Kerchak.

In another first for the ape-man, though Tarzan can stand upright, he is often shown walking on all-fours. It both makes sense and works visually. More dubious an innovation is his cruising down tree trunks and branches as though riding a wave. Though visually pleasing, this tree surfing brings another cinema-created nonsense to his arboreal travel mode in addition to the vine-swinging (also depicted). This is particularly absurd when considering his gorilla environment: they are amongst the few apes not comfortable in trees; the only extended periods of time they spend in branches are when sleeping in nests.

The family demographic (at least in these squeamish times) rules out Tarzan becoming anything like the blood-drenched, battle-scarred figure of the books: when as an adolescent he kills a menacing leopard with a spearhead he has fashioned to bring down fruit, the combatants are conveniently out of sight when the weapon is plunged into the animal's hide.

When Tarzan is an adult, a small group enters the jungle on a mission to study gorillas. Professor Porter and his daughter Jane – both English – are two of the trio. The third is a man named Clayton. This latter character has nothing to do with the Greystoke clan, for there is no Greystoke clan in this film and Tarzan's heritage remains as murky as in the opening scene. Clayton is ostensibly here for the same anthropological purposes as his companions, though he is troublingly trigger-happy. When Jane gets detached from her party, Tarzan rescues her from a pack of baboons of the lesser-known Hades variety. He is entranced by the first hairless ape he can remember meeting and subsequently angry at Kala for not informing him that he is of a different species. There is an awkward moment when he tells Jane his name, which humanistic enunciation sits oddly with the simian jabbering in which he had just been engaging with the hell-baboons.

A montage follows in which the ape-man is taught by Jane of the world beyond the jungle via amongst other things a slideshow. (This is a Victorian-set tale, although the period is not laid on thick.) She also instructs him in the English language and good manners, and naturally Tarzan picks them up with the traditional speed convenient to plot. With the prospect of Jane's departure looming, a smitten Tarzan persuades her to stay by giving in to her entreaties to take her to see his tribe, something Kerchak has expressly forbidden. After a fight with Kerchak, Tarzan broods on his identity. Kala enlightens him on this somewhat by taking him for the first time to the cabin in which she discovered him. Deciding that this place holds the key to the real him, Tarzan puts on his dead father's clothes and prepares to set sail with Jane for civilisation.

On board ship, he walks into a mutiny engineered by Clayton, keen to acquire the bounty achievable through captured gorillas. Tantor and Terk come to the rescue. Tarzan realises his true place as he goes back to land ('I came *home*') and saves his tribe from the trappers, assisted by the demon baboons, who recognise a common enemy. In the battle, Clayton fatally wounds Kerchak, then falls to his own self-inflicted death in a clash with Tarzan in the tree-tops. Before his life ebbs away, Kerchak awards Tarzan the accolade of calling him 'my son.'

Jane makes to leave, but in the rowboat heading for the ship at anchor her father points out, 'But you love him.' She swims back to shore. Her father decides to join her. Cut to Tarzan, Jane and a loinclothed Professor Porter joyously swinging and tree-surfing, watched and assisted by Terk, Kala and Tantor. The movie ends with Tarzan and Jane high up on a branch and the ape-man beating his chest as he yodels across the jungle.

The film's moody poster art was rather misleading. The animation – directed by Chris Buck and Kevin Lima – benefits from computer techniques not in existence in the days of *The Jungle Book*, a process called Deep Canvas enabling the deployment of CGI backdrops that have the lushness of an oil painting. However, the characters superimposed on that rich, often gothic backdrop are possessed of the primary colours, doe eyes, toothpaste smiles, unthreatening anthropomorphism and tendency to comic pratfalls that we have long come to expect from Disney. We are also presented with the studio's customary playful incongruities such as elephants bickering over whether or not piranhas are indigenous to South America and Terk remarking that the dress she has borrowed from Jane is too revealing.

The only deviation from the Disney pattern is a bowing to current animation trends for the jaggedly exaggerated, and even ugly, that gives Tarzan a projecting nose and pointy chin. (Curious considering the apparent template. Micheline Keller: 'I think the look copies our Joe Lara. As did Joe Lara, because everyone was telling Joe Lara that it looked like him.') The most *Jungle Book*-like moment, incidentally, is a scene in which the apes and Tantor use objects from civilisation such as saucepans and a typewriter as instruments in a musical interlude at the landing party's camp.

Speaking of music, *The Jungle Book* is studded with memorable and iconic tunes like 'The Bare Necessities,' 'I Wan'na Be Like You' and 'That's What Friends Are For'. It would have been reasonable for Disney to assume they would be delivered a soundtrack just as whistleable when they commissioned rock star Phil Collins to complement Mark Mancina's score: the ex-Genesis man and solo superstar had not shifted umpteen million albums for no reason, even if songs like 'In the Air Tonight' and 'Another Day in Paradise' are cut from darker cloth than the aforementioned jolly Terry Gilkyson and Sherman Brothers numbers. What Collins came up with was a set of the most perplexing anonymity: five bland songs – only two of which were sung by characters, the others commentary on the action – that nobody could remember once they left the cinema. Astoundingly, one of them – 'You'll Be In My Heart' – garnered Collins an Academy Award for Best Song.

Though the cast was, of course, unseen, it was still star-studded, including amongst its number Minnie Driver (Jane), Rosie O'Donnell (Terk), Nigel Hawthorne (Professor Porter), Brian Blessed (Clayton) and Glenn Close (the woman who was once the voice of Andie MacDowell's Jane here playing Kala). Yet having gone to the trouble of gathering together a bunch of largely English thesps, the producers lazily sagged into the old, illogical he's-got-to-sound-American thought process by picking the very Californian Tony Goldwyn to voice Tarzan. On top of that, the ape tribe have a cacophony of working class American accents.

As well as continuing the character's co-option by purveyors of fare to the juvenile market (Burroughs can't have envisaged how marked that process would be even despite his being in favour of a Disney adaptation), the film takes far more liberties with the source material than Sony Wonder's *Enchanted Tales Tarzan of the Apes*. Those liberties, therefore, can't be put simply at the feet of it being pitched to a young audience. On the plus side, a Disney cinema release is by definition a major entry in the franchise. Accordingly, it put Tarzan culturally centre-stage again.

Through *Tarzan* had a large $150m budget, it achieved impressive returns as parents weaned on the likes of the Ron Ely series (but probably not the Burroughs books) dragged their kids to see it. A new wave of Tarzan merchandise specifically related to the film emerged, including a soundtrack, action figures, interactive computer software and McDonald's Happy Meal giveaway toys. There were also books for juveniles, aimed at a demographic even younger than that of the Tarzan Twins brace, a typical example being the *Tarzan Jungle Jam* instalment in the Mouse Works Chunky Roly-Poly Board Book series. However, the real measure of the film's commercial accomplishments is provided by the mildly astonishing number of spin-offs: a sequel (albeit for the home video market), two further video games (*Disney's Tarzan Untamed*, 2001, for PlayStation 2 and GameCube and *Disney's Tarzan: Return to the Jungle*, 2002, for Game Boy Advance), a TV series and even a Broadway musical. Though the ape-man could never recapture the period in the first half of the century when swinging on a pretend vine was a nigh-universal childhood rite of passage, he exited the 20th Century on a cultural high.

To the Burroughs fan fraternity, Disney's *Tarzan* was admirable more in theory than in reality: that new generations were being introduced to their hero via a blockbuster movie was nice, but it was still kid-stuff. Their ideal was a new Tarzan novel for adults containing an original story. Almost unbelievably, in June 1999 they got their wish. Ratcheting up the dream-come-true factor for some was the fact that in authorising the first all-new, non-adapted adult Tarzan book, ERB, Inc finally acknowledged the Tantor in the room, otherwise known as Philip José Farmer.

Though he had racked up over 50 published novels and was an acclaimed if always controversial novelist, Farmer must have thought his chance had long gone: lifelong ambitions tend not to come true anyway, but are even less likely to be fulfilled when one is over 80. However, whatever his earthy leanings and even arguably his desecrations of the ape-man in his previous books, the corporation decided they could no longer ignore Farmer's credentials.

Via his agent, Farmer had been lobbying Ballantine books about the possibility of writing a new Tarzan novel since the mid-1990s. Initially, he had been rebuffed by Ballantine editor Steve Saffel, who had opted for the Salvatore novelisation. Farmer subsequently wrote to the fan magazine *Burroughs Bulletin* that his hopes of penning an original Tarzan novel had been 'blown away.' He elaborated, 'It's evident that the Ballantine editors are looking for stories to tie in with the TV Tarzan series, which will be science-fictional and futuristic.' Judging by the tone of the rest of the letter, this was a matter of no little dismay to Farmer, who lest we forget had already seen the *Lost Adventure* gig go elsewhere: 'My novel would take place in 1918, would be traditional, and would, I had hoped, sum up the Tarzan mythos and the Tarzan character. Also, since I've been reading the Tarzan books since 1928 and believe, in a sense, that Tarzan really exists, I'd hoped to add some insight into the persona of the Lord of the Jungle. But it's not to be.' That wistful comment however turned out to be not the last word. In 1997, Robert R Barrett, friend of both Farmer and Danton Burroughs, was rung by Danton and informed that Saffel had contacted ERB, Inc with a proposal for a new Tarzan novel. Barrett was asked by Burroughs' grandson who would be a worthwhile author of such a book. 'I immediately told him that I thought that nobody but Phil Farmer should be chosen,' recalls Barrett. 'Dan agreed with me and [said that he] would pass on that recommendation to Ballantine Books.' Of course, this was an action replay of the situation with *The Lost Adventure*. This time, though, the relevant publisher did not ignore the endorsement. On 17 March 1997, Farmer wrote a thank-you letter to Barrett in which he said, 'I'm convinced that you played a large part in Ballantine deciding to let me write a new Tarzan novel.' Asked why the corporation had never authorised an all-new Tarzan novel before, Barrett says, 'Basically those in charge at ERB, Inc didn't think that anyone could match Ed's original Tarzan novels. Which, in my opinion, is correct.'

As someone who had long been poring over Tarzan novels as obsessively as a teenager re-reads pop magazines, Farmer was prepared for the task at hand. Like plenty of Burroughs readers, he had been puzzled by the passage in *Tarzan the Untamed* wherein the ape-man discovers an ancient skeleton and beneath one of its hands a cylinder containing a map and a manuscript written in Spanish. Having set up a plot development, Burroughs had abandoned it. For a man like Farmer who had displayed a fixation with trying to reconcile the Tarzan novels' internal contradictions, it was a loose strand begging to be tied up. Having said that, the incident and its ramifications formed only a small portion of Farmer's book rather than its crux, a change of plan that was the type of thing, Farmer explained to Barrett in a letter in November 1997, that was 'part of the fiction-writing process.' When finally published in 1999, the book bore the title *The Dark Heart of Time*.

Tarzan being preoccupied with his search for the abducted Jane – Farmer's story taking place between *Tarzan the Untamed* and *Tarzan the Terrible* – he naturally doesn't take time out himself to try to solve the mysteries of the cylinder stashed at the bottom of his quiver. However, when he is captured by a safari he inexplicably finds on his trail, he is informed of its contents by one of his Spanish-speaking abductors. Even at this point, the apparently mystical babble in the manuscript is an irrelevance compared with the fact that Tarzan has been taken prisoner and, more importantly, has been distracted from his hunt for his beloved. It gradually emerges that the man who has ordered his abduction is American tycoon James D Stonecraft, who is dismayed that his status as the richest man in the world cannot revive his fading health. He is pursuing Tarzan because he is convinced that he possesses the secret to immortality. One of Stonecraft's employees is a being named Ben-go-utor, a halfway house between man and bear whose species is on the brink of extinction. Though Ben-go-utor initially uses his Tarzan-level spoor-following powers to help ensnare the ape-man, it is under duress: his own beloved is being held prisoner. He finally teams up with Tarzan. (The ape-man learns Ben-go-utor's language preposterously quickly – one aspect of the book at least that is truly Burroughs-like.) At this point, Tarzan comes by chance across the lost city detailed in the Spanish manuscript and there discovers an ancient priestess called Rafmana who, as it happens, possesses immortality. (The coincidence is something else Burroughs-like.) She is the guardian of the Glittering Tree, which contains the mystical Dark Heart of Time.

The omission of the word 'Tarzan' from the arty-farty title was a mistake Burroughs would never have made. Farmer had drawn up a list of 11 possible titles, all containing 'Tarzan', but it was he – not Ballantine – who ultimately decided to truncate *Tarzan and the Dark Heart of Time*. A minor misstep, perhaps, but the writing presents more serious ones. Finally getting the chance to fulfil what he describes in the dedication as 'a 70-year-old ambition', Farmer turns in a work less exciting than his pseudo-Tarzan material like *Lord of the Trees* and *Lord Tyger*. Though his plot is action-packed and often excitingly piles staggering quantities of peril on the ape-man, his narrative abilities prove unequal to those of Burroughs. Far from being marked by the smooth-flowing and evocative style of the latter at his peak, they are characterised – at least by this late point – by a fussiness that works against the action he depicts. Though never quite as momentum-crushingly pedantic as J T Edson in his Bunduki books, Farmer can't resist remarking on irrelevant matters during action sequences. His prose is bitty, repetitious and sometimes confusing. The book could have happily lost a chunk of its nearly 300 pages.

Leaving aside the style, the content is speckled with things that give the reader pause. Explains Barrett, 'A whole series of letters between Phil, Dan and [me] were sent, beginning in early 1998. Dan had asked me to read Phil's Tarzan novel and to point out any discrepancies between Phil's characterisation of Tarzan and Edgar Rice Burroughs'. I had told Dan that I would be happy to do this but only if Phil was able to write the novel as he saw fit and not try to write it as Burroughs would. I pointed out a few instances in which I felt that he had Tarzan doing things that did not match up with Burroughs' characterisation. Phil changed most of these. [He disputed] only ... a couple on which he did not agree with me, and [neither] I, nor Dan, argued with him about them, letting them stand ... I'd rather not discuss what I suggested that he change in the manuscript or which of my suggestions he chose to ignore. There really weren't that many and they changed nothing in the story.'

Some of Farmer's tweaks to the Tarzan template are reasonable. Burroughs was an old-fashioned 'proper' man even for his times and would never have shown Tarzan eating a rat or a rotting elephant. When Farmer does, we understand that this is exactly what someone with Tarzan's bestial upbringing would have done, even if we accept the notion of inherited nobility. Ditto for Tarzan's incredible cold-bloodedness and sadistic mischief: he wreaks havoc with his pursuers and former captives via such methods as killing one of their porters and tossing his decapitated head into their midst. There is a difference between logical projection, however, and making a character behave in ways that are not in his established nature. Farmer has the ape-man weeping when he sees Kala via the aegis of the Dark Heart of Time. Surely the world's self-declared foremost expert on Tarzan knows that he never cries? The other major liberty taken with the Tarzan template is dragging the ape-man into the realms of hardcore science fiction. It's interesting that Farmer had read Roddenberry's Tarzan screenplay, because he commits the same mistake the *Star Trek* creator did in introducing a stranded alien species, and logic dictates he may have got the idea for this from Roddenberry's work. One of the two lost cities in the book is the City Beneath the Waters, established long ago by extra-terrestrials. Their Dark Heart of Time enables people who touch it to see beyond the confines of mortals. (Tarzan chooses to look at where Jane is being held as well as at his ape step-mother.) Rafmana answers to the Ghost Frog, a hideous alien monster. People sacrificed to it end up in a living death in the belly of their devourer. All of this out-of-place fantastical stuff simply feels an impertinence on Farmer's part. Though the strictures of writing an authorised Tarzan book meant that he had to 'behave', and so his customary sexual frankness, scatology and extreme violence are absent, Farmer throws in a sadistic ending that Burroughs would never have: Tarzan causes Stonecraft to drop dead of a heart attack by ringing him up and virtually saying 'Boo!'

Most importantly, the story doesn't make sense: there is no reason for Stonecraft to believe that the ape-man possesses the secret of immortality either through his appearance (he is stated as being a mere 30) or – had Farmer chosen to go postmodern – the published chronicles of his adventures: this all takes place a decade and a half before the appearance of *Tarzan's Quest*, the first place Stonecraft might have read that the ape-man does not age like the rest of us. Some have suggested that Farmer was leaving some dangling plot threads for a sequel. That the inconsistencies were more likely the product of ineptitude was revealed when the author stated his lack of interest in a second book in a September 1997 interview after *The Dark Heart of Time*'s completion but almost two years before its publication ('I just wanted to write one, so I could fulfil a childhood ambition').

Some might assume that Farmer's book was commissioned because of the forthcoming arrival of the Disney movie, but their appearance in the same month was not the original plan. Farmer explained in a letter to *Burroughs Bulletin* that *The Dark Heart of Time* was originally due to hit the shelves not too long after *Tarzan and the Lost City*: 'It was rescheduled because the new

Tarzan movie bombed so badly. Ballantine didn't want the book to come out on the movie's heels. Bad association. So the novel was reset to appear with the new Disney Tarzan animated film and the flood of children's items, games, T-shirts, toys, etc. The reasoning was that the book would be the only Tarzan item for adults to turn to.'

ERBivores (as they were now decreasingly called) had waited a long, long time for an all-new adult Tarzan novel – 35 years to be precise. Compounding their general disappointment when it did emerge was the fact that it was a dead-end. Some follow-ups to this book by other authors were envisaged by Del Rey but none appeared. 'Danton told me that the book did not sell that well, and because of that Ballantine/Del Rey chose not to commission further Tarzan novels,' says Barrett. The flat, unrevealing title of *The Dark Heart of Time* and the underwhelming cover art (a shaded human face and a couple of big leaves) can't have helped the novel's chances. (The phrase 'A Tarzan novel' appears in a banner at the bottom, although one might uncharitably conclude this was less to provide clarification than to pointedly slap a registered trademark symbol next to the character's name.) Following this book, the prose Tarzan once again sputtered to a halt.

The first of the several spin-offs from the Disney Tarzan movie was a TV series from the same company, *The Legend of Tarzan*, which began airing on the United Paramount Network on 3 September 2001 and ran every day of the week except Saturdays. After a first season of 36 half-hour episodes, its second season was more of a coda, consisting of three episodes broadcast in the first week of February 2003 that had previously been released on a home video called *Tarzan and Jane* in July 2002.

As with just about all successful movies that become television shows, *The Legend of Tarzan* was more of the same but diluted: the occasional ferociousness of the parent movie was not going to be appropriate for a show aired on a children's channel and its lush animation not possible in the context of TV budgets and production timeframes. None of the film's stellar cast reprise their roles, Michael T Weiss taking over as Tarzan. Nonetheless, the kids of the Noughties were treated to a much higher grade of animated television Tarzan than their parents had seen as children when sat in front of Filmation's *Tarzan Lord of the Jungle*, even if the new series was shot through with more comedy and aimed at a younger age-group. This upgrade was partly the consequence of CGI having made high-quality animation cheaper and quicker to produce and partly because of a raising of audience expectations that had long rendered olde-worlde the flavourless, formulaic nature of '70s

American television.

The series is set after the events detailed in the Disney *Tarzan* movie, taking place in the African home to which the ape-man returned with his new love at the end of that production. Terk, Tantor, Kala, Professor Porter and of course Jane form the supporting cast. The series opener is rather unpromising, consisting of an episode in which Tarzan is bitten by a venomous spider. Though it gives writer Gary Sperling a chance to depict Jane as a woman of action as she goes off in search of the antidote, the passive scenario for the ape-man rather works against the heroic Tarzan template. Subsequent episodes introduce Opar and La, the Waziri, the Leopard Men, Pellucidar, Nikolas Rokoff, 'One Punch' Mullargan and Stanley Obroski, although in forms little like the way Burroughs first presented them. Keeping with the film's period setting, a pre-presidency Theodore Roosevelt also puts in an appearance, but a truly surprising guest appearance is that of Burroughs himself in the episode 'Tarzan and the Mysterious Visitor'. In real-life, Burroughs never visited Africa, but this story sees an author referred to as 'Ed' (later, his full name is displayed on the manuscript of his first Tarzan book) searching Africa for a missing link about which he has read. We are introduced herein to the man 'who had no business to tell it to me, or to any other' from whom Burroughs originally wrote that he 'had this story'. He turns out to be – at least according to episode writer Madellaine Paxson – a down-on-his-luck Samuel T Philander, friend of Archimedes Porter in the *Tarzan of the Apes* novel. The episode naturally takes liberties with inconveniently undramatic facts but is also well-researched, correctly identifying *A Princess of Mars* and *The Outlaw of Torn* as Burroughs works that pre-dated *Tarzan of the Apes*. Another episode – 'Tarzan and the Silver Screen' – recalls the postmodernist plot of the book *Tarzan and the Lion Man*, with Tarzan finding himself cast in a movie about himself. The displaced thespian seeks revenge.

Twenty-six different writers contributed episodes (sometimes in combination). Whatever the series' occasional sweetness and evident love for its source, this is a surprisingly high number for such undemanding fare. The show's mix of semi-seriousness and profound lack of gravity are demonstrated by the episode 'Tarzan and the Rift', which juxtaposes a story about the ape-man tackling sinister trappers with another about a wedge driven between Tantor and Terk by Tantor's new girlfriend.

In the middle of the roll on which Tarzan had been propelled through the aegis of Disney came another new live-action television depiction of the ape-man. *Tarzan* was an American series of one-hour episodes that debuted on 5

October 2003 on the new-ish WB Television Network. Writer/co-executive producer Eric Kripke seems to have been the person chiefly responsible for the complexion of another show that sought to update and urbanise the ape-man. WB's pre-publicity claimed that it was in the tradition of *Smallville*, their extremely successful edgy, knowing Superman updating. Perhaps significantly, the *Tarzan* pilot was originally titled *Tarzan and Jane*, for it also seems to bear more than a tinge of another TV re-imagining of Superman, namely the 1990s ABC series *Lois & Clark*, which put a contemporary and slightly feminist slant on the franchise.

In WB's rejig, John Clayton is the nephew of billionaire Richard Clayton (Mitch Pileggi), CEO of Greystoke Industries. John was proclaimed dead when his parents' plane crashed in the Republic of Congo. Unbeknownst to the outside world, he was kept safe and raised by jungle animals, chiefly apes. Twenty years later, he was discovered alive and unwell (traumatised by his experiences, he initially barely speaks). Richard Clayton keeps John – who goes by 'Tarzan', although the word is rarely uttered – locked up, ostensibly for safety reasons related to his savagery but in fact more to maintain control of the corporation to which John is the rightful heir. John's aunt Katherine, played by *Xena: Warrior Princess* star Lucy Lawless, takes Tarzan's side against her brother in the latter's quest to 'rehabilitate' John by civilising him.

Jane Porter (Sarah Wayne Callies) is an NYPD detective who lives with her younger sister Nicki (Leighton Meester) and works alongside black renegade Sam Sullivan (Miguel A Núñez Jr). She stumbles upon Tarzan after he has escaped his uncle's clutches and is living on the streets. Following an incident in which he saves her from falling off a building, Tarzan and Jane are smitten with each other (not altogether convincingly). Tarzan proceeds to follow Jane around this urban jungle and help her solve cases. She often finds herself having to rein him in as he spurns society's laws and tries to mete out the sort of justice that prevails in the terrain with which he is more familiar. All this is underscored by a soft rock soundtrack that is an integral part of a show whose intended demographic is largely teenage girls.

The show's star Travis Fimmel was a first on a couple of counts. Never before had an actor playing Tarzan had an Australian accent (albeit ineptly disguised) and never before had one looked like a girl. A Calvin Klein model turned thespian, Fimmel is not handsome but pretty, with sensual lips and cat-like eyes framed by cascading blond tresses. The androgyny is part of an approach that seeks to undermine expected conventions.

Not that conventions can be completely subverted. The trouble with transplanting Tarzan to the big city is that the only way to meet a television drama series' necessity for conflict is to pit him against bad guys, and the easiest way to do that is to make what is effectively a cop show. A crime-fighter who has massive upper body strength, refined tracking skills and a guileless perspective on morality and politesse is ultimately not too dissimilar from an official policeman: he still has to catch the villain in less than an hour against a concrete backdrop punctuated by wailing sirens. Micheline Keller says, 'We tried to give them advice. One of them called us and we said, "You know what? We found that the world really wants to see Tarzan in the jungle, not in the city." But they had their own concept that they were going with.' However, the producers sought to do more than the Kellers had clearly intended if their *Tarzan In Manhattan* had bequeathed a series wherein the ape-man worked for Jane's private investigator dad. That Tarzan is officially dead after an incendiary climax to the first WB episode, and subsequently wrongly accused of murder, adds a tinge of *The Fugitive/The Incredible Hulk* to the show, especially considering the uncle on his trail. Also a cut above the standard is the overall gloomy ambience and slow-burning character development, even if the intended class is slightly undermined by such logic lapses as Tarzan not offending Jane's nostrils at any point and the jungle boy sometimes being unaccountably familiar with technology and social custom.

The enterprise was a noble failure that was gone in the blink of an eye. Though a respectable audience figure of 5.5 million watched the pilot, this had tumbled to 2.84 million by the fifth airing, at which point WB pulled the plug, though it did broadcast the three other episodes on which production had wrapped. In contrast, *Smallville* outlasted *Tarzan* by eight years and triumphantly departed the stage at a time of the creators' own choosing.

Disney's animated sequel *Tarzan II* would perhaps have been more appropriately titled *Tarzan ½*, its events occurring part-way during the studio's first Tarzan film when the title character is still a young boy.

Only Glenn Close and Lance Henriksen (Kerchak) reprise their vocal roles from the first outing, with Alex D Linz replaced as young Tarzan by Harrison Chad. Brian Smith directed this 60-minute affair, which required the efforts of two writing teams, Jim Kammerud and Brian Smith and Bob Tzudiker and Noni White.

The film finds young Tarzan brooding over the fact that he is a substandard 'ape'. Subsequently, his lack of climbing prowess puts Kala in danger in an incident in which he is temporarily beyond contact and therefore presumed dead. When he is about to return to his tribe, he hears some of the other mothers regretfully state that Kala is probably better off without him. Distraught, he flees into the jungle. There he meets a gorilla family consisting of hulking but dim-witted brothers Uto and Kago and their controlling mother Mama Gunda. They are stranded in a barren valley by their fear of Zugor, a legendary monster reputed to guard its only entrance. Zugor is really a gnarled and lonely old ape practising a deception. He and Tarzan strike up a rapport when they realise they were both deemed burdens by their respective former tribes, although that doesn't stop Tarzan falling out with him long enough to utter a playful line nodding to decades of ape-man heritage: 'Me Tarzan, you grouch.' Tantor and Terk realise Tarzan is still alive and come to collect him, as does Kala when she belatedly hears the news. A battle royale ensures between all the parties before a spanner is thrown in the works by Mama Gunda and Zugor falling in love. The film ends with some of the tree-surfing that was such a feature of the previous one followed by a variation of the first film's finale: Tarzan on a high branch emitting a yodel.

There's a feeling of grand pointlessness to the enterprise: we know how Tarzan's life and problems were resolved from having seen the parent film. However, the young intended audience were probably not agonising over that, nor the fact that this follow-up is no *The Godfather: Part II*, and instead were delighted by the above-average animation, good-heartedness, funny characters and amusing scenes. Their mums and dads were probably more distracted by the two new songs Phil Collins contributed in the well-crafted-but-characterless style of the first film.

Ambitions seem to have been low for this project, as epitomised by the fact that its June 2005 release was not to cinemas. Notwithstanding the large market for such products, especially bearing the Disney brand name, issuing a film 'direct to video' (in fact, by then, DVD) is the embodiment of a lack of confidence in its quality and/or commercial viability. Even so, Disney still saw further mileage in the character. Having portrayed Tarzan on film, television and home video/DVD, they were preparing to return him to the stage.

Once upon a time, Disney stage shows were limited to such delights as *Walt Disney's World on Ice*, wherein anonymous individuals dressed as the likes of Goofy and Donald Duck skated across rinks while performing vignettes from the studio's films. This all changed with *Beauty and the Beast*, the high-value 1994 production that in reworking a preceding movie for Broadway showed that a property could both have its life significantly extended and its cachet raised. Having found a new way to embed themselves into the American culture that they, to many, already epitomised, Disney mined that seam with a vengeance, their 1997 show *The Lion King* being particularly mind-blowing in its success. The Noughties saw their stage musicals achieve an even higher plateau, both domestically and abroad. In 2006/07, the number of Disney musicals on Broadway doubled to four. One of them was a production based on their 1999 animated *Tarzan* movie.

Tarzan: The Broadway Musical was reported to be one of the few Great White Way shows containing songs to turn a profit before it opened. This was quite a feat: it was also reported to be one of the most expensive Broadway productions of all time, with a budget between 15 and 20 million dollars racked up over the four-and-a-half years required to bring it to the stage. Nor was the demand for tickets a phenomenon that tapered off when the public got to see either it or the reviews after the 10 May 2006 official opening: its theatre's 1,368 seats continued to be filled for every performance. By September, Disney's Dusty Bennett was informing Danton Burroughs, 'We broke the Richard Rodgers Theatre box office record in July and then went on to break our own record two more times throughout the course of the summer.'

The receipts were the result of the customary care the company lavished on the show. Disney did not lazily stage the film script. Instead, they started from scratch, hiring heavyweight dramatist David Henry Hwang (*M. Butterfly*, *Aida*) to provide an original 'book'. Hwang admitted to *Disney Insider* that he wasn't too familiar with the Tarzan legend and that the previous multiple versions in different media had served to obscure the original story. 'So I read the original novel by Edgar Rice Burroughs and looked again at the Disney movie, which I'd always loved,' he said. 'This was a story that excited me … As a Chinese American, I particularly related to a man caught between two worlds (in Tarzan's case, between human and ape families), taking elements from each to become his best self.' The producers also packed the show with songs, commissioning nine more numbers from Phil Collins. The greatest amount of work that went into the show, however, related to the arboreal facets.

Edgar Rice Burroughs had once expressly agreed with the proposition that the people who staged the first Tarzan stage play had taken upon themselves an 'impossible' task. However, times – and what was and was not impossible – had changed since 1920, with the talents of director/scenic designer/costume designer Bob Crowley and choreographer Meryl Tankard meriting credit alongside technological progress. Bungee cords, nigh-invisible wires, hidden harnesses and a crevice-pocked bouncy castle-like set not only enabled the actors to give the impression of tree-swinging but even facilitated a facsimile of the movie's tree-surfing. Dramatically, the actors also flew out over the audience. All of this was done without real leaves: deep green lighting and hanging artificial fronds created the jungle ambience. (Natasha Katz was nominated for a Tony Award for Best Lighting Design of a Musical.)

A measure of the success of these effects is provided by the overwhelmed reaction of the presumably show-hardened reviewer of the *Daily Telegraph*, who gushed, 'The opening minutes of *Tarzan* are among the most exciting and inventive I have ever witnessed in the theatre. Bob Crowley has conjured up an astonishing succession of *coups de theatre*. They whisk us from a thrilling shipwreck to an amazing underwater rescue sequence, from a bird's-eye view of a tropical beach to a jungle full of gorillas swinging around like kids in an adventure playground.' Some things, though, clearly remained impracticable: the character of Tantor was jettisoned.

Daniel Manche and Alex Rutherford were the younger versions of Tarzan (loinclothed for the sake of decency if not logic), with Josh Strickland taking over as the adult ape-man. The latter's mane of dreadlocked hair somehow worked, and if the lack of bulge to his muscles seemed incongruous it was also understandable: the spectacular flips, swinging and movie-style knuckle-dragging would likely have been beyond the abilities of somebody carrying around more bulk. Jane was played by Jennifer Gambatese, agreeably so according to critics, though she had to struggle against her frumpy if period-correct costume. The apes (gorillas not Mangani again) were represented more by suggestion than costume, with performers like Merle Dandridge (Kala) made simian only by furry tops, skirts and head-pieces.

The show bequeathed the behind-the-scenes book *Tarzan: The Broadway Adventure* and a soundtrack album plus new souvenirs and merchandise. The domestic euphoria turned out to be relatively short-lived, with the Broadway show closing on 8 July 2007 after 35 previews and 486 performances. However, the show fanned out across the globe to appreciative audiences, with productions mounted in Holland, Sweden and Germany in the next few years. There have also been regional US productions.

As with the animated movie, that *Tarzan: The Broadway Musical* was not a faithful Burroughs adaptation was offset by the benefit that it kept the Tarzan franchise alive. Nor did it merely introduce the ape-man to new generations: being the subject of a Broadway show meant Tarzan was taken to a higher grade of people than those to be found in the multiplexes.

Underlining the way that Tarzan had to some extent become a Disney rather than an Edgar Rice Burroughs character in the first decade of the 21st Century is the fact that whereas the distinctive Disney logo appears above the title on the promotional poster for *Tarzan: The Broadway Musical*, nowhere is Burroughs' name in evidence. Meanwhile, the Tarzan name is rendered in an unfamiliar uneven typescript, not in that distinctive double-outlined trademarked Tarzan logo. Having said that, the Disney production bequeathed one Tarzan logo that is superior to the 'real' one: a version where the 'Z' in the word is strikingly provided by a jack-knifed ape-man swinging on a vine.

In the run-up to the year that marked the centenary of Tarzan's first appearance, the announcement that there was to be a new series of Tarzan novels did not come as much of a surprise to ERB aficionados. However, a look beyond the surface facts threw up two unexpected details. The first was that the resumption of the franchise was not the idea of ERB, Inc but of an author who was initially unaware of the 100-year milestone. The other was that the new Tarzan novels – the first authorised by the estate since Philip José Farmer's *The Dark Heart of Time* in 1999 – were to be geared toward children.

Liverpool-born Andy Briggs – the first British writer to chronicle the adventures of the English Lord Greystoke – started off in screenwriting, making contributions to projects like *Judge Dredd*, *Freddie vs. Jason*, *Aquaman* and the *Highlander* TV series (not all of which made it to the screen), and graphic novels. Prose-wise, he created two intersecting series for Oxford University Press called *hero.com* and *villain.net*, revolving around kids who discover a website from which they can temporarily download superpowers.

'I've always had this thing about Tarzan, thinking it would be cool to do something,' says Briggs. As with most people under 50 (particularly in the UK), Briggs had only ever known a drought situation with Tarzan books when he was growing up. 'I got into Tarzan through the TV and the movies,' he says. The transition from idly thinking it 'would be cool to do something' with the ape-man to actively considering taking on the character came by chance. Briggs: 'I originally saw it on a list of titles that I got from a TV company who were looking for out-of-copyright properties that they can reinvent and do something with. I thought "Wow! Cool. It didn't occur to me that this is out of copyright." Then I looked into it and I discovered the hideous copyright mess where it's only out of copyright in America but in copyright the rest of the word. And then the word Tarzan is a trademark, so you can't do anything with that. That's what got me interested, and then I just started thinking about how it can be rejuvenated, how it can be brought to a new audience. This was well before I was even aware of the centenary. This was just a bit of a passion project.

'Originally I was noodling around with how to do it. I write movies, I go to the studios all the time, so do I go in at that level?' With a putative Tarzan movie from Warner Brothers having been in turnaround for several years, Briggs turned his thoughts in a different direction: 'I thought, "If I owned Tarzan, what would I do?" You need to get in at the grassroots. You need to rebuild the brand up almost from scratch, with that wonderful legacy, so I thought a book would be the best way to do it. You could go straight in and do an adult book. Fine, it might find a market, but the smart way to do it is what they've done with the Young Bond series, the Charlie Higson books. If you want a property to survive, you start with the youngest audience you can feasibly work with.' Briggs decided that the field of Young Adult – a latterly-defined genre for readers roughly 14 to 21 featuring protagonists of a similar age-group – 'makes sense, because then there's a refurbished brand that you can build everything else on top of.' He initially met resistance: 'I talked to all the major publishers and everyone thought it was really cool. Everybody knows Tarzan, everyone's looking for a brand. They just didn't think the estate would go for it. It was very demoralising. Eventually, I just thought, "Screw this, I'm just going to contact the estate directly." Contacted them, got my agent in LA to send samples over of my work, my résumé and things, and a half-a-page pitch of what I had in mind, and almost immediately got a reply back saying, "This sounds great. Come over to Tarzana." So I went over, I met with people from the office there, and it wasn't even a battle. There [are] obviously lots of protections, lots of caveats around what you can do with the character. I left very stunned, because I'd had such an uphill struggle with the publishers originally.' With ERB, Inc's imprimatur obtained, publisher Faber signed on the dotted line for Briggs' new Tarzan series. 'We're looking at three for now and then [we'll] just take it from there,' he says. 'Nobody in this day and age can commit to anything more than that.' Some in fact can't commit even to that: rather ominously, the series failed to find an American buyer.

Perhaps surprisingly, Briggs has found that the paucity of new movies and other manifestations of Tarzan in the media in recent times has not caused the character to drop completely off the cultural radar even for the young. 'When I've been doing all the visits around the country with my superhero books, I've been talking to younger readers … I could go to a school or a college and say, "Do you know who Tarzan is?" Everybody knows who Tarzan is. Everyone knows his backstory, everyone knows the famous yodel, but very few of them have ever seen a film and virtually none of them has ever read the book. I find that fascinating, because I suddenly realised how imprinted Tarzan is on popular culture. I just think it's an image that you see subliminally. And some kids … you play them the Tarzan yodel and [they] go, "Yeah, that is George of the Jungle", and that yodel's not in the *George of the Jungle* film. It's a very strange thing. It's a kind of collective consciousness that's built around this character.'

The Tarzan Twins books excepted, Burroughs only ever wrote commercially for adults, but Briggs denies that aiming his Tarzan books at adolescents demeans the character: 'Let's put it this way. *Tarzan of the Apes*, it's a classic. Adults will read it. [But] the majority of people who'll read that book will be kids in school studying English Literature or American Literature. Same way, they are the majority of people who are reading Charles Dickens. They might have been written for an adult audience a hundred or whatever years ago, but that's not who reads them now. If Warners get round to doing this movie, this movie is not going to be a dark, adult movie. It's not even going to be *Greystoke*. It's going to be a *Pirates of the Caribbean*, aimed at the younger generation, adults inclusive.' He says of his Tarzan series, 'To say it's a kids' book – and this is the constant battle I've had with the publisher – is absolutely incorrect. We're just aiming it at the people who are actually just reading *Tarzan of the Apes* … If you do that and later down the stream a movie comes out, kids who are 12 are going to be 19 when that movie comes out. Some people have [said] it should be for diehard fans, which is completely selfish because Burroughs himself was the master [of] flogging it off, licensing it off, as much as possible. It's incorrect to say he's a character for adults anymore. He's just become a character for everybody. Whether the book's marketed in the children's section, whether it's marketed in the adults' section, is irrelevant. In an ideal world, it will pick up in the YA section and then it'll just do what they did with *Twilight*, what they did with Harry Potter: they just stick a different jacket on it and it goes straight into the adults' section.'

Briggs reveals, 'This [project has] taken a year of just going through things with the estate to make sure that Tarzan feels like Tarzan, [that the stories] take all the best elements that the public love, leave some of the things that may have been taking Tarzan in the wrong direction and obviously a lot of the stuff that you can't do now. The essence of Greystoke – his background, lineage – all of that: exactly the same. Raised by the apes in exactly the same way. We've still got Kala, Kerchak.' No doubt even diehard Burroughs fans can comfortably live with some of Briggs' changes. '[Burroughs' original] was written at a time when there were certain assumptions made about racism, sexism,' he says. 'The world has changed in a hundred years.' Similarly, his deliberate avoidance of a wannabe ERB prose style – 'That would be a sham. I never, ever, ever wanted to impersonate Burroughs' – will generate few grievances. However, other aspects of a series that Briggs describes as a 'reboot' are bound to create controversy.

Briggs' changes start with the fact that Tarzan is no longer a man born circa 1888. 'If we were going to set it when Tarzan was born, the same age, it [would be] a pointless exercise,' he says. 'You might as well just say, "Look, read the [original] book." Why do that? Why not just say, "If we're going to refresh this then it's going to have to be appealing to a contemporary audience." In that case we're going to have to bring it up to date and set it now and make sure we've preserved the original flavour of Tarzan." However, Briggs seems to be hedging his bets somewhat when he insists that the period is left a little ambiguous: 'It's irrelevant when this is set. You really don't know, 'cause you're in a jungle.' Up to a point, anyway. Of Jane, he notes, 'She is a modern girl, therefore she has an iPhone.'

Briggs has dispensed with the concept of the Mangani almost completely. 'Because of the influence of the movies, we're just not going to get away with that,' he reasons. 'A new generation of people who've never read the original book [would] struggle to get into that, because [in] every movie, or most of them, they are gorillas, that's all they are.' This of course is completely incorrect – only the Disney products feature gorillas as Tarzan's tribe – but Briggs has done his research a little better on wildlife: 'You're talking about a book that was published in 1912, when Burroughs had never been to Africa, there was no research done out in the wild on how great apes actually behaved, so there [were] a lot of liberties taken in the book that people just are not going to buy now.' With the example of Cheeta in mind, Briggs did investigate the possibility of portraying Tarzan as raised by chimpanzees. Briggs: 'Every zookeeper and animal expert I spoke to referred to the chimpanzees basically being vicious bastards. They just seemed too extreme for their natural behaviour to take in this infant.' A small element of Burroughs' vision of apes one step closer to man does remain. Explains Briggs, 'The estate didn't want [me] to say they are just gorillas, so there are hints in the first book of them being a lot more intelligent.' However, this doesn't address all the continuity issues his decision creates. Chimps may be too nasty to willingly raise a human child but gorillas – a gentle species, albeit with much loud bravado – are too nice for this franchise, making the bloodlust implicit in the victory cry of the bull ape anomalous. Meanwhile, his caving in to the assumptions (allegedly) instilled by movies over this issue seems to contradict his statement, 'The TV and the movies have taken it in a certain direction that ERB was originally never very happy with. I approached [this] from a completely different point of view.'

Orientating the book toward the Young Adult market has necessitated another example of hedge-betting, this one concerning the ages of the central characters. Briggs: 'Again, this was a huge conversation. The ages have been not addressed – skirted around, if you want to be very critical – but it's been done in such a way that it doesn't lock the character [of Tarzan] down. It's trying to get the reader just to interpret it and put their own age on the character.' Doesn't such evasiveness run the risk of blanding out the writing? 'You could say that, but then I would say to you, "Show me the page on *Tarzan of the Apes* where it tells you their exact ages". In point of fact, as the letter Jane writes to her friend when stranded in Africa is dated 1909, that establishes Tarzan at that point as around 21.

Briggs has exploited Burroughs' vagueness about Tarzan's country of origin. 'It's set in the Congo because it's the one wide space which borders Rwanda and everywhere else,' he says of his series. 'It's the last, biggest rainforest in Africa.' Citing the theory that *Tarzan of the Apes* was set, if anywhere, in Gabon, he continues, 'All [the other] countries are all industrialised. Gabon is an oil-rich nation now and there is no rainforest there, so it pushes it back to where you can set it. Having said that, the world in the Congo, the jungle side, the political plight of the Congo, the whole environment, the whole social structure, is much more akin to what Burroughs wrote than any other place you can locate it today. So you can get away with a lot of high action adventure, tick all the same boxes that Burroughs did. It is a perfect location for him.'

Burroughs of course had trouble soon after the series started finding dramatic devices for a jungle-based character, but Briggs sees no reason for him to use Burroughs' fallback of ill-fated safaris trekking to lost cities. 'I just think the modern world allows you to do that automatically,' he says. 'You replace those savage tribes with savage guerrillas, Rwandan radicals, that kind of thing. The world has changed to such a degree, it perfectly fits what Burroughs was always striving for with Tarzan. Plus I'm deliberately holding back the whole Greystoke thing. It's seeded throughout this [first] book because obviously it's an important aspect of his character, but it's not just delivered to you: "There you go, that's everything you want to know about the Greystoke [clan], about his parents and about him." It gives us a little bit more mileage as far as how we can push the stories forward.'

Environmentalism will be a big part of the new series. 'Tarzan was for all intents and purposes the world's first eco-warrior,' Briggs asserts. 'He was the protector of the wild. He kills for food, he kills for safety, for protection. He doesn't go out and kill the animals just for the sake of it … If you go in and start cutting down all the trees in Tarzan's territory, he's not going to stand there. He's going to destroy you. He's going to put you off as much as possible, which is how we enter the story. His home so happens to be the trees, it so happens to be the rainforest. That's the eco side of things.' However, Briggs does concede, 'It would be horrible if he vocalised this. If he went out saying, "Stop! Preserve the environment!" That would be hideous. He is the world's first eco-warrior, but that doesn't mean he's a guy who's attending rallies.'

Though Burroughs never set foot in Africa, Briggs did exploit the limited opportunity afforded him by finite publishing budgets to travel to what he says he won't be calling the Dark Continent. However, 'The best part of the research was over here, talking to zookeepers who have actually gone out into the jungle and interacted with those wild animals and brought them back and lived with those animals day in, day out. I've made sure everything's as authentic as possible.' His penchant for the authentic has also led him to sidestep Burroughs' recourse to unlikely coincidence: 'It's a reboot to make it more credible. That it's not the same beach out of the whole of Africa where people are getting abandoned and shipwrecked.'

The first of the books, *The Greystoke Legacy*, appeared in June 2011. Briggs resisted the obvious publication date of 2012: 'I was banging my drum saying, "Look, surely what you want to do is build up a new fanbase, so when you go into the centenary, you've got all the diehard fans and then you've got this whole wave of new people".'

Briggs admits, 'As a fan, instantly, you're going to spot everything that's changed.' A *Star Wars* fanatic, he can sympathise to some extent. 'For a lot of things, I am a purist and I love the original, I hate people tampering with it.' However, at the end of the day, he makes no apology for his fine-tuning of Tarzan. 'There [are not] enough purists who are going to keep this alive,' he states. 'When all those purists die, Burroughs' original book is dead.'

The Tarzan story as told by Briggs has the aeroplane carrying Lord and Lady Greystoke – an English couple known for championing environmental causes – crashing in the country then known as Zaire, now the Democratic Republic of Congo. Her ladyship is five months pregnant and, though she lives long enough to give birth to a son (their name for him is not revealed), both she and her husband perish. The baby is brought up by a band of gorillas (referred to by Tarzan as Mangani) who make the planewreck their home. The boy next interacts with a human when a United Nations peace-keeper named D'Arnot enters his territory and is saved by him from a lioness. D'Arnot teaches him English. Making his way back to civilisation, D'Arnot tries to alert the Greystoke family to the existence of an heir. When he is disbelieved, he returns to the jungle in search of Tarzan but dies there.

These events are not presented sequentially or directly, but rather pieced together across the course of the story by Jane Porter, teenaged daughter of an illegal logger who encounters the ape-man when she gets lost in the jungle after a fire at the logging camp. Another teenager at the loggers' camp, Robbie, has a troubled past. The loggers' uneasy pact with local guerrillas comes to an end when each side start suspecting the other of acts of sabotage and mischief: in fact, the culprit is Tarzan, taking out his anger at their despoilment of his locality. The book climaxes with a scene in which Tarzan calls upon lions, elephants and gorillas to demolish the guerrillas' camp and rescue the imprisoned loggers, about whom he has taken a more lenient view due to his fondness for Jane. The latter feels the same way for him, shaken out of her insular adolescent mentality by the beauty and danger of the jungle, demonstrated to her by her brave but lonely new friend. The narrative ends with Tarzan disappearing back into the jungle but with Jane feeling she has not seen the last of him.

It is rather intriguing observing Briggs decanting the Tarzan legend into the modern world, although – as ever with tampering with the original story – some of his changes are irritating. Additionally, in changing elements, Briggs gets into trouble. He has Tarzan eating meat because Burroughs' ape-man was raised by the omnivorous Mangani – but how would a man raised by gorillas, a species whose consumption of living things extends only so far as insects, have developed a taste for animal flesh? Though Briggs' depictions of Tarzan's arboreal abilities (a matter of downwards jumping as much as swinging) are impressive, they are again not consistent with ground-based gorilla behaviour. Briggs even paints himself into a corner with the character's very name. 'Tarzan' is not ape-speak for 'white-skin' but is simply not explained, nor are human-sounding handles like Kerchak and Kala. (The likes of Sabor, Numa and Tantor, incidentally, are here names of individual animals, not generic.) For the first time ever in any adaptation in any medium, Tarzan doesn't sport something resembling a loincloth. Instead, in the most gruesome piece of updating, he is clad in a ragged pair of cargo shorts, origin unstated. He is, in other words, a wild variant on a cool teenager.

Briggs is at least able to provide from first-hand experience a verisimilitude of which homebody Burroughs was rarely capable, from dense, accurate detail about wildlife (if sometimes dropped in heavy-handedly and/or didactically) to the simple fact of him appreciating what a sticky, sweaty place Africa is. Meanwhile, he has clearly done his research well on logging outfits, capturing their diesel stink, fly-by-night nature and mercenary ambience. His gorillas are lovely and admirable without being sentimentally anthropomorphic, and his portrayal of the Greystokes' moss-covered, wrecked plane being used as a base by gorillas is evocative and charming. In contrast to this believability, Briggs' depiction of a lion zigzagging to dodge a gunman's bullets is the kind of nonsense that Burroughs, even with his limited knowledge, would never have written.

Briggs writes competently enough, although never particularly sparklingly. Though he is an omniscient narrator, this only fails to work when he goes over the top and shows three different points of view in the space of a single paragraph. There are however occasional examples of sloppiness ('Hacking things apart with a chainsaw was exactly the kind of fun a teenager should be having, or so he thought') and instances of crushing, soap opera-level blandness ('I just wanted to say, if you ever need to talk …')

There are two severe faults with *The Greystoke Legacy*. First, Briggs doesn't actually seem to know what to do with Tarzan. The character is virtually a guest in his own book. Admittedly, the inclusion of lengthy material about jungle interlopers that not only keeps Tarzan off the stage but is in itself rather boring is something of which Burroughs himself was frequently guilty. However, the ape-man at no point drives the narrative here: he is unseen until past the 60-page mark, and when he does appear is presented through the eyes of others. Not until gone 200 pages are we made privy to Tarzan's point of view. Irritating enough for an adult reader, Tarzan's low profile must be tedious and bewildering for the intended young readership.

The other glaring problem is the restrictions imposed on the author by that orientation toward the young. Briggs includes things the uptight Burroughs never would (a use of the word 'crap,' a reference to toilet paper) and goes half-way toward Philip José Farmer-style unflinching realism in depicting Tarzan happily eating live crickets and caterpillars. Elsewhere, though, he is coy even for kids' fare. For instance, there is no real hint of sexual attraction between Tarzan and Jane. The most absurd manifestation of this U-certificate territory is Briggs' refusal to show Tarzan killing animals in any circumstance except when obtaining food. The ape-man fights lionesses but miraculously manages to triumph over them without recourse to fatal wounds, while a battle for supremacy with the gorilla character Terkoz is settled – Filmation cartoon-style – by him causing his opponent to punch himself in the face by lassoing a rope around his wrist. The nadir of the pussyfooting is a passage wherein Tarzan slashes a lioness across a flank with a rare use of his knife and Briggs feels compelled almost to apologise for it, insisting it is 'fair retaliation' for the big cat having raked its claws across the ape-man's back. The morality is moreover a strange one, for human deaths of a grisly nature are quite happily presented for the young readers' edification.

All of this seems to demonstrate the fallacy of Briggs' theory of keeping the character alive via YA. Raising the young on Tarzan is of no use whatever if targeting them necessitates undermining the character's whole savage, bloody premise.

PART TEN: SWINGING INTO AN UNCERTAIN FUTURE

In addition to the second of Andy Briggs' YA Tarzan books, *Tarzan: The Jungle Warrior*, there were some projects of considerable interest to Burroughs fans looming in 2012.

The first was *John Carter*, the March 2012 big budget Andrew Stanton-directed movie adaptation of *A Princess of Mars* from the golden-touch studio Pixar. Many Burroughs fans had literally died waiting for a John Carter motion picture: it took fully 100 years for one to make it to the screen from the character's first appearance. As ever, it was an adaptation that was a cross between lovingly faithful and infuriatingly tampered-with, starting with that boring title whose 'of Mars' had been lopped off because – according to one actor involved – the character hadn't yet 'earned' the regal-sounding appendage. The latter logic seems particularly wrong-headed considering that several months before the movie's release, its producers were stating that it would not be granted a sequel unless it grossed at least $700 million (i.e. it needed to be one of the 50 highest-grossing films of all time). As things transpired, not long after its release, Disney admitted it expected to suffer a $200m loss on *John Carter*. Nonetheless, Burroughs' name and creation were kept alive by a film that generated newsprint and web stories in which asides like 'based on a book by the man who created Tarzan' were inevitably prominent.

A multiple-author collection of short stories titled *The Worlds of Edgar Rice Burroughs* edited by Mike Resnick and Robert T Garcia was scheduled for publication in 2013, following 2012's *Under the Moons of Mars: New Adventures on Barsoom*. It was due to have some Tarzan content, if minimal. Planned for September 2012 was a full-length Tarzan novel for adults, if one that, like the Andy Briggs books, suggests publishers have no confidence in the existence of the once-considerable adult male Tarzan prose demographic. *Jane: The Woman Who Loved Tarzan* by Robin Maxwell is both the first Tarzan novel told from Jane's point of view and the first written by a woman.

Maxwell was once a screenwriter. Though her success in that field seems to have been limited (CBS Movie of the Week *Passions* is the only example she lists on her website at the time of writing), she has subsequently enjoyed considerable success in the field of historical fiction with such works as *The Secret Diary of Anne Boleyn* and *The Queen's Bastard*. In 2010, she published *O, Juliet* in which she told the story of Romeo and Juliet as a novel. As with the Andy Briggs series, her Tarzan tome was not the idea of the not-very-proactive ERB, Inc. 'I really enjoyed instead of historical characters taking literary characters, and I still felt like I wanted to write a great love story,' says Maxwell. 'My agents and editors were saying, "Well, what's your next book?" My husband said, "What's another literary love story?" and about three seconds later I just blurted out, "Tarzan and Jane." He kind of laughed it off. I thought, "This is a real great idea." Nobody's better at doing a woman's point of view of either history or literature than I am.' However, Maxwell was cognisant of the difference between reworking the unequivocally public domain Shakespeare and taking on Tarzan: 'I knew that you messed with Edgar Rice Burroughs' estate at your own peril.' She instructed her lawyer to write to ERB, Inc president Jim Sullos. Maxwell: 'Before I knew it, Jim and my lawyer were on the phone and Jim was asking me, "Well okay, what's your great idea?" 'Cause all I had said in the letter was that I had a new twist on the Tarzan story. I just said, "The Tarzan story from Jane's point of view," and he went through the roof. He just said, "Oh, that's fantastic." He liked the romantic angle of it. He read some of my work, so I went in and pitched to him in Tarzana for five hours.'

Of course, to some extent, Maxwell's idea was merely the literary equivalent of John Derek's 1981 *Tarzan the Ape Man* movie. That picture being such a sore point with the corporation, some might be surprised that ERB, Inc were so receptive to her proposal, but she reasons, 'I have a track record. I'm considered one of the queens of historical fiction, and I have a body of work behind me. Having heard my take on the story, he knew I wasn't going to make it into a mash or something they were going to be ashamed of.' By this point, Maxwell had read *Tarzan of the Apes*, but she admits that when the idea first came to her she had not consumed any Burroughs, though she had enjoyed Tarzan comic books as a girl and seen many Tarzan movies from the Weissmuller era onwards. For those who doubt the suitability for adventure works of someone with her back catalogue, Maxwell asserts that her grounding as a screenwriter taught her how to write action-orientated narrative.

Maxwell was pleasantly surprised at the serendipity of her timing: 'The day that [Jim Sullos] asked me on the phone "What's this about?", that's when he told me the hundredth anniversary was happening.' Perhaps less of a pleasant surprise were the terms to which she was required to agree. 'For the first time in my book-writing career, I will not own the copyright,' says Maxwell. 'I had to give up a percentage of my royalties and the copyright. ERB insist on owning any Tarzan novel.' She was also required to conform to the estate's Tarzan Universe dictates: 'There [are] about 20 rules which you may not break: Tarzan cannot drink, he cannot smoke, he cannot be a racist, Tarzan cannot do anything to harm another human being unless they're bad. Things like that.' This caused a temporary hiccup: 'The last one was Tarzan may not have illicit sex. This was going to be an adult novel and it was going to be a romance between a sexy man and a virgin but a full-blooded woman. Here they are alone in the jungle going through incredible adventures and they were going to make love, there was no two ways about it. I said to Jim, "If they cannot make love in this book, then I'm not writing a book." So he had a talk with the Burroughs estate and came back with a compromise: Tarzan may make love, but it must be done tastefully.'

However, these were merely the first hurdles to publication. Maxwell found that despite her track record and having 'top agents' in her employ, obtaining a publisher was difficult. 'The rejection letters were, "We don't think there's a market for Tarzan books" or, "We don't know how to sell this", she recalls. Though the book found a buyer following a reworked pitch and a second round of applications, science fiction and fantasy specialists Tor are not the level of publishing outlet to which she is used. Surprisingly, though, *Jane* was perceived as a far more attractive talking book: 'Audio books are huge and getting huger, and there was actually an auction for *Jane* and I ended up getting a huge audio book deal.'

'I took tremendous liberties with my telling of the story, but it was all authorised by the estate,' says Maxwell. 'Being a historian and a bit of a science buff, I wanted to keep it as close to reality as possible. I felt that it was really implausible that if Tarzan was taken by the Mangani at age one, he would have been able to relearn the English language. So I decided Tarzan was four years old when his parents got murdered in front of him. Jane … helps him remember who he is. When he meets her, he doesn't have anything but Mangani language.' Another alteration revolved around the implausible coincidence with which adapters had had problems as far back as the 1918 *Tarzan of the Apes* movie: that a party that happens to include a Greystoke is marooned on the very shore on which Tarzan's parents had been stranded. Instead, a party devoid of Greystokes but containing Archibald Porter and his half-English, half-American daughter Jane – herself an heir to a title – come upon Tarzan's home in what Maxwell renders as Gabon because Porter 'is an enthusiastic amateur paleoanthropologist who has already been to Africa on six different expeditions looking for Darwin's missing link.' Jane – herself a budding scientist – is fascinated by the mysterious feral man who saves her from a leopard, for a couple of reasons. Maxwell: 'The Mangani are Darwin's missing link but they're still alive. So as a scientist she's beside herself. But she's also discovered this incredible man.' Maxwell went with the flow of scientific discovery: 'Right when I was about to start writing the section where Jane meets the Mangani, where Tarzan takes her to see them, a *National Geographic* magazine came out and it was about a missing link fossil that they found in

PART TEN: SWINGING INTO AN UNCERTAIN FUTURE

Ethiopia. This one was called *ardipithecus ramidus*. It was an erectus. From the neck down it looked human except the fingers were simian and the big toe was perpendicular to the rest of the toes. The face looked like a chimpanzee. So I used that as the basis of the Mangani.'

Though Maxwell's book is set in the same period as *Tarzan of the Apes*, her Jane is somewhat different from Burroughs' heroine, starting with the fact of her education. Says Maxwell, 'During those years women could not graduate. They could only audit classes at the University. During the week she lives on campus with the women attending Newnham College. She is allowed to audit Professor Archimedes Porter's gross anatomy laboratory – human anatomy – for medical students because Archie is her father. He moved mountains to make that happen, and it's causing quite a stir among the male students. When she goes home to their Cambridge greathouse on weekends, she is, and has been for some years, his assistant in the home laboratory where he works as an enthusiastic amateur in palaeoanthropology ... Jane is a very precocious woman of her time ... She's dissecting a human cadaver when we first meet her ... She was a one-off as an Edwardian woman. Didn't care for the life of the peerage. They had a name for it: a new woman.' However, this is no anachronistic ladette: 'She's a lady. She's of the peerage herself. She's a dignified woman.' Though the narrative is 'all in Jane's point of view', Tarzan features in the bulk of the story.

Other changes Maxwell has made include Tarzan becoming a solitary outcast from his Mangani tribe in his early teenage years after a run-in with Kerchak when the latter (as opposed to natives) kills Kala. Kerchak is also the killer of both of Tarzan's human parents.

Some of Maxwell's changes seem to stem partly from an inchoate and incomplete knowledge of the Burroughs Tarzan. For instance, in her retelling, Tarzan has an adoptive half-sister and playmate (an ape child mothered by Kala after she rescues him) to whom Maxwell gives the name Jai. 'That was a character in something else,' she says vaguely, unaware of the *Tarzan Goes To India*/Ron Ely TV series origin. Further changes clearly derive from our modern PC culture. 'There are no cannibals in this,' says Maxwell. 'The Waziri are the only native tribe in it. They are peaceable because there's no other tribe around and Tarzan has a friendly relationship with them. I did not want to show him killing native people.' Is that realistic? 'Well, the way I have it written it is.' Maxwell's text refers not to the 'jungle' but to the 'forest'. As for Tarzan killing animals, Maxwell explains, 'He does, but not in the same way that he does in the ERB books. He's kind of indiscriminate in the ERB books. He's a kinder, gentler Tarzan. He does kill the leopard that is trying to eat Jane alive. You don't ever see it because it's from Jane's point of view and she blacks

279

out before she knows he's there. But they hunt together and he kills for food.' Despite all this, in some respects Maxwell paints a more bloodthirsty tableau than did Burroughs: 'At that climatic moment of the book, he kills Kerchak and he cuts his heart out and takes a bite out of it.'

Maxwell says, 'The thing that I am so grateful for [is that] Jim and the estate have allowed me a literary conceit. The book opens in April of 1912 in Chicago. Jane is giving a lecture in a public hall and she is displaying the bones of Kerchak, who she claims to be a missing link species. In the audience is Edgar Rice Burroughs and after the lecture – which she is booed out of – he comes up to her and says, "I'm fascinated".'

'It's upmarket commercial fiction,' Maxwell says of *Jane*. 'It's not historical fiction, although I did my research.' As for the potential audience for a book she admits is not being pitched at her usual readership, she says, 'I've done a lot of demographic research. I discovered that only people over 60 had even possibly read the ERB books. Virtually all of them had seen the Weissmuller-Maureen O'Sullivan movies. They had a very distinct and sometimes passionate admiration for Tarzan. If they read the books, they thought highly of ERB too. Then the next down is the 35-60 age group. They were young and watching movies at the time of *Greystoke* and that abomination starring Bo Derek. They did not mostly read the ERB novels. Then the youngest age group, 18-35, they certainly didn't read the books, but what they saw movie-wise was the Disney animated features. They saw *George of the Jungle*, but a lot of them can't even make the distinction between Tarzan and George of the Jungle … Luckily the 60-plus men and women happen to be a big group of readers.' However Maxwell and Tor are not aiming exclusively at the oldies. For instance, *Me, Jane* was nixed as a component of the title because it was felt it would only have resonance for them. As for the question of more Jane-orientated Tarzan books, Maxwell says, 'I'm only planning more if *Jane* is successful.'

Al Bohl's documentary *Lord of the Louisiana Jungle* was planned for an April 2012 premiere. It revolves around the filming of the first Tarzan movie in Bohl's home state. He explains of its genesis, 'I was having breakfast with some men in South Louisiana and one of them told me he was from Morgan City and that they'd made the Tarzan movie there in 1917. Then he said, "Do you know, they brought in monkeys and apes for that movie just for background? When they got ready to leave, the [animals] wouldn't get back in the cages so they just left them." So that just really excited me to realise that there might still be monkeys down in the South Louisiana jungle. That just stuck with me for a long time … I always really liked Tarzan as a kid. I came to Tarzan through Johnny Weissmuller. But also I had really been looking for a subject to do a documentary on. My daughter's a documentary film-maker and I want to do something with her. I realised this story would not only be about my state but have international interest.' Bohl says of his research, 'I've interviewed actors, I've interviewed Tarzan fans, I've interviewed authors, I've interviewed biology professors from universities, I've interviewed the primate person at the Audubon Zoo, I've interviewed a lot of people from the Morgan City area with shared second-hand knowledge, and I've interviewed quite a few African-Americans who knew, first-hand, people that were in the film. I have 70 hours of footage. I'm also writing a book version of it, because it wasn't long into it that I realised you couldn't really tell the complete story in just a film.'

German company Constantin Film were reported to have acquired the animated rights to the Tarzan character. Theoretically, their proposed film could be even lusher than parts of Disney's, even though that movie is relatively recent: it was projected to use new performance-capture and 3D advances. Kellan Lutz, familiar from the *Twilight* movie franchise, was cast as Tarzan and Spencer Locke as Jane in what was trailed as an updating in which the ape-man's foes are those who would seek to destroy jungle habitats, including the Greystoke Energies corporation to which Tarzan does not know he is heir.

There was also the pleasing prospect of a new Tarzan live-action movie, but Burroughs fans would probably be hard-pressed to remember a time when there wasn't talk of such. Producer Jerry Weintraub had been trying to get something off the ground in this area through the aegis of Warner Brothers for just about all of the early years of the 21st Century. In 2003, John August (*Charlie's Angels*, *Big Fish*) was commissioned by Warner Brothers to write a Tarzan screenplay. Nothing came of it. Come 2006 and it was John Collee (*Master and Commander*, *Happy Feet*) in the frame to turn in a screenplay to the studio, with the intention of Guillermo del Toro (*Cronos*, *Mimic*) directing it. 'I'd love to create a new version that is still a family movie, but as edgy as I can make it,' enthused Del Toro. 'There are strong themes of survival of a defenceless child left behind in the most hostile environment.' Two years later, Del Toro had left the picture – in both senses – and it was writer/director Stephen Sommers (chiefly known for the Mummy films and *Van Helsing* but, perhaps more pertinently, the director of the 1994 live-action *Jungle Book* movie) who was set to helm the project. A tidal wave of groans erupted across the Burroughs fan fraternity at the news that Sommers and his screenwriter Stuart Beattie (*Australia*) envisaged a Tarzan film that combined the romance and plushness of *Pirates of the Caribbean* with the spectacular arboreal feats of the adherents of the currently-fashionable parkour, the extreme and categorically urban climbing sport. The fans' concern turned out to be unnecessary as, with grim predictability, Sommers did nothing visible with the project for a few years before stepping aside for a new man. Or, rather, two new men. In a peculiar move, Warner Brothers next commissioned competing Tarzan scripts, one by Adam Cozad, the other by Craig Brewer (*Water's Edge, Black Snake Moan*, the 2011 remake of *Footloose*). Though talk was of the two men's scripts being combined, the latter seemed the favourite to take the project forward as director. In late 2011, Brewer told collider.com, '...I'm a purist ... I'm going to keep Tarzan grounded in the period of the original books.' He had only recently denied reports that he envisioned a Tarzan trilogy, though had admitted, 'I can see multiple movies.'

The assumption with just about all of these proposed cinematic Tarzan projects is that they would be 'reboots', terminology for a fresh start deriving from the computer age seven decades into the future when Tarzan first saw air. In cinema terms it has come to mean a darker, edgier and more knowing variation on previous movies in a franchise (for example, the way 2005's *Batman Begins* superseded and made seem pedestrian all previous Batmans). In some cases, cinema reboots have been thought necessary not because a previous attempt was out-of-date but because it was deemed inadequate by a new hand (for instance, *The Incredible Hulk* succeeding and in effect repudiating the only-five-years-prior *Hulk*). However 'purist' his aims, it's difficult to see Brewer's film(s) not adhering to certain modern parameters: cinema audiences today would find any adult movie without a certain level of grittiness, sexual frankness and banter about assumptions of gender roles to be bland, old-fashioned and even in a way dishonest.

Perhaps the delay in bringing a new live-action Tarzan picture to the big screen is symptomatic of a deeper problem than studio politics. Tarzan never seemed a figure of the Edwardian era that very slightly preceded his first appearance, nor of any other specific timeframe. Whereas Sherlock Holmes is rooted in Victoriana, Tarzan has lent himself to endless updating. At any given point in time, there was somehow always something contemporary about him, even if his muscular values far predated and were often in opposition to those of soft modern society. That situation no longer prevails. The low cinematic profile in recent decades of a character who once dominated the flicks is startling when examining the statistics. In the 52 years between 1918 and 1970, there were 42 official Tarzan cinematic ventures, including the two Ron Ely pseudo-movies and the two marginally differentiated Herman Brix films but not including the two questionable Steve Hawkes films nor serial versions of ventures also released as features. Since 1970, there have been four, one of them not live-action. From once being perceived by movie studios and producers as a sure thing commercially, Tarzan is now a figure viewed with financial scepticism. Roy

PART TEN: SWINGING INTO AN UNCERTAIN FUTURE

Thomas, Marvel Tarzan comics writer, says 'Several decades ago I remember reading that the three most famous characters on the face of the planet Earth were Tarzan, Superman and Sherlock Holmes. Even if Superman might still be in there – I don't know about Sherlock Holmes – I doubt if Tarzan is. And if he is, it's just a faint memory of him, 'cause he's an idea whose time has gone.'

If the fictional character of Tarzan was dropped into the world for the first time today, he would surely seem antediluvian. The idea of a man who is a friend to all those creatures of the jungle with whom he is not tussling to the death is anthropomorphic sentimentality and illogicality of the kind that people now accept only in cartoons. Furthermore, the careless approach to zoology that went hand in hand with the movie Tarzan for the sake of spectacle no longer washes. Though it's probably true to say that modern audiences no more care about the nonsensical throwing together of plains and jungle animals (and sometimes African and Asian wildlife) than those in the first half of the 20th Century, such lapses would be more readily pointed out by modern critics, and like it or not, critical derision does have an effect on the standing of films. And yet, what kind of Tarzan would it be without lions and elephants in the frame? Additionally, many people feel that the whole Tarzan story is rooted in the assumptions of imperialism. Even leaving aside the frequent racism to be found in Burroughs' prose, the very notion of a white man being king of the jungle is one that seems, in some way that is perhaps not fully explainable, to be critical of black races. Completing Tarzan's antiquatedness is the fact that an inherited title like Lord Greystoke does not imply the exalted position in society it did even until relatively recently. The number of hereditary peers permitted to sit in Parliament's second chamber was reduced to a mere 92 in 1999, massively diluting the allure of the peerage. Stripped of the implication of passed-on power, 'lord' is little more than a fancy-pants title.

Moreover, Tarzan's stamping ground of Africa does not have the mysterious associations it once did. 'I've been in Africa, I spent a couple of weeks in Kenya driving around,' says Thomas. 'You'd be hard-pressed to find much jungle there. The animals have to get used to you driving within 50 or a hundred feet of them or else they wouldn't survive, 'cause there wouldn't be any tourism there if you couldn't drive around and suddenly around a corner see a pride of lions or an elephant. You just can't [set] it in Africa anymore. If you do, you're ignoring the facts that any half-way intelligent schoolchild would know. You might be able to find a way to do a story or two now and then and assume that there's some jungle somewhere that's been kept away, but it wouldn't be that vast.' Moreover, Tarzan is limited today in what he can do in that jungle. As far back as in the mid-'80s, Hugh Hudson was apprised of the fact that the public did not find depictions of the death of animals at Tarzan's hands acceptable, regardless of the imperatives of realism. In the early 20th Century, carnivorous African wild animals had associations of menace. In the latter part of that century, as the dwindling of their numbers caused by hunting and habitat-destruction became public knowledge, that perception underwent such a change that they actually became objects of pity. In an age where wildlife is seen through a prism of the imperatives of conservation, the idea of an animal being killed by a man wielding a knife is not exciting but grisly. Yet a Tarzan who cannot plunge his father's blade into the hide of Bolgani, Sabor or Mangani even in self-defence is truly a pointless Tarzan. The loinclothed backwoods policeman role to which this would reduce him has been tried before – principally in the Ron Ely TV series – and been found wanting.

Then there is a matter of cultural time and tide. The oldest-surviving movie Tarzan is a professional habitué of nostalgia events. Denny Miller notes, 'We go mainly to Western film festivals. They're coming to see people they watched with [their] grandmother and grandfather and their mother and father on black-and-white television. Some of them bring their kids, and their kids aren't interested in cowboys. Their heroes are straight up and wear helmets, they're astronauts and spaceship guys. Those are the cowboys and the Tarzans of yesteryear. The youth of today, in this country anyway, are no longer [into] cowboys or Tarzans because they've grown up without them.' Bo Derek's *Tarzan the Ape Man* co-screenwriter Gary Goddard puts it in the more clinical terms of an industry insider, saying, 'A fundamental paradigm shift happened after *Star Wars*. Most people tell you Westerns died because of *Star Wars*, because *Star Wars* is to some degree a Western but it's disguised as something else and the kids didn't want six-shooters anymore after that, they wanted lightsabers. *Star Wars* spoke to a generation. The nature of the Tarzan-type hero is perhaps a product of its time.' 'I think other noble savages have taken his place to a degree,' says Michael Moorcock. 'Conan and various other fantasy creations. The appeal is a powerful one and in American literature goes back at least as far as Fenimore Cooper. *Star Wars* has taken over to a degree, but the role of romantic hero as some kind of outcast seems to have been taken over by various vampires and wolfmen for the moment … I'm not sure his time has passed, but he would probably operate better in the denser parts of the Amazonian forest. Somewhere we could find a lost city or two without losing our sense of wonder.' Moorcock – who 'absolutely' endeavoured to inform the readership of *Tarzan Adventures* of the fact that Burroughs' Tarzan was not the ape-man of the films – also says, 'It has always [proved] hard to make an ERB [adaptation] that's true to the book, and even when we did write *The Land that Time Forgot* with the blessing of ERB,

Inc the director was able to change the ending and get rid of some of the story's idea through editing. I suspect such disappointments will be forever with us … I'd love to see an intelligent movie or HBO series, say, which dealt with the shrinking Congo and the plight of the great apes in the ongoing civil wars in that region. Tarzan is still a good poster boy for ecological preservation, respect for wild animals and our duty to be good stewards for the planet. He doesn't have to be pious about it. He, of all people, can get angry and fight against armies conscripting boy soldiers and so on – maybe having been asked to come by the Waziri. Maybe the only way it could be done would be by a black author. Readers seek their escapism in different ways these days in fantasy and SF, but if Tarzan became more up-to-date he might turn into something less escapist, better able to face the Matter of Africa.'

Regardless what happens with Tarzan in the cinema, the prose Tarzan will never be as big again, and not merely because its originating author is dead. The impending centenary and the forecast attendant publicity saw a new interest in reissuing ape-man novels on the part of mainstream publishers. Gollancz planned a deluxe affair in the shape of the hardback *Tarzan of the Apes & Other Tales: A Centenary Edition*, embossed with iconic Tarzan-with-lion J Allen St John image and the double-outlined, letter-melding Tarzan logo. There were also of course digital editions, the concept of which when *Tarzan of the Apes* was serialised in 1912 would have been no more comprehensible to civilised man than the Mangani. However, nobody was expecting a '60s-style Burroughs boom from this activity. One publisher is reputed to have paid ERB, Inc a mere £100 advance for each ape-man title.

Tarzan's prose decline began with the waning of the pulps, an extended freefall that actually started not long after Burroughs had placed his first story with Munsey. The paper shortages of the Second World War further damaged a declining market. Over the coming years, the decline was exacerbated by the greater entertainment options available to increasingly affluent Americans. Pulps did not survive to the '60s in a recognisable cultural form or newsstand format. Possibly the primary type of mass entertainment in 1912, they are now all long gone.

The '60s may have seen a Burroughs boom but it was also the end of the line for mass market Tarzan books. In the 1970s, men's adventure novels briefly became a flourishing industry. One might have thought this was the perfect backdrop for another ERB boom, or at least a Tarzan boom in which a chosen author could continue the ape-man's adventures in the manner of L Sprague de Camp's extrapolation of Robert E Howard's Conan stories. However, the paperbacks shifting huge quantities at this point in history were gratuitously violent, profane and exploitative of human foible – in other words, full of all the things Burroughs' square-jawed, moralistic prose was not. In any case, the men's adventure novel wave ebbed away rapidly: the market was decimated in the next decade by the home video. Even without that invention, the prose Tarzan would have suffered along with all other literary characters: books have now been completely eclipsed by film, comics, television and digital games in a culture where reading is not cool.

Copyright law in the States has changed since the upheavals of the 1960s, with authors' works protected until 70 years after their deaths if published in 1978 or thereafter. This does little good for Burroughs' heirs, though. Copyrights on works published before 1923 have unequivocally expired. Although works published after that date but before 1978 are protected for 95 years, it all rather becomes meaningless in light of differing copyright laws in different countries and the ability to circumnavigate the notion of sales territories created by the World Wide Web. In 2008, Danton Burroughs was anxious to emphasise to this author, 'We're still protected in England until the year 2020,' a reference to the fact that in Britain the copyright situation is life-plus-70 years. By the last years of Danton's life, increasing numbers of Burroughs' works were falling into the public domain in territories that included his native United States. This, the internet and the rise of inexpensive print-on-demand technology that requires no retaining of stock on hand gave opportunities for Burroughs fans and the merely opportunistic to offer their own versions of ERB books. Said Danton, 'We don't like it, but this is the way copyright law is.' At the time, Danton had little to worry about, as most print-on-demand books were shoddy and by definition not bookstore stock items. However, in 2011, Sterling imprint Fall River began releasing unauthorised versions of the Tarzan novels in sequence. Printed via the conventional litho process, each book came replete with a classy painted cover by Daryl Mandryk. The care devoted to them was underlined by the elegant sub-title 'The Adventures of Lord Greystoke Book __', a welcome exterior nod to the little-known nuances of the character featured within (and, surely, an allusion to one of the few media phenomena to surpass Tarzan at his peak, *Star Wars*, which famously boasted the strapline, 'From the Adventures of Luke Skywalker').

Perhaps, though, this is a rather over-dramatic analysis of the health of the Tarzan franchise. It is not just the Tarzan logo that is a registered trademark but also the very word. ('John Carter' and some place names from Burroughs' books are similarly trademarked.) This should ensure a legal deterrent to too much unauthorised exploitation. As Bill Hillman points out, 'If you're endangering contracts with Disney, MGM or major comic book companies, you have to defend it.' Certainly when comics publisher Dynamite inaugurated an unofficial new Tarzan title in December 2011, they were careful to call it *Lord of the Jungle*, with the name Tarzan mentioned nowhere on the covers (although that didn't prevent ERB, Inc issuing a writ).

Moreover, Danton certainly didn't feel any particular financial pinch on the part of ERB, Inc in 2008, with the John Carter movie in preparation, the live-action Warner Brothers Tarzan being discussed and even a Carson of Venus movie on the theoretical horizon. 'It's never-ending,' he said. 'It still keeps us busy. There's still interest out there.' It is, when one thinks about it, astonishing that movie studios are seriously contemplating both animated and live-action new versions of Tarzan, only recently the subject of a very successful animated version, that a programme of Burroughs reissues and Andy Briggs' and Robin Maxwell's books are on the publishing schedules, that the Tarzan stage show is still playing in parts of the world and that a 2012 Google Alert for mentions of 'Tarzan' on the internet yields new results every day, ranging from a London man relocating to Africa to live like his ape-man hero to a Tarzan slot-machine to a reality show star who calls his manhood 'Tarzan' to debates about Tarzan's skin colour to a generic description of couples falling in love as 'Tarzan finding his Jane' to 'Tarzan economics' of the digital age (companies clinging to the vine that keeps them off the jungle floor while having to reach for the next vine to move them forward). Astonishing because when Tarzan first appeared a century ago, it was in a world with vastly different technologies, assumptions, traditions and points of view. The world in 1912 had no radio or television, nor motion pictures that we would not find risible. Universal suffrage existed in neither America nor Britain. Courtesy of pre-industrialisation dense jungle, Africa was a largely unknown continent. With the exception of just two countries, that continent was the property of far-off white European nations and would remain in that colonised state for four decades. The concept of racism as a pejorative was in its infancy, as were the notions of ecological preservation and animal rights, thus enabling attitudes toward the worth of the lives of the people and wildlife indigenous to Africa on the part of Burroughs that almost nobody would think of purveying today and that are now only justifiable in his works via the fact of historical context and aversion to rewriting history. Life for most of the people in the industrialised West was poverty-stricken and drab. That they sought out adventures set in a far-flung and more colourful land was as much to do with obtaining solace as with aesthetic pleasure. In light of all of that, it can be posited as a triumph that Tarzan has not gravitated to the status of a creation about which a consensus has emerged that he is merely historical like the Three Musketeers or simply offensive like Fu ('Yellow Peril') Manchu, Bulldog (enemy of 'wogs' and 'dagos') Drummond and the Scarlet (friend of the decadently cruel) Pimpernel. Additionally, this might be the ideal moment for a Tarzan revival, for, a century on, only now does the technology exist for the cinema to portray the Burroughs Tarzan accurately and convincingly. It's astonishing to realise that *Greystoke*, the yardstick for a modern cinematic live-action interpretation of Tarzan, is a movie made more than a quarter of a century ago. Just as superheroes have come into their own in cinema since the advent of computer technology that can finally replicate on screen anything seen in comic books, so modern capabilities could do justice to the Tarzan novels' tree-swinging and jungle peril for the first time on film. Witness the way the title character in *X-Men Origins: Wolverine* (2009) bounds across a battlefield employing all four limbs in a motion startlingly animal-like. The increasing sophistication of cinema and its consumers should hopefully ensure that the soul is not forgotten in all of this. A 2011 Kerala Tourism television commercial with the strapline 'Your Moment is Waiting' contained the best scene never to appear in a Tarzan movie: a closing image of a woman beatifically leaning her head against the trunk of an elephant that is resting on its belly, ears contentedly flapping. Though it was strikingly like a transplantation of several scenes written by Burroughs wherein Tarzan is indolently lying on Tantor's back scratching his ears, no Tarzan movie has ever contained anything so beautiful and so suggestive of oneness with nature as this mere advert.

Notwithstanding his comments above, Goddard says, 'There's always a key to bringing a character back and I think Tarzan could come back. I think all the themes still work, stories work. What would bring it back is a re-telling that would speak to today's audiences. It wouldn't even be *Greystoke*. I think *Greystoke*'s even a little too formalised, a little too stiff. Look what they did with [Guy Ritchie's 2009 film] *Sherlock Holmes*. They basically kept Sherlock Holmes but they added almost a steampunk quality. That was a huge hit. Sherlock Holmes is a pretty stuffy character as written. All of a sudden he's embraced by a new generation. A filmmaker has to come along who has a voice, an interesting point of view, who retains the Tarzan basic mythology, the basic elements of the character, and then layers in something that speaks to today's generation. Certainly there [are] enough stories of Tarzan you could actually do that. Tarzan is perennial and the basic idea is very strong. I believe Tarzan is timeless.'

Joe Kubert, DC Comics Tarzan writer, shares that conviction of timelessness. He says, 'The character is so strong and so potent and so ingrained in most young people's and older people's minds that he'll be back again I'm sure, with as much vigour, with as much as strength as ever before.'

APPENDIX: TARZAN IN THE MEDIA

Note: only works authorised by Edgar Rice Burroughs or his estate are listed.

TARZAN BOOKS

By Edgar Rice Burroughs
1914 *Tarzan of the Apes* (McClurg)
1915 *The Return of Tarzan* (McClurg)
1916 *The Beasts of Tarzan* (McClurg)
1917 *The Son of Tarzan* (McClurg)
1918 *Tarzan and the Jewels of Opar* (McClurg)
1919 *Jungle Tales of Tarzan* (McClurg)
1920 *Tarzan the Untamed* (McClurg)
1921 *Tarzan the Terrible* (McClurg)
1923 *Tarzan and the Golden Lion* (McClurg)
1924 *Tarzan and the Ant Men* (McClurg)
1925 *The Eternal Lover* (McClurg) Note: Tarzan makes cameo appearance only
1927 *The Tarzan Twins* (Volland) Note: book for children
1928 *Tarzan, Lord of the Jungle* (McClurg)
1929 *Tarzan and the Lost Empire* (Metropolitan)
1930 *Tarzan at the Earth's Core* (Metropolitan)
1931 *Tarzan the Invincible* (Burroughs)
1931 *Tarzan the Triumphant* (Burroughs)
1933 *Tarzan and the City of Gold* (Burroughs)
1934 *Tarzan and the Lion Man* (Burroughs)
1935 *Tarzan and the Leopard Men* (Burroughs)
1936 *Tarzan and the Tarzan Twins, with Jad-bal-ja, the Golden Lion* (Whitman)
Note: book for children
1936 *Tarzan's Quest* (Burroughs)
1938 *Tarzan and the Forbidden City* (Burroughs)
1939 *Tarzan the Magnificent* (Burroughs)
1947 *Tarzan and the 'Foreign Legion'* (Burroughs)
1964 *Tarzan and the Madman* (Canaveral)
1965 *Tarzan and the Castaways* (Canaveral) (Features 'Tarzan and the Castaways', 'Tarzan and the Champion' and 'Tarzan and the Jungle Murders')

Note: with the exception of *The Tarzan Twins* and *Tarzan and the Tarzan Twins, with Jad-bal-ja, the Golden Lion, Tarzan and the 'Foreign Nation'* and

Tarzan and the Madman, all the above initially appeared in magazines first, often in significantly different form and sometimes under different titles.

By Fritz Lieber
1966 *Tarzan and the Valley of Gold* (Ballantine) Note: novelisation of motion picture of same title

By Douglas Niles
1985 *Tarzan and the Well of Slaves* (TSR, Inc.) Note: role-playing book

By Richard Reinsmith
1986 *Tarzan and the Tower of Diamonds* (TSR, Inc.) Note: role-playing book

By Edgar Rice Burroughs and Joe R Lansdale
1995 *Tarzan: the Lost Adventure* (Dark Horse) Note: Burroughs' uncompleted manuscript finished, amended and expanded by Lansdale; initially appeared in magazines.

By RA Salvatore
1996 *Tarzan: The Epic Adventures* (Del Rey) Note: novelisation of television pilot of same title

By Philip José Farmer
1999 *The Dark Heart of Time* (Del Rey)

By Maude Robinson Toombs
2006 *Adventures of Tarzan* (ERBville Press) Note: collation of newspaper serialisation of novelisation of serial of same title

By Arthur B Reeve
2008 *Tarzan the Mighty* (ERBville Press) Note: collation of newspaper serialisation of novelisation of serial of same title

By Andy Briggs
2011 *Tarzan: The Greystoke Legacy* (Faber and Faber) Note: book for children
2012 *Tarzan: The Jungle Warrior* (Faber and Faber) Note: book for children

By Robin Maxwell
2012 *Jane: The Woman Who Loved Tarzan* (Tor)

TARZAN MOTION PICTURES

Tarzan played by Gordon Griffith (as a boy) and Elmo Lincoln
1918 *Tarzan of the Apes* (National Film Corp.)
1918 *The Romance of Tarzan* (National Film Corp.)

Tarzan played by Gene Pollar
1920 *The Revenge of Tarzan* (Numa Pictures)

Tarzan played Gordon Griffith (as a boy) and P Dempsey Tabler
1920 *The Son of Tarzan* (National Film Corp.) Note: serial; also released in feature format

Tarzan played by Elmo Lincoln
1921 *Adventures of Tarzan* (Great Western) Note: serial; also released in feature format

Tarzan played by James Pierce
1927 *Tarzan and the Golden Lion* (R-C Pictures)

Tarzan played by Frank Merrill
1928 *Tarzan the Mighty* (Universal) Note: serial
1929 *Tarzan the Tiger* (Universal) Note: serial

Tarzan played by Johnny Weissmuller
1932 *Tarzan the Ape Man* (MGM)

Tarzan played by Buster Crabbe
1933 *Tarzan the Fearless* (Principal) Note: serial; also released in feature format

Tarzan played by Johnny Weissmuller
1934 *Tarzan and His Mate* (MGM)

Tarzan played by Herman Brix
1935 *The New Adventures of Tarzan* (Burroughs-Tarzan Enterprises) Note: serial; also released in feature format

Tarzan played by Johnny Weissmuller
1936 *Tarzan Escapes* (MGM)

APE-MAN

Tarzan played by Glenn Morris
1938 *Tarzan's Revenge* (Principal)

Tarzan played by Herman Brix
1938 *Tarzan and the Green Goddess* Note: largely footage previously seen in *The New Adventures of Tarzan*

Tarzan played by Johnny Weissmuller
1939 *Tarzan Finds a Son!* (MGM)
1941 *Tarzan's Secret Treasure* (MGM)
1942 *Tarzan's New York Adventure* (MGM)
1943 *Tarzan Triumphs* (RKO)
1943 *Tarzan's Desert Mystery* (RKO)
1945 *Tarzan and the Amazons* (RKO)
1946 *Tarzan and the Leopard Woman* (RKO)
1947 *Tarzan and the Huntress* (RKO)
1948 *Tarzan and the Mermaids* (RKO)

Tarzan played by Lex Barker
1949 *Tarzan's Magic Fountain* (RKO)
1950 *Tarzan and the Slave Girl* (RKO)
1951 *Tarzan's Peril* (RKO)
1952 *Tarzan's Savage Fury* (RKO)
1953 *Tarzan and the She-Devil* (RKO)

Tarzan played by Gordon Scott
1955 *Tarzan's Hidden Jungle* (RKO)
1957 *Tarzan and the Lost Safari* (MGM)
1958 *Tarzan's Fight for Life* (MGM)
1959 *Tarzan's Greatest Adventure* (MGM)

Tarzan played by Denny Miller
1959 *Tarzan the Ape Man* (MGM)

Tarzan played by Gordon Scott
1960 *Tarzan the Magnificent* (Paramount)

Tarzan played by Jock Mahoney
1962 *Tarzan Goes to India* (MGM)

1963 *Tarzan's Three Challenges* (MGM)

Tarzan played by Mike Henry
1966 *Tarzan and the Valley of Gold* (Banner Productions-Allfin, A.G.)
1967 *Tarzan and the Great River* (Banner Productions)
1968 *Tarzan and the Jungle Boy* (Banner Productions)

Tarzan played by Ron Ely
1970 *Tarzan's Deadly Silence*
1970 *Tarzan's Jungle Rebellion*
Note: above two releases spliced episodes from television series.

Tarzan played by Steve Hawkes
1970 *Tarzan En La Gruta Del Oro* (*Tarzan in the Golden Grotto*)
1972 *Tarzan Y El Arco Iris* (*Tarzan and the Rainbow*); also known as *Tarzan and the Brown Prince*
Note: above two releases of questioned legality.

Tarzan played by Miles O'Keeffe
1981 *Tarzan the Ape Man* (MGM)

Tarzan played by Daniel Potts (as a boy), Eric Langlois (as a teenager) and Christopher Lambert
1984 *Greystoke: The Legend of Tarzan, Lord of the Apes* (Warner Bros.)

Tarzan played by Casper Van Dien
1998 *Tarzan and the Lost City* (Warner Bros.)

Tarzan played by Tony Goldwyn
1999 *Tarzan* (Disney) Note: animated motion picture.

TARZAN TELEVISION PRODUCTIONS

Tarzan played by Gordon Scott
1966 *Tarzan and the Trappers* (NBC) Note: TV movie; also released in cinemas

Tarzan played by Ron Ely
1966 *Tarzan* (NBC)
Duration: two seasons (57 episodes)

Tarzan played by Robert Ridgely
1976 *Tarzan Lord of the Jungle* (title changed to *Batman/Tarzan Adventure Hour*, then *Tarzan and the Super 7*) (CBS)
Duration: four seasons (36 episodes)
Note: animated series.

Tarzan played by Joe Lara
1989 *Tarzan in Manhattan* (CBS)
Note: TV movie

Tarzan played by Wolf Larson
1991 *Tarzan* [First-run-syndication in US]
Duration: three seasons (75 episodes)

Tarzan played by Joe Lara
1996 *Tarzan's Return* [First-run-syndication in US]
Note: TV movie, pilot for *Tarzan: The Epic Adventures*

Tarzan played by Joe Lara
1996 *Tarzan: The Epic Adventures* [First-run-syndication in US]
Duration: one season (20 episodes, excluding pilot)

Tarzan played by Michael T Weiss
2001 *The Legend of Tarzan* (United Paramount Network)
Duration: two seasons (39 episodes)
Note: animated series.

Tarzan played by Travis Fimmel
2003 *Tarzan* (WB Television Network)
Duration: one season (8 episodes)

TARZAN VIDEO/DVD RELEASES

Tarzan played by [unknown]
1999 *Tarzan of the Apes* (Sony Wonder)
Note: animated feature.

Tarzan played by Michael T Weiss
2002 *Tarzan & Jane* (Disney) Note: animated feature

Tarzan played by Harrison Chad
2005 *Tarzan II* (Disney) Note: animated feature

TARZAN RADIO SHOWS

Tarzan played by James Pierce
1932 *Tarzan of the Apes*
Duration: 77 episodes.

Tarzan played by Carlton KaDell
1934 *Tarzan and the Diamond of Asher*
Duration: 39 episodes
1936 *Tarzan and the Fires of Tohr*
Duration: 39 episodes

Tarzan played by Lamont Johnson
1951 *Tarzan, Lord of the Jungle*
Duration: 75 episodes

Tarzan played by Rod Taylor/Ray Barrett/Lloyd Berrell
1950s *Tarzan, King of the Apes*
Duration: 1,000+ episodes (estimated)
Note: Australian production.

TARZAN STAGE PRODUCTIONS

(Excludes regional productions)

Tarzan played by Ronald Adair
1920 *Tarzan of the Apes* (London)
Duration: unknown.
1921 *Tarzan of the Apes* (New York)
Duration: 14 performances

Tarzan played by Josh Strickland
2006 *Tarzan: The Broadway Musical* (New York)
Duration: 486 performances

TARZAN NEWSPAPER COMIC STRIP

Daily strip
1929 *Tarzan* (Metropolitan Syndicate/United Features Syndicate)
Duration: has run continuously since 7 January 1929 with the exception of 17 March-9 June 1929

Sunday strip
1931 *Tarzan* (Metropolitan Syndicate/United Features Syndicate)
Duration: has run continuously since 15 March 1931

TARZAN COMIC BOOKS (USA)

(Note: regularly-published titles only; reprints of newspaper strips excluded; guest appearances in other titles excluded; related titles – e.g. Korak – excluded)

1947 Dell 131 Issues
1962 Gold Key 75 Issues (note: numbering continued from Dell title)
1972 DC 52 Issues (note: numbering continued from Gold Key title)
1977 Marvel 29 Issues
1996 Dark Horse 20 issues

SELECTED BIBLIOGRAPHY

BOOKS

Star Trek Creator: The Authorized Biography of Gene Roddenberry; David Alexander; Boxtree; 1994

Gene Roddenberry: The Myth and the Man Behind Star Trek; Joel Engel; Virgin; 1995

Tarzan of the Movies; Gabe Essoe; Citadel; 1968

Mother was a Lovely Beast: A Feral Man Anthology; Philip José Farmer; Chilton; 1974

The Big Swingers; Robert W Fenton; Prentice-Hall; 1967

Kings of the Jungle; David Fury; McFarland & Co; 2001

Master of Adventure: The Worlds of Edgar Rice Burroughs; Richard A Lupoff; University of Nebraska Press; 2005

The Battle of Hollywood; James H Pierce; House of Greystoke; 1978

Edgar Rice Burroughs: The Man Who Created Tarzan; Irwin Porges; Ballantine Books; 1976

Tarzan Forever: The Life of Edgar Rice Burroughs; John Taliaferro; Scribner; 1999

Tarzan – Giant Book; Various; Williams; 1971

On Tarzan; Alex Vernon; University of Georgia Press; 2008

The Tarzan Novels of Edgar Rice Burroughs; David A Ullery; McFarland & Co.; 2001

MAGAZINE ARTICLES

'Tarzan's Travails'; Joe Brancatelli; *Eerie* #79; November 1976

'James Bond of the Jungle!'; Anthony Petkovich; *Filmfax* #127; 2011

WEBSITES/WEBPAGES

boxofficemojo.com

collider.com

disney.go.com/disneyinsider

edgarriceburroughs.blogspot.com/2011/08/filmations-tarzan.html

epguides.com

erbzine.com

ibdb.com

ibelongwithyou.com

leylander.org/intercom/Tarzan (from an article originally published in *Comic Book Marketplace* #42)

APE-MAN

moviehole.net
newspaperarchive.com
philsp.com/magazines.html
pjfarmer.com
tarzanmovieguide.com
terrororstralis.com
weirdscifi.ratiosemper.com/tarzan/cartoon.html

ABOUT THE AUTHOR

Londoner Sean Egan has contributed to, amongst others, *Billboard*, *Book Collector*, *Classic Rock*, *Record Collector*, *Tennis World*, *Total Film*, *Uncut* and RollingStone.com. He has written or edited 18 books, including works on the Beatles, Jimi Hendrix, the Rolling Stones, *Coronation Street* and Manchester United. His critically acclaimed novel *Sick of Being Me* was published in 2003, while *Don't Mess with the Best*, his 2008 collection of short stories, carried cover endorsements from Booker Prize winners Stanley Middleton and David Storey.